DURABLE PEACE
CHALLENGES FOR PEACEBUILDING IN AFRICA

Edited by Taisier M. Ali and Robert O. Matthews

The African continent has been racked with civil war in the years since decolonization. Even after negotiated settlements of violent conflict, true and lasting peace has been difficult to attain. In *Durable Peace*, Taisier M. Ali and Robert O. Matthews have brought together leading scholars to discuss the experiences of ten African countries – Angola, Ethiopia, Liberia, Mozambique, Rwanda, Somalia, South Africa, Sudan, Uganda, and Zimbabwe – in recovering from war.

In this series of thought-provoking essays, the contributors shed light on the process of peacebuilding. Collectively they demonstrate that, to be successful, attempts to restore peace in war-torn societies must be wide in scope, involving security and political measures, as well as economic development and socio-psychological reconciliation. In addition, these efforts must be extended over long periods of time and, above all else, anchored in the local community.

Peacebuilding is a difficult process, subject to frequent setbacks, and sometimes outright failure. *Durable Peace* argues that any peacebuilding effort must include four basic elements: a secure environment, new political institutions that are broadly representative, a healthy economy, and a mechanism for dealing with injustices of the past and future. How these elements are put together will vary, but if they are arranged to fit the specific local circumstances, the outcome will likely be self-sustaining peace.

TAISIER M. ALI is an independent scholar living in Toronto.

ROBERT O. MATTHEWS is Professor Emeritus in the Department of Political Science at the University of Toronto.

Durable Peace

Challenges for
Peacebuilding in Africa

Edited by
Taisier M. Ali and
Robert O. Matthews

UNIVERSITY OF TORONTO PRESS
Toronto Buffalo London

© University of Toronto Press Incorporated 2004
Toronto Buffalo London
Reprinted in paperback 2015

ISBN 978-0-8020-3614-8 (cloth)
ISBN 978-0-8020-8463-7 (paper)

Printed on acid-free paper

National Library of Canada Cataloguing in Publication Data

University of Toronto Press acknowledges the financial assistance to its
publishing program of the Canada Council for the Arts and the Ontario Arts
Council.

University of Toronto Press acknowledges the financial support for its
publishing activities of the Government of Canada through the Book
Publishing Industry Development Program (BPIDP).

The cover photo on the paperback edition was taken by Andrew Stawicki as
part of an advocacy campaign titled *HIVpositive: AIDS through a New Lens* to
humanize the efforts of Africans coping with the HIV/AIDS crisis. The
project was undertaken by CARE Canada, one of the world's larges
international development organizations, and PhotoSensitive, a group of
distinguished Canadian photojournalists. The full photo exhibition can be
found on-line at www.care.ca..

For Cranford Pratt
who encourages, supports, and stimulates

Contents

Maps

The maps of Africa, Ethiopia, Rwanda, Uganda, Liberia, Mozambique, Somalia, Sudan, and Angola are reproduced from Raymond W. Copson, *Africa's Wars and Prospects for Peace* (Armond, NY: M.E. Sharpe, 1994). Copyright © 1994 M.E. Sharpe, Inc. Reprinted with permission.

The map of Zimbabwe is reprinted with permission from Larry Diamond, Juan Linz, and Seymour Martin Lipset, eds., *Democracy in Developing Countries* (Boulder: Lynne Rienner, 1999).

The map of South Africa is reprinted courtesty of maps.com

Preface

This collection of essays explores efforts by Africans to rebuild their countries after lengthy and costly civil wars and grows directly out of our earlier volume, *Civil Wars in Africa: Roots and Resolution* (1999). Once civil wars had come to an end, it seemed to us that the next logical step was the regeneration of their economy, society, and polity.

With encouragement from many of our colleagues and generous support from Oxfam-Canada, Project Ploughshares, the Steelworkers of America, the United Church of Canada, and the Department of Political Science at the University of Toronto, we held a one-day workshop in May 1999 to develop a common framework for the case and thematic studies we then envisaged. A year later, in June 2000, we convened a two-day conference on peacebuilding in Africa.

We are extremely grateful to a number of organizations without whose support it would have been impossible to hold that conference and to numerous individuals whose participation ensured its success. The organizations included the International Development Research Centre (and especially Necla Tschirgi), the Canadian Centre for Foreign Policy Development, and the Department of Political Science at the University of Toronto. The list of individuals contributing to the conference is too lengthy to include here, but we would be remiss not to mention the following who served as commentators on the papers that now form the chapters in this volume: Adekeye Adebajo, Ali Abdel Gader Ali, Douglas Anglin, Gerry Barr, Pierre Beaudet, Merle Bowen, Francis Deng, Gerald K. Helleiner, John Hirsch, Roger Hutchinson, Paul Idahosa, Nelson M. Kasfir, Martin Murray, Tim Shaw, Richard Simeon, Janice Gross Stein, Zenebeworke Tadesse, and I. William Zartman.

Finally, we would like to thank a number of people for their stimulating comments on various parts of this manuscript, including James Busumtwi-Sam, Hevina Dashwood, Anita Krajnc, Paul Martin, Kristiana Powell, Mark Raymond, Richard Simeon, Ian Spears, and two anonymous readers for the University of Toronto Press. Susan Krajnc's assistance in formatting and putting together this volume was invaluable.

In dedicating this volume to Cranford Pratt we want to give recognition to the special impact he has had on this and earlier projects. He truly was, and continues to be, a stimulating teacher, a wise counsel, and a good friend.

Abbreviations

ACC	Administrative Committee on Coordination (UN)
ADF	Allied Democratic Forces (Uganda)
AFL	Armed Forces of Liberia
ANC	African National Congress
ANDM	Amhara National Democratic Movement
AWG	Afrikaner Weerstands Beweging
CFU	Commercial Farmers' Union (Zimbabwe)
CIC	Centre on International Cooperation
CIDA	Canadian International Development Agency
CODESA	Convention for a Democratic South Africa
COSATU	Congress of South African Trade Unions
CP	Conservative Part (Uganda)
CSOs	civil society organizations
DAC	Development Assistance Committee of the OECD
DDRs	demobilization, demilitarization and reintegration programs
DESA	Department of Economic and Social Affairs (UN)
DFAIT	Department of Foreign Affairs and International Trade (Canada)
DP	Democratic Party (South Africa and Uganda)
DPA	Department of Political Affairs (UN)
DPKO	Department of Peacekeeping Operations (UN)
ECOMOG	Economic Community of West African States Ceasefire Monitoring Group
ECOWAS	Economic Community of West African States Economic Recovery Plan (Uganda)
EFFORT	Endowment Fund for the Rehabilitation of Tigray

EPLF	Eritrean Peoples Liberation Front
EPRDF	Ethiopian Peoples Revolutionary Democratic Front
ERP	European Recovery Program (United States)
ESAF	Enhanced Structural Adjustment Facility
ESAP	Economic Structural Adjustment Program (Zimbabwe)
EU	European Union
FAA	Angolan Armed Forces
FAO	Food and Agriculture Organization
FDRE	Federal Democratic Republic of Ethiopia
Frelimo	Frente da Libertacao de Mocambique (Front for the Liberation of Mozambique)
GATT	General Agreement on Tariffs and Trade
GEAR	Growth, Employment and Redistribution
GEF	Global Environment Facility
GNU	Government of National Unity
GPA	General Peace Agreement (Mozambique)
GURN	Government of Unity and National Reconciliation (Angola)
HIPC	Highly Indebted Poor Countries
HRFOR	Human Rights' Field Officer in Rwanda (UN)
IBDC	Indigenous Business Development Centre (Zimbabwe)
IBRD	International Bank for Reconstruction and Development (World Bank)
IBWO	Indigenous Business Women's Organization (Zimbabwe)
ICTR	International Criminal Tribunal for Rwanda
IDA	international development association
IDPs	internally displaced persons
IFIs	international financial institutions
IFP	Inkatha Freedom Party
ILO	International Labour Organization
IMF	International Monetary Fund
IOM	International Organization for Migration
KZN	KwaZulu/Natal
LPC	Liberian Peace Council
LRA	Lord's Resistance Army
LRRP-2	Land Reform and Resettlement Programme, Phase 2
MDC	Movement for Democratic Change (Zimbabwe)
MPLA	Movimento Popular de Libertacao de Angola (Popular Movement for the Liberation of Angola)
NCA	Norwegian Church Aid

NCUR	National Commission on Unity and Reconciliation (Rwanda)
NDA	National Democratic Alliance (Sudan)
NGO	nongovernmental organization
NIF	National Islamic Front (Sudan)
NPFL	National Patriotic Front of Liberia
NRA	National Resistance Army (Uganda)
NRM	National Resistance Movement (Uganda)
OAU	Organization of African Unity
OCHA	Office for the Coordination of Humanitarian Affairs (UN)
ODA	official development assistance
OECD	Organization of Economic Cooperation and Development
OIC	Organization of Islamic Conference
OLF	Oromo Liberation Front
ONC	Oromo National Congress
OPDO	Oromo Peoples Democratic Organization
ORH	Operation Restore Hope
PBSO	Peacekeeping Support Offices (UN)
PEAP	Poverty Eradication Action Plan (Uganda)
PFDJ	Peoples Front for Democracy and Justice (Eritrea)
PRE	Programma de Reabilitaçao Economica (Mozambique)
RCs	resistance councils (Uganda)
REST	Relief Society of Tigray
RPF	Rwandan Patriotic Front
RUF	Revolutionary United Front (Sierra Leone)
SACP	South Africa Communist Party
SADF	South African Defence Force
SAERT	Sustainable Agricultural and Environment Rehabilitation of Tigray
SAF	Structural Adjustment Facility
SAPs	structural adjustment programmes
SNF	Somali National Front
SNM	Somali National Movement
SPLA/M	Sudan Peoples Liberation Army/Movement
SPM	Somali Patriotic Movement
SSDF	Somali Salvation Democratic Front
SRF	Strategic Recovery Facility (UN)
SRSG	Special Representative of the Secretary-General (UN)

SWAPO	South West African Peoples Organization
TDA	Tigray Development Association
TGE	Transitional Government of Ethiopia
TPLF	Tigray People's Liberation Front
TRC	Truth and Reconciliation Commission
UDF	United Democratic Front (South Africa)
ULIMO	United Liberation Movement of Liberia for Democracy
ULIMO-J	ULIMO faction headed by Roosevelt Johnson
ULIMO-K	ULIMO faction headed by Alhaji Kromah
UNAMIR	United Nations Mission in Rwanda
UNDAF	United Nations Development Assistance Framework
UNDG	United Nations Development Group Office
UNDP	United Nations Development Programme
UNESCO	United Nations Educational, Scientific and Cultural Organization
UNFPA	United Nations Food and Population Agency
UNHCR	United Nations High Commission for Refugees
UNICEF	United Nations Children's Fund
UNISOM	United Nations Operation in Somalia
UNITA	Uniao Nacional para a Independencia Total de Angola (Union for the Total Independence of Angola)
UNITAF	Unified Task Force (Somalia)
UNOHAC	United Nations Office for Humanitarian Assistance Coordination (Mozambique)
UNOMIL	United Nations Observer Mission in Liberia
UNOMOZ	United Nations Operation in Mozambique
UNTAC	United Nations Transitional Authority in Cambodia
UPC	Uganda Peoples' Congress
USAID	United States Agency for International Development
USC	United Somali Congress
WDC	World Diamond Council
WFP	World Food Program
WHO	World Health Organization
WPE	Workers Party of Ethiopia
ZANLA	Zimbabwe African National Union, military wing
ZANU	Zimbabwe African National Union
ZAPU	Zimbabwe African Peoples Union
ZCTU	Zimbabwe Congress of Trade Unions
ZIPRA	Zimbabwe African Peoples' Union, military wing
ZNA	Zimbabwe National Army

DURABLE PEACE
CHALLENGES FOR PEACEBUILDING IN AFRICA

Introduction

Taisier M. Ali and Robert O. Matthews

The idea for this book emerged from our earlier publication *Civil Wars in Africa: Roots and Resolution.*[1] In that volume we examined the causes of civil wars in Africa and the manner in which they were resolved, if at all. In at least three of the cases examined – Ethiopia, Mozambique, and Uganda – where the fighting had stopped several years before, the authors devoted a portion of their chapters to a discussion of the steps taken by the states and international agencies involved in the earlier peace-making efforts and by the post-conflict governments to build an enduring peace. For us and for them, the logical next step was to study attempts being made to restore long-term stability and peace in Africa.

We were further convinced of the need for such a study after undertaking a review of the literature. It became apparent that most empirical studies of peacebuilding limited their analysis to a transitional period during which short-term measures incorporated in a peace settlement were implemented. The focus of this literature tends to be on political negotiations and accommodation among leaders of the rival parties, with emphasis on such short-term tasks as the signing of a ceasefire, the demilitarization and reintegration of former combatants, the resettlement of displaced persons, the approval of a new or revised constitution, and the holding of nation-wide elections. Most analyses do not include the longer-range goals of socio-economic transformation and socio-psychological reconciliation. Yet these are centrally important to lasting peace.[2] The success or failure of peacebuilding is not likely to be determined in the two to three years that follow a negotiated settlement, as the reappearance of fighting in Sudan in 1983, eleven years after the first phase of the civil war ended, so aptly illustrates. Peacebuilding is of necessity a lengthy process that involves security and political arrangements as well as socio-economic measures.

Almost by definition the study of peacebuilding has limited itself in another fashion, restricting the cases studied to civil wars that have ended through negotiated settlement, thus excluding from examination those that have ended through military victory. And yet, as John Kiyaga-Nsubuga observed in his study of Uganda in our earlier volume, the victorious Yoweri Museveni could not avoid the difficult task of peacebuilding. Had he not broadened the political process, promoted economic development, and been sensitive to the historical legacy of the civil war, he would in all probability have faced the resumption of widespread fighting. No matter how civil wars end, the task of building an enduring peace cannot be escaped.

In the spring of 1999, we organized a one-day workshop around the general theme of peacebuilding, bringing together some twenty-eight scholars, government officials, and representatives of non-governmental organizations to help us develop a set of questions to inform our subsequent research. From this workshop emerged a framework that shaped the papers that were subsequently presented at a conference on peacebuilding in Africa which was held in Toronto in June of the next year. We then further refined the conceptual framework to serve as a guide to the contributors as they revised their individual contributions.

We needed to address two questions first. 'What do we mean by peacebuilding?' And very much related to that, 'How can we discern whether the steps taken by newly formed governments to rebuild an enduring peace have been successful?' Clearly if the concept of peacebuilding is to be useful, we need to be able to distinguish it from normal political activity and everyday economic development. While the instruments used in both sets of activities may be similar, the context of a country just emerging from a lengthy and destructive civil war is quite different and thus requires a different response.

Imagine a country where a significant percentage of the population has died and even a greater number has been forced to leave their homes, farms, and villages in search of safety; where people live in constant fear for their lives; where communities have been weakened or destroyed and families splintered; and where children have been orphaned and often pressed into military service. Add to this cost in human terms (what one author described as 'a global disaster'[3]) economic losses measured in terms of the expenses incurred in running a war; the disruption to agriculture, mining, and industry; the lost opportunities for economic growth (estimated by one Organization of African Unity study at 2 per cent per annum[4]); and the destruction of its physical and social infrastructure – in

Africa
(Political boundaries of countries under study are highlighted.)

Mozambique alone, over one-third of all rural clinics and 70 percent of its schools were destroyed or abandoned. Civil wars are, as the World Bank reminds us, one of the main causes of poverty in Africa. The new leadership assuming responsibility for governing a country at the end of a civil war must thus not only address the underlying causes that gave rise to the civil war in the first place, but do so when it is further handicapped by tens of thousands of displaced persons, a shattered economy, a fragmented society, weak and ineffective political institutions, and many demobilized combatants from both sides searching for alternative forms of peaceful employment.

Peacebuilding is often defined as the last phase in the cycle of conflict, beginning when a ceasefire has brought an end to fighting and efforts are initiated to revive a country's economy, to rebuild its society and to restore its polity. It was in this sense that we used the term in our earlier volume and how we initially began work on this study. We came to recognize, however, that the peacebuilding process can begin while a conflict is still ongoing or even before civil war had begun in earnest. Structures that are created and events that occur prior to and during civil war can shape the way in which peace is rebuilt after the fighting has stopped.[5] As one of our contributors reminded us all, peacebuilding is a complex historical process of socio-economic and political renewal involving global as well as local dynamics of coercion and consensus. Consequently, all the cases examined in this volume are set within an historical context and outline the roots of the civil war (including the impact of colonial rule), the principal parties, and the manner in which the war ended – through negotiations, by military victory or not at all.

Not only can peacebuilding be understood as a phase in the conflict cycle and as a long term-process, it can also be seen as a set of challenges facing war-torn societies. Countries emerging from a long period of civil war are confronted by a number of problems that must be dealt with successfully if the recurrence of war is to be averted. While the particular shape of the policies and programs developed to respond to those problems may differ from one country to another, there are a set of challenges with which each country hoping to regain peace and stability after a period of civil strife must contend. These include: bringing an end to generalized fighting, demobilizing and disarming the warring factions, and creating a general environment of trust and confidence; building a set of institutions and political arrangements that assure the establishment of a political process that is open, inclusive, and able to cope with conflicts in a peaceful manner rather then through resort to

arms; fostering reconciliation among previously warring communities
and thus helping to build a sense of community and common identity;
and, finally, eliminating abject poverty and gradually easing the economic inequalities that may have been at the heart of the conflict.

What this suggests is that peacebuilding is best construed as a continuum extending along two different axes. One depicts what might be
thought of as thickening layers of peace, as a dynamic process during
which the previously warring parties lay down their arms, learn to resolve
their differences through non-violent means, develop a common set of
goals and a common identity, and move towards the creation of a just and
equitable society. The second axis is one that measures time and may be
broken down into at least two periods: a transitional phase of several
years, followed by a period, less well demarcated, during which peace is
consolidated. It should then be possible, with the aid of figure I.1, to trace
the movement of any given country over time, depicting the thickness of
its peace or the extent to which it has fallen back onto violent times.

Peacebuilding thus constitutes effecting movement from what is sometimes called a condition of negative peace – one in which the principal
characteristic is the mere absence of violence – to one of positive peace,
a condition of stable and widening shared values. It often results from
two sets of pressures. Driven by government policies and actions, the process is seen as a top-down approach to peacebuilding. Alternatively, pressures resulting from attitudes and socio-economic circumstances of
ordinary people and from the actions undertaken by the groups, organizations and smaller communities that make up the larger society may
lead to the superseding of conflict from the bottom up. Government policies and a vigorous civil society can, of course, complement, reinforce,
or conflict with each other.[6]

To ensure that the studies undertaken in this volume generated comparable material, the contributors were invited to address a similar set of
questions, designed as general guidelines for framing each of their chapters. In the first place, what kind of peace has been established? Is it one
where the peace is solely negative? Or has the country made more
progress in deepening relations between previously warring parties? Secondly, what peacebuilding measures or components have been introduced? To what extent do these peacebuilding strategies include:
security policies, such as demobilization, demilitarization and reintegration of ex-combatants into civilian life; political arrangements, such as
power-sharing, a new constitution, federal structures, and decentralization; measures for social reconstruction, embracing the rebuilding of

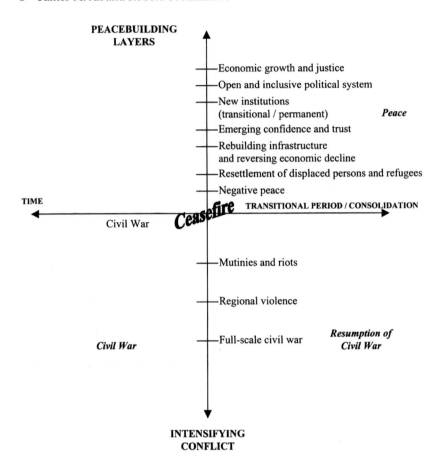

Figure I.1. Peacebuilding

local institutions and the implementation of social policies in health and education; steps to encourage economic development such as a jump-start to the weakened economy, an attack on abject poverty, and the easing of economic inequalities; and finally, policies to encourage justice and reconciliation such as the active promotion of human rights and the treatment of crimes committed by the previous regime? Were these measures introduced during a short period of transition or over a longer period of consolidation?

Thirdly, and here particularly is where the case studies intersect with the theme chapters, to the extent that at least a modicum of peace has been established, what factors contributed to this successful outcome? If, on the other hand, little or no progress is evident, what forces have acted as obstacles to peacebuilding? To what extent can one attribute slow progress to such things as a faulty agreement, the presence of such spoilers as disappointed parties and hegemonic neighbours, inadequate resources and personnel, the lack of a comprehensive vision of where the process is going, or economic measures imposed by international financial institutions?

Fourthly, what role has the international community played in the peacebuilding process, taking care to distinguish between such forces as international capital and international actors, and among a whole range of actors such as immediate neighbours, other regional states, global powers, regional and international organizations, and NGOs? How effective has this involvement been? And to what extent do international actors work at cross purposes with each other?

Lastly, in our earlier study of the roots of civil war we concluded that leadership had often played a key part in either causing the outbreak of violence or in preventing its occurrence. We might expect to find that leaders have had a similar impact on the process of peacebuilding. Nelson Mandela and Yoweri Museveni, for instance, stand out as leaders who have been successful in transforming intense and violent conflict into peaceful relationships, while Charles Taylor's predatory nature was largely responsible for the recurrence of civil war in Liberia. How effective has leadership been, both at the local and national levels, in ensuring that the countries under investigation do not relapse into civil war?

The primary focus of this volume is on the efforts made by ten different African countries to build a structure of peace after a lengthy civil war. Initially we intended to limit our selection to the same set of countries we had chosen for our earlier volume. By limiting our choice to those countries in which widespread fighting had ended, our cases would have been limited to Ethiopia, Liberia, Mozambique, Rwanda, Uganda, and Zimbabwe. (Note that these cases are divided equally between countries where the fighting stopped as a result of negotiations and in those where the civil wars ended through military victory.) Although a political settlement has not been reached at the national level in Somalia, we decided to include it as one of our cases as it provides an interesting contrast between successful peacebuilding in northern Somaliland and the collapse of efforts to build peace in the south and at the national level. We also have added South Africa because of its overall importance for the entire continent, its interesting parallels with Zimbabwe, and its unique character as a civil war that ended through negotiations but without direct third-party involvement. Finally, we thought it would be instructive to include Angola and Sudan, cases in which a peace settlement had been reached but had subsequently broken down. Comparing the collapse of two negotiated agreements in Angola, in 1991 and 1994, with what ultimately proved to be a failed experiment in peacebuilding in Sudan between 1972 and 1983, we hope to reflect on the fragility of such settlements and to draw lessons for present-day experiments in peacebuilding.

The peace that brought an end to the civil wars in Ethiopia, Rwanda and Uganda emerged as a result of military victories rather than negotiated settlements. In chapter 1, John Young describes how the Ethiopian Peoples Revolutionary Democratic Front (EPRDF), along with the Eritrean Peoples Liberation Front (EPLF), forced Mengistu to flee the country and the government to surrender. Though successful in the period of transition, lasting from 1991 until the mid-1990s, in establishing stability throughout the country, in setting up regional governments, in demobilizing the guerrilla forces and creating a national army, the EPRDF had to face a war with Eritrea and now confronts the serious challenge of broadening political participation and consolidating democracy. Ironically, the very factor that accounted for Ethiopia's success in making the transition from war to peace, the highly disciplined and ideologically coherent nature of the ruling Tigrean Peoples Liberation Front, may make the country less adaptable to the forces of change and thus serve to undermine its future stability.

Timothy Longman, in his study of Rwanda in chapter 2, describes a country where peace has remained elusive. The newly established regime of the Rwandese Patriotic Front (RPF) has not even succeeded in creating a negative peace, as armed opposition to it has continuously erupted, flaring up as recently as June 2001. The political leadership is intolerant of dissent and offers little more than token representation in government to the majority Hutu community. Tensions both between and within the two main ethnic groups remain high. Many of the difficulties facing Rwanda's peacebuilding efforts can, in Longman's view, be attributed to 'the legacies of the one-sided victory that brought an end to Rwanda's civil war.' The case illustrates that if an unrepresentative government imposes peace from above and subsequently fails to open up the political system to allow for popular expressions of resentment and frustration, continuing and growing violence is the most likely outcome.

In chapter 3, John Kiyaga-Nsubuga builds on the piece he wrote in our earlier volume in which he described how Museveni attempted to establish representative institutions and reconstruct Uganda's economy without losing control of the political process at the same time. In this chapter he focuses on the consolidation phase of the National Resistance Movement's (NRM's) peacebuilding efforts, beginning with Museveni's landslide victory in the 1996 presidential elections. During this latter period the NRM regime has engineered a transformation of the country's economy, further expanded political space, and introduced effective institutional reform. At the same time, however, Museveni has continued to place severe limits on the activities of political parties and failed to develop a mechanism for leadership succession and regime transformation. Concerned that their fortunes may be drastically affected if they were to be removed from office, Uganda's present leaders seem not to be prepared to take the next steps in liberalizing the political process. By controlling that process indefinitely, they risk generating 'a backlash that could unsettle the regime and undo whatever good it may have achieved.'

The next four chapters focus on peacebuilding processes that follow on or flow from negotiated settlements to civil war. In chapter 4 William Reno describes how in Liberia even though the Abuja peace accord of 1997 provided a measure of stability and order in the daily lives of most Liberians, the peacebuilding process that followed was in reality a 'fake.' The newly elected president, Charles Taylor, behaved in much the same way as his predecessor, Samuel Doe, using the resources under his control to promote his own personal security and welfare and acting 'more like a private entrepreneur than a ruler of a state.' His regime's behaviour was, in Reno's view, the direct result of the state of collapse in which Liberia found itself in the late 1980s, aided and abetted by an international community that was anxious to distance itself from continuing disorder in Liberia and therefore all too quick to seize on the mere end of fighting as evidence of a more permanent peace. In the end, Taylor was forced to take refuge in Nigeria and was replaced by a transitional government backed up by a UN peacekeeping force.

Building peace in Mozambique, a process described by Alexander Costy in chapter 5, is widely perceived as having been a success story. Politically there was an end to fighting, while many of the combatants were demobilized, over a million refugees were integrated into Mozambican society, and a centralized socialist state was transformed into a liberal democracy. Mozambique's leaders also succeeded in adjusting the country's economy to the imperatives of the global economy. And yet, Costy argues, over the longer term, structural change has resulted in the erosion and even reversal of many of the gains achieved in the immediate postwar period, thus posing a threat of renewed instability. Indeed, by the late 1990s Mozambicans were experiencing chronic social unrest and increased levels of crime, resulting in what one international NGO referred to as a 'lawless society.'

In chapter 6, John S. Saul portrays in a similar vein South Africa's ambiguous success story in peacebuilding. On one hand, South Africa has made the shift from the violent and authoritarian society that had been apartheid to a constitutionally-based democratic order, a stability that has been sustained through five years of Nelson Mandela's rule and now four years of Thabo Mbeki's presidency. And yet, seen from the perspective of political economy, South Africa's record is far less impressive. Indeed, Saul argues, the vast majority of South Africa's population has been 'sacrificed on the altar of the neo-liberal logic of global capitalism.' If the quality of their lives further deteriorates, not only will South Africa continue to experience surging crime rates, but it may become witness to what President Mbeki recently referred to as 'the danger of a mounting rage.'

Drawing on the Zimbabwean case, in chapter 7 Hevina Dashwood challenges the prevailing view that following a civil war, peace can be restored through the deployment of short-term political and security measures. Instead, she argues, successful peacebuilding must involve an 'inter-related package of security, political and socio-economic arrangements that provide for the ability to manage social conflict without resort to violence.' Although the civil war ended over twenty years ago, and consequently Zimbabwe has been considered a success story in peacebuilding, such a judgment now seems to have been premature. Recent events in Zimbabwe, which place it on a 'civil war watch,' can in fact be traced back to the root cause of the earlier civil war, the mal-distribution of land. The failure to deal adequately with that issue, both at the time of the Lancaster House agreement in 1979 and in its subsequent implementation, has contributed to the violent upheaval of recent years. Other factors played a part in the current violence, notably Mugabe's unpopularity, his willingness generally to condone the resort to violence, and his total disregard for the rule of law in solving the land issue; the growing influence of the military in Zimbabwe's political life; and the harmful impact the international community has had on Zimbabwe's capacity to implement a program of land distribution. But these were intervening variables that contributed to the escalation of violence in Zimbabawe, not the root cause.

   The last two case studies offer examples of partial or failed peacebuild-ing. In chapter 8, Hussein Adam details the collapse of the Somali state, the role played by the international community in restoring order to that country, and the contrasting peacebuilding experiences in northern and southern Somalia. Somaliland, Puntland, and the Bay area have brought an end to generalized fighting, restored an atmosphere of confidence and trust, and created political arrangements that are relatively open and inclusive. Previously warring communities have learned to resolve their differences, developed a common set of objectives and a common iden-tity, and moved towards the development of a just society. Elsewhere, in the capital of Mogadishu and the central and southern regions, the situ-ation is far less stable. At best, it can be described as a condition of nega-tive peace, where violence, if not effectively controlled, is at least limited in scale. If peace is ever to be consolidated in the south, it will likely arise from spontaneous developments in civil society, much as it did in the north, rather than from internationally imposed solutions. Finally, chap-ter 9, written by Ian Spears and the two editors, focuses on a comparison of two instances of peacebuilding failures – Sudan's experiment with peace between 1972, when the Addis Ababa agreement was signed, and its annulment in 1983; and the reaching of agreements to end fighting in Angola on two separate occasions, in 1991 and 1994, and their subse-quent collapse into renewed fighting. This study points out that the dif-ficulty of reaching a negotiated settlement and maintaining the resulting peace is related to the sense of physical, economic, and political insecu-rity that the parties to the civil war feel, both as individuals and as collec-tivities. Specifically, this insecurity found expression in the difficult task the parties faced in reaching and sustaining an agreement on the forma-tion of a new national army; in the efforts undertaken to fashion a mutu-ally agreed-upon mechanism for the sharing of natural resources in an environment of scarcity; and in the lengthy process of establishing polit-ical institutions that were broadly based and open.
   In addition to these case studies found in the first nine chapters, this volume includes several chapters that focus on broad common themes that cut across all the cases. Even though we will touch on some of these ideas in our conclusion, these chapters, which focus on individual themes, allow us to highlight and explore at greater length what are prominent and, in some cases, controversial issues, and to do so from dif-ferent perspectives. To have a political economist write about the role of economics in the peacebuilding process and a trio (an activist, an inter-

national public servant, and an academic) reflect on the role of the international community should add new dimensions to our understanding of the peacebuilding process.

James Busumtwi-Sam explores the relationship between development and peacebuilding in chapter 10. He begins by outlining a conception of the particular development challenges a country faces when it is engaged in peacebuilding, challenges that differ from those involved in either humanitarian relief or traditional development. Only when there is a clear understanding of the type of development needed to build and sustain peace can the international community hope to contribute successfully to that enterprise. Instead of moulding countries in the image of Western market democracies, international assistance for peacebuilding should be 'about helping local actors establish the conditions that will enable them to make choices in an atmosphere free of large-scale violence, fear, deprivation, and privation.'

Finally, in chapter 11, James Busumtwi-Sam, Alexander Costy, and Bruce Jones discuss the historical and structural obstacles which hinder a more effective involvement of international institutions, both official and unofficial, in managing post-conflict interventions. Developed in response to the very different challenges of the post–Second World War era, the present international structures are poorly equipped to deal with the issues surrounding contemporary peacebuilding. The consequence is 'a structural deficit manifest in a confusion of roles, vagueness of purpose and weak co-ordination among leading states and international organizations.' One adaptation to the inadequacies of international institutional arrangements has been the increasingly important role played by civil society organizations (CSOs) in post-conflict situations. The presumed operational advantages and strategic functions attributed to CSOs by the aid policy community may help to explain why post-conflict aid has increasingly been channelled through the civil sector in the 1990s. Yet, this option has raised several critical concerns. In recent times, the United Nations has assumed a more robust political profile in post-conflict recovery, reflecting a revival of support for UN leadership in post-conflict settings. While ultimately solutions for civil wars will have to come from African countries themselves, a more constructive engagement by the international community can facilitate the transition from war to lasting peace.

In our conclusion, we reflect on the peacebuilding enterprise in the context of the growing literature on this subject. Through a comparative analysis of peacebuilding efforts in ten different African countries and an examination of two broad cros-scutting themes of relevance to this process of reconstruction, we hope to shed more light on the concept of peacebuilding and to identify the factors that both hinder and facilitate its progress.

NOTES

1 Taisier M. Ali and Robert O. Matthews, eds., *Civil Wars in Africa: Roots and Resolution* (Kingston and Montreal: McGill-Queen's University Press, 1999).
2 An exception to this general rule is found in the work of John Paul Lederach, in particular his volume entitled, *Building Peace: Sustainable Reconciliation in Divided Societies* (Washington, DC: United States Institute of Peace, 1997).
3 Raymond W. Copson, *Africa's Wars and Prospects for Peace* (Armonk, NY: M.E. Sharpe, 1994), 4.
4 Ali Abdel Gadir Ali, *The Costs of Conflict in Africa: Some Estimates* (Addis Ababa: Organization of African Unity, April 2000).
5 Mark Duffield made a similar point in his recent volume *Global Governance and the New Wars* (London: Zed Books, 2001), 138, when he argued that UNITA's adaptation to the loss of great power patronage in the early 1990s and 'the resulting local-global linkages' formed around the illicit diamond trade will be an organic part of any post-conflict regime.
6 Kees Kingma describes how 'support by the [local] communities was critical for the success of the reintegration of the ex-combatants.' See K. Kingma, ed., *Demobilization in Sub-Saharan Africa* (London: Macmillan, 2000), 233.

Part One

Peacebuilding after Military Victory

1
Post–Civil War Transitions in Ethiopia

John Young

Ethiopia's development from an ancient autocracy to a modern state in the last half of the twentieth century has been difficult, prolonged, and beset by violent conflict. During the country's thirty-year-long civil war there were numerous attempts at mediation and negotiation, but in the end the war concluded in 1991 with the military victories of the Eritrean Peoples Liberation Front (EPLF), which led to the establishment of the independent state of Eritrea, and the Ethiopian Peoples Revolutionary Democratic Front (EPRDF). Power-sharing was attempted in Ethiopia during the initial transition period, but failed and the EPRDF has since ruled alone. The EPRDF also rejected any merging of its armed forces with those of the ousted Derg, or military regime.

Nonetheless, the transitional period of peacebuilding attained some successes. The EPRDF achieved military control and ensured general stability, carried out a successful demobilization of the guerrilla forces and created an effective national army, established a workable constitution and regional governments, implemented programs of economic and political reform, overcame a revolt of the Oromo Liberation Front (OLF), developed a viable system of foreign relations, gained international legitimacy, and initiated and carried forward a limited program of democratization. This transition period can be dated from the coming to power of the EPRDF in 1991 to the mid-1990s when the country was largely at peace, the new political leadership secure, and the institutions of government in place and functioning. But the dramatic changes in the EPRDF leadership in mid-2001, even though they were achieved without violence, makes clear that the term 'transitional period' is not easily defined.

That said, the relative success can be attributed to a number of factors that will be explored in this chapter. First, achieving an outright military victory meant that the EPRDF faced little opposition. Thus the new government did not have to contend with state collapse as in Somalia, torturous negotiations such as in Mozambique, the instability of failed attempts at power-sharing as in Angola, or the kind of difficulties in constructing a national army as these and other countries have had to take up. Military victory also meant that the EPRDF could gain the approval of its proposed constitution and pursue largely unhindered its programs of political and economic reform.

Second, it will be seen that the successful transition had much to do with the character of the Tigray People's Liberation Front (TPLF), which was instrumental in forming the EPRDF and provided the ideological direction of the government, as well as much of its leadership. The Leninist-structured TPLF has maintained a high degree of unity (at least until divisions broke out in the Front's Central Committee in the spring 2001), discipline, ideological coherence, and a peasant-based focus. As a result, the post-1991 Ethiopian government has maintained stability and had the capacity and commitment to pursue its programs, foremost of which have been administrative decentralization and rural economic development. These measures were designed to overcome the destitution of the majority of the country's population, strong resistance to change, and as a means to reduce the prospect of discontented urban-based elites making common cause with aroused peasants, the very means by which the TPLF came to power.

Lastly and ironically, the defeat of the socialist bloc and the emergence of a new order dominated by the United States and Western international financial institutions have given the still Marxist-leaning EPRDF a measure of international legitimacy. The EPRDF pragmatically adapted to the hegemony of the market and continued Ethiopia's historical role as an opponent of expansionist Islam. In return, the West, led by the United States, has not seriously challenged the EPRDF's human rights record, continued control over much of the economy, and slow progress to democratization. Indeed, with the military defeat of Eritrea and continuing concerns over Islamist-led Sudan, the United States has little option but to recognize the military dominance of Ethiopia in the Horn of Africa and to appreciate that the EPRDF is the only force in the region that can provide stability.

The very strengths of the EPRDF as demonstrated in the transitional period, however, point to subsequent difficulties and the possibility of future failure and a return to instability and civil conflict. Most notable,

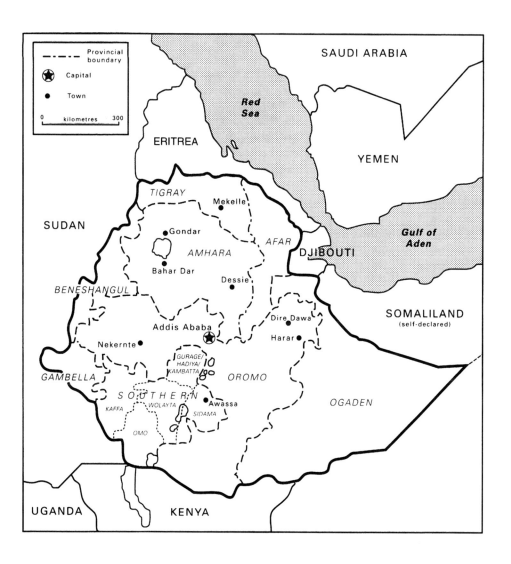

Ethiopia

a successful transition cannot be complete without progress towards democratizing the state, and probably more significantly for such an ancient land, the society. Unlike all other countries in Africa, Ethiopia has not had what can now be recognized as the benefit of the liberalizing values and institutions of colonialism. As a result, the country has carried forward strong societal traditions of authoritarianism and one-man rule through 150 years of the reigns of emperors Twedros, Yohannes, Menelik, and Haile-Selassie, and the military dictatorship of Mengistu Haile-Mariam.

The EPRDF has moved away from such patterns of personal leadership and has thus far resolved political disputes without the state murders of the past. The Front has also ended the aspirations of generations of Ethiopian leaders to centralize the state and instead has given a measure of expression to ethnic and regional sentiments. But ultimately the EPRDF has made little progress in overcoming an historical legacy that provides powerful obstacles to democratic development. Indeed, at the end of a decade of rule, as at the beginning, the governing party effectively constituted the state and there were concerns that Ethiopia would succumb to one-man rule. In any case, the weak state of civil society, the dominance of undemocratic values among both the customary and modern elites, the society's fierce resistance to change, and the conservative weight of traditional institutions like the Orthodox Church, together with the country's overwhelming poverty mean that there have not been significant moves to achieving democracy.

Although democratic progress has been limited, even incremental successes depend upon the unity of the government. After a remarkable twenty-six years without major divisions, conflict broke out in the TPLF Central Committee in March and April of 2001. These divisions, which probably began with personal ambitions but developed ideological dimensions, spread to other components of the EPRDF, the armed forces, and the central organs of the state. In a society where power is worshipped and compromise held to be indicative of weakness and tantamount to an invitation to rebel, significant political change invariably threatens to spill over into violence. It may well be that a second transition has begun, but at the time of writing it has not proceeded far enough to map out its direction or scope.

One element of the confusion is the contradiction between the TPLF's definition of itself as a vanguard party of the peasants, and the discourse it employs which emphasizes legality and parliamentarinism and its attempts to win the support of an uncompromising urban middle class. On the one hand, many of the inteligentsia from Ethiopia's traditional ruling class, the Amharic typically deny the legitimacy of the EPRDF government, oppose the Front's central objectives of decentring the Ethiopian polity or even recognizing ethnic rights, and maintain an imperial vision of a greater Ethiopia that includes Eritrea; on the other hand, many intellectuals from Ethiopia's Oromo community, who claim to represent the country's largest ethnic group, deny the legitimacy of both the EPRDF and the Ethiopian state and are committed to establishing their own independent national entity. A decade of EPRDF rule has not moved the political positions of these factions.

In addition, the EPRDF faces the problem that confronts all revolutionary parties that come to power: increasing signs of atrophy as officials enjoy the fruits of political office. And indeed, raising the cry of corruption, TPLF leader and Prime Minister Meles Zenawi launched a campaign of renewal in mid-2001, which saw the displacement of many members of the Front's Central Committee and various other state and party officials. While there is appreciation of the receptivity of the TPLF and EPRDF to launch such a campaign, the timing makes clear that it was also a critical element of an internal power struggle. It appears to have been designed as a vehicle to tarnish the image of Front veterans, and a means to protect Meles against widespread accusations that he had not sufficiently protected the sovereignty of Ethiopia in the lead up to the war with Eritrea and during the war itself.

Historical Context

Alone in Africa (with the possible exception of Liberia), Ethiopia was never colonized and has thus carried forward its ancient polity, feudal-like system of land tenure, ruling classes, ethnocratic patterns of domination, and authoritarian political culture into the modern era. Unable to reform and facing a growing challenge from the forces unleashed by a modernization Emperor Haile-Selassie initiated but could not control, the regime exploded in 1974 in the closest example of a classic revolution yet witnessed in Africa. But an opposition united only in its desire to overthrow the old regime was soon hopelessly divided along class, ethnic, and ideological lines. The Eritrean revolt that began in 1961 intensified, war with Somalia broke out, and the Derg's military administration spawned numerous rebellions, first in the urban centres and, when those proved impossible, in the countryside.

Foremost among these revolts was the one led by the TPLF. Operating from isolated areas in the largely marginalized northern territory of Tigray, the student-led TPLF was avowedly Marxist and committed to Maoist-like notions of protracted people's war based on the peasants. But in spite of its Marxism (which characterized virtually all the opposition movements of the day as well as the Derg), the TPLF was surprisingly pragmatic on issues such as land tenure and trade and commerce, which directly impacted upon the peasants on whom the movement depended. The Front was not pragmatic, however, in its conviction that Ethiopia's primary contradiction arose from state domination by the Amhara over the country's oppressed nations, including Tigray. It further concluded that only national (that is, ethnic-based) movements could successfully confront the Derg and provide the means for replacing the centralized state with the desired nation-based federation. This analysis proved effective in mobilizing Tigrayan peasants. It provided an organizational structure for uniting militant elements from other oppressed nations in the struggle (the EPRDF was formed in 1989), and a basis for establishing the post-Derg Ethiopian federal state. Indeed, commitment to national self-determination formed the core of its program and united the otherwise initially disparate elements that formed the TPLF.

Equally important in conducting war and developing a bond with the peasants, was the development of a system of evaluation of plans and programs and accountability of its leaders known as *gim gima*. First taken up by intellectuals who have always dominated the movement, it then spread to the guerrilla army and was soon held to be crucial in developing military skills as well as making commanders answerable to their fighters. From the army gim gima spread to the liberated territories and was introduced to the local councils, mass associations, and militias where it gained popularity as the best means of ensuring the accountability of leaders and administrators. With the formation of the EPRDF the system developed a wider base and was given a critical role in the current administration of Ethiopia, although its future is in some doubt, as will be seen.

In a protracted war against the Mergistu government the TPLF entered short-term tactical alliances with groups that shared its opposition to the Derg even if they did not have compatible political programs. But the TPLF's long-term view of the conflict remained firm and ensured that its objectives were not subject to alteration because of these alliances. Thus the TPLF was quick to develop cooperative military relations with a number of other movements, including the more experienced EPLF and the

OLF, even though they did not share strategically compatible long-term objectives. As long as the TPLF accepted its role as junior partner to the EPLF these differences were kept under wraps, but the rapid expansion of the TPLF in the mid-1980s and the leading role it increasingly saw itself assuming in a post-Derg Ethiopia, brought these differences to the fore in 1985 and the movements ended their relationship.[1] With the Derg's demise in sight, the relationship was resumed in 1988, but the differences remained and would figure in the war a decade later between Eritrea and Ethiopia.

The war of liberation and the importance given by the TPLF to its political program also meant that the movement gave little attention to peace negotiations. Moreover, until the late 1980s the TPLF did not have the military strength to ensure that negotiations could be used to fulfill its objectives. Instead, negotiations were largely viewed as a means to spread propaganda, weaken the Derg politically, and support the TPLF and EPRDF's military campaign that alone would achieve the desired objectives. In the event, there were repeated attempts by former US President Jimmy Carter to facilitate contacts between the TPLF (and later the EPRDF), and the Derg and some meetings were held in Rome. But the Derg's failure to recognize the seriousness of the challenge posed by the TPLF until very late in the day, its concentration on negotiations with the EPLF, and its own unwillingness to compromise its program or share power meant that there was little scope for a peaceful settlement of the war in any case. The May 1991 meetings held in London under US auspices between the various opposition forces and the Derg took place against the background of Mengistu fleeing the country and in retrospect amounted to little more than government surrender.

Post-1991 Attempts at National Reconciliation

After the EPRDF entered Addis Ababa in May 1991 it organized a conference to map out the country's future, but significantly those organizations invited were predominantly national-based, liberation fronts, or groups recently organized, frequently at the behest of the Front.[2] Class-based movements, such as the leading parties of the student movement and the Derg's Workers Party of Ethiopia (WPE), were not allowed to attend and to date have not been permitted to participate in the political life of the country, thus reducing the prospect of opposition to the EPRDF's vision of a national-based Ethiopia. Constraints on participation in the conference were in part due to the unwillingness of predominantly Amhara intellectuals and groups to accept the right of Eritreans to self-determination and their demand that the war against the EPLF continue. And it is noteworthy that more than a decade later a considerable part of the opposition to the EPRDF continues to hold an imperial vision of a greater Ethiopia and rejects the Front's commitment to the principle of national self-determination. Indeed, political obstinacy and the refusal to compromise are core values of Ethiopian political culture and hence major obstacles to democratization.

Thus the Addis Ababa conference revolved around the rights of the country's nationalities and a set of principles were approved, including the right to secession. The EPRDF's outright military victory and its domination of the transitional conference ensured that its will prevailed. The conference established the Transitional Government of Ethiopia (TGE) and the TPLF chairman, Meles Zenawi, assumed the presidency of the new construct. An EPRDF-dominated Council of People's Representatives was set up and it adopted the resolutions of the Addis Ababa conference as an interim constitution.

Against much domestic and foreign advice, the EPRDF did not integrate the existing forcibly conscripted Derg army with its own forces to form a national army. The leadership held that discipline had broken down in the army, it had a history of bad relations with the country's peasants, and its political training by the WPE and its allies from the eastern bloc was wholly inappropriate for the role that a national army rooted in the peasantry must now assume. Indeed, there is no doubt that EPRDF forces were better motivated, superior in political leadership, and had an affinity for the peasants that was lacking in the Derg's army, and this might well have been undermined by integrating the two forces.

In any case, by the time the EPRDF took power much of the army had disintegrated; some soldiers went to the countryside as bandits, many sold their weapons and others hid them, most returned to their villages, and some became destitute in the cities. In response, the government began organizing programs to integrate former soldiers into civilian life and appealed abroad for financing such endeavours. But before much progress could be made on these plans, regional elections were organized for June 1992 and this served as the stimulus for the OLF to revolt and for some ex-army Oromo soldiers to turn their weapons on the new government.

The OLF had played an important but secondary role in the Addis Ababa conference, was given the next largest group of seats in the Council of People's Representatives after the EPRDF, and was promised that its forces would be integrated with those of the national army. But it grew increasingly disenchanted with the EPRDF's domination of the transitional government. It seriously doubted the movement's commitment to the right of secession and, after alleging intimidation and other irregularities in the elections, withdrew from the government and launched an insurrection. Joined by thousands of disaffected ex-army Oromo soldiers the revolt quickly spread through eastern Ethiopia. But almost as quickly the EPRDF army brought it to an end, capturing some twenty thousand combatants against minimal army losses. Although small numbers of OLF guerrillas continue to eke out an existence in eastern Ethiopia and had their hopes raised by Eritrean support during the Ethio-Eritrean war, their forces were defeated in Somalia even before that war ended.

While some have seen the insurrection of 1992 as evidence of the failure of the transitional government to integrate the former army with its own and to resolve disputes over power in the new federal system, the EPRDF leadership concluded that the rapid containment of the revolt was evidence of the capacity of its army to neutralize opposition movements. In addition, it held that its policies to devolve powers to ethnic-based regional administrations were correct and should be rapidly pursued. And lastly, while the EPRDF maintained that only its own disciplined army, with close relations with the peasants, could have successfully overcome the insurrection, it nonetheless moved quickly to provide and solicit foreign help for the retraining and support of the demobilized ex-Derg soldiers. Programs to reintegrate former army members into civilian life by providing them with land and cattle appear to have been successful, but some did not want to return to the countryside and have stayed in the urban centres, sometimes reduced to begging and crime to support themselves.

As well as taking up the problems of the former Derg soldiers, the EPRDF also had to demobilize a considerable number of its own forces, develop an ethnically balanced army commensurate with its political objective of restructuring the Ethiopian state, and train and prepare what had been a guerrilla army as a conventional force. On balance, the EPRDF has made progress in all of these tasks, but not without problems. Many ordinary EPRDF peasant fighters were only too happy to return to their families and state-guaranteed plots of land. Others were given academic and vocational training and some, because of their war-sustained injuries, have had to receive extensive rehabilitation. Because of conservative values, it has proved difficult to reintegrate into village life the many young women who joined the EPRDF and they have been given lengthy and often separate training so they can take up occupations in urban centres. Whether it was a policy or not, the army went from having a large contingent of women (estimated to be one-third of the TPLF fighters) to virtually none within a couple of years of the EPRDF taking power. For all of these programs the government has received foreign funding. But the EPRDF also established a wide range of party-affiliated companies and among their objectives initially included giving ex-fighters priority in jobs, providing money for their rehabilitation, and giving pensions to dependants of severely wounded or dead fighters.

Achieving a rough ethnic balance in both the rank and file and leadership of the new armed forces has been a political priority of the EPRDF, even though it has meant a disproportionate demobilization of Tigrayan fighters, who are usually the most experienced and committed, and the advancement into higher positions of sometimes less qualified non-Tigrayans. In particular, there were major efforts to recruit from historically disadvantaged communities, such as those inhabiting the lowlands east and west of the country's central plateau. While hard statistics are not available, there is reason to believe that progress was made in broadening representation in the army. As a result of the war with Eritrea, a number of demobilized Tigrayan army leaders, such as Siye Abraha, resumed leading positions in the service, thus perhaps changing the ethnic balance with the leadership, although again the evidence is not available to draw hard conclusions. When the war ended some quickly returned to civilian life and Siye was jailed and purged for his anti-Meles stance in the TPLF division of 2001.

During the guerrilla campaign conducted from 1975 to 1991 the culture of the EPRDF's army was open, and questioning of authority was encouraged through the institution of gim gima. Well after liberation in 1991, a senior member of the armed forces assured me that the national force was not a 'yes sir, no sir' kind of army and that the rights of the rank and file to challenge their officers were guaranteed.[3] While efforts to introduce greater formality into the army were made, it appears that a degree of democracy and equality remain: saluting was slow to become regularized, the orders of superiors can be questioned, political perspectives of individuals are important, and evaluations, including self-criticism, remain important elements of army life. Like the rest of Ethiopian society under the EPRDF, ethnicity figures highly, can be disruptive, and Tigrayans – irrespective of their formal ranks – have a disproportionate influence. It is unclear what the impact of the Ethiopian-Eritrean war or the TPLF leadership dispute of mid-2001, which spread to the army and led to the dismissal of Chief of Defence Staff Tasdkan and other senior officers, will have on the character of this unique army. It may be that the army's democratic values acquired during its formative guerrilla period will be undermined. If this proves to be the case it will be a considerable loss because in a largely authoritarian and highly polarized Ethiopia the army has been a force for democracy and one of the few secular institutions to have a measure of popular respect.

Attempts at formalizing gim gima in the transitional period corresponded with the realization that a movement with roots in guerrilla struggle did not always have the skills and experience to operate the increasingly sophisticated equipment of a modern conventional army. As a result, all seven hundred Ministry of Defence officials were retained, and after investigations for abuses, three thousand former Derg officers were kept.[4] However, there was a wholesale dismissal of pilots from the national airforce because of their record of terrorist attacks on civilian targets, particularly in the EPRDF heartland of Tigray. And it was not until the outbreak of war with Eritrea in 1998 that the weakness of the airforce was recognized as a serious problem and objections to the former Derg pilots and other specialists were overcome, after which many were rapidly mobilized. Moreover, the Eritrean war intensified moves to utilize more sophisticated military hardware and this entailed importing not only the technology, but also experts from Eastern Europe to train and advise Ethiopian army personnel.

The OLF insurrection of 1992 not only brought about the end of the military threat posed by the movement, but also marked the beginning of the end of power-sharing in Ethiopia. The OLF and EPRDF have engaged in periodic negotiations in the years since the revolt over a possible role for the OLF in the government, but they have not been successful. The Southern Ethiopia Peoples Democratic Coalition, which represented a coalition of non-EPRDF ethnic-based parties from the ethnically diverse southern region of Ethiopia, had a minor presence in the early transitional government, but after holding meetings with various opposition movements in Paris in 1993, it was summarily removed from the government.

Instead, the EPRDF has worked in government with groups officially called allies and independents. These are typically small, ethnic-based liberation movements that had close relations with the EPRDF during the war years. They usually have programs almost identical to the EPRDF and for practical purposes are members of the ruling party, or members in waiting. A small number of independents are represented in the Council of People's Representatives, but some are independent only in name and are in reality under the control of the EPRDF. Outside the Council there are a large number of legal but weak opposition parties that operate in the centre with considerable freedom, but usually have little presence beyond the capital, where in any case their activities to date have been circumscribed.

A similar pattern can be found in the media, with the state and the EPRDF having an overwhelming position and the private and opposition media largely restricted to Addis Ababa. The state media includes the sole television and radio stations and a wide range of newspapers and periodicals. The EPRDF in turn has two radio stations (Radio Woyene in Tigray and Radio Fana), and many newspapers and periodicals. Although nominally independent, the news agency Walta Information Center is controlled and managed by EPRDF members and sells material to the EPRDF, state, and private media. There were some indications at the end of the Ethio-Eritrean war and during the May 2000 general elections that government and Front media were giving wider attention to opposition views, but the coverage of the internal TPLF dispute has been blatantly pro-Meles.

The private media includes a range of newspapers and periodicals that usually express an opposition point of view. Typically under-financed, unprofessional, and backed by political interests, they are often harassed by the authorities, but nonetheless continue to provide a vibrant commentary on political life in the country. They are virtually all based in Addis Ababa and while the situation is improving, even reading the opposition press outside the capital can lead to harassment or arrest, although such measures are not permitted by law. Interestingly, some of the most outspoken opposition papers which express Amhara or pan-Ethiopian sentiments became strong proponents of the war with Eritrea and as a result were far less critical of the EPRDF and faced few government constraints. With the war over this honeymoon quickly ended and leading elements in the media again questioned the EPRDF's loyalty to Ethiopia, challenged the Front's decentralization program, and accused the TPLF of an alliance with the EPLF. They also urged a militarist approach to Eritrea and advocated the capture of the Eritrean Red Sea port of Assab, again making clear their continued unwillingness to accept Eritrean independence.

Apart from some traditional elements, civil society was essentially denied any existence in Ethiopia until the EPRDF took power in 1991 and since then its emergence has been slow and difficult. All NGOs have to be registered with the government and because of an inefficient bureaucracy, but mostly because of government concerns that such organizations represent political interests – a not always unfounded suspicion – bringing them into existence is a daunting, task. Western governments and NGOs have devoted considerable resources to governance (although this was often suspended during the Ethio-Eritrean war), which frequently goes to bolstering government agencies, courts, or on civil society, but the results of these efforts are limited and questionable. There have been demonstrations in Addis Ababa and for the most part they are not interfered with, but are most often ignored by the government. Exceptions included demonstrations by university students in opposition to the 1993 Eritrean referendum on independence and against land reform in the Amhara state, and in both cases participants were forcibly stopped, jailed, and beaten.

Against the background of divisions within the ruling party's leadership, a dispute at Addis Ababa University spilled on to the streets on 18 April 2001 and was quickly taken over by criminal elements that looted the business areas of Addis Ababa before being brutally put down by the police with the loss of more than thirty lives. There were also minor disturbances and support for the reformist demands of the students at other post-secondary institutions in the country. Whether politically aroused students can form a viable opposition to the government in the manner of the previous generation is at this time doubtful since they are divided ethnically, have no common ideology or political platform, and no history of struggle. But if the divisions within the EPRDF are not soon resolved, then even a weak student movement in combination with street lumpin can be a destabilizing influence.

Elements of an independent civil society are far more likely to be permitted in Addis Ababa than elsewhere in the country, though this is in some ways surprising because opposition to the government is much stronger in the capital than elsewhere in the country. This can probably be explained by the more developed character of political life in the only truly urban centre of the country, greater unwillingness of conservative regional politicians to permit opposition, the limited presence of foreigners to report on the situation outside Addis Ababa, and the fact that there is little indication that the EPRDF faces much opposition in the countryside. Indeed, the frequent disdain with which the EPRDF responds to the opposition can in part be attributed to the view that as a party that professes to represent alone the interests of the peasants, it is sensitive to the concerns of the masses, while their urban-based critics are not. While the EPRDF has viewed democracy as being class-based and has been openly disdainful of Western notions of liberal democracy, even this principle was being questioned by mid-2001.

In an Ethiopia with a weak civil society and a history where powerful men and not laws have defined the relationship between subjects (there were no citizens) and the state, the present constitution must be recognized primarily as a symbol of the regime and part of an effort to achieve domestic and international legitimacy. However, while sometimes ignored in practice, unlike many constitutions, this one is grounded in values fought for during revolutionary struggle. In particular, the war aimed to end Amhara hegemony and bring historically marginalized groups into the state, or at least ensure that they did not launch national-based anti-state armed struggles. That said, nothing in the constitution or the democratization process in general in any way detracts from the EPRDF's further unstated commitment to maintain hegemony in the Ethiopian state.

While the EPRDF has not closed the door to power-sharing, throughout the period being examined here it held that forces such as the OLF must accept the 1994 Ethiopian constitution before such a relationship could be entertained. Since the constitution broadly reflects the values of the EPRDF, power-sharing is thus dependent upon an acceptance of the status quo. Moreover, since it is inconceivable that the EPRDF would accept a power-sharing relationship in which the other party or parties had anything close to half the representation in government, it could not produce a major alteration in the balance of political power in the country. Once again, the convincing military victory of the EPRDF and the fact that opposition forces, whether legal or illegal, do not or are not permitted to provide a serious challenge to the government means that the Front has little incentive to give up any of its hard-won power. Since the mid-1990s EPRDF leaders have argued that political development in the country is dependent upon the emergence of a constructive opposition. However, while traditional Ethiopian political culture does not encourage pluralism, and the parties that have developed in the post-1991 period are typically factional, opportunist, and poorly led, after thirteen years in power the Front must also bear some responsibility for the weak state of the opposition forces and the continuing stultifying political culture of the country.

The May 2000 elections generally did not challenge this conclusion, but there were some positive developments. For the first time the government media presented opposition views and for many in Ethiopia the highlight of the campaign was a long and hard-hitting debate between party leaders carried on national television and radio. Second, the Ethiopian government demonstrated a level of technical competence in the conduct of the election that had not been seen in previous elections. Third, the National Electoral Board demonstrated some independence by cancelling votes in a number of southern regional constituencies because of irregularities and the rescheduled vote resulted in the election of eight candidates from the opposition Southern Ethiopia Peoples Democratic Coalition led by Dr Beyene Petros, who subsequently become the de facto leader of the parliamentary opposition.

Indeed, the southern region, and in particular the Haddiya zone (the area in which the Southern Front won almost all its seats), stood out for the level of violence. This appears to be due to the extra-legal efforts by EPRDF officials, whose positions were weakened by the conviction of their local leader for corruption, the popularity of Beyene who is a native of the zone, and the capacity of his party to overcome official harassment. Although working from a small base, Beyene's party will have an opportunity to present its very different views from the EPRDF on land tenure; it supports land not being marketable but wants written guarantees of possession. The party also favours pluralism, opposes the right of national groups to secession, and objects to the EPRDF's notion of revolutionary democracy.[5] Most surprising in the national election was the failure of the Oromo National Congress (ONC), which only elected one candidate in spite of the fact that there was little evidence of government interference in the region and it is assumed that the EPRDF affiliate, the Oromo Peoples Democratic Organization (OPDO), is widely unpopular. The ONC came across as a one-man party of Merera Gudina, who pursued a timid campaign that emphasized Oromo nationalism and appeared to be competing with the OLF. The new National Assembly thus looks much like the previous one and the election must at best be seen as only a small step towards achieving accountable government. In any case, to date the Assembly remains only a minor focus of power in the country.

To some extent parallel to, but reinforcing the formal administrative structure, is the EPRDF's developed system of gim gima. Widely practised and supported in the liberated territories during the revolution (particularly in Tigray) this system of evaluation met resistance when the EPRDF introduced it into all levels of government after 1991. But with the support of peasants, fighters, and leaders, who are themselves subject to it, gim gima was, at least until recently, spreading to all manner of government and non-government associations throughout Ethiopia. Plans and programs and the personnel carrying them out are – ideally – critically and openly evaluated on regular basis, and changes and improvements are recommended for the administering bodies to carry out. The impact of the system has been most notable on the political life of the country: for example, a deputy prime minister and governments for the Somali, Gambella, and Benishangual regions, as well as officials from numerous district administrations and public agencies, have been dismissed and many imprisoned as a result of gim gima conferences that exposed maladministration and corruption. Indeed, regional government auditors interviewed by the author typically acknowledge that gim gima is one of the best tools in bringing corruption to light. But there is little doubt that the institution operated best in a revolutionary context and can never have the same impact under present conditions.

In addition, beginning with Tigray and moving south, gim gima is being introduced into the schools. In Tigray it begins in the first grade when students regularly meet to evaluate their teachers and the results are passed on to the principals for action. Although there is a danger of individuals being assessed on grounds other than their work performance, anecdotal evidence suggests that even in the early grades these sessions do produce a measure of accountability, quicker response to problems, and added responsibility among students. While teachers often have mixed views about gim gima, students I have interviewed in Tigray and the Amhara region all strongly endorse it.

This is not a feature of democracy as it is known and practised in the West, but it does have two elements that are critical to democratic government: giving people a voice in their administration, and making leaders responsible to the citizens. Moreover, in an Ethiopia where secrecy is valued and openness is viewed as akin to innocence and simplicity, gim gima in theory encourages transparency. While to date the scope of the system has not included consideration of core EPRDF values, these are probably not of major concern to those for whom the institution was principally designed – namely the peasants. The peasants' primary concern is with achieving responsible, effective, accountable public administration and gim gima appears to provide a means to achieve these objectives.

Of course, when major programs and leading figures in government are dismissed as a result of gim gima, there is a significant measure of orchestration and planning by higher authorities to ensure that broad political objectives are achieved. With few safeguards and in a culture with little tolerance for diversity, there is always the danger of human rights abuses. Practical problems also exist, such as introducing an institution developed in the army and peasant milieu of Tigray to other regions and spheres of society. In addition, there is an appreciation of the need to reduce the time devoted to it: pre-1991 gim gima sessions among Tigrayan peasants would often go on for months and as late as 1993 the government of Tigray was effectively closed down for two months while gim gima was being conducted.[6] Moreover, it is very difficult to make a conclusive assessment of gim gima because its effectiveness varies enormously across organizations and geographically as one moves south in the country, and as well there has been no serious research into the institution. Another problem, noted by a leading theoretician in the EPRDF, is the particular weakness of gim gima in the federal government where civil service rules tend to predominate.[7] There is also a distinction between hard and soft versions on gim gima, with the former largely confined to Front members and involving extensive self-criticism. Softer versions are increasingly being used to win the support of the generally conservative middle classes.

National Self-determination to Federalism

At the core of the ideology of the TPLF, and later the EPRDF, was the conviction that for at least a century before 1991 Ethiopia had been an ethnocratic dictatorship under Amhara ruling classes from the central state of Shoa. Therefore, the primary objective of the revolt was to end this dictatorship and ensure that all of the country's nations would have the right to freely associate with or leave a newly constructed federal state. The TPLF assessment was also meant to serve as a military and mobilizing strategy, and indeed the EPRDF was established to build up a viable ethnic-based coalition that would mobilize the country's disparate population, and serve as a model for the post-Derg organization of the Ethiopian state. This ethnic-based coalition also had the effect of providing a means by which the TPLF, representing Tigrayans who constitute less than 5 percent of the population, could maintain a leading position in the country's political life.

In addition, this model was designed to promote a convincing alternative to the centralized state that had produced a legacy of war and poverty under successive Ethiopian emperors and the Derg. The EPRDF held that a far-reaching decentralization was the only means to maintain the territorial integrity of the country and ensure that the debilitating wars that had torn Ethiopia apart in the recent past would not recur in the future. The first step towards achieving this was the 1992 regional elections (noted above) and they were followed in 1994 with elections to the Constituent Assembly to complete and ratify a new constitution. In both cases there was evidence of human rights violations and most of the thirty-nine parties participating were supporters of the government, while the major opposition parties boycotted the elections. A constitution was nonetheless approved in December 1994 by the Council of People's Representatives, which led to the creation of a federal state of ten regions. This paved the way for national elections in May 1995 that in the absence of major opposition parties produced a massive victory for the EPRDF and its allies. On August 24 the country was formally proclaimed the Federal Democratic Republic of Ethiopia (FDRE).

While the sincerity of the Constitution's pledge that 'Every nation, nationality, and people in Ethiopia has an unconditional right to self-determination, including the right to secession'[8] is as yet untested and regional governments have varying levels of autonomy, the EPRDF's program of decentralization has been at the core of its program and represents the most dramatic change in Ethiopian government policy in over a century. It must, however, be stressed that power is being devolved to regional units controlled by members and allies of the EPRDF and thus devolution does not threaten the Front's hegemonic position in the state. Nonetheless, while critics outside the country point to this fact to dismiss Ethiopian federalism, it is noteworthy that most domestic critics fear that the TPLF-implemented system has been so far-reaching as to threaten the dismemberment of the country.

It would appear that real political and economic power, based on constitutionally guaranteed rights to funds and local authority to raise some taxes, is being devolved. While agents of the central government and the TPLF play varying roles in regional governance, local administrators and judges are usually from indigenous communities and speak local languages, unlike the imposed Amharigna of the past. Most impressive has been the cultural renaissance that is taking place, based in particular on the introduction of indigenous languages in regional schools. A primary stimulus for decentralization was local-level development and, while this is hard to evaluate, there is no doubt as to the growing importance of regional-level economies. This, too, suggests a genuine shift in power from the centre to the peripheries. While the Ethiopian federal model assumes a measure of central direction, it has proved sufficiently flexible that each region has followed its own particular pattern of political development. For example, the Tigray and Amhara regions of Ethiopia's northern highlands have the strongest regional administrations, the southern region (because of its great ethnic diversity) has the most developed zonal administrations (that level of administration which falls between the region and district), and the Amhara region is proving most effective at devolving powers to the districts.

Not surprisingly, Tigray with its skilled political leadership and mobilized population has proved adept at local government.[9] Indeed, the end of the war and the establishment of the federal state led to a loss of autonomy in Tigray as it moved from the status of a virtual sovereign state to that of a province that had to operate through frequently obstructive central government agencies. Moreover, the central government personnel who returned to Tigray brought with them the practices, values, and assumptions of the old bureaucracy which frequently conflicted with the popular democratic procedures developed by the TPLF and supported by the people. Also, a suspicious urban population and business community which had had little contact with the TPLF during most of the years of struggle was slow to accept a movement associated with Marxism. But political stability, the TPLF's long-established relations with the peasants, and the growing prosperity of the province overcame any simmering resentment.

Both governance and the rapid levels of economic development were disrupted between May 1998 and May 2000 when northern portions of Tigray became battle zones in the war with Eritrea. In addition, a dispute within the TPLF Central Committee led to the dismissal of the Tigray Regional President, Gebru Asrat, who [was] widely respected and proved a capable and popular leader in the region since 1991. Despite the widely held belief, both inside and outside Ethiopia, that a disproportionate amount of central government resources are directed to Tigray, the continuing high levels of underdevelopment in the region suggest otherwise. For example, according to national statistics for the year 1999, Tigray had the lowest per capita income of any regional state in Ethiopia and indices show that the region also had, along with the Amhara region, the country's highest levels of underweight children.[10]

After a slow start in the Amhara region, which contains approximately one-third of the country's population, the regional affiliate of the EPRDF, the Amhara National Democratic Movement (ANDM), is providing capable administration and making even more progress than the TPLF in carrying out the EPRDF's program of further devolving powers from the regions to the districts. Although the ANDM was established in the late 1970s, it soon fell under TPLF domination and has not gained the same legitimacy of the latter movement, nor does it have close relations with the peasants, or the experienced leadership. The jailing of ANDM leader in deputy prime Minister and defence minister, Tamrat Layne, for corruption is indicative of that weakness, but the regional leader Adisu Legesse has led a generally competent and stable administration from 1991 until early 2001 when he was reassigned to the central government. Moreover, while Amhara intellectuals in Addis Ababa often oppose the EPRDF, my visits to the region in 1992, 1995, and 1998 indicate a steady decline in hostility in the urban centres to the government, almost certainly because of improving material conditions and effective administration.

The administration and development of Oromia region, which accounts for almost 35 percent of Ethiopia's population, has been beset by problems from its inception. Given the size of the population it is arguably the biggest threat to the viability of the EPRDF's system of ethnic-based federalism. The region's population is largely ethnically homogeneous, has some of the country's richest lands, and with Addis Ababa serving as its regional capital has access to the best infrastructure and skilled personnel in the country.[11] But in spite of these advantages, economic and political development has been limited and as a result many Oromo intellectuals retain sympathies for the OLF, even if thus far it has not proved militarily effective and there is little indication the region's peasants are prepared to actively oppose the regime. Because of its late establishment and weak leadership, the regional EPRDF affiliate, the Oromo Peoples Democratic Organization (OPDO), has largely proved ineffective, prone to corruption, and unable to meet the demands for development. And indeed this was tacitly acknowledged in the removal from power of the region's president, Kuma Demeksa, and a number of other top officials in July 2001.[12]

The southern region had an estimated population of 11.3 million in 1994, which is divided among more than forty nationalities,[13] but this heterogeneity has not proved an insurmountable obstacle to development. Nonetheless, it has produced tension and sometimes violent conflict over the distribution of scarce economic resources (principally land) and political power. With such ethnic diversity the region has devolved more powers to zonal administrations than elsewhere in Ethiopia. Indeed, the TPLF-developed notion of national self-determination is being sorely tested in this region, which started out with forty-four recognized ethnic groups; at the time of writing this had increased to fifty-six. Under a regime where power is based on ethnicity, the demand for ethnic recognition is bound to increase and this problem will have to be confronted.

While Amharigna is used at the regional level, the language is not employed below that and this has caused some resentment among Amharas and others from the north living in the south. However, generally the development of the local languages that have replaced Amharigna is proceeding well and is producing a cultural renaissance among peoples who have long been marginalized in the Ethiopian state. The southern region, however, suffers from a lack of political unity, in part because its ruling party was established at the behest of the EPRDF and only after 1991. Initially there were many changes in the administration at the regional, zonal, and district levels of government, largely as a result of leaders being removed for corruption and maladministration, which can be attributed to limited education, experience, and loyalty to their respective parties. The behind-the-scenes role of TPLF cadres appears more active than in the Oromo and Amhara regions and in the 2000 elections the south recorded the most abuses. Unlike the three more developed, ethnically homogeneous, and politically conscious regions to the north, the enormous ethnic diversity of the south means that it could not realistically consider separation as a unit and thus can be expected to be a strong supporter of a united federal Ethiopia.

Although not constituting major populations, the lowland states of the Somali and Afar in the east and Gambella and Benishangul-Gumuz in the west have made only slow progress, although the difficulties in developing strong governments in these backward areas was readily anticipated.[14] Many of the people inhabiting these territories are pastoralists with no tradition of indigenous settled administration and in fact little experience with central government, apart from largely tribute-demanding regimes before the advent of the Derg. Moreover, the present extremely low levels of economic and political development in these states are the result of the failure of past centralized regimes. As a result, there have been high levels of corruption, maladministration, and considerable political instability.

Demands have been made that the central government, which provides more than three-quarters of the budgets of these states, take a more active role in their administration, but this creates a major problem for the EPRDF. On the one hand, to rule from the centre would undermine the principle of national self-determination and might

reduce the capacity of these states to gain the necessary skills in government. On the other hand, permitting the flagrant waste of public
resources is untenable in conditions of scarcity and would be politically
damaging, even if the parties ruling in these regions are only nominally
allies of the EPRDF. In the event, a two-tier or even more graduated system of federalism appeared to be emerging, with the central government playing a much more active role in the affairs of these lowland
states than elsewhere in the country. This caused resentment in the eastern Somali and Afar regions where national consciousness runs high,
but in the western Gambella and Benishangul regions local governments until recently acknowledged their weakness and both they and
the general population welcomed a greater central government role.
However, it is indicative of the growing unwillingness to accept TPLF
tutelage that even in these regions there are demands for more autonomy. Whether such underdeveloped regions can cope without outside
political and organizational assistance, however, is by no means clear.

As well as providing regional states the right to secede, the Ethiopian
constitution allows nations, nationalities, and peoples (terms referred to
in the constitution, but not defined) within regional states the right to
establish their own states. The Silte, who are associated with the Gurage
people of the Southern Region, were the first to test this provision and
demand that the central government recognize them as a separate people with the right to their own administration. Initially the local EPRDF
affiliate did not permit a vote on the matter, but in March 2001 a referendum was held, and the overwhelming majority decision was to recognize a separate status for the Silte, although at the time of writing this
status has not been given constitutional expression. Consequently, the
Silte case received a lot of attention but there have been many cases,
particularly in the Southern Region, where ethnic-based rights have
been conferred on communities.

Generally the Ethiopian experiment with federalism is proving successful in meeting the EPRDF's goals of ending the hegemony of the
Amhara ruling class in the centre and giving a role in administration to
the marginalized nations, while at the same time ensuring the unity of
the country. Indeed, such a program of decentralization was probably
crucial in preventing the break-up of Ethiopia after 1991 and the spawn-
ing of a series of civil wars. Nonetheless, the results of decentralization
are mixed, with some regions and some areas demonstrating considerable skill in local administration and others falling behind. Moreover,
Ethiopian federalism has not eliminated ethnic-based struggles, as dem-

onstrated by violent conflicts in recent years between the Amhara and Oromo in Arsi, and between Gujis and Sidamas, Borena and Hammer, Oromo and Somali, and many others. But such struggles have been localized and not threatened the viability of the system.

Ethnic federalism is not the ultimate answer to Ethiopia's problems of equity and governance, but nonetheless it seems a necessary response to a history of state centralism and systemic denial of the rights of minorities. Moreover, the system is demonstrating sufficient flexibility that regions are developing their own priorities and authority is being devolved to regional and sub-regional government units deemed capable while the central government is endeavouring to reinforce other regions with weak administrations and the EPRDF is engaged in training regional affiliated cadres in these areas. Although the regional components and allies of the EPRDF vary enormously in strength and experience, the Front as a whole has maintained its unity and discipline and this has thus far ensured that locally generated nationalist sentiments and demands have not to date become destabilizing. This has been a difficult balance to achieve and at the time of writing it is facing its most serious threat as a result of the crisis within the TPLF, which is the linchpin in the governance structure.

Economic Policy

Much of the success of the transitional period can be attributed to the EPRDF's economic policies and the capacity of the Front to carry them out. While the TPLF's early Marxist rhetoric and admiration for Albania initially caused anguish among the business community, the Front's long experience in the liberated territories made clear its pragmatism and readiness to respond positively to the concerns of the peasants. Indeed, peasant opposition to the Derg's establishment of state and cooperative farms and interference in trade and commerce was used by the TPLF to mobilize opposition against the regime. Ideological support for this apparent pragmatism was initially provided by the Front's acceptance of a two-step model in which Tigray would first be freed from Amhara domination, feudalism would be eliminated, and capitalism introduced; only then would a socialist transformation commence. This model and the secret organizations which were to oversee its implementation in the country's regions were officially disbanded in 1991, but a decade later the EPRDF felt it necessary to pass a series of widely publicized conference resolutions endorsing capitalism.

Like all revolutionary movements, the TPLF needed funds to support its struggle, but there is little evidence that it was acquired from foreign sources, coercing peasants, or crime, apart from some early bank robberies. Financing was acquired through taxation in the liberated territories, voluntary contributions from the business community, and donations from Tigrayans living abroad. Almost certainly a portion of relief assistance provided by NGOs was also used, and in the final stages of the war money was obtained from companies organized by the TPLF. The movement's first experience with party-affiliated organizations was the establishment of the Relief Society of Tigray (REST) in 1978, which served both to ensure the effective distribution of foreign and locally provided aid and to reap the political benefits of distributing grains directly to those to whom the movement was appealing for support.

As the struggle advanced and more skilled personnel joined the TPLF, the movement acquired the capacity to start its own businesses. Typically these first businesses were in the area of transport, usually on a small scale, and were designed to contribute to the war effort or provide services for which the private sector did not have the will or capacity. This experience, however, not only proved profitable politically and financially, but served as the conceptual and practical basis for much of the TPLF's model of reconstruction and development in Tigray, which in turn has provided the direction for all the regional states in the post-1991 period, an issue that will be taken up shortly.

Upon assuming power in May 1991 the EPRDF was confronted with an economy near collapse, a state devoid of funds, and an Amhara-dominated civil service in virtual rebellion. The immediate need was to provide stability and the army quickly accomplished this. International loans and funding from the EPRDF's own coffers staved off the financial crisis of the state, but reforming the economy has proved a more daunting task. The Derg's command economy, which eliminated markets in trade and labour, directly interfered in commerce, and established state and cooperative farms that consumed enormous resources with poor results, was already being challenged by an aroused peasantry across Ethiopia by the time the EPRDF took power. A movement that had come to power claiming to represent the peasants was not about to openly challenge them. In any case, the TPLF's liberated territories had long accepted markets, and by 1991, with the collapse of the economies of Eastern Europe and the Soviet Union, state socialism was no longer a viable option.

The in-coming government encouraged markets, initiated moves to privatize state farms and other largely bankrupt state holdings, the hated state agricultural marketing corporations were wrapped up, and a campaign against the deeply entrenched corruption was undertaken. From the peasantist perspective of the EPRDF much of the Derg's 'socialism' was not designed for the majority population of peasants, but intended to benefit the WPE leadership and, to a lesser extent, a parasitical urban population that had always plundered the peasants. Thus in a curious way elements of the EPRDF's economic policy meshed closely with the anti-state, new liberalism of the international financial institutions and the ideology of the West led by the United States. And indeed, no less an organization than the World Bank, in an unpublished 1997 report, gave high praise to the government's administration of the economy and the leadership of Prime Minister Meles Zenawi in particular.[15]

However, the match is not perfect: many TPLF and other EPRDF leaders had been activists in the student movement and challenged the Haile Selassie regime with the slogan of 'land to the tillers.' They were not about to introduce a free market in land that could be expected to foster the kind of class and ethnic tensions that had helped produce the revolution of 1974. Moreover, in the wake of the overthrow of the Derg, the peasant cry was not for a free market in land, but for security of land tenure. The model developed in the liberated territories therefore went some way to creating conditions that met the peasants' needs. Rural land thus remained nationalized, peasants were guaranteed rights to land, and while security of holdings was ensured and leasing of land was permitted, no market in land was permitted. Nonetheless, the model has proved sufficiently flexible that peasants can acquire mortgages through leasing their land, and in Tigray peasant demands that they be given written documentation confirming their rights to land have been accepted and this practice is likely to be duplicated elsewhere in the country.

Moreover, there is no doubt that a major reason for the EPRDF's emphasis on rural development and its refusal to permit a market in land is to slow down the destructive effects of urban expansion devoid of industrialization. Indeed, the Addis Ababa riots of 18 April 2001 which were dominated by the unemployed, will likely give the EPRDF further resolve not to bend to international pressures for privatizing rural land, which would lead to an even greater influx into the cities. But unless there can be sufficient capitalization in the countryside – largely through better agricultural methods, fertilization, and irrigation – to significantly increase production and raise the standard of living of a largely destitute population, the pressures will be difficult to contain and the migration to the cities will continue, irrespective of the official policy. Overcoming rural poverty will prove to be one of the greatest challenges facing the EPRDF, and indeed, government officials never fail to argue that this is the biggest threat to the security of both Ethiopia and the region.

Within this system of land tenure the EPRDF has concentrated on a multifaceted program of rural development. Among the priorities is building up one of the weakest infrastructures in Africa and one that has made Ethiopia's northern peasants repeatedly vulnerable to famine in this century. The construction of clinics, schools, and particularly roads, which are critical to alleviating famines, are proceeding apace. Where feasible, micro-dams are opening up new opportunities for multi-cropping and marketing surplus produce in nearby towns. Agricultural extension was practised in the liberated territories and has undergone a marked expansion since 1991. The emphasis is on introducing chemical fertilizers to peasants where practical and careful studies have been made on how to match crops and production levels with local conditions. Together these moves have led to increases in production and higher standards of living for peasants in most parts of the country. But the picture is mixed, with chemical fertilizers having the best results among the predominantly grain growers of the north. Moreover, while fertilizers were initially heavily subsidized, they are now largely sold at market prices. Many peasants have to go into debt to pay for them and this is causing resentment. Once again the critical variable in rural development is proving to be administration. As would be expected, the most effective rural governments are found where the anti-Derg revolution had the deepest roots, which in descending order are Tigray, much of the Amhara region, parts of the south, much smaller areas in Oromia, and, bringing up the rear, the eastern and western lowland states.

Moreover, famines are not a thing of the past. In 1992–3 areas of northern Ethiopia were afflicted. The government's response was quick and effective and contrasted positively with the experience of the imperial and Derg regimes. This famine could in part be attributed to the economic dislocation and weakness of the country after decades of war. However, such excuses cannot be used to explain the famine of 2000, which included some parts of the north, but was largely concentrated in the east and south of the country. Nor can it explain the famine overtaking the country in 2003. Indeed, EPRDF leaders acknowledge their government's failure to end Ethiopia's infamous cycle of famines and consider it to be perhaps their central challenge.[16] This has led to consideration being given to relocating peasants,[17] an approach that would have been unheard of only a few years ago because of peoples' memories of the disasters associated with the Derg's resettlement efforts. That this famine coincided with the Eritrean war has been widely noted and comparisons with the experience with the Derg are inevitably, if mistakenly, drawn. However, as has been the case with many famines in the Horn of Africa, the pastoralists were the major victims and the ruling party with its roots among the northern peasantry has arguably been less than understanding of the plight of this long-oppressed community.

The Front's industrial policies are devoted to agro-industrial development, which largely means processing agricultural goods. To stimulate this development the EPRDF removed most price controls, encouraged monetization, and launched a massive program of road construction. However, apart from a vast expansion in the country's service sector after 1991, the agricultural-based industrialization that the TPLF hoped would provide employment for the province's growing and land-starved population was largely ignored by the typically small and cautious investors. As a result, the TPLF concluded that its objectives for the Tigrayan economy could only be realized by the establishment of a community-based fund that would draw on the experience of the party-affiliated organizations established during the war. Called the Endowment Fund for the Rehabilitation of Tigray (EFFORT), it began operations in 1995.[18]

EFFORT's start-up capital included non-military equipment captured from the Derg by the TPLF or donated by foreign donors to REST's truck fleet. Funds were also made available by the TPLE from companies it had established during and after liberation. Limited financial contributions came from supportive NGOs, from investment capital derived from joint ventures with private companies, and from money borrowed from the government-owned Commercial Bank of Ethiopia against the Fund's assets. The fund is nominally a non-government holding company whose thirty-two member board of directors are elected from the TPLF's mass associations. It is managed by seven sitting members from the Front's Central Committee. As a holding company the various sitting members on the board of directors in turn have been appointed as chairmen of other companies owned by EFFORT. Recognizing that the failure of many state-owned companies derives from their being immune to the demands and discipline of the market, EFFORT-held companies operate as private enterprises.

Among EFFORT's holdings are textile and clothing plants, a leather tannery, a marble quarry, a cement plant, a major construction company, a diversified agricultural company, a bank, reputedly the largest truck transport company in Africa, and a partially owned pharmaceutical fac-

tory. REST, which is now officially an NGO, is also involved in the commercial sector, and is joined by the Tigray Development Association
(TDA), another NGO with a close relationship to the TPLF. The TDA has
established a number of enterprises, including a bus service and an Addis
Ababa-based travel agency (now held by EFFORT). This development
model is increasingly being taken up by EPRDF affiliates throughout
Ethiopia. Indeed, the TPLF's program was almost completely adopted by
the neighbouring Amhara regional state and this includes counterparts
to EFFORT, REST, TDA, and the Sustainable Agricultural and Environment Rehabilitation of Tigray (SAERT), a para-statal largely concerned
with constructing micro-dams and irrigation projects. A similar pattern is
being followed in Oromia and the southern region, with only the lesser-
developed lowland states not having the capacity as yet to follow suit.

  This innovative approach has not, however, escaped controversy. First,
it is frequently asserted that while many party-affiliated activities are taking place in areas of the economy ignored by private businesses, in other
cases they are competing with the private sector and there are charges that
the government favours these companies. The TPLF/EPRDF response is
that EFFORT and its emerging regional counterparts are specifically targeting areas of the economy ignored by private enterprise and that in
some areas their companies are almost alone in paying taxes on an orderly
basis.[19] Nonetheless, there is alarm in some business sectors at the scale
of involvement of the party-affiliated companies; for example, according
to conservative estimates made in 1997, EFFORT's assets alone are valued
at over US$160 million, making it, along with the private Alamoundi con-
glomerate, the leading components of the Ethiopian economy. But perhaps the biggest concern with such party-affiliated companies is the
danger that its Front officials will succumb to corruption, and indeed
accusations of this kind have been made.

  Generally economic development has followed political development. Thus, in spite of recent events, the politically more advanced
regions of Tigray and Amhara have seen the most development since
1991, both rural and urban, as the various regional administrative centres have flourished. In spite of its potential, Oromia has witnessed little
economic expansion and the south falls between these regions. The lowland states to the east and west of the highlands have seen considerable
infusion of central government resources and have advanced, but much
of the resources have been squandered through weak and corrupt
administration. Addis Ababa has also experienced poor government
and has been a magnet for the poverty-stricken fleeing the countryside.

Peasants have been the main beneficiary of EPRDF-directed development, but again this breaks down by regions. The urban middle class
was plundered to such an extent during the final years of the Derg that
the impact of the EPRDF's structural adjustment program was probably
less debilitating than elsewhere in Africa. Moreover, it would appear
that the proliferation of professional government employment opportunities in the regions have led to their expansion at a time when middle
classes throughout Africa have contracted. In spite of an emphasis on
agro-industrial development, Ethiopia remains heavily dependent upon
the export of coffee and international prices for this commodity have
been falling for some years. Add to this the war with Eritrea, which led
to the relocation of resources from development to the army and to
reduced financial support from the international community and the
World Bamk. That said, projected growth rates (before the political crisis of mid-2001) of 6.5 percent and 7.0 percent for the years 2001 and
2002 respectively[20] did not suggest an economic crisis, although Ethiopia's poverty is so great that even these rates will not induce the structural change that is required and to which the EPRDF aspires.

Foreign Relations

It is the fate of successful revolutionary movements that they invariably
come to power under conditions that could not have been anticipated
when their struggles were launched. Thus when the TPLF took up the
armed struggle the Cold War was at its height, the Soviet Union was the
dominant foreign power in Ethiopia, Sudan was at peace, the Somali
state had not disintegrated, and an independent Eritrea did not exist.
Adding to the difficulty in understanding the dramatically changed
international and regional contexts was the long isolation of the TPLF.
With no foreign alliances apart from a difficult relationship with the
EPLF, the leadership looked to Marx, Stalin, Mao, and Albania's Enver
Hoxha for inspiration. Moreover, the TPLF leadership took pride in
their presence in the field rather than relying on foreign begging expe-
ditions like many other revolutionaries. Partly because of its internal
focus, the movement was slow to grasp international changes; indeed,
Meles Zenawi was singing the praises of Albania only months before its
collapse and the EPRDF assumption of power in 1991.

The same Meles, however, was among the first in the movement to
appreciate the unchallenged global dominance of the United States and
was instrumental in developing a working relationship with the Ameri-

cans. Indeed, Meles has proved an effective administrator and spokesman and is generally respected internationally. Holding positions as
chairman of the TPLF, EPRDF, and prime minister grant him considerable authority, but this authority is easily over-estimated and the Front
has always prided itself on the collective character of its decision-making.
With a few exceptions, such as the TPLF leaders in Tigray, the EPRDF
leaders, including Meles, are not popular figures in the country. They
are far more distant from ordinary Ethiopians than either Mengistu
Haile Mariam or Emperor Haile Selassie. Moreover, while the dimensions of the crisis within the TPLF Central Committee are not clear at the
time of writing, it would seem that one result of it is that TPLF officials
holding leading positions within the government, including and especially Meles, have gained a disproportionate amount of power in comparison to Front officials whose efforts have been focused at the cadre
and party level.

The West generally has an interest in the stability of Ethiopia, ensuring that its citizens' television screens are not filled with pictures of starving children, and that state socialism be dismantled and the market
given prominence. The EPRDF has gone some way to providing these
assurances, although both the famine in recent years and the internal
political struggles of 2001 will give pause for thought. But the West, and
more particularly the United States, is also concerned with the spread of
Islamic fundamentalism in the region and containing the National
Islamic Front (NIF) government in Sudan. The EPRDF opposed the
NIF and was given military assistance, along with Eritrea and Uganda,
for its support. However, the front came to that position circuitously,
indicating its lack of experience in conducting international relations in
the transitional period.

In the final phase of its war against the Derg Sudan made a big display
of support for the movement and implied that it had been a crucial element in that victory. The EPRDF was not deceived, but its policy of ending the long history of antagonistic relations in the Horn and having
good relations with its neighbours meant the expulsion of the Derg-sup-
ported Sudan Peoples Liberation Army (SPLA) from Ethiopian territory. Not surprisingly, this move was warmly welcomed by the Sudan
government because it almost brought about the defeat of the SPLA.
The NIF also saw in the policy of its good neighbour a means to introduce its Islamist politics to Ethiopia's large Moslem population. Very
quickly the expanded Sudanese embassy in Addis Ababa and the many
'Islamic NGOs' were making their presence felt while the NIF's media

broadcast its propaganda and Ethiopian Moslems were encouraged to pursue their education in Sudan. The regional government of the western state of Benishangul with its large numbers of Moslems was virtually taken over by Islamists under the influence of the NIF and experienced growing instability on its border with Sudan. Meanwhile, other Islamists infiltrated various organs of the central government, including the foreign service. Islamist intrigue reached its height in the attempt on the life of Egyptian President Hosni Mubarak on the streets of Addis Ababa in 1995, and while the complete story of that event may never be known, the links to Khartoum are widely accepted.

Only then did the EPRDF act, dramatically reducing the size of the Sudanese embassy and closing the consulate in Gambella. The front also expelled the Islamist NGOs, arrested and deported many Sudanese in the country, and conducted a widespread purge, particularly of the infiltrated regional government of Benishangul. Not stopping there, the EPRDF reconciled with the SPLA, allowed it to establish military bases on its western borders, trained its forces, and supported the movement's capture of territory in Sudan's South Blue Nile area and even as far afield as western Equatoria. As a result, the instability on Benishangul's borders quickly ended. The EPRDF's Sudan policy had come full circle and resembled that of the Derg. But the changes were not over: after the outbreak of war with Eritrea there was again a warming of relations with Khartoum and the SPLA's military presence in Ethiopia was circumscribed. Regional relations have a habit of changing with bewildering speed and also to be characterized with a high degree of duplicity, so although recent moves towards reconciliation appear to be genuine, they will have to be closely watched.

Moreover, the Sudanese opposition's sympathy for Eritrea during the Ethio-Eritrean war, and the EPRDF view that elements of the National Democratic Alliance (NDA) were largely controlled by the Eritrean government, together with the growing economic ties between Sudan and Ethiopia based on the import of Sudan's oil and the use of Port Sudan, do give credence to the reconciliation between the two regimes. However, while on the one hand Ethiopia's convincing victory over Eritrea gives the EPRDF increased confidence to develop its relations with Khartoum, Sudan's civil war and the continuing Islamist stance of the regime place limits on how far that reconciliation can proceed. It is already clear, however, that relations between an oil-derived economically expansive Sudan and the militarily dominant Ethiopia will be the key factors determining the future of the Horn.

Relations with the EPLF have likewise gone through contortions. The TPLF was quick to develop relations with the militarily superior EPLF after it took up arms in 1975 and this meant that it did not in the early years want to highlight their growing political and military differences. But by the mid-1980s these differences were becoming increasingly diffi-cult to ignore and the TPLF was rapidly approaching the EPLF in size and experience, even if the Eritreans did not accept this. Although the EPLF characterized Eritrea's historical circumstances as colonial, under the Italians its infrastructural development was far superior to moşt areas in Ethiopia, including Tigray, and this continued under Haile Selassie's post Second World War administration. The result was that Eritreans typically viewed themselves as more developed and even supe-rior to their neighbours to the south and this thinking did not change under the EPLF. As their confidence grew in the struggle, however, the Tigrayans came to reject their role as junior partners to the Eritreans. While consistently affirming the right of Eritrea to independence, the TPLF held its relationship with the EPLF to be merely tactical, by which it meant that the movements were linked in their common goal of over-throwing the Derg, but not in terms of their strategic ends.

The movements disagreed on matters of internal democracy (the TPLF viewed the EPLF as authoritarian), military policy (the TPLF favoured guerrilla tactics as opposed to the conventional army approach of the EPLF), relations with the superpowers (the TPLF condemned both, while the EPLF only attacked the United States), and most signifi-cantly, they disagreed over the issue of national self-determination. It is this difference that remains contentious. The TPLF held that all nations (i.e. ethnic groups) had the right to national self-determination up to and including the right to independence, whether in Ethiopia or Eri-trea. The EPLF just as forcefully rejected this for Ethiopia, and insisted that the nine or more groups that make up the Eritrean population col-lectively constituted a nation and hence they did not have separate rights to national self-determination.

Making clear just how strongly the EPLF felt about these differences, it broke relations with the TPLF, shut down its radio station in Eritrea, and expelled Tigrayans from its liberated territories. More surprising, the EPLF closed the only road linking Sudan through Eritrea to Tigray at the height of the 1985 famine, thus putting at risk hundreds of thou-sands of starving peasants dependent upon relief being delivered over that road – a decision which is still the cause of resentment in the prov-ince. There was a rapprochement in 1988, but it did little to resolve the outstanding political disagreements between them, much less the distrust. But with the Derg's demise in sight such problems were temporarily set aside.

None of those differences were publicly on display during the Eritrean independence referendum of 1993 that was supported by the EPRDF, or generally in the period from 1991 to the end of 1997. Indeed, the EPRDF went to such lengths to accommodate the EPLF that many Ethiopians drew the conclusion that their government was little more than an agent of the Eritreans. The trend began when in the aftermath of the EPLF coming to power in 1991, it summarily ejected tens of thousands of Ethiopians and even Eritreans married to Ethiopians. Not a word of reproach was made by the EPRDF of this massive human rights abuse, which caused Ethiopians enormous distress. In fact the expulsions continued while Eritreans in Ethiopia held leading positions in the civil service and the EPRDF tacitly accepted a form of dual citizenship that only applied to Eritreans. Eritrea's import of coffee purchased in Ethiopian birr and exported for US dollars and the many smuggling operations that were overlooked until Eritrea introduced its own currency in 1997 all served to increase Ethiopian resentment and fuel suspicions of the EPRDF.

These conditions could not continue indefinitely and the spark for the violent turnaround was the introduction of the Eritrean currency and the EPRDF's rejection of the EPLF's demand that it be treated at par with the Ethiopian birr. With its historically more developed economy, the Peoples Front for Democracy and Justice (or PFDJ, the post-1991 name given the EPLF) aimed to have Eritrea serve as the industrial centre to an Ethiopian hinterland, which would provide raw materials and serve as a market for Eritrea's finished goods. But largely through the EPRDF-affiliated companies, Ethiopia had made major inroads into traditional areas of Eritrean dominance, notably textiles, clothing, and food processing. As a result, Ethiopia's decision on the currency gave weight to the growing economic crisis in Eritrea and notice that the EPRDF would no longer accept the Eritrean tail wagging the Ethiopian dog. And this in turn stimulated a widening crisis that focused on long-ignored or played-down differences over their joint border that became the stated reason for the Eritrean invasion of Ethiopian territory in May 1998. That such differences should produce war, however, speaks more strongly to the growing economic crisis in the country and to the failure of the PFDJ to oversee a democratic transition, even of the weak kind being carried out in Ethiopia, than of border disputes that were never a problem for the people who lived in the areas in question.

The ferocity with which the Eritrea-Ethiopia war was fought speaks to political cultures in both countries that leave little room for compromise and the fact that the ultimate fate of the PFDJ and EPRDF could depend on the outcome of the conflict. Moreover, Ethiopia's expulsion of citizens of Eritrean decent and the xenophobic statements of some government leaders make clear the shallowness of pluralism in the country. The war led to a shift in resources from development to the military and finances being expended in developing port facilities to replace those previously used in Eritrea. This was a factor in the famine of 1999–2000 and the massive reduction in funding seriously undermined the effectiveness of the country's regional governments.

An assessment of the EPRDF's foreign relations in the transitional period based on this brief overview of selected cases would be at best mixed. At the global level the Ethiopian government has largely been successful in adapting to the new world order on conditions that have allowed it far more autonomy than most developing countries. On the surface it is surprising that Ethiopia was one of the largest recipients of international assistance in Africa and, until the war with Eritrea, gained the support of the United States, particularly when the country is ruled by a vanguard party that has made only limited progress in democratization, rural land remains nationalized, and party-affiliated companies dominate the formal economy. But, as noted, the EPRDF has gone far in reforming the state and economy. It has demonstrated its administrative competence in containing the drought of 1993, its land policy responds to practical needs, and the country has been a bulwark against Islamist incursions in the region. Human rights abuses are being raised by international NGOs, but geopolitical concerns have thus far meant they have not been taken up seriously by the Unites States or other leading Western countries. While the war with Eritrea, moves towards rapprochement with Sudan, the famine of 2000, and the turmoil that broke out in the TPLF leadership in mid-2001 have probably shaken US confidence in the EPRDF, the fact that the front alone is a force for stability means that the Americans have nowhere else to turn for allies to protect their interests.

While the EPRDF has demonstrated considerable skills at the global level, the examples of its relations in the Horn of Africa expose its inexperience. Moving beyond rhetoric to applying a policy of good neighbourly relations in a region as turbulent as the Horn was naive. Accepting the bone fides of the NIF and giving support to the PFDJ to the extent that it produced growing dissent within Ethiopia were also mistakes of considerable magnitude. Running down its military, while no doubt attractive to Western donors, was clearly mistaken when civil wars were in progress in neighbouring Sudan, Somalia, and Djibouti, and Eritrea continued to strengthen its military forces and maintain conscription. And the price has been high, as clearly neither the political leadership nor the Ethiopian armed forces were prepared for the Eritrean invasion.

As a result of concerns for its security and possibly popular pressures, the EPRDF deported large numbers of Eritrean residents and Ethiopians of Eritrean decent that gained it further negative international publicity and encouraged domestic anti-Eritrean racism and the takeover of Eritrean-owned enterprises. Having said and done nothing in 1991 when the EPLF carried out much larger expulsions of Ethiopians, the EPRDF's criticisms of the Eritrean deportations of Ethiopians in 1998 appeared hypocritical. It was also not lost on Ethiopians that while EPRDF officials of Eritrean ancestry have maintained their positions, their private counterparts without political connections suffered daily discriminations. It was hoped that the EPRDF would have the courage to conduct a *gim gima* of its leadership whose bad judgment was responsible for leaving the country so ill-prepared for the destructive war with Eritrea, but that now seems unlikely.

Ethiopia's victory ended the military threat of Eritrea, but opened the door to a continuing and contentious political relationship between the two countries. Moreover, the decision by the international arbitrators to award Bedame, a central area of the border dispute between the two countries, to Eritrea will be politically difficult for the Meles government to stomach. That said, with PFDJ military pretensions put to rest, it will be clear that Ethiopia is incontestably the dominant military power in the region and there is reason to believe that the Front will now be more prepared to use that power to defend and advance Ethiopia's interests beyond its borders. Good neighbourly relations will be balanced by realpolitik, and the EPRDF may conclude that its security in the turbulent Horn can only be ensured by becoming the regional hegemon. In any case, it is now widely accepted, both in and outside the Ethiopian foreign policy establishment, that the initial enthusiasm of the EPRDF for friendly neighbourly relations that emphasized regional peace, cooperation, and economic integration was unduly optimistic. But support for Ethiopian militarism is far greater at the societal level than among the EPRDF leadership, as was evidenced by the army's limited objectives in the war.

The EPRDF's seeming distain for any international involvement in the Ethio-Eritrean war that did not produce an Eritrean retreat led to Western resentment that was symbolized by the ineffective UN arms embargo placed on Ethiopia. But talk of isolating Ethiopia was quickly shelved. Moreover, the United States will not likely oppose the EPRDF's limited regional aspirations since it will be recognized as the only viable and non-threatening state in the area and the only one through which it can realistically pursue its own interests. More complicated will be Ethiopia's relations with the Arab Middle East and in particular with Egypt. The Arab world has long been antagonistic towards Ethiopia and generally favoured Eritrea during the war, and the scale of Ethiopia's victory will cause alarm. Most upset will be Egypt, whose concern with defending its interests in the Nile basin has also suffered a loss through Ethiopia's victory. The outcome of the Ethio-Eritrean war thus has many dimensions that will unfold in the years to come.

Domestically it is noteworthy that in spite of what is acknowledged to be a major military victory over Eritrea, the EPRDF reaped few political gains. Indeed, the war had barely been completed when many of the opposition groups condemned the EPRDF for not capturing Assab and absorbing it into Ethiopia,[21] even though the port is internationally recognized as an integral part of Eritrea and its capture was probably not an Ethiopian objective. Such criticisms demonstrate the chauvinist character of much of the opposition and their attachment to an imperial vision of Ethiopia that would be enormously destabilizing for both Ethiopia and the region should they come to power. At the same time the persistence of an opposition which after a decade continues to deny the legitimacy of the government and claims the TPLF to be in league with the PFDJ places constraints on both the government's pursuit of foreign policy, and on any realistic hopes of a national reconciliation.

Conclusion

A complete military victory over the EPRDF's opponents, the Front's administrative competence, a measure of pragmatism, the invaluable experience of developing a close understanding of the country's peasants, and a belated appreciation of the changed international context have ensured – at least until war with Eritrea – a generally successful transition. Nevertheless, the EPRDF would not have come to power without a vanguard party and a revolutionary project. In part through ideological conviction and also through recognizing the limitations of the civil service and of the opposition of significant elements within Ethiopia, the notion of the vanguard party prevailed. Moreover, to give it up and move too quickly towards a Western-style democratization that Ethiopian culture was ill-adapted to accept was never seriously entertained in the transitional period. In addition, while some among the EPRDF leadership recognize the weaknesses of a vanguard party, they cannot fail to appreciate that in Ethiopia and in the Horn of Africa, where enemies outnumber friends, their political survival depends upon the party's hegemony, discipline, and unity.

But not to democratize, the EPRDF risks increasingly taking on the political appearance of the Derg, holding back the political development of Ethiopia, and losing its domestic and international legitimacy. To the extent that peacebuilding can be understood as making progress towards deepening relations between previously warring parties, then the EPRDF has made little headway. From its refusal to integrate the defeated Derg army with its own, to the breakdown in relations with the OLF, through its limited willingness to permit opponents to play a meaningful role in the political process, the EPRDF has clung to its hegemonic position in the state. It must be recognized, however, that in giving its opponents little quarter the EPRDF was confronted by political forces that had few claims to legitimacy and little genuine commitment to democracy. Moreover, the EPRDF's behaviour was entirely consistent with Ethiopian cultural values that place high emphasis on strength and consider compromise as weakness.

But if hopes for pluralism and peacebuilding in Ethiopia are severely constrained by these obstacles, there has still been progress. First, by ascribing to the right of national self-determination, together with its commitment to a radical decentralization of the state, the EPRDF has helped ensure that the country is not again torn apart by ethnic-based disputes. Moreover, even though there has been varying amounts of party manipulation of regional governments during the transitional period, the EPRDF's commitment to decentralization represents a radical break with the centralizing projects of Ethiopian rulers for 150 years. Second, the EPRDF has moved cautiously, but considerably further than any other country in the Horn, to accept opposition parties, a free media, and the birth of a civil society (albeit with considerable constraints). And again, while these moves can be seen as limited, against the deeply entrenched authoritarian traditions of the country they cannot be dismissed. Lastly, the EPRDF is attempting to introduce throughout Ethiopia a system of accountability developed during the revolution, which has democratic elements.

The future of gim gima or the form it takes as the EPRDF increasingly moves beyond its revolutionary origins must be in doubt. Nonetheless, it is a mistake to assume that democracy in Africa can only be measured against Western experience and practices or that cultures like that of Ethiopia are conducive to foreign imports like liberalism. In the absence of evidence to the contrary, gim gima does appear to go part of the way to achieving accountable governance. It may not always provide assurances against human rights abuses, but such concerns do not figure highly in Ethiopian society or to date in the EPRDF, which devoted its struggle to achieving group rights that have a central place in its constitution. Moreover, with the exception of the church and mosque, civil society outside the urban centres of Ethiopia exerts few controls on the government, and gim gima, even with its dangers of manipulation and human rights abuses, can make a contribution to democratic governance even though it cannot in itself be interpreted as constituting democratic governance. The fear – and this is acknowledged by some TPLF cadres – is that opportunism, the desire to win the favour of the intelligentsia, the very different conditions faced after achieving state power in 1991, and the obstacles posed by the central state's backward civil service are undermining a valuable institution in Ethiopia that can be used to attack privilege and the undemocratic values that still figure highly in society. Perhaps the biggest failure of gim gima, however, is its inability to resolve the dispute that broke out in the TPLF Central Committee in mid-2001.

That said, the EPRDF's international acceptance and the support from democratic elements in the middle and urban classes will depend upon the Front's willingness to deepen its thus far limited moves to democratization, open government, respect for human rights, and acceptance of civil society. The emergency situation created by the war with Eritrea temporarily reduced this pressure, but the dispute that broke out in the TPLF in 2001 makes clear that the Front must make a greater commitment to democracy, resist Ethiopian cultural conservatism, and endorse and practise transparency. And this will (and is) bringing to the fore debate over fundamental precepts such as the vanguard status of the party, revolutionary democracy, and Meles's contention in mid-2001 that the TPLF was forming an independent and exclusive class standing above the society.

While mobilizing and empowering the peasants was critical to the EPRDF assuming power, many in the Front's leadership are preoccupied with gaining the support of the generally disaffected middle classes. Efforts to date have focused on convincing these classes that the rural-oriented policies of the EPRDF and its establishment of ethnic-based regional governments better represent their interests than the loosely formulated programs of the opposition parties. However, the failure of the EPRDF to win the favour of these groups, even after its impressive defeat of Eritrea, makes clear that these strategies are unduly optimistic, particularly in Addis Ababa where opposition to the regime is concentrated. After a decade, the middle class led by a vocal intelligentsia is not completely reconciled to either a Tigrayan dominated government or its political agenda. Moreover, to open the party to mass membership and give it a pluralist character would result in domination by an urban middle class that opposes its program and commitment to the peasants. Historically, peasant-based parties that come to power are led by a middle-class intelligentsia who soon become urban-focused and increasingly turn away from their origins in the countryside. There is no doubt that these processes are at work in the EPRDF, but as yet they have not completely worked themselves out.

Beyond Ethiopia, the turbulent regional scene will remain a problem for the EPRDF and one that threatens internal disorder as well. Having acknowledged its early naivety, the EPRDF remains committed to regional good neighbourliness, but now retains, as one official noted, an axe in reserve. Ethiopian and Western (primarily US) interests in the Horn until the war with Eritrea were fairly closely matched, but that war and the rapidity of the changes in the region mean that Ethiopia's relations with the West will be problematic. American growing strategic interests in the neighbouring Middle East as exemplified by the war in Iraq are likely to prove more beneficial to Ethiopia's enemy, Eritrea, which is better placed geographically to assist Washington and is anxious to assume the role of a regional partner. Another potential area of contention is over the economy. In spite of rhetoric to the contrary, the EPRDF retains restrictions on foreign investment (notably over its moribund financial and telecommunications sectors); it opposes a free market in rural land, and, most significantly, it has made party-affiliated companies the dominant feature in the formal economy. While the EPRDF is not likely to dramatically alter its policies any time soon, particularly with respect to land, it may restrict the role of party-affiliated companies and be more welcoming of foreign investment in telecommunications and banks if these moves are not deemed to compromise the country's sovereignty. But traditional Ethiopian values and culture, probably more than the current regime, are the biggest obstacles to Ethiopia fully integrating itself into the international community.

The EPRDF's great experiment in giving legitimacy to ethnic national-ism, which has brought decades of war to Ethiopia, together with the for-mation of ethnic-based regional administrations, must remain in doubt. Tempering, but not controlling, these forces which threaten further the dismemberment of Ethiopia (Eritrea having taken the first step) was due to the control of the EPRDF over its ethnic components and public bureaucracies. The fact that this model almost certainly ensured that the Oromos and other groups did not seriously attempt to establish inde-pendent entities makes clear that there was probably no viable alterna-tive. While the ethnic genie cannot be put back in the bottle, as some Ethiopian intellectuals would like, there will have to be reforms to the system. In particular, the proliferation of recognized ethnic groups under a regime where ethnicity is the main road to power, and the polit-ical domination by one ethnic community, the Tigrayans, are not sus-tainable in the long term.

While TPLF dominance of the polity was an inevitable result of the long revolutionary struggles in Tigray, means will have to be developed to share power more broadly among other ethnic groups. This, however, raises two basic problems. First, having led the anti-Derg revolution, made great sacrifices, and demonstrated a level of personal commitment and political skills largely absent in the rest of the country, TPLF leaders, cadres, soldiers, and ordinary Tigrayans will have to give up power in cru-cial areas and this will only be done with great reluctance. Second, TPLF involvement in the central and regional governments was in part due to the Front's superior political and administrative skills, and to give more power to other groups, particularly in the less-developed regions, may well lead to increased mismanagement and corruption and, in the case of Oromia, increased pressures for independence.

And lastly, the question must be raised as to how the EPRDF and its TPLF core should be characterized after the initial goals of overthrowing the Derg and consolidating power have been achieved. It must be stressed that, unlike most African governing groups, the TPLF/EPRDF came to power after a lengthy armed struggle, on the basis of peasant sup-port, and committed to a revolutionary transformation of society. The TPLF/EPRDF core still asserts its revolutionary character, and its con-tinuing commitment to rural land nationalization, national self-determi-nation, gim gima, and democratic centralism give some credence to this claim. But after a decade in power there was increasing recognition in the TPLF of the need to evaluate the Front's past performance, and indeed, it was during discussions on how to proceed with this exercise that the

Central Committee divided. Apart from broader questions of policy, it seems clear that many in the TPLF and EPRDF are enjoying the fruits of victory and high standards of living. Some are also succumbing to the dominant values of Ethiopian society, which stress hierarchy, status, and social and physical distance from perceived inferiors. To some extent this assimilation of conservative practices is being done consciously. In the early period the EPRDF won the support of the peasantry and is now directing its energies at winning legitimacy among an urban middle class. But this class has consistently opposed the EPRDF's objectives and, demonstrates little willingness to achieve reconciliation. Should a genuine reconciliation take place, it would signify the end of the EPRDF as a party of the peasants.

NOTES

1 See John Young, 'The Tigray and Eritrean Peoples Liberation Fronts: A History of Tensions and Pragmatism,' *Journal of Modern African Studies* Vol. 34, no. 1 (1996).
2 Sarah Vaughan, 'The Addis Ababa Transitional Conference of July 1991: Its Origins, History and Significance,' *Occasional Papers*, Centre for African Studies, Edinburgh University, 1994.
3 Interview with Brigadier Assiminew Bedane, Addis Ababa, 26 January 1996.
4 Interview with Yemane Kidane, chief of the minister's cabinet, Ministry of Foreign Affairs, Addis Ababa, 1 May 2000.
5 Interview with Beyene Petros, president, Southern Ethiopian Peoples Democratic Coalition, Addis Ababa, 15 August 2000.
6 John Young, *Peasants and Revolution in Ethiopia: The Tigray Peoples Liberation Front 1975–1997* (Cambridge: Cambridge University Press, 1997).
7 Interview with Abai Tsheye, TPLF Politburo, Mekelle, 22 February 2000.
8 Federal Democratic Republic of Ethiopia, *The Constitution of the Federal Democratic Republic of Ethiopia*, article 30(1) (8 December 1994).
9 John Young, 'Development and Change in Post-Revolutionary Tigray,' *Journal of Modern African Studies* 35, no. 1 (1997).
10 Ministry of Economic Development and Cooperation, 'Poverty Situation in Ethiopia' (Addis Ababa, February 1999), 10; Central Statistical Authority, 'Report on the 1998 Health and Nutrition Survey' (Addis Ababa, October 1999), 229.
11 State of Oromia, Bureau of Planning and Economic Development, *Socio-Economic Profile of Oromia* (Finfine, November 1996).

12 Walta Information Center, 'Oromia Regional State Endorses Kuma's Resignation' (Addis Ababa, 24 July 2001).

13 Southern Nation, Nationalities and Peoples' Regional Government Bureau of Planning and Economic Development, *Socio-Economic Profile* (Awassa, 1996).

14 John Young, 'Along Ethiopia's Western Frontier: Gambella and Benishangul in Transition,' *Journal of Modern African Studies* 37, no. 2 (1999).

15 World Bank, Memorandum of the President of the International Development Association to the Executive Directors on a Country Assistance Strategy for the Federal Democratic Republic of Ethiopia (19 August 1997).

16 Interview with Abai Tsheye.

17 'EPRDF Second Five Year Peace, Democracy, and Development Draft Program' (Addis Ababa, 2001).

18 Young, *Peasants and Revolution.*

19 Interview with Yemane Kidane.

20 Economist Intelligence Unit, 'Ethiopian Economic Forecast 2001' (March 2001).

21 'Joint Statement of Six Opposition Parties,' All Amhara Peoples' Organization, Oromo National Congress, Joint Political Forum, National Democratic Union, Ethiopian Democratic Party, Ethiopian Democratic Union Party (Addis Ababa, 25 July 2000).

2

Obstacles to Peacebuilding in Rwanda

Timothy Longman

The genocide and war that ravaged Rwanda in 1994 represent one of the most intense periods of violence ever to sweep across an African state. In a three-month period after President Juvénal Habyarimana died in a plane crash on 6 April 1994, more than one-tenth of Rwanda's population perished. Most of the victims of the violence were members of the Tutsi ethnic minority group, who were driven into places of presumed refuge, such as churches and schools, then systematically slaughtered by civilian death squads, usually organized by government officials and backed up by soldiers or police.[1] In addition to sparking the genocide, President Habyarimana's death reignited the civil war between government forces and the Rwandan Patriotic Front (RPF), a Ugandan-based rebel army comprised primarily of Tutsi refugees from earlier waves of violence in Rwanda. With so much of the government's attention focused on eliminating a supposed 'internal enemy,' the regime left itself vulnerable to the RPF assault. By July, the RPF had driven the government forces along with over one million refugees, across the border into the Democratic Republic of the Congo (then still called Zaire) and was able to install a new government in Kigali.

In the years since 1994, peace has remained elusive for Rwanda. The RPF has struggled to extend its control throughout Rwandan territory and to establish public security, but it has continued to face considerable opposition and unrest. In the years immediately after the genocide, Hutu militia, many of them former government soldiers based in the refugee camps in Congo, raided Rwanda, targeting government officials and Tutsi survivors of the genocide for assassination. In part to eliminate this security threat, the RPF invaded Congo in support of a Congolese rebel movement that eventually drove from power long-time Congolese dictator Mobutu Sese-Sekou. After violence again flared in

Rwanda in 1997–8, with Hutu rebels once more attacking civilians in Rwanda, the RPF invaded Congo a second time. Within the borders of Rwanda, the RPF has used extensive force to subdue the Hutu population. The government has imprisoned over 120,000 Hutu under accusations of participation in the genocide, and government forces have killed thousands of other civilians. During the 1997–8 uprising, the government forcibly relocated tens of thousands of civilians into monitored villages. Although the level of violence in Rwanda has diminished since 1998, the level of tension in the country remains very high, the government continues to rely on heavy use of coercion to maintain control, and many people, both Rwandans and outside observers, believe that there is a strong possibility of renewed inter-ethnic violence.[2]

In seeking to explain the difficulties of establishing peace in Rwanda since 1994, most observers have focused on Rwanda's status as a 'post-genocidal' society.[3] Severe and generalized violence has a major impact on a nation's psyche, leaving individuals traumatized and creating a polarized society. Rwanda today has to deal both with the social legacies of that violence and with the cultural problems that made genocide possible in the first place. Both the Rwandan government and the international community have placed substantial emphasis on legal proceedings – the International Criminal Tribunal for Rwanda, domestic trials, and now community-based courts – as means of combating the culture of impunity and promoting the healing process among survivors of the genocide. The United Nations High Commission for Human Rights established a mission in Rwanda to help promote respect for human rights. Considerable international attention and resources were also directed towards rebuilding the physical infrastructure of the country, as numerous UN agencies and international non-governmental organizations such as Oxfam and Concern rebuilt bridges and roads and rehabilitated water and electrical systems. Many NGOs and UN agencies also focused on providing assistance to civilians who had suffered in the violence: such facilities as medical treatment and trauma counselling, housing construction, and children's services. In fact, the amount of international attention devoted to rebuilding Rwanda in the aftermath of genocide has been truly remarkable, given the international community's usually tepid interest in African crises.

Despite all of attention to peacebuilding by the Rwandan government and the international community, Rwanda has made little progress along the peacebuilding continuum. The political system remains intolerant of dissent and offers little more than token representation of the majority Hutu community in government, and the gradual reform of

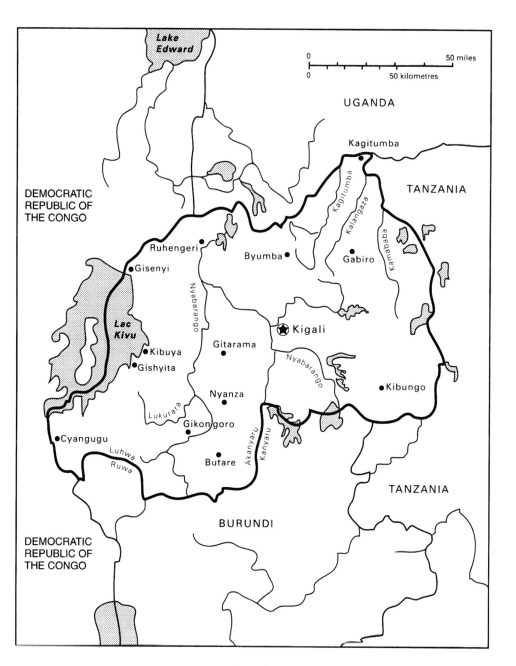

Rwanda

public institutions is occurring without popular consultation and support. The level of confidence and trust in the government is limited, and tensions both between the two main ethnic groups and within each of the groups remains high. Armed opposition to the government has occurred periodically, flaring most recently in May and June 2001 along the northwest border with Congo, and the RPF has responded with violence of its own, not only targeting rebel militia, but also forcibly displacing thousands of civilians. The Rwandan intervention in two bloody wars in Congo also powerfully demonstrates the limited success of peacebuilding efforts in Rwanda.[4]

While many of the problems with peacebuilding in Rwanda clearly must be attributed to the lingering effects of the severe violence that the country experienced, in this article I wish to explore another factor that has received little attention – that is, the legacies of the one-sided victory that brought an end to Rwanda's civil war. In contrast to cases such as South Africa, Mozambique, and Zimbabwe, Rwanda's civil strife did not end with a peace settlement, but rather, as in Uganda and Ethiopia, with a military victory by rebel forces. As many analysts will point out, peace agreements do not guarantee an easy process of peacebuilding, because they require substantial compromise and the struggle for former combatants to learn to live peacefully together is never easy.[5] The failed peace settlements in Sierra Leone and Angola are clear evidence of this danger. Yet the case of Rwanda highlights the difficulties of building peace following a military victory. While the Rwandan Patriotic Front has been able to act forcefully to implement programs to confront the legacies of genocide, from legal proceedings to re-education camps, the effectiveness of these efforts has been compromised by the fact that the Front is not representative of the population. The Rwandan case shows that the effort to impose peace from above has serious limits, and the absence of political compromise in the aftermath of war promotes both increasing public resentment and authoritarian rule. It should not be surprising, thus, that the presidents who came to power through force of arms in Uganda, Rwanda, Ethiopia, Eritrea, and Congo, once heralded as 'Africa's new leaders,'[6] have not only taken up arms against one another, but appear increasingly like the old dictatorial presidents with which Africa is all too familiar.

Ethnic Conflict and the Civil War in Rwanda

Ethnic violence first broke out in Rwanda shortly before independence in 1959. Ethnic identities had gained increasing political significance during the colonial period, as the German and Belgian colonial administrations used ethnicity to organize indirect rule.[7] Political power became concentrated in the hands of an elite segment of the Tutsi, the ethnic group that constituted around 15 per cent of Rwanda's population.[8] Hutu felt increasingly powerless and exploited, and as Rwanda approached independence, the Hutu feared being shut out of new power arrangements. A Hutu uprising in November 1959 drove many Tutsi chiefs from power and initiated a process of transferring power to Hutu that led to the deposition of the king in 1961 and the establishment of an entirely Hutu government at independence in 1962. The violence directed against Tutsi drove thousands to flee the country. Some of these Tutsi exiles tried to regain power through force and to destabilize the new Hutu government by launching a series of attacks against Rwanda between 1961 and 1965. After each of these attacks, government troops and armed civilians massacred Tutsi still living in Rwanda, driving thousands of additional Tutsi to seek refuge in neighbouring countries.[9] Anti-Tutsi violence broke out again in Rwanda in 1973, following a 'selective genocide' of Hutu elite in neighboring Burundi,[10] and again thousands of Tutsi fled Rwanda. In part in response to the instability created by the ethnic violence, the military intervened in government a few months later, replacing Rwanda's first president with the army chief, Habyarimana, in a coup d'état.[11]

The 'War of October,' as Rwanda's civil war that began on 1 October 1990 came to be known, had its roots in Rwanda's history of ethnic violence in the 1960s and early 1970s. By 1990, thousands of Rwandan Tutsi had been living outside Rwanda for as long as three decades, and their status as refugees left them politically vulnerable. When the Obote regime persecuted Tutsi refugees and other Rwandans living in Uganda in the early 1980s, a number of Tutsi joined the National Resistance Army (NRA) in its fight against Obote and helped bring Yoweri Museveni to power in 1986. Despite their importance to the new Museveni regime, the Rwandan Tutsi remained vulnerable because of their foreign origins. Hence, a group of Tutsi National Resistance Movement (NRM) officers organized the Rwandese Patriotic Front, hoping to replicate in Rwanda the movement's success and thereby to gain the right for Tutsi refugees to return home.[12]

Believing the Habyarimana regime to be vulnerable because of challenges it faced from a pro-democracy movement within Rwanda and apparently believing that Rwandans of all ethnicities dissatisfied with Habyarimana would flock to support them, the RPF invaded Rwanda in 1990. While this first attack on Rwanda's northeast frontier failed miser-

ably, it did draw attention to the RPF, and in subsequent months hundreds of Tutsi refugees from around East Africa flocked to Uganda to
join the Front. When the RPF attacked Rwanda again in January 1991
under its new leader, Paul Kagame, it was much more successful, briefly
occupying a large area in northwest Rwanda.[13]

Ethnic conflict was at the heart of the War of October from its inception. Although the RPF portrayed itself as a multi-ethnic movement fighting for democratization for all of Rwanda, and did include several Hutu
in prominent positions, most RPF leaders and soldiers were Tutsi, and the
fire that drove the rebellion was the aspiration of Tutsi refugees to gain
the right to return home. The Habyarimana regime, for its part, had initially gained both popular and international support in part by decreas-
ing ethnic tensions in the country and focusing political energy instead
on economic development. However, popular support for the regime
began to decline in the late 1980s as the economy slumped, and in 1990
a movement for political reform emerged in Rwanda, drawing its support
primarily from those excluded from power under Habyarimana: that is,
Hutu from regions other than Habyarimana's home region in the northwest and Tutsi from throughout the country. When the War of October
broke out, Habyarimana's allies quickly moved to portray the war as a
Tutsi plot to reverse the 1959 revolution and reinstall a Tutsi monarchy
and to discredit anyone who opposed the president as an ally of the RPF.
In the weeks after the October attack, the government arrested thousands
of Tutsi and held them for months without formal charges, accusing
them of complicity with the RPF. In several parts of the country, government officials organized massacres of Tutsi in their communities and
more anti-Tutsi violence followed the January 1991 attack. The Habyarimana regime hoped to polarize Rwanda along ethnic lines by portraying
the conflict as purely ethnic in nature and thereby characterizing Hutu
opposition activists as traitors to their ethnic group.[14]

Although initially the opposition movement forced Habyarimana to
accept political concessions, including the legalization of opposition parties and the installation of a multi-party coalition government, the strategy of reinserting ethnicity into Rwanda's conflict gradually began to pay
off for the regime. As the RPF experienced increasing success on the battlefield, with major assaults in June 1992 and January 1993, they seriously
disrupted the economy and displaced tens of thousands of Rwandans,
making themselves increasingly hated by the Hutu public. Most Tutsi
within Rwanda, finding themselves a growing target for violence and discrimination by the regime, became increasingly sympathetic to the RPF.

Regime supporters played on this expanding ethnic polarization, portraying themselves as the defenders of Hutu interests and Hutu opposition figures as unwitting allies of the RPF.[15] The peace accords signed by the government and the RPF in Arusha in August 1993 were designed to end the war, to create a new coalition government inclusive of the RPF, and to integrate the RPF into the Rwandan armed forces. But the Arusha Accords were widely unpopular within Rwanda. Rifts emerged within the opposition parties between supporters and opponents of the accords, and after the first Hutu president of Burundi, Melchior Ndadaye, was killed in a coup attempt in October 1993, a full-scale political realignment occurred. A large portion of Hutu politicians formerly opposed to Habyarimana joined with the president's supporters in a broad coalition known as 'Hutu Power,' leaving politically vulnerable the small remaining group of moderate Hutu and the Tutsi, who nearly universally supported the Arusha Accords.[16]

Despite the history of recurrent ethnic violence in Rwanda, genocide was never a pre-determined outcome of the country's political processes but instead occurred as a result of conscious decisions by powerful individuals. Ethnic scapegoating proved an effective tool for associates of President Habyarimana to regain popular support, and they carefully sought to foster anti-Tutsi sentiment in the population in order to reap political gains. Hutu extremists effectively used the media, particularly the radio, to create paranoia among the Hutu,[17] and they used various forms of popular mobilization to create solidarity among their supporters, such as creating civilian militia groups and providing them with military training. It is unclear exactly when plans were drawn up to wipe out perceived opponents of the regime, both Tutsi and moderate Hutu, but it is clear that a plan was already in place by April 1994. Within hours after President Habyarimana's death, members of the presidential guard and other elite troops spread out into the capital with lists of prominent regime opponents to kill: opposition politicians, civil society activists, and well-known Tutsi. When it became clear after a few days that the international community would not intervene to stop the violence, Hutu extremists systematically spread the killing throughout the country, focusing it more specifically on Tutsi in an effort to wipe out once and for all what they perceived as a 'Tutsi threat.'[18]

Just two days after Habyarimana's death, the RPF again took up arms and began a rapid advance on Kigali. RPF leaders quickly perceived that the new government was composed of Hutu extremists opposed to the implementation of the Arusha Accords, and the renewal of anti-Tutsi violence spurred them to act. Within less than a week, the RPF had advanced on Kigali and forced the new government to flee to Gitarama. Over the next several weeks, the RPF rapidly advanced across the north and east of the country. With massacres of their fellow Tutsi going on in areas of Rwanda under government control, the RPF sometimes took vengeance against the population of the communities they conquered, and hundreds of thousands of Hutu fled as the RPF pushed forward, with over one million crossing the border into Tanzania. By July the RPF had taken control of nearly the entire country, except a portion of the southwest controlled by a French military operation. As the war came to a conclusion, a million Rwandans fled into Congo and another two million took refuge in the French-occupied zone.[19]

Reconstruction and Reconciliation Efforts

RPF and Rwandan Government Initiatives

The Rwanda the RPF assumed control of in July 1994 was a country in ruins. As the United States Department of State noted, 'The 1994 genocide destroyed the country's social fabric, human resource base, institutional capacity, and economic and social infrastructure.'[20] Over 10 per cent of the population had been killed either in the genocide or in the war, and over half of the Rwandans still alive were displaced, internally or as refugees in neighbouring countries. The national infrastructure was in shambles, with roads and bridges destroyed, water and power lines cut, and the economy – overwhelmingly dependent on agriculture – at a standstill. At least as serious as the physical legacies of war were the cultural and social legacies of the violence. The 1994 genocide was the culmination of a process of ethnic polarization that left Rwandan society deeply divided along lines of identity, and the violence traumatized the Rwandan population. The Tutsi survivors of the genocide not only lost their families but were left with memories of the betrayal and severe cruelty they experienced at the hands of former friends and neighbours. The large number of Hutu who participated in the massacres of Tutsi and the many more who were complicit through their tacit support or inaction were traumatized in other ways by their involvement in the violence.[21] The experience of Hutu internally displaced or in exile was also often quite traumatic, as thousands died of hunger, disease, and violence. After taking power, the RPF thus faced major challenges in re-establishing the bonds of civility and creating sufficient unity in Rwandan society to make governing possible.

A major initial task of the RPF was to extend its control throughout Rwanda and to establish security within the country. In the first months after taking office, Front soldiers used extensive coercive force to subdue the population. Some of the attacks on civilians appear to have been revenge killings in response to the genocide, while others seem to have been more calculated to demonstrate the power of the new regime and gain obedience from the population.[22] The RPF viewed as a particular security threat the continued concentration of Hutu in camps both for the internally displaced (IDPs) in the former French zone and in refugee camps in Congo and Tanzania. In early 1995 the RPF began forcibly to close the IDP camps, even opening fire on the camp in Kibeho, leaving several thousand dead. By mid-1995, however, the RPF had tempered its use of raw coercive force, shifting to imprisonment as a strategy for maintaining order.[23]

The other initial task of the RPF after taking power was to install a government. Having replicated the NRM's military success, the RPF hoped to replicate its political success as well, so Front leaders developed a political system modelled after Museveni's 'no-party democracy.'[24] As in Uganda, the RPF did not outlaw political parties per se, but it severely curtailed political party activity and indefinitely postponed elections, while its armed wing became the national army of Rwanda. The RPF named a multi-ethnic, multi-party government based loosely on the Arusha Accords, with the positions originally allotted to Habyarimana's party taken instead by the RPF. Kagame, the military chief of the RPF, became vice-president and minister of defence, but most other cabinet positions, including the president and prime minister, were allocated to civilians, equally divided between Hutu and Tutsi. At lower levels, however, Tutsi and the RPF heavily dominated positions of authority.[25] Although formally taking responsibility for rebuilding the country, in practice the new government worked closely with the RPF.

The government of Rwanda and the RPF have undertaken a number of programs to promote peacebuilding in the country. One major focus for the new government has been on rehabilitating the domestic justice system in order to prosecute perpetrators of genocide, a goal that the government considers essential to eradicating the culture of impunity that made genocide possible. Almost immediately after taking office, the government began to arrest Hutu under accusations of involvement in the genocide. Although it was widely assumed that most of the chief organizers of the genocide were outside Rwanda, in the refugee camps in Congo or elsewhere, the government had arrested over seventy thousand people even before the closing of refugee camps in Congo in late

1996 forced a mass return to Rwanda.[26] By 1999 the number of people in prison exceeded one hundred and twenty thousand. Unfortunately, the judicial system had been so thoroughly devastated by the genocide and war, with a vast number of judges, prosecutors, lawyers, and police investigators killed or in exile, that even investigating the cases was difficult, much less prosecuting them. The international community dedicated substantial funds to rebuilding courts and judicial offices and to training new judicial officers. Even with trials for the chief organizers of the genocide being conducted by the International Criminal Tribunal for Rwanda, the number of accused within Rwanda was far beyond the capacity of the legal system to process, and many delays occurred before the first genocide trials took place in December 1996. Since then, several thousand prisoners have been tried, but this still represents only a small portion of those accused.[27]

In part as a means of responding to the overwhelming numbers of accused and in part in an attempt to develop a system of justice more rooted in Rwandan society, the government has developed an alternative system of local courts to try many of the accused. These local courts are called *gacaca* after a type of community court used to settle minor disputes (usually over property) in precolonial Rwanda, and they are composed of elders chosen by their communities then given limited legal training. The gacaca courts will have jurisdiction over lower-level accused – those who killed following orders or who committed property or other lesser crimes – and they are expected to represent not just the opinions of the elders but those of the wider communities. Rwandan officials have worked closely with international agencies in developing the gacaca courts, attempting to ensure that they will remain within the bounds of legal principles. The first gacaca trials were held in 2001.[28]

Government peacebuilding efforts in Rwanda, of course, have not been limited to the judicial domain. The government named in July 1994 included a minister 'for the Rehabilitation of Those Displaced by War and for Demobilization,' who was charged with organizing the return of refugees to Rwanda. Initially this Ministry of Rehabilitation focused on 'old case load' refugees – Tutsi who fled Rwanda in the 1960s and 1970s – but the ministry later became involved in efforts to convince Hutu refugees to return from Tanzania and Zaire and attempted to deal with problems when they did. Many other ministries have been involved in reconciliation efforts as well. For example, the Ministry of Primary and Secondary Education (now known simply as the Ministry of Education) has not only undertaken a massive program to rebuild schools but has also made significant curricular reforms. In the aftermath of the genocide, the teaching of history was eliminated from primary and secondary school curricula, because many people felt that the ethnically biased history taught previously in the schools had supported the ideology of genocide. Courses on political education have been introduced to allow an opportunity to discuss politically sensitive issues.[29]

In addition to the various ministries, the government has created two national commissions to deal with aspects of social reconstruction. The National Commission on Human Rights, charged with monitoring human rights conditions in Rwanda and making recommendations to the government on improving its human rights record, began operations in 1999 but was slow in getting its work underway and has had little impact on the country. In contrast, the National Commission on Unity and Reconciliation (NCUR) has been very active. The NCUR has departments charged with conducting civic education, mediating conflicts, and organizing community reconciliation initiatives, and among other activities, it has taken a lead in organizing annual national commemorations of the genocide.

One of the major initiatives undertaken by the NCUR has been the 'solidarity camps,' generally known by the Kinyarwanda appellation *ingando*. These camps were initially created in 1996 and 1997 to help reintegrate into Rwanda Hutu refugees returned from camps in Congo, but they have been expanded to include a variety of Rwandan citizens. They serve as an opportunity for the RPF to promote its vision of Rwandan society and to provide political re-education. Lasting from one to three months, the ingando maintain a quasi-military discipline and generally provide limited military training, which is linked to civil self-defence organizations established throughout the country. The camps also include extensive education programs, with presentations on Rwandan history and politics that seek to promote the RPF's vision of national unity. Participation in solidarity camps has become a requirement for all students prior to enrolling in university, and government officials and military personnel have also been required to participate.[30]

In addition to these and other governmental initiatives, Rwanda's civil society has taken an active role in peacebuilding efforts. A number of domestic human rights organizations in Rwanda have documented both the genocide and ongoing human rights abuses. Survivor organizations have defended the interests of those most affected by the violence. Churches and women's groups have sponsored countless reconciliation programs. The National University of Rwanda and various community organizations have sponsored conferences on the genocide and on means to promote peace.

International Initiatives

Numerous international agencies – bilateral, multilateral, and non-governmental – have joined with the new Rwandan government and civil society in the task of reconstructing the country. Most of the initial international interventions focused on providing basic emergency relief such as food, water, health care, and housing. The United Nations Mission in Rwanda (UNAMIR) took a lead in the physical rehabilitation of the country's infrastructure, working with organizations such as Oxfam and Concern to rebuild roads, bridges, water and electric lines, schools, hospitals, and other public facilities. Various international groups worked with orphans, victims of rape, widows, and other vulnerable populations. Over time, international attention shifted from emergency relief to economic development, since the disruptions of the war exacerbated the problems facing Rwanda's already weak economy.

In addition to the physical and economic reconstruction of Rwanda, the international community has taken an interest since immediately after the war in rebuilding the broken bonds of community in Rwanda and in seeking to prevent future violence. The most significant and sustained international peacebuilding efforts have been in the area of justice, with the international community not only providing substantial support to Rwanda's domestic justice systems but also establishing an international tribunal to try main organizers of the 1994 genocide. The international community has emphasized justice as a means of building peace for two primary reasons. The first justification came from a belief that trials could help to reform Rwanda's culture and eradicate the social sources of genocide. According to many analysts, genocide was possible in Rwanda because of a culture of impunity in which people were given licence to commit reprehensible acts without fear of consequences. To create a culture which respects rule of law requires holding accountable those responsible for the genocide by bringing them to justice. As William A. Schabas contends, 'prosecuting the perpetrators of genocide is a most urgent priority. It is essential for the restoration of Rwandan society that the wheels of justice begin to turn with respect to the crimes committed during 1994.'[31] The Rwandan government itself declared in debates in the UN Security Council over the creation of the International Criminal Tribunal for Rwanda (ICTR) that 'it is impossible to build a state of law and arrive at true national reconciliation [without eradicating] the culture of impunity ... [Those] who were taught that it was acceptable to kill as long as the victim was from a different ethnic group or from an opposition party, cannot arrive at national reconciliation unless they learn new values.'[32]

A second justification for investment in legal responses is the idea that victims and perpetrators will not be able to live together in peace until justice has been achieved. Trials can serve to demonstrate the social condemnation of the crimes committed and to give survivors of the crimes the sense that those responsible have been justly punished. As Alison Des Forges explains in the conclusion to her comprehensive report on the genocide for Human Rights Watch:

> Demanding justice is morally and legally right and it is also politically sound. Without justice, there can be no peace in Rwanda, nor in the surrounding region. This truth, widely acknowledged in 1994, has become even clearer in the four years since: insurgents, including some responsible for the 1994 genocide, and RPA soldiers are killing and will keep on killing civilians until they become convinced that such a course is futile and costly.

The most visible of the judicial responses to the Rwandan genocide has been the International Criminal Tribunal for Rwanda (ICTR), which was established by the UN Security Council in November 1994 under the direction of the same chief prosecutor as the tribunal created for the former Yugoslavia in 1993. While the government of Rwanda initially supported the creation of a tribunal, it refused to back the final proposal in the Security Council, because the ICTR was to be based in Arusha, Tanzania, rather than in Rwanda, because it would not have capital punishment as a penalty, and because Rwanda felt that more emphasis should be placed on supporting its own courts. Despite this resistance, the ICTR set as its goal prosecuting the chief architects of the genocide and opened offices in Kigali. The operations of the Tribunal were slow in getting started, suffering from insufficient funding and incompetent leadership, but by 2001, more than twenty individuals had been indicted and nine trials had been completed or were under way. The Tribunal has been successful in gaining extradition of those indicted and, despite continuing institutional problems, seems likely to prosecute successfully a number of the main leaders of the genocide.[33]

In addition to the ICTR, the international community has taken a leading role in rehabilitating the domestic justice system. Foreign donors contributed substantial funds to refurbish courts, police stations, and prosecutors' offices damaged in the war. Various NGOs have organized training for judges, magistrates, and police investigators, and international lawyers have worked closely with the Ministry of Justice and the national legislature to write a genocide law for prosecuting people for crimes against humanity. Avocats sans Frontiers (Lawyers without Borders) has provided defence lawyers for some genocide trials. More recently, both governmental and non-governmental support has been essential to the creation of gacaca courts.

Another major, if short-lived, international program to help combat impunity and promote human rights in post-genocidal Rwanda was the United Nations High Commission for Human Rights' Field Operation in Rwanda (HRFOR). Established in Rwanda shortly after the genocide, HRFOR was charged with investigating the genocide, monitoring ongoing human rights abuses, and helping to 're-establish confidence, and thus, to facilitate the return of refugees and displaced persons and rebuilding of civil society.'[34] At the height of its operation, HRFOR had over one hundred field officers and had branch offices in nearly every prefecture of the country. The actual activities of the HRFOR changed over time. After the creation of the ICTR, its officers focused more on ongoing human rights abuses, including following the fate of returned refugees and monitoring prison conditions. As a result, HRFOR ran afoul of the Rwanda authorities; in 1997 the government withdrew its support for HRFOR and expelled it from the country.

The United Nations High Commission for Refugees (UNHCR) worked closely with the Rwandan government to facilitate the repatriation of both old and new caseload refugees to Rwanda. The UNHCR housed over two million Rwandan refugees in its camps in Tanzania and Zaire and mounted an extensive program to encourage them to return home voluntarily. It also financed large-scale production of housing, initially for old caseload Tutsi refugees, but it later built accommodation in responce to a housing shortage and to eliminate conflicts over housing that were discouraging voluntary repatriation of new caseload refugees. Various other governmental and non-governmental organizations also contributed millions of dollars to housing construction designed to help reduce community conflict.[35]

International organizations have supported literally hundreds of other programs aimed at peacebuilding and promoting reconciliation. A simple search on the worldwide web produces more than twenty thousand web pages that discuss reconciliation in Rwanda. Numerous churches

and charitable institutions have sponsored community-building and reconciliation programs with names such as 'The Healing through Connection and Understanding Project,' 'The Peacebuilding among Rwandan
Youth Project,' and the 'Social Transformation Program.' Programs
range from trauma counselling for victims of rape to solidarity camps
organized by the Catholic Church to promote dialogue among young
people to a project for prisoners to raise crops for the families of genocide victims. The diverse projects are united by the common goal of
diminishing the divisions that keep Rwanda's population separated.

The Legacies of Victory

Despite the numerous domestic and international peacebuilding programs and the millions of dollars already spent in Rwanda, peace has
remained elusive. In the years immediately after the RPF took power,
Hutu extremists launched periodic raids on Rwanda from their bases in
refugee camps in the Democratic Republic of the Congo. The RPF's
1996 invasion of Congo and attacks on the refugee camps only briefly
stopped armed Hutu rebellion within Rwanda. Hutu rebel incursions
into northwest Rwanda in 1997–8 nearly constituted a full-scale rebellion and were quelled only with extensive use of force by the RPF both
inside Rwanda and in Congo. Rebel incursions from Congo began again
in mid-2001. For its part, the RPF has used violence regularly against the
Rwandan population in order to eliminate threats to its authority. While
levels of violence were highest during the first year of RPF rule, assassinations, disappearances, torture, and other forms of violence have continued as everyday facts of life in Rwanda. Rwanda's two incursions into
Congo have in some ways diverted conflict from Rwanda into its large
neighbour, but the relative calm within Rwanda cannot be considered a
durable peace, since it is based on a foundation of extreme violence.
The bombing of refugee camps and pursuit of Hutu civilians in late
1996 are only the most visible acts of violence perpetrated by the RPF in
Congo. The most basic requirement of peacebuilding, the cessation of
armed conflict, thus remains still to be accomplished in Rwanda.[36]
   The failure to establish peace in Rwanda can be attributed in part to
the lingering destructive effects of the genocide that Rwanda experienced in 1994, but I contend that the peacebuilding process has also
been hampered by the authoritarian character of the government that
took power in Kigali at the end of the war. Without denying in any way
the terrible tragedy that the Tutsi community in Rwanda experienced, it

is important to acknowledge that not all of Rwanda's current problems can be attributed to the genocide. Tragically, the genocide itself has been used by the current regime as a cover to allow it to violate human rights, and this has undermined reconciliation efforts and contributed to the culture of impunity. If, as this book claims, peacebuilding requires creating an environment of generalized trust, establishing open political institutions, fostering reconciliation, and diminishing economic inequality, then Rwanda's failure to advance along the peacebuilding continuum must be attributed as much to the current regime's resistance to democracy and failure to respect human rights as to the legacies of the genocide.

In the aftermath of the 1994 genocide and war, the international community came to a simplistic understanding of the sources of conflict in Rwandan society, blaming violence in the country exclusively on the ousted government and its supporters. Since the RPF was comprised primarily of Tutsi, the ethnic group that suffered most in the genocide, since the RPF was the enemy of the former regime, and since it brought an end to the genocide, the international diplomatic community regarded the RPF as a moral actor and was therefore willing to excuse any abuses on the part of the RPF as somehow necessitated by the post-genocidal situation.[37] The RPF and the new government that it installed claimed to hold as their goals the elimination of ethnic divisions in Rwandan society and the installation of a democratic regime that was respectful of human rights, and much of the international community (diplomats, aid workers, many scholars) has been willing to take these claims at face value. As René Lemarchand explains:

> There is a temptation, in writing about the genocide, to tell a story of good and evil. This is understandable: the evil committed in the name of Hutu power numbs the mind. But there is more to the story than Tutsi victimhood and Hutu guilt. ... Guilt and innocence do not run parallel to ethnic lines. But in Rwanda today, guilt and innocence are increasingly becoming ethnicized: because the Tutsi were so thoroughly victimized, they are now beyond reproach.[38]

The failure of the international community to hold the RPF and the current government accountable for their human rights record and their resistance to democratic reform is a major obstacle to peacebuilding in Rwanda today.

Despite the failure of most of the international community to take note, strong evidence implicates the RPF in human rights abuses dating back even to before they took power. As Gerard Prunier writes in the revised edition of his analysis of the genocide, 'It is now obvious, from a variety of sources, that the RPF carried out a large number of killings first during the genocide itself and then later during the end of 1994 and even into early 1995, with a diminishing intensity.'[39] Interviews that I conducted in Rwanda in 1995–6 confirm the assertions of Amnesty International, Human Rights Watch, and other groups that as the RPF advanced across the country in 1994, they opened fire on civilians in many communities and carried out myriad summary executions and revenge killings in the months immediately after taking power.[40] The level of violence perpetrated by the RPF diminished after their first year in power, but politically motivated assassinations, disappearances, torture, and other abuses have continued even to the present. The move to quell the uprising in the northwest of the country included extensive use of violence against unarmed civilians. The RPF's involvement in the wars in 1996–7 and 1998–2001 involved widespread abuses of human rights, including attacks on refugee camps that killed hundreds of civilians.[41]

In discussing human rights violations by the RPF and the Rwandan government, I do not mean to lend support to those who would claim a parity between the violence perpetrated on each side in the Rwandan civil war, most notably expressed in assertions of a 'double genocide.' The term genocide has been evoked too easily in Central Africa in recent years. For it to retain its usefulness as a moral and legal category, it must be defined narrowly.[42] The killing carried out by the RPF was not sufficiently systematic or targeted to constitute genocide.

Nevertheless, the RPF is clearly guilty of violations of the rules of war and gross human rights abuses, and the failure to hold the Front accountable for its actions has seriously undermined efforts at peacebuilding. While institutions such as the ICTR and the Rwandan courts have ostensibly sought to combat the culture of impunity, the fact that human rights standards have been applied only to one side in Rwanda's conflict has in fact fostered that impunity, promoting the idea that only the defeated will be punished. Because the ICTR has to date only brought charges against members of the former regime accused of abuses against Tutsi and has brought no charges against members of the RPF for their abuses, the Tribunal appears to many Hutu to be an example of victors' justice. According to many Rwandans, the domestic legal system has even less to do with justice, because it has been used as a tool for silencing opposition. Because the legal system is overwhelmed by the number of accused and takes years to investigate allegations of involvement in the genocide, accusing someone of participation in the genocide has been an effective means of removing them from society. In the years immediately after the genocide, hundreds of people were falsely accused for personal revenge or for political reasons. Hutu who rise to prominence in Rwanda continue to be in danger of facing genocide accusations unless they adhere strictly to the government's line of discourse. As a result, the Hutu population has been largely silenced, and in the past several years, most public criticism of the regime has come from Tutsi, particularly survivors of the genocide.[43]

While the RPF has been able to use military force to end generalized fighting, its actions have in fact undermined trust and confidence. The Front has implemented major reforms to political institutions, but it has retained tight control over the operation of government. Since first naming a government immediately after the war, the RPF has always given an image of inclusion by naming Hutu as ministers and including various political parties in the government. In practice, however, real power remains in the hands of a limited group, particularly Tutsi RPF members repatriated from Uganda. Hutu ministers have regularly complained of being accorded little real control over their ministries, as the second or third in command in each ministry – invariably a trusted RPF officer – actually calls the shots. In mid-1995, five Hutu ministers, including Prime Minister Faustin Twagiramungu, quit the government in protest over their lack of power. In early 2000, Rwandan President Pasteur Bizimungu resigned, stating his frustration over the authoritarian nature of the government, and Paul Kagame, long said to be the actual power behind the thrown, assumed the presidency. Even Tutsi survivors of the genocide or other Tutsi not closely linked to the coterie surrounding Kagame are allowed little power. Joseph Sebarenzi served as speaker of the National Assembly but was forced to flee into exile in late 1999 when he showed evidence of developing an independent power base.[44] Mahmood Mamdani observes, in an understated fashion, that 'even if the majority of the cabinet in Rwanda is from outside the RPF, its identity more Bahutu than Batutsi, one suspects this majority is in government at the behest of the RPF.'[45]

Restrictions on political parties have likewise undermined the façade of democracy in Rwanda. The RPF has consistently claimed to use the Arusha Accords as a basis for its government, and so it has always included representation from the political parties mentioned in the accords. Yet in practice, parties other than the RPF are not allowed to function. They cannot recruit members or hold rallies or conduct other business associated with the ordinary operation of a political party. Further, the RPF has outlawed parties not mentioned in the Arusha Accords. When former president Bizimungu, longtime a member of the RPF, attempted to found a new political party in May 2001, he was placed under house arrest. Restrictions on party activity seriously undermined the validity of local elections held in March 2001, since the campaign was almost entirely devoid of political debate.

In practice, the regime has allowed very little freedom of speech, and the resulting lack of free discussion has seriously compromised the ability of Rwanda's population to seek reconciliation and develop a sense of common identity. The regime effectively uses the rhetoric of national unity to preserve its own political power by presenting a public discourse that insists on the unity of all Rwandans and denounces ethnic discrimination and hatred, while at the same time actively discriminating in favor of its central power base (Tutsi from Uganda). Anyone who complains about inequality or discrimination can easily be dismissed as supporting the politics of ethnic division. Criticism of the government is equated with support for the genocide. As a result, there is no room in Rwandan politics for the airing of independent political ideas. As Brauman, Smith, and Vidal claim,

> this radical transformation of the foundational discourse has impeded the repression of extreme ethnic behavior on only one side: when it targets Tutsi. In reality, in all domains of the society, most particularly in the politico-administrative sector and that of modern activities, weighs on Rwandan Hutus the threat of being despoiled, arrested, assassinated, without those responsible of these exactions or these murders ever being the object of pursuit.[46]

The current government has also exacerbated the economic sources of conflict in Rwanda. The genocide and war clearly devastated Rwanda's already weak economy, but the conduct of the regime has led to a serious growth in income disparities. While much of Rwanda languishes in poverty, Kigali has become increasingly well off, and Rwandans with links to the regime have had access to numerous opportunities for enriching themselves. Initially, they were able to benefit from privileged access to international trade and to the numerous international agencies that came to provide aid to Rwanda in the aftermath of the genocide. Since 1996 those with links to the regime have been able to profit from the invasions of Congo, as Rwanda has become a major transit point for diamonds, gold, and other products mined in Congo.[47] Most of the population, particularly Hutu and Tutsi genocide survivors, are relegated to low-paying positions in manual labour. The increasingly evident enrichment of state functionaries and their families – visible in the construction of elaborate new homes and in the launching of new business ventures – contributes to the tensions within the country.

Sadly, the international community's general willingness to forgive the human rights abuses and authoritarian practices of the Rwandan government has contributed substantially to the climate of impunity that has encouraged more and more abuses on the part of the government. Effectively using the genocide to claim moral advantage, the regime has actually been able to use the international community to advance its agenda. The program of forced villagization (*imidugudu*) was funded largely by the international community. Claiming that they needed to move people into villages not only for greater security but to facilitate the provision of services, the RPF drove thousands of people into the new villages, often destroying perfectly good homes in order to force people into inferior housing with fewer services, rather than more, available. The first invasion of Congo in 1996 similarly gained international support, as the RPF claimed it had legitimate security concerns as well as a humanitarian interest in protecting Congo's persecuted Tutsi minority.[48]

Lessons of the Rwandan Case for Peacebuilding

My point in briefly reviewing some of the deficiencies of the current Rwandan regime is to suggest that peacebuilding in Rwanda has been hampered not simply by the legacies of the genocide, which have largely been acknowledged both within the country and abroad, but also by ongoing authoritarian practices, which have generally been overlooked or excused. As Rony Bauman, Stephen Smith, and Claudine Vidal assert, 'The current Rwandan government does not escape the law of its military origins: to the detriment of other modes of action, it resorts to the use of arms to manifest and reinforce its superiority, in particular – but not exclusively – in reference to Rwandans.'[49] In short, the Rwandan case highlights the difficulties of peacebuilding after a decisive military victory. Because the RPF took over Rwanda through force of arms and remains sufficiently militarily strong to preserve its hold on power, the RPF has little incentive to promote the process of peacebuilding.

The Rwandan case demonstrates the importance to peacebuilding of including all sides of a conflict in political settlements. The principle of consociational settlements to conflicts, most consistently advocated by Arendt Lijphart, requires a compromise between warring parties that guarantees representation to all sides. In the Rwandan case, the RPF has given token representation to Hutu and to various factions of the Tutsi population, but as a military movement that gained an absolute victory in the Rwandan war in 1994, the Front has been able to retain near complete control of the Rwandan political system. Excluded from political channels to express their frustrations and aspirations, the Rwandan population remains susceptible to violent movements. Much of the population evidently cooperated with Hutu rebels during the rebellion in the northwest in 1997–8, and unless the political system opens up in a meaningful fashion, Rwandans are likely to support other armed opposition movements in the future. The Rwandan case thus shows the obstacles to peacemaking arising from both the legacies of severe violence and the legacies of a one-sided settlement to armed conflict.

NOTES

1 Alison Des Forges, *Leave None to Tell the Story: Genocide in Rwanda* (New York: Human Rights Watch, 1999), provides an excellent description of how the genocide was carried out, both at the national and local levels. According to the research of the Human Rights Watch research team (of which I was a part in 1995–6), the killing was so intense and well organized that most major massacres were completed by the first week of May, and the focus of state-sponsored violence shifted to flushing out survivors. On the genocide, see also Gerard Prunier, *The Rwanda Crisis* (New York: Columbia University Press, 1997).

2 Cf. Filip Reyntjens, 'Talking or Fighting? Political Evolution in Rwanda and Burundi, 1998–1999' (Uppsala: Nordiska Afrikainstitutet, 1999); Amnesty International, 'Rwanda – The Hidden Violence: Disappearances and Killings Continue,' AFR 47/023/98 (London: Amnesty International, 1998); Amnesty International, 'Rwanda: No One Is Talking About It Anymore' (London: Amnesty International, October 1997); Human Rights Watch, 'Rwanda: The Search for Security and Human Rights Abuses,' Human Rights Watch Short Reports 12, no. 1(A) (April 2000).

3 For example, Mark A. Drumbl, 'Punishment, Postgenocide: From Guilt to Shame to *Civic* in Rwanda,' *New York University Law Review* 75, no. 5 (1999), writes that 'Rwanda finds itself in a stage of social and historical develop-

ment, which this Article refers to as the "postgenocidal" stage, in which it seeks to come to terms with the violence and initiate a very complex healing process' (1224).

4 See, for example, Rony Brauman, Stephen Smith, and Claudine Vidal, 'Politique de terreur et privilège d'impunité au Rwanda,' *Esprit* (August-September 2000); Reyntjens, 'Talking or Fighting?'

5 In reference to South Africa, for example, see Heribert Adam, 'Trading Justice for Truth,' *World Today* (January 1998), argues that 'a purchased revolution amounts to a compromise that satisfies neither side.'

6 Philip Gourevitch, 'Letter from the Congo: Continental Shift,' *New Yorker* (4 August 1997); Marina Ottaway, 'Africa's "new leaders": African solution or African problem?' *Current History* 97, no. 619 (1998).

7 Some scholars question whether ethnicity is the appropriate term to discuss Hutu and Tutsi, since the two groups share a common language and religion and have lived in integrated communities for centuries. But it is clear that as a result of a process that began shortly before colonialism, Hutu and Tutsi, whatever their previous meaning, were transformed into ethnic identities.

8 Exact ethnic percentages are difficult to determine, because of the historically flexible nature of identities and the degree to which they have been politicized. The most frequently cited figures estimate the Twa at 1 per cent, Tutsi at 14–15 per cent, and Hutu at 84–85 per cent.

9 The best account of the late colonial and early independence period is René Lemarchand, *Rwanda and Burundi* (New York: Praeger, 1970). For a general historical overview, see also Gerard Prunier, *The Rwanda Crisis: History of a Genocide* (New York: Columbia University Press, 1995, 1997).

10 The term 'selective genocide' comes from René Lemarchand and David Martin, *Selective Genocide in Burundi* (London: Minority Rights Group, 1973). Burundi had a similar ethnic composition to Rwanda, but the Tutsi remained in control of the country after independence. Since the 1960s ethnic violence and other political events in each country have had a profound impact on events in the other country.

11 Filip Reyntjens, *Pouvoir et Droit au Rwanda* (Tervuren: Musée Royale de l'Afrique Centrale, 1995).

12 Prunier, *The Rwanda Crisis*, 61–74, 90–2; Catherine Watson, *Exile from Rwanda: Background to an Invasion* (Washington: US Committee for Refugees, February 1991).

13 'Rwanda/Uganda: A Violent Homecoming,' *Africa Confidential* 31, no. 23 (12 October 1990); Prunier, *The Rwanda Crisis*, 93–120.

14 Africa Watch, 'Rwanda: Talking Peace and Waging War, Human Rights Since the October 1990 Invasion,' *Human Rights Watch Short Report* 4, no. 3,

(27 February 1992) 7–11; Filip Reyntjens, *L'Afrique des Grands Lacs en Crise: Le Rwanda et le Burundi (1988–1994)* (Paris: Karthala, 1994), 94–5; Fédération Internationale des Droits de l'Homme (FIDH), Africa Watch, et al., 'Rapport de la Commission internationale d'enquête sur les violations des droits de l'homme au Rwanda depuis le 1er octobre 1990 (7–21 janvier 1993): Rapport Finale' (Paris: FIDH, March 1993), 18–22.

15 After the installation of a multi-party government in April 1992, to speak of the parties opposed to Habyarimana as the opposition may seem confusing, since they held half of the cabinet posts in the government, including the position as prime minister, but this was the terminology used by Rwandans themselves to distinguish between pro- and anti-Habyarimana parties.

16 Des Forges, *Leave None to Tell the Story*, 96–128; Reyntjens, *L'Afrique des Grands Lacs en Crise*, 122–5, 202–6, 248–56; Prunier, *The Rwanda Crisis*, 149–212.

17 Jean-Pierre Chrétien, *Les Medias du Génocide* (Paris: Karthala, 1995); *Broadcasting Genocide: Censorship, Propaganda, and State-Sponsored Violence in Rwanda 1990–1994* (London: Article 19, 1996).

18 Des Forges, *Leave None to Tell the Story*, 141–274; Prunier, *The Rwanda Crisis*, 229–68.

19 Prunier, *The Rwanda Crisis*, 281–355.

20 US. Department of State, 'Country Reports on Human Rights Practices for 1999: Rwanda' (Washington, February 2000).

21 See Father Michael Lapsley, *Priest and Partisan* (Capetown: Michael Worsnip, 2000) on the impact of violence on those who perpetrate it.

22 Amnesty International, *Reports of Killings and Abductions by the Rwandese Patriotic Army (April–August 1994)* (London, October 1994).

23 Prunier, *The Rwanda Crisis*, 358–65.

24 On the NRM political system, see Nelson Kasfir, 'No Party Democracy in Uganda,' *Journal of Democracy* 9, no. 2 (April 1998).

25 Prunier, *The Rwanda Crisis*, 328–33; Bauman, Smith, and Vidal, 'Politique de terreur et privilège d'impunité au Rwanda,' 149.

26 Even several members of the RPF acknowledged as much to me in conversations in 1995–6. One RPF soldier told me in early 1996 that he estimated fully 80 per cent of those in prison at that time were not guilty of murder.

27 Drumbl, 'Punishment, Postgenocide,' 1279–92; Leo J. DeSouza, 'Assigning Blame in Rwanda: How to Break the Cycle of Revenge in Ethnic Conflict,' *Washington Monthly* 49, no. 9 (1997); Lawyers Committee for Human Rights, 'Prosecuting Genocide in Rwanda: A Lawyers Committee Report on the ICTR and National Trials' (Washington: Lawyers Committee for Human Rights, July 1997).

28 Farah Stockman, 'The People's Court: Crime and Punishment in Rwanda,'

Transition 9, no. 4 (2000), 20–41; Drumbl, 'Punishment, Postgenocide,' 1263–7.

29 This information is based on interviews conducted in Kigali and Butare, Rwanda, in March, May, and June 2001.

30 Eugene Rucogoza, head of Department of Civil Education, National Commission on Unity and Reconciliation, interviewed in Kigali on 1 June 2001; Human Rights Watch, 'The Search for Security,' 20.

31 William A. Schabas, 'Justice, Democracy, and Impunity in Post-Genocide Rwanda: Searching for Solutions to Impossible Problems,' Crim L F, 1996, 534.

32 Rwandan representative to the United Nations, quoted in Payam Akhavan, 'The International Criminal Tribunal for Rwanda: The Politics and Pragmatics of Punishment,' *American Journal of International Law* 90, no. 3 (1996), 501–10.

33 Lawyers Committee for Human Rights, 'Prosecuting Genocide in Rwanda'; Akhavan, 'The International Criminal Tribunal for Rwanda,' 502–8; Brenda Sue Thornton, 'Notes from the Field.'

34 Agreement of cooperation between HCRC and the Government of Rwanda, quoted in Todd Howland, 'Mirage, Magic, or Mixed Bag? The United Nations High Commissioner for Human Rights' Field Operation in Rwanda,' *Human Rights Quarterly* 21, no. 2 (1999), 1–55.

35 Human Rights Watch, *Uprooting the Rural Poor in Rwanda* (New York: Human Rights Watch, May 2001).

36 Jeff Drumtra, *Life after Death: Suspicion and Reintegration in Post-Genocide Rwanda* (Washington: US Committee for Refugees, February 1998); Filip Reyntjens, *La Guerre des Grands Lacs: Alliances mouvantes et conflits extraterritoriaux en Afrique Centrale* (Paris: Harmattan, 1999).

37 Samantha Power, for example, notes that, 'while human rights watchdogs cry foul, American and European governments take the opposite stance – keeping largely mum over these abuses, emphasizing the unparalleled obstacles the Tutsi regime must overcome, and pumping in aid to help them do so.' see 'Life after Death: Barriers to Reconciliation in Rwanda,' *New Republic* (6 April 1998): 16–19.

38 René Lemarchand, 'Hate Crimes: Race and Retribution in Rwanda,' *Transition* 9 nos. 1 and 2 (2000), 118–19.

39 Prunier, *The Rwanda Crisis*, 359.

40 Amnesty International, *Reports of Killings and Abductions by the Rwandese Patriotic Army*; Human Rights Watch, 'Rwanda: The Crisis Continues' (New York: Human Rights Watch, April 1995); Amnesty International, 'Rwanda: Two Years after the Genocide – Human Rights in the Balance. An Open Letter to

President Pasteur Bizimungu,' AFR 47/02/96 (London: Amnesty International, 4 April 1996).

41 Amnesty International, 'Rwanda: The Hidden Violence'; Human Rights Watch, 'Rwanda: The Search for Security and Human Rights Abuses'; Brauman, Smith, and Vidal, 'Politique de terreur'; Reyntjens, 'Talking or Fighting?' See also my report on the first war coauthored with Alison Des Forges, 'Attacked by All Sides: Civilians and the War in Eastern Zaire' (New York: Human Rights Watch; Paris: FIDH, March 1997), and my report on the second, 'Eastern Congo Ravaged' (New York: Human Rights Watch, May 2000).

42 For definitions of genocide, see Frank Chalk and Kurt Jonassohn, *The History and Sociology of Genocide: Analyses and Case Studies* (New Haven: Yale University Press, 1990), 8–32; Irving Louis Horowitz, *Taking Lives: Genocide and State Power*, 4th ed. (New Brunswick, NJ: Transaction Publishers, 1997); and Helen Fein, *Genocide: A Sociological Perspective* (London and Newbury Park: Sage, 1993), 8–31.

43 Cf. Human Rights Watch, 'The Search for Security and Human Rights Abuses.'

44 Brauman, Smith, and Vidal write that 'In only a few years, a small group has succeeded in constituting a politico-military network at the heart of the RPF that, controlling the principle positions of power, exploits all occasions for corruption' ('Politique de terreur,' 151).

45 Mahmood Mamdani, 'From Conquest to Consent as the Basis of State Formation: Reflections on Rwanda,' *New Left Review* 216 (March–April 1996), 31.

46 Brauman, Smith, and Vidal, 'Politique de terreur,' 149.

47 Bjørn Willum, 'Civil War Financed by Diamonds and Donors,' *Aktuelt*, 18 January 2001; Kristi Essick, 'A Call to Arms: How the Demand for Cell Phones and Computer Chips Is Helping Fuel a Bloody Civil War in the Democratic Republic of Congo,' *Industry Standard* 11 June 2001.

48 Filip Reyntjens, 'Briefing – The Second Congo War: More Than a Remake,' *African Affairs* 98 (1999), 241–50.

49 Bauman, Smith, and Vidal, 'Politique de terreur', 150.

3

Uganda: The Politics of 'Consolidation' under Museveni's Regime, 1996–2003

John Kiyaga-Nsubuga

In an earlier essay on Uganda's political transition under Yoweri Museveni's National Resistance Movement (NRM) regime,[1] I argued that restoring normalcy in a country which has been devastated by civil war requires strong, nationalistic leadership. Such a regime must have several abilities: drawing a broad range of contending elites into the political process to minimize polarization; generating intra-elites consensus on the fundamentals of political discourse; pursuing policies that focus on reversing economic decline; and improving the well-being of the majority of the populace. I also stressed that the efforts of regimes that are trying to establish order out of chaos should not be measured against some preconceived yardstick but by the steps, however measured, that are taken in the *direction* of political liberalization – taking the context into account.

I did not think then, and I still do not think now, that regimes that inherit highly polarized political systems whose institutions and structures are already in shreds can realistically be expected to stabilize politics immediately, given that they have to contend with disruptive actions by vanquished elites, and overbearing pressure for political inclusion from previously disenfranchised groups. In such contexts, political stability can only be achieved through a long-term process because of the difficulty of putting in place workable and broadly acceptable institutions, coupled with the obvious need of the liberalizing regime not to lose control of the process altogether. The problem is compounded if the economy is also in shambles, because the regime must simultaneously deal with heightened and often unrealistic expectations from the long-suffering population against a background of severe resource constraints. The challenge for the regime, then, is how to establish accountable and representative political institutions and structures, and to reconstruct the economy in a meaningful manner without allowing the process to be captured by political adversaries.

I want to build on that argument in this essay in which I examine the consolidation phase of the NRM regime, in order to draw attention to the dilemma of political transition that proceeds in a context of severe intra-elite discord. We have been cautioned not to imagine that political transitions in Africa follow a uniform pattern, but to make allowance for innumerable 'uncertainties, complexities, contradictions, ambiguities, and downright enigmas which exist.'[2] That notwithstanding, I want to suggest that political events in Uganda since the outset of the NRM regime highlight the general problem of reconstructing broken-down societies which several other countries also face, but the unique manner in which they have unfolded underlines the inherent conflict in trying to rebuild and democratize society while struggling to retain control of the political process at the same time.

This essay examines the political dynamics in Uganda, when the regime sought to strengthen its hold and carry out its agenda without the support of the traditional political parties, particularly the Democratic Party (DP), that it had enjoyed previously. The first ten years (1986–96) could be called the stabilization phase, when the regime tried to anchor itself by including various contending groups in its political and military structures.[3] This period ended when the DP left the alliance and, together with the Uganda Peoples' Congress (UPC) faction led by Cecilia Ogwal, fielded DP leader Paul Ssemogerere against Museveni in the country's first presidential elections in 1996.[4] The consolidation phase can, then, be said to have started with Museveni's landslide victory in the 1996 presidential elections when his regime abandoned its earlier all-inclusive approach and began to rely more on political capital from the processes and institutions that it had fostered, particularly decentralized governance, the revamped parliamentary system, press freedoms, economic recovery, and effective intervention in the social sector.

I will examine three elements in this essay. First, I will highlight the regime's handling of the political process after the 1996 presidential election, to draw attention to the extensive political liberalization that was undertaken and the attendant controversies it generated. By this I hope to elaborate on my earlier point that political transitions that take place against a background of severe intra-elite discord are likely to generate a paradox in which the liberalizing regime might apply liberalization and control measures simultaneously to ensure that it remains in control of

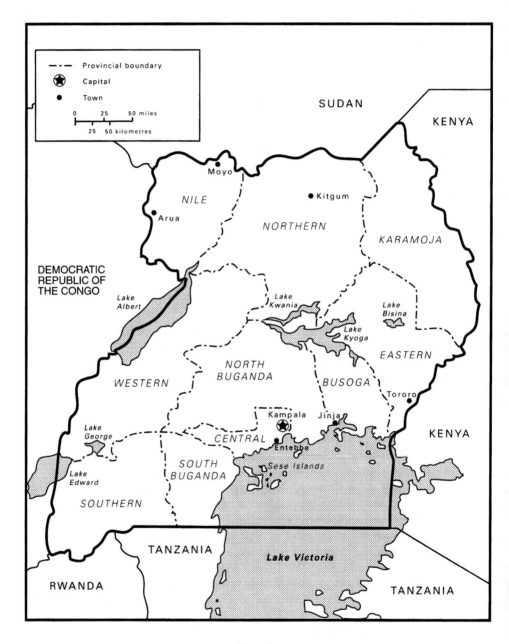

Uganda

the political process. Second, I will highlight the main elements of the NRM regime's socio-economic policies to show why the regime's somewhat controversial views on democracy found considerable resonance within Uganda, and aroused only perfunctory protestations from the donor community. The point I hope to make is that evaluation of a regime's performance during the transition from chaos to normalcy should take account of the regime's entire regimen of initiatives, as well as the context in which it is operating, in order to obtain a meaningful understanding of the possibilities and limitations of guided transitions. Finally, I will draw attention to the danger reformists may face in trying to control the political process for too long. While firm control of the political process early on may be necessary to revive the country, set it on a sound footing, and prevent it from relapsing into chaos, prolonging the control indefinitely may generate a backlash that could unsettle the regime and undo whatever good it may have achieved.

Background

When the NRM regime seized power in 1986 after a bruising five-year guerrilla war against Milton Obote's second regime (1981–5), and that of General Tito Okello Lutwa (1985), it inherited a country whose economy was in ruin and whose political and administrative institutions were in tatters: The infrastructure was dilapidated, especially the roads; social services, particularly health and education, were in a sorry state; inflation was running at over 120 per cent annually; government was running a large budgetary deficit due to financial indiscipline; the country had a serious balance of payments problem, which was compounded by over-reliance on coffee exports for foreign exchange earnings; the exchange rate was overvalued by almost ten times the market rate; and income per capita was only 59 per cent of its 1971 level.[5]

Parallel to this, the population had lost faith in government because of its inability to provide adequate social services. Government lacked transparency and accountability in its operations, and the civil service was bloated, poorly paid, inefficient and dispirited. The political system itself was highly fragmented with nine major players on the scene comprising four political parties and five armed groups – excluding Museveni's National Resistance Army (NRA).[6] Furthermore, civil-military relations were very strained because previous regimes had long used the security agencies to brutalize the population into submission. All this created a chaotic environment in which security of person and property was not guaranteed, which had a very negative impact on the economy as a whole.

From the start the NRM leadership took the view that the country's long-term stability lay in successful economic reconstruction, and in incorporating the diverse armed groups into the army and their political leaders into cabinet and the National Resistance Council. The leadership's argument was that the disintegration the country had suffered in the past had originated from associational politics based on ethnic, religious, and regional cleavages that had developed during the colonial period, and that the transition to normalcy required rearranging politics on a different basis in the interim period.

To that end, the regime undertook a series of measures, including the appointment of appointing leading personalities from contending groups to ministerial positions (except Obote's UPC for which the regime had a special dislike), drafting a new constitution through a broad consultative process that started with the appointment of a constitutional commission in 1988 (the constitution was enacted in 1995), and requiring political competition to take place under an umbrella movement that emphasized individual merit and downplayed partisanship. The reasoning was that these measures were essential for facilitating the healing process because they would stabilize the highly volatile situation, minimize tension, generate some minimum consensus, and provide the basis for intra-elite collaboration without which the country's reconstruction would be impossible to achieve.[7]

As it turned out, however, the intra-elite cooperation that was expected to result from the sharing of power between the NRM and its rivals did not last long, because the parties had very different agendas right from the start. While the NRM leadership looked at the movement as a mechanism for conflict management within which different tendencies could participate in running the country without resorting to the divisive politics of the past, the DP leadership considered it to be merely a temporary arrangement for allowing ideal conditions for multiparty politics to emerge.

Clearly, in retrospect, the initial decision by the DP leadership to ally with the NRM regime was made largely for reasons of expedience and not out of conviction over the soundness of the NRM's political agenda. For all intents and purposes, the DP seems to have gone into the alliance to strengthen and deepen its influence countrywide in readiness for the inevitable struggle for power in the future. Apparently, its calculations were based on the strong support it had generated during the

1980 elections, when had used its power to extract six important cabinet positions from the NRM during the distribution of the spoils in 1986.[8] On the other hand, the NRM leaders had apparently assumed that the DP would perpetually accept its junior status in government. More than anything else, it was this difference in perception and strategy that led the two to part ways in 1995, and to the NRM regime's abandonment of inclusion as a stabilization mechanism.

Thus the NRM's stabilization phase could be said to have ended with the formal rupture in relations between the DP and the NRM, and the consolidation phase to have begun with Museveni's landslide victory in the 1996 presidential elections.

I would like to stress that the specific trajectory of Uganda's political transition under the NRM regime is explicable in terms of the fact that from the outset the various groups differed in perspectives and long-term expectations, did not begin with consensus on the parameters of political discourse, and were vastly unequal in power and influence. Although they collectively believed in the need to reconstruct the economy, to rebuild public institutions, and to establish democracy in the country, they lacked common understanding of the political direction that was to be taken and how political power was to be competed for in the long run. This initial lack of consensus over the fundamentals of political discourse increased the need for control of political activity to be a key factor if the NRM was to retain control of the transition.

The Consolidation Phase

The Absence of Consensus and Its Impact

The NRM leadership appears to have concluded after the 1996 presidential elections that the grounds which had earlier made the DP an indispensable ally no longer obtained. Not only had the DP allied with the UPC, its former arch-enemy, to oust Museveni from power (a move which was seen by the NRM leadership as betrayal of the highest order), but even the hollowness of its claim over control of the central and southern regions had been brutally exposed by Museveni's landslide victory. Furthermore, its alliance with the UPC had sharply divided its ranks and substantially reduced its stock as a crucial partner in the running of government.

The UPC was not a big threat to the NRM regime either, having split into two factions: a hard-line pro-Obote faction led by James Rwanyarare, which did not want anything to do with the NRM regime, and a more moderate faction, led by Cecilia Ogwal, which believed in constructive engagement. Neither faction was capable of mounting any effective challenge to the regime. Meanwhile the tiny Conservative Party (CP) had also split into two with its leader, Mayanja Nkangi, remaining in government, and the breakaway faction of John Ken Lukyamuzi and Yosamu Nsambu remaining in vocal but ineffectual opposition.

Thus two antagonistic political camps had emerged by the end of the 1996 presidential elections: a strong and apparently cohesive movement camp which was fundamentally opposed to the resumption of multiparty politics, and a weak and divided multiparty camp which conceived the movement politics as no more than a poor disguise of one-party rule. Quite apart from this, the regime also faced armed opposition from two groups: Joseph Kony's Lord's Resistance Army (LRA) in Gulu and Kitgum districts on the border with Sudan; and the Allied Democratic Forces (ADF) in Kabarole and Kasese districts on the border with the Democratic Republic of Congo (DRC). The latter staged its operation from rear bases in the DRC, allegedly with funding and support from the fundamentalist regime of General Bashir in Sudan, and it was this, according to government, which forced Uganda to send troops to the DRC in 1997. However, the attempt to stabilize the country by crossing into the DRC had its unintended and quite unpleasant consequences. Among other things, it led Uganda to fall out with Rwanda, a country that had been seen as a key ally in the region due to earlier support that Uganda had given to the Rwanda Patriotic Front during its capture of power in Kigali. After backing different factions in the DRC, the two countries' armies fought twice in Kisangani. Uganda eventually withdrew from its last oupost in Bunia in April 2003 in fulfillment of an agreement that had earlier been signed in South Africa, leaving the area in control of UN peacekeeping forces. Although the government claimed that the Uganda Peoples Defence Forces (UPDF) had succeeded in neutralizing the Rwanda-supported Peoples Redemption Army (PRA), led by renegade Uganda military officers, which was allegedly holed up in the Ituri region in the DRC, Uganda's image has been tarnished by the misadventure. However, of the two armed opposition groups, it was the conflict in the north that has imposed the largest cost on the country in terms of destruction and human suffering. Between 1986 and 2003 it led to the displacement of over one million people, the abduction of over eight thousand children some of whom were turned into sex slaves by LRA soldiers, and the maiming of thousands of people whose limbs, ears and lips

were cut off by LRA fighters as punishment.[9] Some eight hundred thousand people were living in protected camps. All this generated extensive
stress, recycled hostility and fuelled the conflict further.[10]

The war in northern Uganda had its proximate causes in the lawlessness and revenge killings by some of the NRA soldiers that had been stationed in Kitgum District following the defeat of the Uganda National
Liberation Army, which greatly alienated the local population.[11] The
fundamental causes of the war, on the other hand, were really economic
and geopolitical. The northern region had always been the least developed part of Uganda right from the colonial period and most of its people had long been used to looking for employment in the state sector,
particularly in the security agencies. The defeat of the northern-domi-
nated regimes, therefore, had direct and negative consequences for
thousands of their beneficiaries and provided fertile ground for their
recruitment into rebel ranks. Geopolitically, the long-running conflict in
southern Sudan between the Sudanese Peoples Liberation Army (SPLA)
and the Khartoum government had always had an impact on Uganda,
not least because of the close affinity between the peoples on either side
of the border. The bone of contention in this particular case was the
regimes in Sudan and Uganda accused each other of supporting their
respective rebels.

Initially the NRM had believed that the conflict could be resolved militarily. At one point nearly one hundred thousand people were forced
into protected villages around Gulu town in an effort to isolate and
defeat the rebels. After pressure from several quarters, the NRM regime
tried a conciliatory approach and held talks with rebels in 1994, but the
talks collapsed due to rebel suspicion of government intentions. Government tried another approach and got Parliament to pass an Amnesty Bill
in 1999 under which all surrendering rebels were granted automatic
amnesty from prosecution. The National Rescue Front II, which had
been fighting the government from its bases in Sudan, took advantage of
this amnesty in 2002, but few LRA rebels had surrendered by the time of
this writing. Again, a new initiative was taken by government in 2001 to
isolate Kony by talking directly to his field commanders in a bid to find
an end to the conflict. The Libyan leader, Colonel Muammar Gaddafi,
also brokered a rapprochement between the Ugandan and Sudanese
governments, which led to the reinstatement of diplomatic relations
between the two countries in the same year. The two governments even
reached a rare agreement under which Uganda was granted permission
to engage LRA on Sudanese territory. However, no breakthrough had

been achieved by 2003, and it was not clear whether real stability could be achieved in that war-torn region without significant improvement in the economic fortunes of the local population.

Taking the events described above as a whole, one could reasonably argue that the NRM regime had not achieved the political unity for the whole country that it had set itself out to build. However, the regime was able to extend its legitimacy and political capital, and to consolidate its hold on power on the basis of significant successes it had scored in several other areas, particularly in the socio-economic economic field.

Economic Reconstruction: Phase 1, 1986–1995

The regime's grand objective from the start was to reverse the previous economic ruin, expand production, and improve the people's wellbeing. However, the approaches that were chosen in pursuit of these objectives changed sharply in the first two years due to the regime's quick realization of the difference between ideology and reality.

Initially, Museveni was strongly opposed to the liberalization of the economy under the structural adjustment programs (SAP) that were being advocated by the IMF and the World Bank,[12] but it soon became clear to him and the rest of the NRM leadership that undertaking these policies held the key to the realization of the regime's overall economic objectives.[13] It says much about the NRM leadership's pragmatism and determination to turn the economy around that they quickly agreed to adopt the same IMF/World Bank SAP policies they had been castigating previously, in spite of articulate opposition from some academic quarters and from within the regime itself.[14]

Following this decision in 1987 an Economic Recovery Program (ERP) was launched with the support of an IMF Structural Adjustment Facility (SAF), an Economic Recovery Credit from the International Development Association (IDA), and an assortment of multilateral and bilateral assistance.[15] The ERP's broad aim was to lower inflation and stabilize the currency, to reduce imbalances in the external account, and to provide impetus for rehabilitation and growth. In addition to devaluing the shilling by 77 percent and applying a conversion tax of 30 per cent on all currency and bank deposits, government increased produce and petroleum prices, and liberalized foreign exchange allocation through Open General Licensing to ensure an uninterrupted flow of foreign exchange to key industries.

More vigorous measures were undertaken in the 1988–9 financial year. The shilling was devalued by a further 60 percent, fuel prices were increased, a Special Import Program (SIP) was started to make foreign exchange available for an expanded list of imports, and a 100 per cent retention scheme was introduced for non-traditional exports. In response, the IMF granted the government a much needed Enhanced Structural Adjustment Facility (ESAF).

But it was in the following year that decisive measures were taken to shock the economy out of its lengthy slumber. Following government's adoption of a revised framework, that it had jointly drafted with the IMF and the World Bank – which called for limiting government borrowing from the central bank to 1.3 per cent of GDP; devaluing the shilling by 41 per cent, followed by smaller monthly devaluations; broadening indirect taxation of goods, services and imports; and tightening government expenditure[16] – inflation was reduced to about 30 per cent and GDP expansion exceeded 6 per cent, the rate it had maintained for the preceding two years. By then some of the transport bottlenecks had been addressed with the reconstruction of 1,850 kilometres of all-weather roads and 2,411 kilometres of gravel trunk roads, and the importation of hundreds of trucks, buses and railway wagons, and thousands of cars. By early 1990 the differential between the official exchange rate and the 'Kibanda' (black market), which had reached 1:11 in mid-1988, had been reduced to 1:2. Also, following several increases in price incentives, coffee farmers were able to receive 26.5 per cent of the world coffee price in 1990, compared to the 7.6 per cent they had received four years previously.

Other measures were taken on the institutional front. In 1988 the World Bank sponsored a project to determine the public service's overall size. As a result, a commission was appointed in May 1989 to review the public service and to recommend how to increase its efficiency and responsiveness to the country's needs; the statistics department in the Ministry of Planning and Economic Development was overhauled; an inspector general of government was appointed; and external aid coordination was streamlined by placing this responsibility in the Ministry of Finance (previously external aid coordination was scattered in several places including the Ministry of Foreign Affairs, the Bank of Uganda, the Ministry of Finance, and the Ministry of Planning and Economic Development). These measures, and ones described above, laid the basis for economic recovery that the country was able to register by the mid-1990s.

Economic Reconstruction: Phase 2, 1996–2000

The second phase in the economic reconstruction program involved translating the benefits of the economic recovery into improved livelihood for the populace.[17] The major instrument chosen for this was the Poverty Eradication Action Plan (PEAP). The PEAP identified a set of actions that were to be given priority by governmental and non-governmental sectors in order to realize the government's objective of eliminating mass poverty in Uganda by 2017. These included creating a framework for sustainable economic growth and structural transformation; ensuring good governance and security; increasing the ability of the poor to increase their incomes; and improving the quality of life of the poor.[18] Effective implementation of the PEAP was judged to require intensifying the liberal macro-economic policies that had been started earlier. It also included prioritizing allocation towards poverty related areas; ensuring that aggregate expenditure was in line with sound macro-economic management;[19] and instilling financial discipline in government ministries and departments to fight inflation and to eliminate accumulation of domestic arrears. Attendant measures also aimed at stabilizing the exchange rate, making the export sector more competitive; restructuring and strengthening the financial sector, and recapitalizing the Bank of Uganda and strengthening its lax supervisory mechanisms (two major commercial banks, the International Credit Bank and Greenland Bank, became insolvent in 1998–9 under the Bank's very nose).

The combination of these measures produced a remarkable economic turnaround. Between 1990 and 2000 GDP growth averaged 6 per cent annually, and most of the economic sectors exceeded annual growth rates of 5 per cent, with most of the growth being registered in construction and manufacturing (12 per cent), hotels and restaurants (11.8 per cent), and transport and communications (8.3 per cent). Average inflation fell from an earlier high of 108 percent in 1986–7 to 5 per cent in 2000; the share of non-traditional exports rose from 14 percent of commodity exports in 1990 to over 37 per cent to 1999; and the government's budget deficit, excluding grants, reduced from 8 percent in 1995–6 to 6.6 per cent of GDP 1998–9 (if grants are included, the deficit fell from 1 per cent of GDP in 1996–7 to 0.3 per cent of GDP in 1997–8).[20] Total installed electricity generation capacity increased to 260 megawatts in 2000 (from 180 megawatts), and two private consortia were cleared in 2001 to build more generating capacity at Bujagali and Karuma Falls on the River Nile. Telecommunication was also greatly improved through licensing of three private cellular telephone companies – Mobile Telephone Network (MTN), CelTel and TelCel (belonging to the newly privatized Uganda Telecommunications Limited) – which was a great boost to trade and commerce.[21]

To ensure that PEAP had a definite and beneficial impact on the people, a poverty action fund (PAF) was created to channel resources to five national priority program areas that had a direct impact on poverty alleviation and service delivery – namely, primary education, primary health care, rural feeder roads, water and sanitation, and agricultural extension.[22] Funds for PAF were derived from savings from the World Bank's Highly Indebted Poor Countries (HIPC) debt relief initiative (Uganda was the first country to qualify for this relief due to the depth of her reforms), from the donor community, and from government. As a proportion of the total budget, expenditures under PAF rose from 18 per cent in 1997–8 to 35 per cent in 2001–2.[23] An evaluation of PAF carried out in ten representative districts in early 2000 established that, implementation problems aside, the fund was benefitting its intended beneficiaries in two ways: local people were able to hire out their labour, and they were also receiving services, such as education, (especially universal primary education), water, sanitation, health and road construction.[24] More significantly, the number of Ugandans living in absolute poverty fell dramatically from 56 per cent in 1992 to 35 per cent in 2000.[25] This, of course, is not to suggest that the economy had fully recovered. If anything, it still faced a multitude of challenges, including a very narrow resource base comprised primarily of traditional agricultural exports (coffee, tea, etc.), poor revenue collection,[26] high dependence on donor support, and weak financial management and other systems.[27] The point I am making here is that the economic turnaround that had been registered was of such magnitude as to be instrumental in generating the regime a high level of legitimacy, both locally and in donor circles.

Decentralization and Local Governance

One of the regime's most revolutionary initiatives was the decentralization program, under which a broad range of powers and responsibilities was transferred from the centre to popularly elected local governments.[28] Previously Uganda had operated a local government system in which all district councils were appointed from the centre, and in which virtually all their operations were centrally directed as well. In 1993 government decided to devolve powers to popularly elected local governments, and this was inserted into the constitution and operationalized through the Local Governments Act, 1997, which sharply demarcated the respective roles of central and local governments.[29]

The central government that had all along been overlord in policy implementation was now limited to policy formulation, setting national standards, and monitoring, supervising, and giving assistance to local governments (in addition to its other basic national duties, such as handling defence, foreign affairs, and currency). Local governments were given extensive powers and responsibilities. These included formulating and implementing development plans based on locally determined priorities; making, approving, and executing their own budgets, raising and utilizing resources according to their own priorities; appointing their own statutory committees, boards and commissions; making ordinances and by-laws, hiring, managing, and firing personnel, and managing their own payroll and separate personnel systems. The overall objective of the policy was to democratize society by promoting inclusive, representative, and gender-sensitive decision making; promoting good governance by placing emphasis on transparency and accountability in public sector management; improving service delivery by giving the responsibility for policy implementation to the beneficiaries themselves; and alleviating poverty through collaborative efforts between central and local governments, donors, non-governmental organizations, and the private sector. As a byproduct, of course, it was also intended to increase the regime's political capital by broadening avenues for political participation while providing other outlets through which political ambitions could be satisfied.

The adoption of devolution as the bedrock of the NRM's decentralization strategy can be attributed to three major domestic crises that the regime had to address when it seized power in 1986: an institutional crisis that had long paralysed the functioning of government; a legitimacy crisis that had created a large chasm between the governors and the governed; and the contradiction between the administrative system the NRM had set up in liberated areas during the 1981–5 civil war and the centralized structures it inherited on taking power.[30] Devolution was intended to redesign the function of central and local institutions, and also to increase the legitimacy of government by broadening political participation and improving service delivery and institutionalize the revolutionary changes that were implied by the system of resistance councils (RCs).

The local government system was financed through fiscal transfers from the centre and from locally generated revenue. The intergovernmental fiscal transfers comprised conditional grants for funding devolved services, unconditional grants for financing locally identified priorities, and equalization grants for enabling poorer districts to provide services at a national minimum standard of service delivery. Locally generated revenue comprised a graduated (or head) tax, market dues, property rates and other taxes that could legally be charged. A detailed formula was designed which spelled out how locally raised revenue was to be shared among the various local governments.[31]

A complex set of institutions was superimposed on the local government system to enforce transparency and accountability in its operations, and to ensure that local governments operated within the ambit of the law. These included the Ministry of Local Government, line ministries, the Public Accounts Committee of Parliament, central government resident district commissioners, the auditor general, the inspectorate of government, local government internal auditors, and local government public accounts committees.

From the start the decentralization policy generated tremendous enthusiasm because it gave people unprecedented power to make decisions over matters that affected them directly, and brought matters of governance to the centre stage of national debate. But it also experienced several implementation challenges. Apart from the gross mismatch between the new mandates of local governments and the resources that they received from the centre, there were severe capacity weaknesses at both local and central government levels – particularly in the areas of planning, budgeting, financial management, general management, monitoring and evaluation and tendering and procurement – which generated significant implementation difficulties. This was in addition to recurrent tension between local politicians and civil servants due to confusion of roles and inadequate understanding of the provisions of the Local Governments Act, 1997.

Everything considered, however, the decentralization implementation process had made remarkable progress by 2002, considering the multitude of challenges it was facing. Among other things it received categorical commitment to decentralization by all line ministries.[32] Although there was foot-dragging in the way some aspects of decentralization policy were being implemented,[33] this could be largely attributed to difficulties of adjusting to a new reality rather than to deliberate attempts to resist change. There was also significant improvement in local government skills and competencies.[34] All local governments were able to make their own annual budgets and three-year development plans and there were convincing reports of marked improvement in service provision in many districts, particularly in the road and water sectors.[35] The decentralization process also enjoyed strong government commitment, as indicated by its careful piloting through the District Development Project[36] and its roll out countrywide through the Local Government Development Program (LGDP) in 2000, and by the steady increase in the level of intergovernmental fiscal transfers from 117.8 billion shillings in FY 1995–6 to 329.6 billion shillings in 1999–2000.[37] Further indication of this commitment can be gauged from the steady increase in the budgetary amounts allocated to the Poverty Action Fund (PAF), the main instrument through which the priority program areas of primary health care, primary education, water and sanitation, agricultural extention, and rural roads were financed. Total expenditure under PAF as a percentage of the national budget was 26.5 per cent in 1999–2000, 32.2 per cent in 2000–1, 36.0 per cent in 2001–2 (provisional), and 36.0 per cent in 2002–3 (projected).[38]

Other Social Interventions

On the social front, government introduced the universal primary education program in 1996 to provide equal opportunities to school-age children, after it was discovered that there were more such children out of school than in the system. The policy provided free schooling up to four children per family in order to spread the benefits of education, particularly to rural households. Following its introduction in 1996 the program practically doubled school enrolment from 3.6 million in 1994–5 to nearly 7 million in 1999–2000,[39] and increasing to 7.2 million by 2001. Although, on the downside, the program experienced immense implementation difficulties due to lack of careful forward planning, which resulted in inadequate classroom space and insufficient teachers and books for the sudden upsurge in numbers, it provided great relief to tens of thousands of families in rural areas whose children would otherwise never have seen the inside of a classroom.[40]

Another government intervention that has made a significant social impact is its open and multi-sectoral approach to the HIV/AIDS pandemic. While other countries were denying the existence of HIV/AIDS in their societies for fear the impact such admission would have on their economies, Uganda stood virtually alone in publicizing the nature and extent of the problem. Government mounted a comprehensive program that had strong public awareness, and its preventive and community care elements led to dramatic reduction in infection rates from a high of 30 per cent in the worst-hit urban areas in 1992 to a weighted antenatal prevalence rate of 6.1 per cent by 2001,[41] making Uganda one of the very few countries (with Thailand) where this had happened worldwide.

It must also be mentioned that the government's liberal policies on the media had greatly enhanced the freedom of expression. By 2002, over eighty private radio and six television stations had been registered, where none existed before – although thirty-eight radio stations were already operational – and this led to a broader, deeper and more open discussion of key social issues. Parliament was also revamped and permitted to play its rightful role of balancing the judiciary and the executive – three ministers were censured in 2000. This led to a great deal of popular representation, as indicated by the sharp struggles during the 2001 parliamentary elections.

This picture provides the backdrop against which the bitter 2001 presidential election was contested. The key issues during this election were whether Uganda had made sufficient progress on the democratic and economic fronts under the NRM's leadership and whether Museveni was leading the country in the right direction, particularly with regard to establishing mechanisms for leadership change.

The Struggle for Control: The 2001 Presidential Elections

During the drafting of the 1995 constitution a big debate had raged over the appropriate type of political system to adopt, given that the country had already experimented with both multiparty and movement systems by that time. NRM leaders had argued for continuation of the movement system whereby people sought office on individual merit on the grounds that political parties had previously shown themselves to be sectarian and divisive. Political party supporters had argued, on the other hand, that political parties are an indispensable component of any modern democratic political system because they are formalized avenues of political aggregation and representation, and that past iniquities were due to bad leadership within specific political parties and should not, therefore, be attributed to all political parties as such. They viewed the movement system as the same old single party concept that had been tried in several African countries before and found to be dictatorial and retrogressive.

With the debate so polarized, it was agreed to settle the matter by referendum in June 2000, and this was inserted into the constitution itself. As it happened, by early 2000 the political parties were in a much weakened position as a result of having been prevented from organizing

their activities overtly, while the NRM was vibrant and had a fully functioning secretariat funded from the treasury. With the cards so stacked
against political parties, the DP and UPC leaderships jointly boycotted
the referendum, on the grounds that political association is a fundamental right that cannot be decided on by vote, and had called on their
supporters to do the same. Their call was largely ignored and the country opted through majority vote to continue with the movement system
for another five years up to 2005, following which the matter would
again be put to referendum.

An interesting element in all this was the attitude of donors. While
donors and western governments had pressured other African governments to provide space for political parties, they were lenient with the
NRM regime on this matter, arguing that it was up to the people of
Uganda to determine the political system of their choice. Clearly, a con-
tributory factor to the donors' softness towards the NRM regime was the
remarkable progress it had made on the socio-economic front, the success with which it had established relative peace at home, and the fact
that no credible alternative leadership had yet emerged (due, ironically,
to the regime's constant repression of political party activities).

While opposition to the movement system had been momentarily
contained by the referendum, cracks began to appear within the NRM
itself and dissent began to be expressed openly over the manner in
which the top leadership was handling public affairs. While opposition
to the NRM regime had seriously fragmented by 1996, allowing Museveni to win that year's presidential election by a landslide, the situation
was different in the 2001 presidential election. This time the opposition
coalesced around a retired colonel, Dr Kiiza-Besigye, who sought to
unseat Museveni following internal disagreements within the NRM
regime itself. Colonal Besigye was a member of the army high command
and a historical member of the NRM – in fact he had been the NRM's
first national political commissar. Thus his challenge to Museveni provided a unique opportunity to test the openness and penetrability of the
movement system in matters pertaining to political competition at the
national level.

Besigye's bid for the presidency generated a great deal of excitement
for several reasons. First, it provided the first opportunity for the individual merit principle to be tried in a contest for the country's top job.
Hitherto the principle had only been applied in local government elections, although political party and other affiliations sometimes made
their manifestations even there. The 1996 election had not been based

on this principle at all because Semogerere had been presented as a joint candidate for the DP and UPC.

Secondly, it presented Museveni with a real challenge because Besigye was a senior military officer and an insider who was well acquainted with the NRM's strengths and weaknesses. For this reason he appealed to a cross-section of groups that had been looking for some form of messianic salvation. His candidacy was attractive to the political parties which had hitherto been held on a tight leash, and to the urban youths and traders who were finding it difficult to cope with the effects of the economic reforms. Many blamed Museveni for the continuation of the war in the north, while others, including business people, were increasingly alarmed by the extent of corruption in the public sector and the regime's apparent inability or unwillingness to take decisive action against it. There were four other candidates, but the contest was really between Museveni and Besigye. Interestingly, ethnicity and regionalism, which had previously been major factors in Ugandan politics, were not significant this time because both Museveni and Besigye were from the west.

In the end Museveni proved too strong for the array of forces that had been lined up against him and he won 69.9 per cent of the popular vote as opposed to Besigye's 27 per cent. He was able to appeal to his traditional support among women, to the peasantry in the countryside where over 80 per cent of the populace resided, and to the nascent middle class in order to neutralize Besigye's strong showing among the urban youth. Besigye petitioned the electoral process and results, but the Supreme Court ruled in a majority decision on 21 April 2001 that, although the electoral commission had failed in several instances to comply with the provisions of the Presidential Elections Act, this did not substantially affect the results.

Besigye's unsuccessful bid for the presidency in 2001 drew attention to one important element. The political transition that the NRM regime was directing had not developed a sound mechanism for effecting leadership succession at the national level fifteen years on, although it had done so at the local government level. Coupled with Museveni's strong character and leadership, and the regime's restriction of political space for political parties, this meant that alternative leadership could only arise after undergoing a lengthy process of formation and maturation. Herein lay a paradox: while the movement government had made impressive gains on the political, economic, and social fronts, those gains could apparently only be safeguarded by prolonging the exit of their chief architect since serious internal leadership challenges were considered to be too threatening for the regime's survival.[42] While the movement had proved a useful tool for containing centrifugal forces during the transition's initial phase, its long-term utility as a stabilizing factor was being questioned, not least by prominent people inside the regime itself.

Internal Fracture and the Abandonment of the Broad Consensus Approach

Besigye's bid for power exposed significant disaffection within the NRM movement leadership, which became clear in early 2003. Most observers had assumed that Museveni would be serving his last term of office following his triumph in the 2001 presidential elections, because article 105(2) of the constitution limited the president to two five-year terms and Museveni himself had said on several occasion that he would honour the constitution. Unease began to develop outside and within the regime when it appeared that Museveni and his advisers were beginning to have a change of heart. Matters came to a head in March–April 2003, forcing Museveni to show his hand. During the annual meetings of the government's National Executive Council and National Conference, Museveni changed his position and agreed to the resumption of multiparty politics which he had resisted all along. However, several recommendations were made during those meetings which raised the country's political barometer. It was proposed that the return of political parties be subjected to a referendum (the same issue that had caused an outcry before); that the president should be given powers to dissolve Parliament; that powers to censure ministers should be removed from Parliament; and that the two-term limit on the presidency should be lifted to allow individuals to stand as many times as they wished. The net effect of these proposals was to concentrate powers in the hands of the president and allow Museveni an opportunity to stand for elections after his second term (his second term is to end in 2006 by which time he would have ruled the country for twenty years!).[43]

These astounding developments were met with resistance within cabinet itself. Two senior ministers and Museveni's confidants, Jaberi Bidandi Ssali (minister of local government) and Eriya Kategaya (minister of internal affairs) openly opposed these measures, especially the lifting of the two-term limit on the presidency, arguing that this would allow dictatorial tendencies to creep into the political process once again. In a surprise cabinet shuffle, Museveni dismissed them from the government along with three others who held similar views. Clearly, Museveni had succumbed to the temptation to stay in power even if this ran the risk of undermining his legacy as a visionary who had long stood above his contemporaries in the country.

Conclusion

Uganda's political transition under Museveni's NRM regime highlights the possibilities and limitations of guided liberalization in the context of severe intra-elite discord. It is an incontrovertible fact that the regime engineered a remarkable transformation in the country's fortunes that was manifested in resurgent and robust economic growth, expanded political space and participation, and relatively effective institution building. These important achievements translated into impressive socio-economic indicators, and this generated significant capital for the regime both locally and abroad. But the government continued to restrict political space for political parties, while also failing to develop a clear and viable mechanism for leadership succession and regime transformation. These were worrying developments, considering that the regime had already been in power for fifteen years, and the situation held the potential for undermining the government's otherwise impressive record of achievements.

What this points to is that we need to be measured in our assessment of transitions of this nature. Peacebuilding in countries that have experienced internal strife involves three major elements: reconstructing the socio-economic fabric, broadening political space and rebuilding political institutions. These are difficult to achieve simultaneously in the context of heightened expectations, severe resource constraints, and sharp intra-elite cleavages.

The manner in which peacebuilding is likely to differ from country to country is due to differences in historical and socio-economic circumstances, the character of the regime that is spearheading the transition; and the manner in which it responds to domestic and external challenges. The imperatives of regime survival are much sharper in a political system in which loss of political power can lead to total loss of privilege and influence. Liberalizing regimes may not wish to put themselves at risk because of the indeterminate actions of their rivals. Clearly, institutionalization of intra-elite relations is critical for creating requisite confidence-building measures during political transitions that are centrally initiated and controlled. If those in power could be reasonably confident that their fortunes would not be drastically affected after they left office, it would be possible for them to effect peaceful regime changes and to focus all energies on genuine development issues.

NOTES

1 John Kiyaga-Nsubuga, 'Managing Political Change: Uganda under Museveni,' in Taiser M. Ali and Robert O. Matthews, eds., *Civil Wars in Africa: Roots and Resolution* (Kingston and Montreal: McGill-Queen's University Press, 1999), 12–34.
2 John A. Wiseman, *The New Struggle for Democracy in Africa* (Aldershot, UK: Avebury, 1996), 11.
3 I refer here to the regime's incorporation of opposition groups into the National Resistance Council (as Parliament was called then), cabinet, and the National Resistance Army – the armed wing of Museveni's guerrilla movement.
4 The DP suffered an internal split over this. Several top DP leaders refused to go with Ssemogerere and remained within the NRM regime.
5 See Uganda Economic Study Team, *Uganda* (Ottawa: International Development in Centre, 1986); World Bank, *Uganda: Social Sector* (Washington DC, World Bank, 1993); and J. Ddumba-Ssentamu, 'Liberalization in Uganda: The Recent Experience and Challenges,' a paper presented at the seminar on *Transformations in Uganda*, Nile Resort Hotel, Jinja, Uganda, 2–4 May 2000.
6 The four political parties were the predominantly catholic Democratic Party (DP), Milton Obote's Uganda Peoples' Congress (UPC), the Uganda Patriotic Movement (UPM) Museveni had earlier set up to contest the 1980 elections, and Mayanja Nkanji's Conservative Part (CP), the successor to the traditionalist Kabaka Yekka (KY) of the Mengo Establishment. The five armed groups comprised the Uganda Freedom Movement (UFM) and the Federal Democratic Movement of Uganda (FEDEMU), both of which operated in the central region; the Uganda National Rescue Front (UNRF) and the Former Uganda National Army (FUNA), both of which operated in the north western region; and the Uganda National Liberation Army (UNLA) whose remnants had fled to southern Sudan after its defeat.
7 Museveni even publicly stated that he did not like many of his appointees to cabinet. As he put it, 'The groups which were threatening me would bring me a list of twenty bad people, and in order to preserve peace, I would have to choose two or three of the least bad of them.' See 'NRM Government Not of Museveni's Choice,' *Weekly Topic* (Kampala) 26 October 1988; 1.
8 In an attempt to balance all contending groups Museveni's first cabinet had 33 ministers, 14 ministers of state, and 5 deputy ministers. Of these 16 were from the East, 12 from the West, 18 from Buganda, and 3 from the North. The DP got the powerful ministries of Internal Affairs, Finance, Commerce,

Regional Affairs, Planning and Economic Development, and Agriculture. See James Tumusiime, ed., *Uganda 1986–1991: An Illustrated Review* (Kampala: Fountain Publishers, 1992), 10–11. In addition to acquiring strong representation in cabinet, the DP also tried to control the Resistance Council (RC) system (the precursor to the present local government system), which it had initially opposed together with chiefs, lawyers, state bureaucrats, the police, the court system and political party functionaries because it threatened their traditional dominance over the political process. See Expedit Ddungu and Ernest Wabwire, *Electoral Mechanisms and the Democratic Process: The 1989 RC–NRC Elections*, Working Paper No. 9 (Kampala: Centre for Basic Research, June 1991), 30.

 9 Amnesty International, *Amnesty International Report, AFR 59/01/97, Uganda: 'Breaking God's Command'* (A1). See also Ruddy Doomand and Koen Vlassenroot, 'Kony's Message: A New Koine? The Lord's Resistance Army in Northern Uganda,' *African Affairs* 98 (1999), 5–36; and World Food Programe, *Uganda: Facts and Figures* (Kampala, September 2003).

10 For a detailed assessment of these factors, see Tom Barton et al., *NUPSNA: Northern Uganda Psych-Social Needs Assessment* (Republic Uganda: Ministry of Gender, Labour and Social Development & UNICEF 1998).

11 *Africa Confidential* 27, no. 18, (3 September 1988), 3. Following this, two armed groups formed to fight the NRM regime: the Uganda Peoples Democratic Army (UPDA) and the Holy Spirit Movement (HSM) led by priestess Alice Lakwena. Both were eventually defeated by the NRA; however, Kony reorganized the HSM and transformed it into the LRA.

12 While addressing the Zambian ruling party (UNDP) leadership in August 1988 Museveni said: 'If you insist that market forces become the dominant feature in an economy, this method will not permit the state to guide the improvement and modernization of these structures but it will lead to increased liberalization. That is very dangerous if it means that anybody is permitted to import anything they like into the country – all those things bought in scarce dollars. I can compromise with the IMF on other things but not on this one.' See *What Is Africa's Problem?* (Kampala: NRM Publications, 1992), 75; see also his *The Path of Liberation* (Kampala: Government Printer, 1989), 45–6.

13 According to Dr Crispus Kiyonga, the finance minister in 1987: 'To carry out the NRM's programme we needed money. The inputs for the production sector were in short supply and had to be procured from abroad. At the end of the day we were already conditioned to look outside for resources for the rehabilitation and development programme while we strengthened our internal systems. The NRM government therefore decided in 1987 to co-

operate with the World Bank and the IMF in order to attract resources for programme implementation.' See 'The State of Economic as Inherited by the National Resistance Movement Government in 1986: The Economic Challenges and the Direction Taken,' in Republic of Uganda, *A Critical Look at the Economy under the National Resistance Movement (NRM) Government: Papers Presented at the Uganda Government Seminar on the Economy since 1986* (Kampala: Ministry of Finance/Chartered Institute of Bankers, Kampala Centre, June 1990), 13.

14 For opposition to IMF/World Bank structural adjustment policies at the time, see Mahmood Mamdani. 'Uganda: Contradictions in the IMF Programme and Perspective, in Republic of Uganda,' *A Critical Look at Uganda's Economy under the National Resistance Movement (NRM) Government,'* paper presented at the Uganda Government Seminar on the Economy since 1986 (Ministry of Finance/Chartered Institute of Bankers, June 1990), 178–218. This paper is also reproduced in *Development and Change* 21, no. 3 (1990), 427–69; and in Ghai Dharam, ed., *The IMF and the South: The Social Impact of Crisis and Adjustment* (London: 2ed Books, 1991), 183–214. Mamdani's argument is further developed in several newspaper articles, including 'The IMF in Uganda: Celebrating a False Promise, *Weekly Topic* (Kampala), 22 March 1989, 8–9. Continued in *Weekly Topic* (Kampala), 29 March 1989, 8–9; and 'Adjustment Is Not Solution' *New Vision* (Kampala, 17 May 1991, 8–9). Within the NRM regime itself strong opposition to IMF/World SAP was expressed by Chango Macho W'Obanda, a member of the NRM first cabinet. See the lecture he delivered at Makerere University, titled 'The World Bank and IMF as Weapons of Capitalist Domination,' which is reproduced in *Weekly Topic* (Kampala), 12 August 1987, 7, 12; and in *Weekly Topic* (Kampala), 19 August 1987, 7–8. For the NRM government's reasoning, see E. Tumusiime-Mutebire, 'A critique of Professor Mamdani's "Uganda: Contradictions in the IMF Programme and Perspective",' *Discussion Paper No. 4* (Kampala: Ministry of Planning and Economic Development, January 1990), a milder version of which is reproduced in *Development and Change* 22, no. 2 (1991), 339–51. See also Mamdani's article titled, 'Instabilities in the Uganda Economy,' *New Vision* (Kampala), 8 February 1990, 6–7, and its sequel, 'Stabilization and Adjustment Policy,' *New Vision* (Kampala), 9 February 1990, 6–7.

15 See United Nations Development Program, Uganda: *Development Cooperation Report* (New York, 1989), 63–68A.

16 See Uganda Authorities in Collaboration with the Staffs of the Fund and the Bank, Uganda: *Policy Framework Paper, 1989/90–1991/92* (Washington DC; 24 March 1989), 9–10; and World Bank, *Public Choices for Private Initiatives*, vol. 1 (Washington DC, 12 February 1991), 2–3.

17 Museveni had resisted earlier populist pressure to pursue redistributive economic policies, on the argument that wealth had to be created first before
could be distributed. In reply to Mamadani's argument that the NRM regime
should have made land reform and income distribution integral parts of its
reconstruction strategy Museveni had said: 'Unfortunately Mamdani has not
got his focus well. We have not said that we have reached the stage of distributing wealth to the disadvantaged. If Mamdani is able to distribute some surplus which he has got to the poor, he can do it. But we do not have it. The
struggle now is not to distribute. The struggle now is to produce. I am sure
Mamdani knows about those words. Distribute and produce. You cannot distribute what you do not have.' See *Weekly Topic* (Kampala), 5 April 1989, 5.
For Mamdani's argument, see M. Mamdani, 'Uganda in Transition: Two
Years of NRA/NRM,' *Third World Quarterly* 10, no. 3 (1988), 1165.

18 Ministry of Finance, Planning and Economic Development, *Poverty Eradication Action Plan 2001–2003*, vol. 1 (February 2001); Rosetti Nabbumba, 'Government's Efforts to Eradicate Poverty,' *The Reformer* (a quarterly newsletter
of the Second Economic and Financial Management Project), 1, no. 1
(2000), 6.

19 Ministry of Finance, Planning and Economic Development, *Uganda Poverty
Status Report, 1999* (Kampala, March 2000).

20 Ministry of Finance, Planning and Economic Development, *Uganda Poverty
Status Report, 1999*, 2–3.

21 See ibid. 'Indicators of Development in Uganda Supplement,' *New Vision*
(Kampala), March 2001, 21; and *East African*, 2–8 April 2001, 5.

22 A great deal of learning took place during the development of the PEAP.
Following realization that the plan was facing implementation difficulties
due to earlier failure to solicit the beneficiaries' views and priorities on poverty, an evaluation of the PEAP's objectives and modalities was conducted in
nine districts and thirty-six communities in 1998–9. The study found, among
other things, that of the five national priority programme areas that government had identified local people placed the highest premium on water and
sanitation. These findings were incorporated into the Plan for the Modernization of Agriculture (PMA). See Ministry of Finance, Planning and Economic Development, *Uganda: A Participatory Poverty Assessment report: Learning
from the Poor – A Summary of Key Findings and Policy Messages* (June 2000).

23 Minister of Finance, Planning and Economic Development, Hon. Gerald
Sendaula, *Budget Speech: Economic Growth and Structural Transformation* 14 June
2001.

24 The districts in which the evaluation was done were Bushenyi, Rukungiri,
Mpigi, Luwero, Apac, Lira, Mbale, Kumi Kiboga, and Kamuli. See Uganda

Debt Network, *Monitoring the Implementation of the Poverty Action Fund* (March 2000).

25 Minister of Finance, *Budget Speech*, 14.

26 Although tax revenues as a proportion of GDP had doubled from approximately 6 percent in 1987 to 11.5 percent in 2000, this was still well below the sub-Saharan Africa average of 20 percent. See ibid., 26.

27 Two crucial government programs – the Second Economic and Financial Management Project (EFMP II) and the Local Government Development Program (LGDP) – were developed primarily to strengthen public sector planning, budgeting and financial management, following the realization that government underperformance in these areas was jeopardizing all other reform initiatives.

28 There are six types of local governments in Uganda's system of decentralized governance: district councils (56), sub-county councils (903), city division councils (5), municipal councils (13), municipal division councils (34), and town councils (74). There are also county (163), parish (4,375) and village (over 40,000) councils. These are referred to as administrative units. Local governments are body corporate; administrative units are not. See Republic of Uganda, *Local governments Act, 1997* (Entebbe: Government Printer, March 1997), sections 4 and 46. For the functions that were devolved to local governments, see schedule 2 of the same act.

29 The groundwork for establishing decentralization had been started earlier in 1987 with the commissioning of inquiry into the local government system. See Republic of Uganda, *Report of the Commission of Inquiry into the Local Government System* (Kampala, June 1987).

30 I recognize the external factors to which the adoption of decentralization of power to local governments by developing countries is usually attributed, such as mounting donor frustration with the state-centric development approaches that were earlier preferred by most post-independence governments. See, for example, David Hirschmann, 'Development Management versus Third World Bureaucracies' *Development and Change* 30 (1999), 287–305; and Jesse C. Ribot, 'Decentralization, Participation and Accountability in Sahelian Forestry: Legal Instruments of Political-Administrative Control,' *Africa* 69, no. 1 (1999): 27–8. However, my argument here is that domestic factors were decisive in generating the visionary policy direction the regime adopted during the early stages of its life, because there was already an untenable situation on the ground that had to be tackled. During its guerrilla war against Obote's second regime, the NRM had set up popularly elected resistance councils (RCs), which were identical in structure to the current local councils (LCs), to administer the areas it had captured. The

RCs were inconsistent with the centralized structures the NRM inherited after seizing power.

31 See Republic of Uganda, *Local Governments Act, 1997*, section 86 and fifth schedule, part V.

32 This commitment is explicitly stated in the papers that were presented by the various ministries during the *National Forum on the Implementation of Decentralization*, which was held at the Uganda International Conference Centre, Kampala, 15–19 November 1999.

33 Local governments have constantly complained about the reluctance of the Ministry of Finance, Planning and Economic Development to involve them fully in the budgeting process and its foot-dragging in setting up the national planning authority; and about the tendency of the Ministry of Health to increase rather than decrease the conditionalities in its grants. See C.G. Kiwanuka-Musisi, President, Uganda Authorities Association, 'Emerging Issues in the Implementation of Decentralization,' a paper presented at the *National Forum on the Implementation of Decentralization*, International Conference Centre, Kampala, 15–19 November 1999.

34 In a recent comparative analysis of six sub-Saharan African countries (Zambia, Senegal, Ghana, Swaziland, Uganda, and Zimbabwe) along several areas of service provision, Uganda was considered the benchmark against which other sub-Saharan African countries are to be measured. See Jesper Steffensen and Svend Trollegaard, *Fiscal Decentralization and Sub-National Government Finance in Relation to Infrastructure and Service Provision: Synthesis Report on 6 Sub-Saharan African Country Studies* (May 2000).

35 See Uganda Debt Network, *Monitoring the Implementation of the Poverty Action Fund* (preliminary report, 4 March 2000).

36 In FY1999-2000 government embarked on a phased devolution of the development budget to the local government system through the Local Government Development Programme (LGDP), starting with all the districts that were not part of the pilot District Development Project (described below) and those that did not have substantial donor support. The DDP–Pilot, which became operational in July 1998, was a three-year project that aimed at building local government capacity to provide sustainable social services and to alleviate poverty through inclusive participatory planning, allocation, and investment. It was jointly funded by the United Nations Development Program and the United Nations Capital Development Fund through a US $12.4 million grant, and was operationalized in the districts of Arua, Kabale, Kotido, Jinja, and Mukono. It operated parallel to the Peri-Urban Infrastructure Project (PUIP) that had started earlier in 1997, which tested the same mechanisms in urban setting in the municipalities of Mbale, Fort Portal,

Masaka, and Lira. The LGDP is intended to assist government to operation-
alize decentralization of the development budget to local governments, bas-
ing on the lessons learned from the DDP over appropriate funding levels,
conditions of access, accountability, and public sector involvement. These
lessons put to rest earlier fears over local governments' ability to make effective development plans and to allocate and manage financial resources efficiently and effectively. For details, see Ministry of Local Government, *District
Development Project – Pilot – Evaluation Review Report: Findings and Recommendations* (8 January 1999); Ministry of Local Government, *Assessment of the DDP –
Pilot – Local Governments Minimum Conditions and Performance Measures: Synthesis Report – Year 2* (June 1999); and Ministry of Local Government/UNDP/
UNCDF, *District Development Project – Pilot – Evaluation Review: Final Report*
(10 November – 11 December, 1999).

37 See M.C. Muduuli, Director, Budget, Ministry of Finance, Planning and Economic Development, 'Implications of the 1999/2000 budget for local governments with special reference to conditional and unconditional grants,' a
paper presented at the *National Forum on the Implementation of Decentralization*,
International Conference Centre, Kampala, 15–19 November 1999.

38 Minister of Finance, Planning and Economic Development, Gerald M.
Ssendaula, *Budget Speech*, 13 June 2002, table 4.

39 UNICEF, *Equity and Vulnerability: A Situational Analysis of Women, Adolescents
and Children in Uganda 1994* (Government of Uganda / Uganda National
Council for Children, 1994); Nansozi, K. Muwanga, 'The Politics of Primary
Education in Uganda: Parent Participation and National Reform' (Ph D Dis-
sertation: University of Toronto, 2000); Ministry of Education and Sports,
'Policy Paper for the Decentralization Forum', a paper presented at the
National Forum on Implementation of Decentralization, International Conference
Centre, Kampala, 15–19 November 1999; and Uganda Bureau of Statistics,
*Uganda National Household Survey 1999/2000 – Report on the Socio-economic Sur-
vey* (Entebbe: January 2001), 18.

40 Hon. Gerald Ssendaula, *Budget Speech*, 21.

41 Ibid., 22.

42 Following the presidential election, Besigye was prevented from leaving the
country and was placed under twenty-four hour surveillance by the security
agencies. Fearing for his life, he fled the country on 15 August 2001. See *East
African* (Nairobi), 27 August–September, 2001; *New Vision* (Kampala),
26 August 2001; and *Monitor* (Kampala), August 2001.

43 For a vigorous response to these proposals, see *New Vision* (Kampala), 7 April
2003, 41.

Part Two

Peacebuilding after a Negotiated
Settlement

4
Reconstructing Peace in Liberia

William Reno

In July 1997 Charles Taylor, head of the National Patriotic Front of Liberia (NPFL) faction, won 75 per cent of the popular vote for the office of president. Taylor accomplished his goal of becoming the president of the Republic of Liberia, after seven years of fighting (1989–96), the devastation of the country's economy, and a national death toll of two hundred thousand, about 7 per cent of all Liberians. Taylor's election was the culmination of a seven-year-long, convoluted negotiating process, involving at least six indigenous rival militias, a multinational West African expeditionary force, fourteen peace treaties, and over forty ceasefires.[1] It appeared as though, with help from regional and international mediators, Liberia's conflict finally was resolved, and the process of rebuilding Liberia had begun.

In fact, there was not to be a restoration of what many participants in the negotiations conceived of as a pre-1989 normality. Three years later President Taylor was suspected of aiding insurgents in neighbouring Sierra Leone. Meanwhile, he maintained at least half a dozen security forces. These forces, containing many former wartime fighters, attacked Taylor's rivals and members of ethnic groups, particularly Krahn and Mandingo, who had opposed Taylor during the war. Twice in 1998 factional fighting broke out in the capital, Monrovia, followed by retributive attacks on groups opposed to Taylor. Liberian rebels attacked the country from Guinea twice in 1999, while more sustained fighting along Liberia's border with Guinea broke out in July 2000.

Liberia's recent history raises crucial questions for students of conflict resolution, questions which guide the analysis in this paper. First is the recognition that ending violence often requires that facilitators of peace negotiate with those who have guns. Yet this strategy may result in rewarding forces that are strongest at a particular time, even if they lack legitimacy in the broader society in which they operate. Peace defined as the absence of fighting can become a licence for a group to consolidate its hold on power and eliminate its rivals. The second question concerns the nature of insurgent groups that emerge out of collapsing states. Do factions in Liberia (or Sierra Leone, Congo, Congo-Brazzaville, or Haiti) have post-conflict interests in engaging in what most people in the country would recognize as tasks of governance? Or is the absence of fighting an opportunity for them to exploit more efficiently the country's resources for private gain? If it is the latter, insurgents-turned-rulers continue practices and perpetuate grievances that led to war in the first place. Regimes that result from settlements of wars growing out of state collapse can find violence to be a useful tool for personal aggrandizement and for controlling other people.[2] An incumbent ruler's access to external resources and support for his claim of sovereignty may reduce for a time the actual level of violence. Nonetheless, the underlying relation between predator and victim remains much as it was during the war, and may ultimately result in an increase in violence.

This chapter provides a critical analysis of the practice of conflict resolution in Liberia, particularly of the role of international actors involved in this process. Fewer people have died violent deaths in Liberia since 1997 than in the years before. Nonetheless, in the survey below I argue that the decreased intensity of fighting since 1997 leaves intact conditions that promoted the outbreak of war in 1989 and that motivated some of the most important war leaders during the war years. Furthermore, Taylor's regime posed significant obstructions to efforts to end conflict in neighbouring Sierra Leone and threatened the peace and security of people in its northern neighbour, Guinea. These questions call for examination of the role played by outsiders: how do they understand events in Liberia and what are the interests of those who are engaged in conflict resolution, and whose resources and involvement are manipulated to serve the aims of a particular local group?

Background: Conflict amidst State Collapse

Liberia's civil war began on 24 December 1989 with the NPFL invasion from Côte d'Ivoire, led by Charles Taylor. The real origins of the war are found in the collapse of Liberia's government at the hands of Sergeant. Samuel Doe, a junior officer who seized power in a coup in April 1980. Turning his back on his early populist appeals, Doe consolidated power

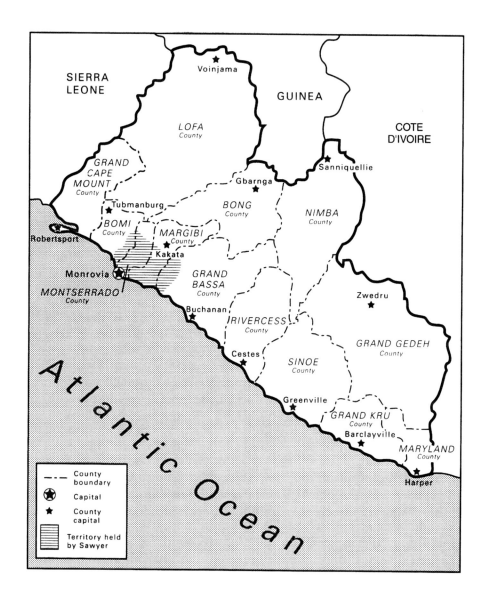

Liberia (1992)

through elevating ethnic kinsmen to high positions in an expanded security force.[3] Aid from the United States, totalling $450 million between 1980 and 1986, freed Doe to pursue his own ambitions without taking into account the interests of others in Liberia. To do so, he built special security units, staffed with supporters from his own Krahn ethnic group of eastern Liberia, and turned to foreign, most notably Israeli, trainers for arms and expertise.[4]

Thus Doe was not merely indifferent to the claims of others; he actively asserted personal control and attempted to impose his directives on others by force. This behaviour antagonized even his close associates, provoking at least five alleged coup attempts between 1982 and 1985. Foreshadowing warfare in the 1990s, these violent episodes resulted from competition among Doe's associates. For example, Doe had his vice president executed in 1982 after an alleged coup attempt. In 1983 Doe's former minister of rural development (a future Taylor ally) attempted to overthrow Doe. In 1984 another future Taylor associate was accused of plotting against Doe. In 1985 the deputy commander of the Executive Mansion Guard tried to assassinate Doe. Later that year, his former military commander invaded Liberia through the route that Taylor would use in 1989. This behaviour contrasted with the stability of the regime that Doe overthrew, which had managed political affairs in Liberia for 133 years prior to Doe's 1980 coup.[5] Doe's anxieties about his personal security, leaving him unable to delegate authority or tolerate effective bureaucracies in which rivals could build power bases, established a pattern of rule that Taylor would adopt after he became president in 1997.

Doe's reliance on support from among his ethnic kinsmen, who constituted no more than 6 per cent of Liberia's population, and his strategy of supporting multiple security forces of less-than-certain loyalties, prompted Doe to arm other groups that were loyal to him. This he did through arming security forces of local politicians and their rivals to serve as a check on the ambitions of each. In the process, regime associates built private armies to pursue their own ambitions, which hastened the collapse of Liberia's state institutions, and which in the 1990s made up the armed forces of competing warlords. The consequence of these tactics was to make Doe's rule progressively more violent. His suppression of dissidents after a 1985 coup attempt, farmed out to an army commander who commanded a private security force for a foreign investor, killed between five hundred and one thousand people in reprisal attacks.[6] In this sense, the collapse of government institutions and the emergence of hostilities constituting Liberia's internal war were integrally connected.

Doe's disruption of local communities even extended to religious affairs. He pursued personal animosities, self-interest, and intimidation in the guise of his supposed command of 'traditional religion.' He undermined the legitimacy and social standing of customary religious authorities as his followers adopted the customs and techniques of local religion – sacrifice, masks, and protective charms – for their own purposes.[7] Taylor and other faction leaders in the 1990s continued using these cultural tools to support their personal power, accounting for the appearance of seemingly bizarre young fighters in wigs, alleged cannibalism, and other references to the supernatural.[8] In this light, Taylor's addition of 'Dankpanah' to his name, a title used among Poro religious society leaders, can be seen either as an honorific title or as a signal of his authority over young fighters who also appropriate religious symbols to buttress their personal power.

'Governance' in this manner left Doe to engage in numerous deals in which he appropriated state assets for himself and his business partners in a manner that Taylor would pursue later. His partners included an Italian organized crime figure under investigation in the United States, an individual representing himself as 'Compte de Vendôme and Possessor of the Sublime Light,' assorted Nigerian millionaires, Indian maharajahs, and other dubious characters.[9] One business deal involved Doe's granting of a timber concession to a South Korean firm in return for an honorary doctorate. The outcome was the rapid contraction of Liberia's economy as legitimate foreign businesses left and Liberian entrepreneurs faced growing economic competition from their president, armed with the commercial advantages of his command of security forces and prerogatives of office. In the first three years of Doe's rule alone (with massive US aid), formal GNP fell from $461 million to $321 million.[10]

Doe's ability to repress societal groups did not translate into security for his regime as threats continued to emerge from among his associates. Charles Taylor, once a member of Doe's government, spent much of 1986–9 travelling around West Africa to secure support for his quest to overthrow Doe.[11] In the context of state collapse, Taylor's claims against Doe appeared more as a bid to take over the opportunities for private enrichment that Doe enjoyed than as a reformist alternative to Doe. NPFL insurgents were very much a product of state collapse, and in this regard bore a striking resemblance to Doe's regime in their conduct and aims, and to insurgents in neighbouring Sierra Leone. Their complaints focused on Doe's tendency to appropriate the country's resources, instead of sharing proceeds with others.[12] Their complaints concerned

Doe's fitness as a controller of patronage and his usefulness to them, not as a provider of public goods or builder of state institutions. Meanwhile, NPFL fighters' tendencies to loot and abuse other people generated pleas and petitions even among the NPFL's local collaborators that fighters receive regular salaries and accept military discipline as measures to halt these predations upon their communities.[13] These appeals that Taylor and his fighters behave in a more state-like fashion, in the Weberian sense of monopolizing the exercise of coercion and in building bureaucratic hierarchies, were incompatible with Taylor's overall means of exercising power, just as had been the case under Doe.

Taylor's political strategy was reflected in the character of the NPFL. A human rights organization reported a popular Liberian perception that 'NPFL "fighters" are a law unto themselves, and many of these fighters are young, undisciplined and unpaid.' Like Doe, Taylor seemed to take little interest in administering areas that his group controlled, nor did he attempt to institutionalize an administrative hierarchy in his organization, relying instead on loyalty to himself to motivate followers. 'There is no central committee or politburo, no political manifesto or party programme,' reported another observer.[14] Ideology and administration were subordinate to a politics driven by the need to acquire resources to ensure Taylor's attractiveness as a patron amidst violence and uncertainty that he helped create. Doe's, then Taylor's destruction of Liberia's economy reinforced rather than undermined this patrimonial political order as alternative sources of economic opportunities for aggrieved Liberians dwindled.

The relation of Taylor's NPFL to people under its control appeared to be highly exploitative, at least for those who did not play a direct role in the NPFL. A US State Department document reported that the NPFL operated involuntary labour camps in Grand Gedeh County and subjected inmates to beatings for refusing to work or attempting to escape. Numerous reports emerged of fighters who used disorder as a means to acquire wealth. A traveller observed NPFL fighters who were like 'human merchants sprung up among the rebels, smuggling people out of the territory at exorbitant fees, usually as high as $300.'[15] The Liberian press contained numerous and persistent reports of systematic looting on the part of NPFL fighters, a practice that survived the 1997 peace agreement.[16]

Taylor apparently profited handsomely from his conquest of Liberian territory. He concluded a deal with Firestone Tire and Rubber, a foreign firm with a long history in Liberia. Taylor also invited logging firms to do business with his organization. These firms soon found that Taylor relied upon them to provide transportation, supplies, and irregular cash payments to his associates. A US official estimated that Taylor personally controlled about $75 million in trade revenues in the period 1990 to 1994.[17]

The primary feature that distinguished Taylor's method of rule and activities from those of Doe was that they occurred in competition with similar groups. Other former Doe officials seized opportunities to advance their own private interests, and to gain a role in running Liberia in the event that peace negotiations were successful. These included the Liberian Peace Council (LPC) under the direction of George Boley, Doe's presidential secretary, and United Movement for Democracy (ULIMO) with Alhaji Kromah, Doe's minister of information as its head, and later called ULIMO-K. ULIMO spawned another faction, ULIMO-J, so named for Roosevelt Johnson, who had been a soldier in the Armed Forces of Liberia since 1971. He had taken part in the 1985 coup attempt, fleeing Liberia after the death of the coup leader, Thomas Quiwonkpa. Hezekiah Bowen led remnants of the Armed Forces of Liberia.

Taken together with the NPFL, United Nations officials initially estimated in 1993 armed forces that included 60,000 fighters. The UN secretary general's office revised this figure to 33,000 in 1997, explaining that original figures included additional faction members, such as young women and girls whom fighters took as 'wives' during war and young children recruited to carry supplies. Of the 33,000, NPFL was the largest faction, accounting for 12,500 fighters. Doe's old Armed Forces of Liberia counted 7,000 fighters, ULIMO-K had 6,800, ULIMO-J, 3,800, and LPC fielded another 2,500. These revised figures show that only about 1.5 per cent of Liberia's population participated as combatants in this war. Of these combatants, the US Department of State estimated that 50 per cent were under the age of nineteen, and 10 per cent were younger than 15.[18]

What grievances prompted Liberians to fight? Some recalled Doe's massacres in Nimba County. Taylor observed: 'We didn't even have to act. People came to us and said: "Give me a gun. How can I kill the man who killed my mother?"'[19] Some faction heads such as George Boley argued that they acted to protect ethnic communities that Taylor's forces had targeted for retribution for their imputed support of Doe.[20] Regardless of their messages, survival as faction heads required that leaders of these groups compete with Taylor to claim a share of Liberia's war economy of predation. To do otherwise would expose the group to defeat in the short term. Building administrations in liberated zones or mobilizing followers would take time to accomplish. Besides, many faction heads were themselves recycled elites from the Doe years, and thus faced little prospect of acceptance among followers, except as patrons capable of allowing them access to the spoils of war.

Others, particularly rank-and-file fighters, were themselves products of the war they fought. One traveller explained this as 'what I would call reverse adulthood syndrome (RAS). RAS comes off as a condition in which the fear of death and humiliation puts the genuine adults and achievers into their shells. The vacuum is then filled in by the young ones who become dare devils, not caring about death or any related end. For them, chance (and not age, valuable time and energy) creates material wealth.'[21] Like their leaders, these individuals discovered that disorder and violence offered them superior prospects for advancing their lot in life, and gave them access to resources from which they believed they had been unjustly excluded.

Many combatants across the factions and hierarchies of age and status (estimated to peak at 45,000 in 1994–6 out of a Liberian population of 2.2 million) shared a common feature of battling to appropriate the remains of Doe's patronage network, the primary source of opportunity amidst the collapse of Liberia as a state. Others took the opportunity to avenge the predations that had been committed in this endeavour. Meanwhile, as a result of the war Liberia's people were either internally displaced (1.2 million), made refugees (750,000) or were killed (200,000) – these conditions accounting for over 75 per cent of Liberia's population.[22] A World Health Organization survey of 334 Monrovia secondary school students in 1994 revealed that 61 per cent had seen someone killed, tortured, or raped. This litany of societal disruption, combined with what many Liberians saw as the anti-social, personal motivations of many of the fighters, was to emerge as a major challenge to negotiating a peaceful settlement of Liberia's war. There would also be much popular lament that the negotiating process would not include the bulk of the population of Liberia, but rather only those who fought to control the Executive Mansion, a process that many saw as rewarding socially destructive behaviour.

The Negotiating Process

Peace negotiations began in mid-1990 as a regional effort. NPFL agents rejected outside mediation and early suggestions that they should participate in a coalition government. They had little motivation to negotiate, calculating that they would soon seize Monrovia and end the war with victory over remnants of Doe's regime. Nonetheless, West African heads of state met in Banjul, Gambia, in August 1990 (without NPFL representation) to discuss solutions to Liberia's conflict. The West African group appointed Dr Amos Sawyer, a professor from the University of Liberia and respected opponent to Doe, as the new head of state of Liberia. Some of West Africa's other heads of state, some of whom came to power through coups, likely feared that a successful NPFL seizure of power in Liberia would embolden associates and army officers in their own regimes to venture similar attacks. It is also likely that Nigerian officials feared that Taylor's victory over his rivals would weaken their country's influence in the region. Out of this group came the decision to sponsor a peace enforcement force, ECOMOG (ECOWAS Monitoring Group), which landed in Monrovia on 23 August 1990 to impose a settlement.

From then to 1995, the peace process encountered numerous obstacles. In September 1992, for example, NPFL received large shipments of weapons from foreign states that supported Taylor's NPFL, including Côte d'Ivoire and Burkina Faso. Well equipped, Taylor launched 'Operation Octopus' in October, and nearly succeeded in seizing Monrovia. ECOMOG responded to the attack by establishing closer military coordination with anti-Taylor factions. In the eyes of NPFL fighters, ECOMOG soldiers had become yet another faction in Liberia's civil war, and reinforced Taylor's statements that any externally monitored peace agreement would be biased against the NPFL.

International support for ECOMOG expanded in 1993. After concluding an agreement from a position of military vulnerability, Taylor signed the Cotonou Accord in July 1993. Three hundred observers of the UN Observer Mission in Liberia (UNOMIL) and about four thousand East African troops, in addition to ECOMOG, were to oversee the encampment and disarmament of combatants. This agreement collapsed as new factions appeared, probably to strengthen the position of their parent organizations in peace negotiations. This volatile situation was compounded by the appearance of Charles Julu, a former AFL commander (and leader of Doe's repression in Nimba County in 1985) as head of a group called New Horizons. Julu snuck into the Executive Mansion and proclaimed himself president, an attempt that was foiled by ECOMOG. Renewed fighting broke out, generating another two hundred thousand displaced persons. NPFL fighters held forty-three UN observers hostage to secure transport and communications. This sort of realignment of increasing numbers of factions would plague negotiations for the next two years.

Failed talks in Accra (1994–5) finally led to a more lasting agreement, negotiated in Abuja in 1995. Unable to take Monrovia, Taylor settled for a position in a 'collective presidency' that contained representatives of all the major factions until an election could be held. After the election, the government would revert to the strong executive organization under the country's prewar constitution. The significant feature that distinguished this agreement from prior agreements was its absence of mechanisms to force NPFL's disarmament and Nigerian president Abacha's apparent willingness to allow Taylor to continue to control significant portions of Liberia's territory (a model that would characterize the 1999 Lomé Agreement in neighbouring Sierra Leone). From a pragmatic perspective, this decision recognized that Taylor's fighters had guns and that ECOMOG could not beat them on the battlefield. Both accepted key insurgent leaders as interlocutors at the price of allowing them to continue to exercise de facto control over economically valuable portions of their countries' territory. The agreements collapsed when outsiders challenged this informal understanding in order to implement formal arrangements that interfered with insurgents' access to resources.

The Abuja agreement collapsed amidst fighting as soon as external monitoring forces made credible attempts to challenge insurgents' control over territory and resources (as did Sierra Leone's Lomé agreement when UN peacekeepers resolved in April 2000 to enter diamond mining areas held by the Revolutionary United Front (RUF). The ECOMOG commander, Major-General J.M. Inienger, and some members of the collective presidency attempted to force Roosevelt Johnson (head of ULIMO-J, a weaker faction) to disarm his fighters. Behind this lay allegations that a local ECOMOG commander had rejected informal arrangements between Liberian fighters and Nigerian soldiers that allowed insurgents to mine diamonds and export them.[23] The arrest of Johnson precipitated street fighting, looting, and the complete breakdown of law and order in Monrovia over Easter of 1996. Taylor used this chaos to infiltrate about seven thousand NPFL fighters into Monrovia. Amidst insecurity, assassination attempts were made against key NPFL dissidents and Michael Francis, the Catholic archbishop who had forcefully denounced all factions. The media were attacked, except NPFL-controlled Kiss FM.

Finding himself in an even better position to join a coalition government and to prepare for elections on his own terms, Taylor cooperated with international attempts to restore the Abuja agreement. Now, threats from West African states and from UN Security Council members that they would abandon their efforts to back negotiations if factional fighting began again would not have served Taylor's bid to take power in Liberia. Strengthened within Monrovia, Taylor now benefited from the order that ECOMOG imposed, which prevented the NPFL's opponents from rearming and allowed Taylor to liquidate them in preparation for the electoral campaign called for under the terms of the peace agreement.[24] To the extent that his forces appeared to keep order, he faced little pressure from external guarantors of the agreement who recognized that Taylor's cooperation was essential to limit disorder without active external military intervention. This shared interest is what enabled Taylor to launch an effort to weaken his rivals under the guise of enforcing the disarmament provisions of the agreement.

Groups within Liberian society criticized the practice of negotiators recognizing warlords who formed factions as legitimate participants in the peace process. Automatic recognition of armed claimants to state power created incentives for others to set up their own groups to assert claims to international recognition and a portion of Liberia's resources. This in turn fuelled the propensity for citizens to arm themselves for self-defence, which became manifest in the proliferation of small home guard units during the latter years of the war. The tendency of officials in other states to support particular factions, such as Côte d'Ivoire's and Burkina Faso's support of the NPFL and Sierra Leone's support of ECOMOG and ULIMO, also weakened incentives for faction leaders to negotiate. But once Taylor emerged in a commanding position in Monrovia, he could play peacekeeper, intimidating and disarming other groups. This occurred in spite of the Abuja agreement's provisions for a power-sharing arrangement prior to the 1997 election. The intimidation of weaker factions and civilian critics went unpunished, probably because external guarantors of the agreement feared that criticism of Taylor would undermine his support for the agreement, given that they had no credible means of coercing him to cooperate.

Taylor proved able to intimidate Liberia's voting population too. When elections were finally held in 1997, Taylor polled a 75 per cent landslide vote. A destitute, starve,d and traumatized population recognized that in these conditions it was preferable to vote for the strongman who could defeat the other factions, and perhaps leave Liberians to their own devices to survive.[25] Taylor thus proved able to manipulate the wishes among outsiders and most Liberians for the return of some stability to Liberia – at least in the sense of an absence of fighting, if not of a government with a particular vision or a specific program of postwar economic reconstruction.

The Abuja agreement highlights a dilemma that faces all externally backed negotiated settlements in the context of state collapse. Insurgents in places such as Sierra Leone, Congo, and further afield, in Chechnya and Colombia, show little evidence of building grassroots bases of support. Instead, they rely upon the selective exploitation of economic opportunities that disorder and violence permit. Leaders of these groups accordingly enjoy little real legitimacy among most of the people they control. The example of outside negotiators recognizing warlords on the basis of their formation of factions during wartime appears to set a bad precedent that could undermine regional stability if their behaviour is not modified in peacetime.

This presents an acute dilemma for conflict resolution efforts. To ignore armed groups means rejecting negotiations with those who control violence in a society and have a capability to disrupt alternative strategies. Therefore, the only reasonable alternative to negotiations would be the military defeat of faction heads. This dilemma really is very serious if, as I argue here, negotiated settlements merely create a pause in warfare, and may in fact lay foundations for expanded conflict as 'winners' in negotiated settlements pursue ambitions farther afield in a violent manner and continue to exploit people under their control. Yet a military resolution would require resources and capabilities that states in the region do not possess, and levels of commitment that powerful states will not produce. Politically, the easiest option for outsiders is to support a peace process that ends shooting for the time being, and allows officials to pronounce the affected region stable, so as to reduce expense and political risk to themselves.

Fake Peacebuilding after the 1997 Election

The way that Taylor exercised authority underwent little change, despite his shift from faction leader to president of the Republic of Liberia. As during the war, he used the bulk of resources under his control to promote his own security and welfare and that of a small clique of associates. The uses of these resources appeared to be geared toward making Taylor more appealing as a patron and eliminating other factions that challenged Taylor's claims to become ruler of Liberia during the 1989–96 war. In this context, Taylor's organization appeared to behave as a government in the tradition of Max Weber only in the most minimal sense of claiming a monopoly over coercion, and in punishing everyone whom it discovers to have used force without its express permission.[26] One might argue with even this minimalist equation of Taylor's organization with a government. Even though Taylor's organization was the dominant security agency in Liberia's territory, it provided security for people only to the degree that their activities contributed to the personal enrichment of Taylor and his associates. Taylor behaved more like a private entrepreneur than a ruler of a state, though his claim of sovereignty and his international recognition as a legitimate interlocutor in the process of conflict resolution provided him with the façade of a state behind which to conduct his operations. In this regard, Taylor's use of state assets and prerogatives for private purposes continued to mirror that of the ruler he sought to overthrow in 1989.

Taylor maintained at least a half dozen security agencies. These included the Anti-Terrorist Unit under the direction of his son Chucky, the Special Security Service, the Joint Security Forces, the National Bureau of Investigation, Counter Force, and the Security Operations Division, along with the previously existing Armed Forces of Liberia. Some of these forces reportedly received training from foreign private, especially Israeli, military service companies.[27] Taylor also managed to use the Abuja agreement's proposals for restructuring the Armed Forces of Liberia and the Liberian National Police as an excuse to pack them with NPFL fighters once he won the July 1997 election. The primary objectives of these organizations appeared to be to protect Taylor personally, and to limit unauthorized entry of insurgents into Liberia, particularly from Guinea's Guéckedou prefecture, the origin of the April 1999 raid on Voinjama, the headquarters of Lofa County, and the larger August 1999 attack. Security duties also included pursuit and elimination of Taylor's rivals, such as the 18 September 1998 attack on Camp Johnson Road, the headquarters of ULIMO-J faction head Roosevelt Johnson. Both of these activities underscored the continuing instability not only of Liberia, but also of the region, so long as losers in the electoral process concluded that Taylor's military power would leave them vulnerable to attack.

The official budget of Liberia showed little concern for operations other than security. In 1999 Taylor announced a national budget totalling only $64 million, up from $55 million the year before, but still just 15 per cent of reported expenditures in 1988, the last year before the start of the war.[28] Internally, Liberia's capital receives only intermittent supplies of electricity, a commodity rarely available outside the city. Popular attention in late 1999 focused on the return of the first traffic signal to service in Monrovia. The project was short-lived, and the signal malfunctioned after several weeks. Foreign donors and Liberian NGOs have borne most of the costs of providing minimal levels of social services since 1997. The government opened 230 health clinics (out of a prewar total of 330 clinics) in 1997–9. However, the Liberian government's total capital expenditure in 1999 amounted to $5.6 million, of which $4.9 million reflected purchases of a fleet of Isuzu Troopers, sedans, and equipment from West Oil for use by government officials. Meanwhile, Taylor directed that $40 million be spent on armed forces 'restructuring.'[29] The national budget in 2000 (which lacked allotments to run local governments) also came to include debts of $26 million incurred by Taylor while acting as head of the NPFL.[30] Revenues for this budget came primarily from taxes on foreign logging operations, fees collected from ships flying the Liberian flag of convenience, and excise taxes (though as noted below, much greater resources appear to have been available for Taylor's personal use).

These resources sustained forces that behaved little differently from the fighters during the civil war, and employed many of the same fighters from that era. They were accused of harassing human rights workers (including a proposed director of a national human rights commission who was personally beaten by Taylor's police director), extra-judicial killings, and maintaining informal detention centres.[31] The crucial difference between the 1990s and more recent years lies in the dominance of these forces. Apart from occasional challenges, they did not struggle with contending groups to control territory, nor have to wage war to gain access to resources. This change permitted others in society to live with greater (if still arbitrary) security than was possible when factions fought against each other – order, if not peace.

This development also enabled Taylor and his associates to continue the appropriation of Liberia's resources for themselves and foreign partners. Taylor's status as a globally recognized ruler of a sovereign state enabled him to make agreements with businesses that others would accept as legitimate. For example, Taylor came to an agreement with the American entrepreneur and television evangelist Pat Robertson for a twenty-year concession to mine gold. Robertson founded the African Development Corporation in 1992 to work a diamond mine in Zaire, an arrangement that blended the air services of Robertson's 'humanitarian' Operation Blessing with commercial practices that attracted attention from authorities in the United States.[32]

Taylor's control of potentially valuable territory attracted other operators who, unlike Robertson, were directly involved in helping to give material support to RUF insurgents in neighbouring Sierra Leone as part of their business operations in Liberia. For example, a former Israeli military officer (wanted by Colombian authorities for aiding insurgents there) reportedly trained and helped equip Sierra Leone fighters via Liberian networks associated with Taylor. The appearance in Monrovia in 1999 of a former South African attaché charged with helping Angolan insurgent leader Jonas Savimbi market diamonds provided more hints that Taylor's organization derived commercial benefit from clandestine diamond exports from Sierra Leone.[33] In turn, credible observers cited persistent reports from Sierra Leone that some RUF fighters were recruited in Liberia and received training there.[34]

Taylor's support for the RUF was an extension of his wartime political and economic strategies, to which he was able to add various prerogatives of sovereignty, such as his capacity to shield these transactions from external interference (if not criticism). In 1991, for example, RUF head Foday Sankoh collected military supplies from the NPFL-held port of Buchanan, in advance of his NPFL-backed incursion into Sierra Leone on 23 March, marking the start of Sierra Leone's civil war.[35] As late as 2003, Taylor continued to host in Monrovia RUF commander Sam 'Masquita' Bockarie, a former professional nightclub dancer and hair stylist. Many Sierra Leoneans suspect that diamond transactions that financed the RUF insurgents occurred through this and other networks leading to Taylor's regime. This assertion is backed up with Liberian diamond export data, showing an estimated production of 150,000 carats in 1997, while Antwerp sources reported the import of 5,803,000 carats from Liberia during the same year, presumably many Sierra Leonean stones from rebel-held territory among them. Foreign journalists report findings in an analysis endorsed by the British government after the collapse of Sierra Leone's peace agreement in 2000.[37] A UN report in late 2000 provided extensive evidence linking Taylor to business operations that marketed diamonds from conflict zones in Sierra Leone and other countries via Liberia.[38]

This connection between personal profit and warfare complicated the role that Taylor played in negotiating an end to Sierra Leone's war. He was seen as personally benefiting from warfare. At the very least, one can conjecture that Taylor prefered that his associates from Liberia's civil war period busy themselves with personal profit from Sierra Leone's war, rather than remain idle in Monrovia to threaten Taylor's hold on power. Circumstantial evidence further hints at Taylor's involvement: his statements in 1999 and 2000 in support of the RUF grew in proportion to the military pressure on these insurgents to leave Sierra Leone's diamond-producing areas.

Taylor was also able to use sovereign prerogatives to permit access to

Liberia's territory to recruit more organized firms to exploit the country's resources. A Malaysian firm, Oriental Timber Company, received a concession to remove timber from eastern Liberia. Even among more established firms, Liberia's uncertain political conditions deterred investment by those that are more transparent in their operations. Côte d'Ivoire's forestry development agency had reportedly earlier rejected Oriental Timber Company's proposals to log timber in that country due to concerns about its operating procedures, but in Liberia, the firm enjoyed the protection of a foreign business partner of Taylor's, a man who was also Doe's business partner. By early 2000, the firm was reportedly exporting timber at a rate matching the prewar peak of one million cubic metres. In the process, the firm destroyed farms and residences in its concession area without compensation, and barred Forestry Development Agency staff from entering its property. In October 1999 Taylor reportedly warned that 'the forest is for the government, and no person or section can claim personal ownership,'[39] a statement that in this context can be interpreted to mean that Taylor considered the forest to be his personal property to dispose of as he saw fit.

Taylor acquired additional resources from his repeated official visits to Taiwan, where his promises to back Taiwanese admission to the United Nations generated modest donations, including Taiwanese payment of the $3.7 million cost of printing new currency. Despite its other expenditures, it appears that Taylor's government did not have enough money to print money. This is suggestive of the priorities of the regime, especially the tendency to privatize state assets and resources for use in personalist politics, rather than in social reconstruction and the provision of public goods.

In practical terms, this relationship with outsiders boosted the income of politically favoured groups in Liberia. It also bode ill for regional stability, since it gave Sierra Leone's insurgents incentives to fight to control mineral resources in Sierra Leone that they could sell to Liberian partners and to abjure commitment to any broad power-sharing agreement to end Sierra Leone's war. In fact, combat in Sierra Leone intensified in May 2000 precisely when a UN peacekeeping force there signalled that they would attempt to force RUF fighters to allow UN peacekeepers and Sierra Leone government administrators to enter the country's diamond mining areas as part of a coalition government envisioned in the peace agreement. This development also points to a flaw in peace agreements that provide incentives for insurgents to hold on to areas with resources. As in Liberia, disarmament of combatants in 1999–2000 in Sierra Leone prescribed paying fighters cash for guns. Mining profits could be used to buy old and defective guns, which were cashed in for further profit. A preferable strategy might have been to give land for guns, which would give ex-combatants a stake in local production and a preference for rulers who provide services to help them go about their business, rather than rulers who provide opportunities for looting and personal profit.

Further evidence suggests that Taylor had a considerable stake in continuing warfare in Sierra Leone. Outside observers have noted that Liberian exports of diamonds (recorded in Belgium where many were shipped) far outstripped Liberian capacity to produce this resource, with some estimates of revenues as high as a half billion dollars. By 1996, for example, Liberia shipped more than 12 million carats of diamonds to Belgium, while reportedly capable of producing no more than 150,000 domestically. Industry experts disagree over the portion and value of diamonds that came from Sierra Leone in these figures. One industry analyst, for example, cites a figure of about $70 million in 'conflict diamonds' from Sierra Leone during the late 1990s. An industry journal, however, cited an overall Liberian diamond export figure of $298 million in 1999, despite Liberia's scant diamond resources.[40]

Even the lower figure suggested for Sierra Leone indicates that Taylor's business partners inside Liberia and their associates in Sierra Leone derived considerable income from the continuation of war in Sierra Leone and the failure of Sierra Leone's government and UN peacekeepers to exercise effective oversight over these transactions. This is reflected in the drop of diamond imports from Sierra Leone from 770,000 carats worth $66 million in 1998 to just 183,000 carats worth $31 million in 1999. Investigations suggest that Taylor continued to host entrepreneurs who did business with RUF after the signing of Sierra Leone's 1999 Lomé peace agreement. The then British foreign minister, Robin Cook, asserted that he had 'continuing evidence establishing close links between the rebels in Sierra Leone and supporters in Liberia, and that Liberians are profiting from illegal diamond smuggling.' More concrete accusations include claims that Taylor permited training of RUF fighters at Gbatala in western Liberia, and that he sent direct aid to Sierra Leone's insurgents, a charge that Taylor's government vigorously denied. In late 2000 the UN reiterated similar claims, and observed that 'Liberia has been actively supporting the RUF at all levels, in providing training, weapons and related *materiel*, logistical support, a staging ground for attacks and a safe haven for retreat and recuperation, and for public relations activities.'[41]

Overall, the outcome of the Abuja peace process in Liberia brought a measure of order to the daily lives of Liberians and created conditions

that enabled foreigners to distribute humanitarian aid. This latter benefit, however, did not apply to all of Liberia. The US Department of State
reported that in 1999 'Government security personnel were involved in
the looting of 1,450 tons of food intended for Sierra Leone refugees' in
northwestern Liberia. Some outsiders took even this reduction of violence within national borders as evidence of peace building. But Taylor's
management of this 'peace' process translated into direct support for
the war in neighbouring Sierra Leone in return for wealth. Violent accumulation of personal wealth among his associates was externalized to the
territory of a neighbouring state and is predicated on the insurgents'
hold on economically valuable territory there. This in turn posed the risk
of further regionalizing Sierra Leone's war. If RUF fighters were forcibly
removed from diamond mining areas, as Sierra Leone's government and
its British military and diplomatic backers had resolved to do, Taylor
faced the loss of personal and political resources that underpinned his
rule in Liberia and his control over NPFL fighters. Under these conditions, it appeared that order was possible in Liberia only if there was war
in Sierra Leone and vice-versa. This reflects the integral connection
between control of natural resources and the nature of Sierra Leone's
RUF and its political and economic partner, Taylor's NPP government.
It also signaled grave consequences for Liberia of any British-backed military offensives against RUF rebels after the British intervention in Sierra
Leone in mid-2000.

By mid-2000, a group calling itself Liberians United for Reconciliation
and Democracy (LURD), composed of Taylor opponents, claimed credit
for fighting that occurred along Liberia's border with Guinea. Nonetheless, it was not clear that Taylor simply faced armed opponents. First, eyewitness reports indicated that much of the violence in Liberia was the
result of Anti-Terrorist Unit predations on local communities. The British and American governments accused Taylor of using the conflict to
resupply RUF rebels under cover of local chaos. More important war is
an apparent attempt to destabilize Guinea. As in Liberia after 1997,
peacekeepers in Sierra Leone and their diplomatic backers would not
fight to force armed groups to comply with agreements or directives.
Nor could British military advisors restructure the Sierra Leone army in
quick order. Thus Taylor's likely strategy was to apply military pressure
on UN peacekeepers in Sierra Leone to force them to negotiate a face-
saving withdrawal that would favour the RUF and, by extension, Taylor's
influence in Sierra Leone and personal access to the country's mineral
resources. The UN peacekeeping force in Sierra Leone (numbering

twelve thousand as of October 2000) faced the withdrawal of its core of Indian and Jordanian troops, though Pakistani and Bangladeshi units replaced them in early 2001.

Signs of the success of this strategy appeared in the 17 October 2000 report of a UN Security Council team that surveyed the security situation in Sierra Leone and subsequent Sierra Leone officials' statements. The team voiced support for negotiating a peace agreement with RUF leaders, despite continuing UN support for a war crimes tribunal that would prosecute RUF leaders.[42] This would be accomplished through prosecuting 'bad' rebels most visibly responsible for atrocities in the breakdown of the 1999 Lomé agreement, while newer leaders such as Issa Sesay would become interlocutors. Were elections to be held in this environment, RUF would be able to intimidate voters on the model of Taylor's 1997 election campaign. Like Liberia, Sierra Leone would be pronounced 'stable' and an end to international engagement would follow.[43]

Meanwhile, Taylor provided refuge for a Guinea rebel leader, a son of a former president of Guinea. Fighting along the Guinea border has created a rebel-held enclave in Gueckedou prefecture in which this rebel group became installed, much like Taylor's sponsorship of RUF rebels in their March 1991 invasion of Sierra Leone.[44] As in Sierra Leone, the introduction of a rebel force exploited factional splits already present in the target country's military. In this case, the rebel leader claimed that he makes common cause with a Guinean army faction that staged an unsuccessful coup attempt in 1996. Heavy fighting between RUF and Guinea's army broke out in December 2001, one month after RUF and the Sierra Leone government agreed to a ceasefire. The UN Security Council accused Liberia of aiding RUF and Guinean rebel groups, and called upon the Liberian government to cease its involvement in destabilizing neighbouring states.

The International Community and Its Preference for Order

Taylor's apparent interference in Sierra Leone's civil war drew regular international condemnation, as did his repression of critics and rivals in Liberia. The US Department of State expressed concern that 'Taylor and his government have not learned to tolerate and deal peacefully with opposition.' Nonetheless, Taylor's economic and political interests in continued conflict in Sierra Leone and Guinea initially received little official criticism from the government. Taylor was able to use his personal relationship with Jesse Jackson, President Bill Clinton's special

envoy to Africa, and with some members of the House of Representatives, to plead his case as an interlocutor capable of influencing RUF
behaviour. But US officials were not insensitive to evidence of Taylor's
complicity in the continuing violence in neighbouring states.[45]

Continued engagement with Liberia, however, appeared to follow
from a conviction that Taylor's behaviour would become more states-
manlike as he was forced to grapple with the demands of governance. A
similar conviction guided the highly specific advice that the US Agency
for International Development's Office of Transition Initiative offered in
setting up Sierra Leone's commission to manage natural resources as
part of the Lomé agreement.[46] RUF leader Foday Sankoh headed this
government agency, but behaved much as his Liberian mentor. Rather
than transforming this organization either into a political party or into an
administrative structure, the commission, like Liberia's 1997 election,
formalized the faction leader's exclusive claim to key natural resources.
This behaviour stood in stark contrast to optimistic expectations of American officials that these strongmen would ultimately prefer to reconstruct
their countries' economies and peace in the West African region as a way
to maximize their own power.

Outsiders in fact helped subsidized Taylor's construction of the sort of
centralized personal economy that had earlier contributed to the breakdown of Doe's regime and the outbreak of war in 1989. The IMF, for
example, engaged in preliminary negotiations with Liberia's government
in an effort for it to begin servicing its arrears on debts. This action shows
further how Taylor's regime was able to derive concrete benefits from its
possession of sovereignty. It was suggested that monthly payments of
$50,000 from the Liberian government against arrears on its overall $3.1
billion debt would suffice initially to regularize the country's relations
with the IMF and give it access to more external resources.[47] Anxious
creditors preferred to work with sovereign regimes that acknowledge the
international obligations of their states, rather than authorities that are
not accredited as sovereign, or which lack the capability to behave as
interlocutors. In Liberia's case, Taylor's regime did not need to demonstrate any real internal capacity to service debts – the payment of $50,000
monthly would do – to potentially qualify for debt relief under multilateral creditors' Highly Indebted Poor Country (HIPC) initiate.[48] IMF officials billed debt relief as part of Liberia's postwar 'reconstruction'
program, despite the regime's lack of interest in providing even minimal
public services such as providing a national currency or basic security
with resources that are already at its disposal.

It was more likely that Taylor and his associates would treat these resources from abroad as private profits derived from his claim of sovereignty as a head of state. Direct aid to Liberian societal organizations would be regarded as a subsidy for essential state tasks. These external resources would free up more local and regional resources that Taylor had the capacity to collect to sustain his personal political network and to intervene violently in the affairs of neighbouring states. Taylor was able to attract other resources since his election, despite his previous poor relations with creditors. From 1997 to 1999, bilateral aid agencies provided Taylor's regime with $159 million in aid, freeing up internal resources for Taylor to direct to his associates. Taylor's regime spent only $12 million of its own resources on capital expenditures during this period, representing a small percentage of overall resources at its disposal if one considers unofficial diamond export earnings and potential profits from other business dealings.

The Tension between Order and Reconstructing Peace

The international society of states is particularly ill equipped to deal with postwar reconstruction in places such as Liberia. The assumption that authorities rationally prefer to end violent appropriations of resources that characterize wars of state collapse is not borne out. Instead, faction leaders who become heads of sovereign states are likely to continue to behave much as they did during wartime. The advantage of sovereignty for the strongest faction leader, however, is that his globally supported claim as head of a state enables him to use the prerogatives of sovereignty to eliminate his rivals, usually by force.

The elimination of armed rivals enables rulers like Taylor to operate more efficiently in the sense of not having to share loot and other resources as widely as during the war. In fact, if subordinates can be controlled, the ruler will favour an extremely small government. The lack of effective agencies reduces dangers to the ruler that subordinates will use state agencies to build their own bases of support and appropriate state assets without the ruler's authorization. Effective agencies also require delegating tasks, which could pose an additional security threat to rulers who are as wary as Taylor of their personal security. Despite this internal lack of capacity, sovereign statehood ensures that both natural resources and foreign aid will be under the control of the ruler, a situation that may hamper growth and postwar reconstruction.

This behaviour might be regarded as desirable from the perspective of creditors. Government budgets will be small, with relatively few civil servants asserting claims on state resources. 'Reform' of this sort mirrors prescriptions from multilateral creditors. The choice facing creditors and donors of aid lies in whether or not they wish to finance social service expenditures in the face of the government's unwillingness to give priority to these tasks. De facto protectorate status for places like Liberia would mean that people there would receive basic services, and that they might someday demand that their government provide these services instead. In the meantime, barring this sort of radical (and costly) external intervention, the propensity of a regime like Taylor's to appropriate resources and assets for itself is likely to continue to disrupt the lives of average Liberians, especially if, as in the case of timber operations, their presence interferes with the accumulation of private wealth. In such cases where international society shoulders most of the burden of providing public goods, the effect is likely to be detrimental to postwar reconstruction: rulers are protected from having to make difficult political decisions about whether resources will be spent on the well-being of the ruling clique, or on building legitimacy among their populations. Though the latter may be arduous and risky, it is at the core of rebuilding governments in places like Liberia that presently lack them.

Short-term concerns about order in international society also pose risks to Liberia's peaceful reconstruction. The initial decision of other West African states to negotiate ceasefires and peace agreements with faction leaders and to exclude societal groups further protected these leaders and their fighters from having to provide services and engaging in normal political activity to attract popular support. One of the primary lessons of the Liberian experience is that elections are not sufficient to create this relationship. Nor are peace pacts that are limited to agreements among armed combatants likely to generate the ties of reciprocity between rulers and citizens. Nonetheless, outsiders wary of disorder in Liberia were quick to greet the cessation of fighting as evidence of peace. Nigeria's government saw the 1997 election as an opportunity to wrap up a peacekeeping mission that it claimed cost $5 billion over seven years.[49] US officials were quick to use Taylor as an interlocutor in support of the Lomé agreement that brought what seemed to them stability in Sierra Leone.

The irony of these anxieties about order and stability was that resources that continued to be made available to Taylor in the name of order in fact undermined regional security. These resources enabled his regime to continue to replicate and spread to other countries the conditions of state collapse that appeared during the Doe regime, and which led to Liberia's war in the first place. This is because Liberia's war was not a civil war in the sense of contention between political positions, or the clash between a regime and rebels establishing liberated zones set up as reformist alternatives, nor was there a true government faction or organization (other than in name) in Liberia. The war was an outcome of state collapse, just as were wars in Sierra Leone, Somalia, Congo-Brazzaville, and the Democratic Republic of the Congo. The resolution of these wars lies in rebuilding civil government. The final irony is that this is something that might be better done with little or no aid, official or private, to particular regimes, where providing it even releases war leaders from responsibility for their own fighters, much less the population as a whole.

Postscript

As predicted Taylor's rule turned out to be extremely precarious. On 11 August 2003 he left Liberia to go into exile in Nigeria. A week later, what remained of Taylor's government signed a peace agreement in Accra with two rebel groups as a prelude to the arrival of a UN peacekeedpign force and elections in 2005. The agreement was signed as rebel forces, including many who had opposed Taylor throughout the 1990s, had fought their way to Monrovia. This latest phase of Liberia's now thirteen-year old conflict showed that some lessons of peacekeeping were learned, but others were not.

International observers recognized that the 1996 Abuja agreement enabled Taylor to continue destabilizing the region. Derek Smith, Britain's high commissioner in Sierra Leon noted, 'It was onlyuin the late 1990s that it was fully realised that Charles Taylor was behind the RUF ... Once this relationship was fully understood, the British Government worked hard to get the United Nations Security Council to impose sanctions on Liberia in an attempt the break Taylor/RUF relationship.'[50] But negotiations in Accra followed the same course as previous agreements. Those with guns dominated the proceedings at the expense of the representation of the great majority of Liberians. Many in Liberia saw in the anti-Taylor rebels the same people who oppressed them in earlier conflicts, and doubted that they would rule Liberia better than Taylor had. Numerous civilian politicians arrived in Accra, including many Liberians who had spent years in exile. Many had overlapping claims to represent factions or communities. With no test of popular backing, the hastily organized conference seated an interim government that will rule Liberia until elections are held in 2005.

It could be the case that with significant economic assistance Liberia's economy will be rebuilt and civic groups will play a major role in politics under UN protection. But neighbouring Sierra Leone's UN peacekeeping bill has come to $3.5 billion since 1999. The enormous bill for the United States rebuilding of Iraq will likely scare other potential donors off extensive state-building exercises in general. Thus reconstructing peace in Liberia most likely will remain a very incomplete process, incorporating some of the same people and processes responsible for conflict in the first place.

NOTES

1 A comprehensive guide to factions and peace agreements is found in Jeremy Armon and Andy Carl, eds., *Accord: The Liberian Peace Process, 1990–1996* (London: Conciliation Resources, 1996).
2 Paul Collier and Anke Hoeffler, 'On Economic Causes of Civil War,' *Oxford Economic Papers* 50 (1998), 563–73; Mats Berdal and David Malone, eds., *Greed and Grievance: Economic Agendas in Civil Wars* (Boulder, CO: Lynne Rienner Publishers, 2000).
3 On Doe's coup and consolidation of power, see Edward Lama Wonkeryor, *Liberia Military Dictatorship. A Fiasco 'Revolution'* (Chicago: Strugglers' Community Press, 1985).
4 Yekutiel Gershoni, 'Liberia and Israel,' *Liberian Studies Journal* 14, no. 1 (1989), 34–50.
5 Gus Liebenow, *Liberia: The Quest for Democracy* (Bloomington: Indiana University Press, 1987).
6 Bill Berkeley, *Liberia: A Promise Betrayed* (New York: Lawyers Committee on Human Rights, 1986).
7 Entrenching power by spiritual means predates Doe. President Tolbert (1971–80) was popularly thought to have sacrificed and enclosed part of the brain of his dead daughter Victoria in an ivory staff, during which he was also president of the World Baptist Alliance.
8 Stephen Ellis, *The Mask of Anarchy: The Destruction of Liberia and the Religious Dimension of an African Civil War* (London: Hurst, 1999).
9 Partly chronicled in letter of Gus Kouwenhoven (a Doe business associate) to Samuel Doe, 7 January 1989, Monrovia, Liberia.
10 Christopher Clapham, 'Liberia,' in Donal Cruise O'Brien, John Dunn, and

Richard Rathbone, eds., *Contemporary West African States* (New York: Cambridge University Press, 1989), 108.

11 Mark Huband, *The Liberian Civil War* (London: Frank Cass, 1998), 14–62.

12 See, for example, Charles Taylor, 'Solidarity Message to the 7th Pan-African Conference,' Gbarnga (Liberia), 28 March 1994.

13 *Report from the National Security Committee*, Gbarnga, 21 April 1992.

14 Africa Watch, 'Liberia: The Cycle of Abuse' (New York, 21 October 1991), 1; 'Liberia: Taylor's One Man Band,' *Africa Confidential*, 27 July 1990, 6.

15 Cited in 'Human Rights Abuses,' *West Africa*, 22 March 1993, 454; see Bayo Ogunleye, *Behind Rebel Line* (Enugu: Delta Publications, 1995), 139.

16 For example, 'Looting in S/western Liberia,' *Monrovia Daily News*, 17 November 1995; 'More Looted Goods on the Market,' *The Inquirer*, 27 October 1995; 'NPFL Men Still Looting,' *Inquirer*, 24 November 1995.

17 National Patriotic Reconstruction Assembly Government, 'Memorandum of Understanding' 16 January 1992, and 'Firestone Restart Timetable, 16 January 1992; Liberia Timber Association, 'Request for Solution to Serious Problems Facing Logging Companies in Southeastern Region,' San Pedro, Côte d'Ivoire, 5 June 1991; 'Appeal for Your Intervention with Other Government Agencies,' 22 November 1991; US Congress, House International Relations Committee, 'Testimony of William Twaddell, Acting Assistant Secretary of State for African Affairs,' 26 June 1996.

18 United Nations, *Twenty-first Progress Report of the Secretary-General on the United Nations Observer Mission in Liberia*, (New York: UN, 29 January 1997), para. 17; annex II; US Department of State, *Liberia Country Report on Human Rights Practices for 1996* (Washington, DC: Department of State, 30 January 1997), section IV.

19 Quoted in Bill Berkeley, 'Liberia: Between Repression and Slaughter,' *Atlantic Monthly*, December. 1992, 54.

20 George Boley, personal communication.

21 K. Moses Nagbe, *Bulk Challenge: The Story of 4000 Liberians in Search of Refuge* (Cape Coast: Champion Publications, 1996), 53.

22 Figures are from US Department of State, *Liberia Country Report*, 2.

23 'UNOMIL Probes Ceasefire Violations,' *Inquirer* (Monrovia), 12 September 1995, 1; 'Fight over Diamond,' *The News* (Monrovia), 28 July 1995, 1.

24 Lt.-Col. Festus Aboagye, *ECOMOG: A Sub-Regional Experience in Conflict Resolution, Management and Peacekeeping in Liberia* (Accra: Sedco Enterprise, 1999), 123–30.

25 An interpretation found in David Harris, 'From "Warlord" to "Democratic" President: How Charles Taylor Won the 1997 Liberian Elections,' *Journal of Modern African Studies* 37, no. 3 (1999), 431–55; Max Sesay, 'Security and

State-Society Crises in Sierra Leone and Liberia,' in Caroline Thomas and Peter Wilkins, eds., *Globalization, Human Security, and the African Experience* (Boulder, CO: Lynne Rienner Publishers, 1999), 145–61.

26 See Max Weber, *Theory of Social and Economic Organization* (New York: Free Press, 1947), 156.

27 'M. Taylor s'oppose au démantèlement de l'unité anti-terroriste dirigée par son fils,' *Marchés Tropicaux*, 5 November 1999, 2228; 'Liberia: Taylorland under Siege,' *Africa Confidential*, 19 February 1999, 6–7.

28 International Monetary Fund, *Liberia: Staff Report for the 1999 Article IV Consultation and Staff-Monitored Program* (Washington, DC; IMF Report 00/52, April 2000), 30.

29 Ministry of Finance (of Liberia) correspondence with International Monetary Fund, 'Memorandum of Economic and Financial Policies,' February. 2000; 'Liberia allocates 40m for Army,' *Jane's Defence Weekly* 33, no. 10 (8 March 2000).

30 'The Case for Suspicion,' *New African*, April 2000, 17.

31 Amnesty International, *Annual Report, 1999*, 42; United States Department of State, *1999 Country Reports on Human Rights Practices: Liberia* (Washington, 2000).

32 'The Promised Land,' *Africa Energy and Mining*, 16 June 1999; 'Liberia: la compagnie américaine Freedom Gold sur le point d'exploiter les grisements libériens,' *Marchés Tropicaux*, 10 December 1999, 2487.

33 'Profession: 'agent de securite,'' *Lettre du Continent*, 11 May 2000, 3; 'Liberia / Sierra Leone: Godfather to the Rebels,' *Africa Confidential*, 23 June 2000, 1–3.

34 United Nations Security Council, *Fourth Report of the Secretary General on United Nations Mission in Sierra Leone*, 19 May 2000, 3. In a January 1999 BBC interview Taylor denied helping RUF insurgents, but suggested that Liberian combatants were fighting in Sierra Leone.

35 Report from an eyewitness, and a BBC interview, 15 April 1991.

36 'Taylor Trouble,' *Democrat* (Freetown), 29 October 1998, 1; 'Rebels Meet in Monrovia,' ibid, 17 February 2000, 1; 'Smuggling Ring Invades Mining Areas,' *For Di People* (Freetown), 2 February 2000, 1. See also Ian Smillie, Lansana Gberie and Ralph Hazleton, *The Heart of the Matter: Sierra Leone Diamonds and Human Security* (Ottawa: Partnership Africa Canada, 2000), 32.

37 For example, allegations that Taylor personally benefited from RUF diamond transactions appeared in 'Staying On,' *Economist*, 17 June 2000, 41; Philip Sherwell, 'Liberia Chief Fuels "Diamond War,"' *Sunday Telegraph* (London), 28 May 2000, 32; Andrew Osborn and Ewen MacAskill, 'Rebel Paymaster Loses Aid,' *Guardian* (London), 14 June 2000, 18.

38 United Nations, *Report of the Panel of Experts Appointed Pursuant to UN Security*

Council Resolution 1306 (2000) (New York: UN, 20 December 2000), paragraph 19 in relation to Sierra Leone.

39 Africa News Online, 20 March 2000.

40 Andrew Coxon of De Beers at 'Technical Forum on the Issue of "Conflict Diamonds,"' Kimberley, South Africa, 12 May 2000. 'Surprises in Antwerp,' *Africa Energy and Mining*, 15 March 2000, 1.

41 Douglas Farah, 'Liberia Reportedly Arming Guerrillas,' *Washington Post*, 18 June 2000, A21; United Nations, *Report of the Panel of Experts* (December 2000), para.20.

42 United Nations, Office of the Secretary General, *Report of the Secretary General on the Establishment of a Special Court for Sierra Leone* (New York: UN, October 2000).

43 This analysis follows the author's discussions via e-mail with British military officials in Sierra Leone and officials of western governments in Sierra Leone.

44 Conversation with a US official source, 12 October 2000, e-mail correspondence with a British military source, 18 October 2000. See also 'Liberia: Cross-border Crisis,' *Africa Confidential*, 21 July 2000, 1.

45 See, for example, United States Senate, Committee on Foreign Relations, 'United States Policy in Sierra Leone,' 11 October 2000.

46 Analysis derived from author's discussion with US officials in Africa.

47 International Monetary Fund, *Staff Report for the 1999 Article IV Consultation and Staff-Monitored Program* (Washington, DC: IMF, 14 February 2000), 25, para.53.

48 International Monetary Fund, *Liberia: Selected Issues and Statistical Appendix* (Washington, DC: IMF, April 2000), 20.

49 'ECOMOG: Wasting of Riches,' *Scrutiny* (Lagos), March 1999, 1-2; Goodluck Ebelo, 'Wasted,' *Tempo* (Lagos), 28 January 1999, 5-7.

50 Derek Smith, 'Statement before the Truth and Reconciliation Commission of Sierra Leon,' Freetown, 2 July 2003.

5

The Peace Dividend in Mozambique, 1987–1997

Alexander Costy

Mozambique is widely perceived as a singular success story in African peacebuilding. Politically, it has successfully kept the peace since 1992, despite the formidable difficulties of military demobilization, the social reintegration of some 1.6 million war refugees, and conversion from a centralized socialist state to a liberal democracy. Economically, Mozambique has been lauded by foreign donors and international financial institutions as a successful 'adjuster,' reflecting a general approval over the country's structural adjustment efforts.[1] By 'succeeding' on both political and economic fronts, Mozambique has provided a rare validation of Western blueprints for postwar recovery in Africa.

Yet despite these apparent successes, building peace in Mozambique has not been without its problems. For many Mozambicans, the expected economic and social benefits of postwar settlement have been only vaguely perceived. And although political stability has been maintained, Mozambique's new structures of liberal-democratic governance appeared, several years into the peace, to be exposed to significant political and social pressures. Indeed, a closer look at the political economy of the war-to-peace transition suggests that while formal peacebuilding objectives were largely achieved under UN mandate in the early 1990s, serious questions arise about the underlying quality and content of the peace itself, and about its implications for the majority of citizens over the longer term.

This chapter analyses peacebuilding in Mozambique from the perspective of long-term developmental choices, and not simply in terms of temporary stabilization strategies. It surveys several key reforms which have underpinned Mozambique's postwar settlement, and assesses their value in terms of building a socially sustainable peace and averting future conflict. Overall, the chapter argues that structural patterns of accelerated liberalization have worked to erode substantially and possibly reverse social and economic gains achieved in the immediate postwar period, and potentially pose the danger of renewed instability.

Mainstream peacebuilding literature generally emphasizes the political dimensions of post-war settlement (e.g. power-sharing solutions, reconciliation mechanisms, democratization, and human rights monitoring). The long-term developmental challenges of building sustainable peace systems have received considerably less attention. In the case of Mozambique, I expressly broaden the conceptual parameters of peacebuilding in a manner that directly connects the formal politics of post-conflict stabilization with deeper, and more problematic, processes of socio-economic transformation. In so doing, some preliminary themes emerge as a basis for discussing the appropriate role of national states and societal forces in post-conflict development, and the value of accelerated liberalization in generating acceptable political, economic, and social peace dividends over the long term.

Roots of War and Peace in Mozambique

The roots of Mozambique's war have been the subject of considerable debate. Supporters or one-time participants of the Frelimo movement's socialist experiment have sought to portray the sixteen-year conflict primarily in terms of a foreign destabilization campaign executed by a proxy force of locally recruited fighters. Critics of Frelimo socialism, by contrast, have depicted the conflict as a 'civil war' reflecting mass popular disaffection with Frelimo's state-driven development schemes and ideological orientations. As Saul has pointed out, interpretations matter, and the evolution and final outcome of this 'inside/outside' debate has indeed had concrete prescriptive implications for peacebuilding in Mozambique.[2] Had it been sufficient to explain the war, an end to South African destabilization may have emerged as a straightforward remedy to the conflict. Instead, the overwhelming attention given to internal factors has provided the necessary intellectual and historical justification for pursuing nothing less than a comprehensive transformation of the Mozambican political economy, its institutions, ideology, and social organizations, as a requisite strategy for building peace. For the purposes of this review, the Mozambican conflict is perhaps best understood by inserting external and internal factors into their historical context.

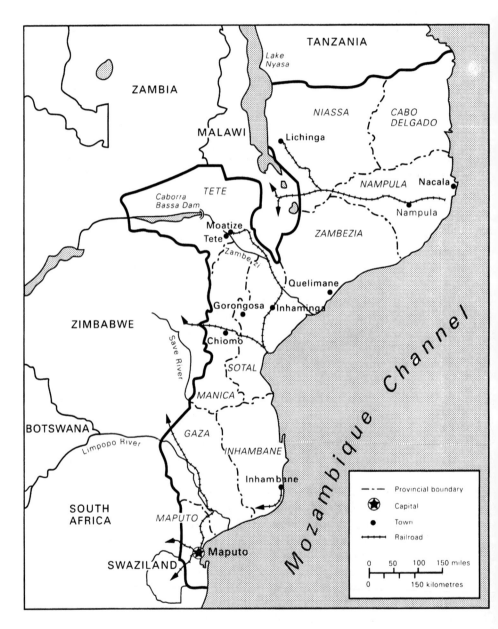

Mozambique

Socialist Choices

When the Frelimo movement took power in late 1974 after over a decade of fighting against the colonial regime, its initial choice of a centrally planned, socialist path towards socio-economic development was motivated by a combination of historical circumstances which shaped both objective needs and policy preferences of the period. Mozambique's colonial political economy had developed around a limited set of extractive and coercive activities which laid little ground for sustainable growth in the newly independent country. Most colonial revenue had flowed from external sources such as payments on foreign land concessions, fees for exported labour, railway transit charges, and agricultural export earnings. Despite belated colonial initiatives to nurture a local African middle class, the economy's reliance on forced labour, and the imposition of rigid standards of social stratification, severely limited Africans' access to education and formal employment. Private enterprise remained overwhelmingly under the control of European and Asian traders, while public administration remained a virtual monopoly of the colony's small strata of whites or *assimilados*. A vast majority of Mozambicans not bound by contract to the plantation or mining economies remained marginal to formal commercial and administrative sectors, surviving on subsistence agriculture and informal seasonal labour.[3] This combination of external economic dependence and weak social infrastructure left the Mozambican political economy highly vulnerable to external shocks, and precluded any prospects of quickly developing a national human-resource base suitable to the developmental needs of a newly independent state.

Portugal's unexpectedly swift handover of power to the Frelimo movement in late 1974 caused widespread panic among the resident professional and commercial classes. By 1976, 90 per cent of the white population had fled the country, taking with them the bulk of its skilled labour force. Businesses and farms were abandoned and tens of thousands were put out of work. Private investment grew scarce while industry, construction and tourism came to a virtual standstill. Rural trade networks connecting town and country threatened to dissolve, and public administration and social services around the country ceased to function.[4] On the external front too, revenues from prior economic arrangements with neighbouring regimes rapidly fell as railway transit was interrupted and annual recruitment to the South African mines was drastically reduced.[5]

From the outset, then, Frelimo's policy choices responded to the contingency of impending national economic and administrative collapse. Ironically, immediate strategies were implemented to uphold existing colonial structures through extended government intervention and centralized planning. Land, social services, and key industries were nationalized, and thousands of Frelimo party members, many of them unqualified, were deployed across the territory to take up local administrative positions vacated by the Portuguese. Hundreds of abandoned shops, farms, and firms were placed under public management in a bid to keep the economy functioning.[6]

At another level, Frelimo's early socialist options reflected deliberate ideological choices within the broader context of Southern African liberation during the Cold War and apartheid periods. In Mozambique as elsewhere in Africa, socialist analysis lent itself generously to the values and objectives of national liberation, anti-imperialism, and majority rule. It had provided the ideological underpinnings of guerrilla resistance against an oppressive Portuguese regime closely connected with South African apartheid and, through NATO membership, with Washington and its allies. Its socialist orientation also gave Frelimo an appealing rhetorical platform to mobilize rural populations in support of a new modernization agenda. But perhaps most significantly, it gave the new Mozambican regime the blueprints for a concrete, long-term experiment in social and economic development which contrasted starkly with recent colonial experiences, and which offered a seemingly viable alternative to the colonial nation-building policies so harshly imposed in much of the region.[7]

Some early Frelimo successes in social policy were recorded in the years immediately following independence, notably in health and education. In practice, however, Frelimo's ambitious efforts to modernize Mozambique according to socialist guidelines were undermined by serious policy errors. The rapid bureaucratization of wide areas of economic life all but quelled independent commercial and financial activity in the country.[8] An excessive centralization of planning and decision-making functions within the state led to the increased disjuncture between public policy and the realities experienced by the majority of Mozambique's rural population. Coercive collectivization of agricultural production, villagization, and the increasing use of force to induce compliance in social and economic life served to drain the socialist project of its initial political legitimacy. Arguably, such errors stemmed from fundamental flaws in a rigorous socialist approach which insisted upon aggregate class analysis and thereby failed to address sufficiently the complex social, economic, and cultural diversities cutting across rural society. By the early 1980s, the 'hardening of the Frelimo state' had reached its apogee,[9] and social resentment, particularly among the peasantry, increased, laying a fertile ground for a new round of civil war.

Destabilization and Peace

Armed incursions into Mozambique began soon after independence, in response to Frelimo's decision to implement full UN trade sanctions and to shelter the guerrilla opposition against the Ian Smith government of Rhodesia. Early Renamo attacks against economic and infrastructure targets were supported by Rhodesian military intelligence and a loose alliance of Frelimo dissidents and Portuguese exiles. When, in 1980, the independence of Zimbabwe was proclaimed, Renamo bases were transferred to locations in South Africa, from which the movement began to prosecute a long, destructive war against the Frelimo state, in keeping with Pretoria's 'total strategy' against regional threats to the apartheid regime. Throughout the following decade, the destabilization campaign grew in scope, sophistication, and intensity, and increasingly involved civilian targets. With sustained South African support and partly through forced recruitment, Renamo's military organization grew from some several dozen men to almost ten thousand, and by the early 1990s had extended its control to almost a quarter of the national territory.[10]

The issue of Renamo's rootedness within Mozambican rural life has been a main focus of the inside/outside debate noted earlier. For many of the war's analysts, social rootedness has helped to explain the growth and longevity of the rebel movement, as well as its ability to constitute an accepted political and administrative authority in areas firmly under its military control. Some sociological analysis has sought to document how Renamo succeeded in constructing solid alliances with local traditional power structures and securing popular support in certain regions of the country. There is also evidence to show that, as the war proceeded though the 1980s, local loyalties for Renamo were boosted by popular dissatisfaction with the increasingly coercive rural policies conceived by distant Frelimo central planners.[11] At the same time, given Renamo's noted lack of a coherent ideology and frequent use of extreme violence against local populations, its success in building a consensual local social base in rural areas has remained somewhat of a puzzle.

Although Renamo was able to capitalize on peasants' adversity to forced villagization, most agree that its relationships with local rural society were both highly complex and regionally variable. One factor under-pinning this relationship was Renamo's early recognition of the importance of traditional local authorities and the cooptation of locally accepted social structures through which authority could be transmitted, and through which some measure of public support could be mobilized. This appears to have been the case particularly in Central Mozambique, where Renamo's connections with local authorities were buttressed also by ethnic affinities. Elsewhere, the strength and integrity of existing tra-ditional authority structures appear to have had some impact on the quality of Renamo's relationship with local communities, notably the level of violence used against them. In Zambezia, where local authority structures had strong and relatively stable historical roots, Renamo appears to have opted for a policy of accommodation, and violence against civilians was relatively less pronounced. By contrast, in southern regions (notably Gaza province) where structures of traditional author-ity had historically been weakened by patterns of migratory labour to South Africa and later by Frelimo's collectivization programs, Renamo authority appears to have been for the most part, exercised directly on the basis of fear of extreme forms of violence.[12]

According to Juergensen, local loyalties toward either of the two war-ring parties were highly susceptible to perceptual changes over time, depending on local understandings of the actions of each warring party, and the message it was able to project locally. He also found that in bor-der areas where local populations possessed the option of moving to internationally protected refugee camps, Renamo was more likely to accommodate the demands of local chiefs in a bid to prevent depopula-tion.[13] Such contrasting findings illustrate the central point that, in the highly fragmented war environment of the 1980s, it is difficult to come to any firm conclusions about the actual extent and quality of Renamo's social base, or rootedness in rural society.

As many have argued, analytical emphasis on the question of Ren-amo's local rootedness should not lead historical inquiry away from the central issues of Renamo's foreign origins, its heavy external opera-tional dependence, and the limited scope of its strategic autonomy. For Minter, Renamo was from its inception 'incorporated within the Rhode-sian and then South African military structure,' and Renamo operations were 'subordinated to defending the white regime's security' against perceived regional threats.[14] For the South African regime, this meant using Renamo to cause as much immediate damage as possible, while exploiting local sensibilities and frustrations to undermine the credibility and ideological appeal of the Frelimo program. That the war later moved on to assume complex local dynamics can in no way be taken to reflect a weakening of links between Renamo and its external sponsors, and may on the contrary signal an increasing sophistication of foreign destabilization strategies over time. In the end, Renamo would never free itself enough from the wider regional geopolitical objectives of its external sponsors to become a genuine national movement with an identifiable political or economic program. This would later be confirmed by Renamo's difficulty in shaping its own identity as it underwent its postwar transition from a fighting force to political party.

The continued pressure of destabilization and the onset of drought in the mid-1980s led Frelimo to launch a succession of external and internal policy reviews. On the external front, Mozambique began diplomatic discussions with South Africa culminating in the 1984 Nkomati Accord, which aimed to curtail each country's interference in the internal political affairs of the other. In the event, although Mozambique effectively ended its support for ANC activities in the South Africa, that country's backing for Renamo actions in Mozambique continued and intensified. The accord did, however, send a strong international signal that Frelimo was not closed to a diplomatic solution to the war, and Frelimo's implementation of its part of the deal showed that it was prepared to take seriously its diplomatic commitments. Mozambique's international profile improved as a result, and emergency appeals for humanitarian aid found increasingly sympathetic ears in the West. Food aid, including from the United States, began to enter the country in growing quantities, marking the beginnings of what would become a long and increasingly unequal relationship with the Western aid community.[15]

Yet despite the influx of new aid, war and economic decline continued throughout the decade. GDP fell by 8 per cent each year between 1981 and 1985, and the volume of marketed agricultural output and industrial production fell dramatically. The value of exports dropped from US $281 million in 1981 to only US $79 million in 1986, and payments arrears reached an amount roughly equivalent to half of the country's GDP.[16] To make up for increasing budgetary shortfalls and maintain expenditures, the government was obliged to seek international credits, and its total foreign debt rose from nil in 1982 to almost US $3 billion in 1985.[17] This prompted Frelimo to apply for IMF and World Bank membership and, under strong pressure from these institutions, to draw up plans for national economic reform. In 1987 Frelimo launched its Programma de Reabilitaçao Economica (PRE), the first structural adjustment program ever to be implemented by any country during wartime. This led to a first round of price liberalizations, privatizations, and currency devaluations. Subsidies to strategic sectors of the economy were cut in a bid to make them more competitive. Income-based rent controls were replaced by new systems based on property value, and public sector employment guarantees were lifted.[18] Together, these measures marked the beginning of Frelimo's practical retreat from its socialist experiment, and signalled the opening of a new era of unprecedented international penetration of independent Mozambique's political, social, and economic institutions.

By the turn of the 1990s, Mozambique's social infrastructure lay in ruins. One-third of all rural clinics and about 70 per cent of schools were destroyed or abandoned. Access to large portions of the national territory was limited by road destruction, landmines, or erosion. One million war-related deaths were counted, and up to six million people became internally or externally displaced during the fighting. In 1992 the UN estimated that overall war costs corresponded to 250 years of the country's export earnings and were fifty times higher than its annual aid receipts. In that year, Mozambique ranked last on the UNDP Human Development index and was listed by the World Bank as having the lowest GNP per capita. The war and related humanitarian emergency left Mozambique among the most aid dependent countries, with official aid as a proportion of GDP rising from 43.7 per cent in 1987 to 115 per cent in 1993.[19]

The signing of the General Peace Accord in October 1992 resulted from a combination of propitious international, regional and national trends. The end of the East-West confrontation weakened the Cold War logic which had fuelled the conflict. Regionally, the dissolution of the apartheid regime in South Africa signalled an end to direct external destabilization, and opened the prospect of enhanced economic and political cooperation across Southern Africa. Inside Mozambique, the economic toll of the fighting, compounded by growing debt, famines, and chronic drought, had rendered continued war-making unsustainable. The peace was equally facilitated by a protracted series of negotiations on various fronts dating back to the early 1980s. But as war continued to rage, other initiatives to maintain open channels of contact between the warring parties were taken up by Mozambique's Protestant and Catholic church leaders. Despite numerous setbacks, the churches eventually positioned themselves to facilitate increasingly regular contacts with Renamo and, later, direct meetings between officials on both sides of the conflict. In particular, the Catholic church of Sofala, which enjoyed privileged relations with the Renamo leadership, proved crucial in securing and maintaining Renamo participation in the peace dialogue.[21]

By 1990, several players had entered what was still technically an informal peace process. The presidents of Zimbabwe and Kenya facilitated talks and added official weight to the process, while South Africa and the United States, supported by a growing chorus of humanitarian organizations, brought increasing pressure to bear upon both parties to agree to formal negotiations. In July, Renamo and Frelimo leaders met for the first time in Rome, launching official talks and shifting the focus of negotiation squarely into the international realm, with the American, Italian, Portuguese, French and British governments playing an increasingly prominent mediating role. The General Peace Agreement (GPA) was negotiated over the subsequent twenty-four months, and covered a remarkably extensive range of issues in detail. Its main protocols related not only to immediate military disengagement and mutual political recognition, but also to press freedoms, the role of political parties, and the socio-economic reintegration of demobilized soldiers. It included a detailed schedule of the modalities and timing of the country's first multiparty elections, and was accompanied by a declaration on agreed principles for humanitarian assistance. Final agreement was reached on 4 October 1992 for a twelve-month peace plan to be implemented under United Nations supervision.

The Peace Operation

The UN Operation in Mozambique (UNOMOZ) was launched in late 1992 with a wide-ranging mandate to monitor the ceasefire, oversee demobilization, conduct mine clearance, support the elections, and coordinate humanitarian assistance. To this end, and despite recurring logistical and administrative delays, UNOMOZ eventually deployed over ten thousand troops, civilian police, and military and electoral observers, at a cost of some US $1 million per day. Its humanitarian unit, UNOHAC, coordinated successive humanitarian appeals for the operation amounting to approximately US $1 billion, sizable proportions of which were channelled through international NGOs.[21]

From a peacebuilding perspective, the operation was judged successful on a number of counts. First, essential political lessons from Angola about the appropriate sequencing of peacebuilding actions were heeded and applied. The timing of refugee resettlement to coincide with the electoral agenda ensured the broadest possible participation in the vote. Critically, the elections themselves were made contingent upon the prior demobilization of former combatants and the creation of a new, unified national army. Thus the option, exercised by UNITA forces in Angola, of returning to war in the event of an unfavourable vote, was effectively eliminated in the Mozambican case. Secondly, UNOMOZ succeeded in pushing the peace process agenda forward despite repeated political challenges from the parties to the agreement, and several operational and administrative setbacks. In this regard, Richard Synge has credited UNOMOZ chief Aldo Ajello with deftly employing a combination of incentives and political pressures to ensure Renamo's ongoing commitment to the peace, temper Frelimo's drive to dictate the terms and pace of implementation, and reduce mutual political suspicions to manageable levels. Through his active diplomacy and consultation with key donors and aid agencies, Ajello likewise succeeded in maintaining the credibility of UNOMOZ and ensuring continued international support for its operation. Third, UNOMOZ produced concrete results in most of the priority areas which it had been tasked to support.[22] Each of these is briefly reviewed here.

Repatriation

A central priority for the UN was to facilitate the resettlement of some 1.6 million Mozambican refugees and an estimated three to four million internally displaced persons. UNOHAC was given overall responsibility for coordinating the repatriation process, while UNHCR, the UN's refugee agency, assumed an operational lead. In 1993 cross-border coordination mechanisms were established with neighbouring governments to facilitate refugees' registration and processing, while agreements between the International Organization for Migration (IOM), the World Food Program (WFP), and UNHCR established a division of labour respectively for refugee transport, food assistance, and resettlement. In the event, improved security conditions and road access after 1992 prompted the spontaneous return of a substantial proportion of the refugee population, thereby accelerating the programming timetable. By late 1994, 1.5 million people had crossed back into Mozambique, marking one of the largest resettlement programs to take place under UN auspices.

Along with improved security, several factors accounted for the success of the repatriation process. The US $100 million UNCHR reintegration program provided strong material incentives for refugee populations to return to their areas of origin. Aid was deliberately targeted towards localities where high rates of return were expected, and ranged from the distribution of relief items and agricultural implements to the rehabilitation of infrastructure. In conjunction with forty-seven NGOs, between 1993 and 1996. the UNCHR implemented over fifteen hundred projects to repair clinics and schools, improve access to water, facilitate rural transport, and raise agricultural production. Despite well-founded worries about the long-term sustainability of these efforts, the immediate objective of making tangible improvements to living conditions in areas of expected return was generally achieved. The UNHCR projects thus provided a psychological and material draw powerful enough to attract not only refugees from the outside, but also significant numbers of internally displaced persons away from urban centres towards depopulated rural areas. Moreover, despite the speed and intensity of the resettlement process, relatively few tensions were registered, as might have been anticipated, over such issues as land tenure and housing. This lack of conflict was attributed, on one hand, to the stabilizing economic effects of the aid projects themselves, particularly in terms of short-term job creation and stimulation of local markets. On the other hand, the UNHCR noted contextual factors of success, including war-exhaustion, the absence of localized war-lordism, a relative abundance of productive land, and importantly, the use of informal resettlement strategies by the returnees themselves.[23]

Demobilization

The decommissioning of Frelimo and Renamo fighting forces represented perhaps the most sensitive component of the peace-support operation, both because of its central importance to the consolidation of the postwar settlement and because the process itself, which involved the quartering, disarming, and resettlement of over ninety-one thousand troops, remained constantly exposed to political disagreements. The selection of forty-nine UNOMOZ-supervised assembly areas, to which troops would be relocated for registration and demobilization, was marred by mutual political suspicions and by the desire of each party to retain military control over its respective territories. As a result, it was not until more than a full year after the ceasefire that all assembly areas became operational. Demobilization was further complicated by the slow pace of assembly at the designated areas (stemming from the reluctance of both parties to alter existing troop deployments), and technical delays in the registration and processing of soldiers, which lengthened the period of cantonment or caused overcrowding. Violent protests over living conditions, inadequate supplies, and especially over the issue of demobilization payments, were registered in several camps throughout 1993 and 1994, in some cases spilling into nearby communities and prompting interventions by UN peacekeeping units. However, tensions were successfully contained or defused through timely action at both political and operational levels, and the overall integrity of the demobilization process was maintained.[24] Final figures indicate that 87 per cent of registered combatants were demobilized by August 1994, while an additional 11.5 per cent (amounting to just over 12,000 soldiers) were voluntarily recruited into the new national army.[25]

Several factors account for the ultimate success of the demobilization program. One, as noted elsewhere, was that conditions in Mozambique appeared to be ripe for a final resolution of the conflict. In the final months of the conflict, both sides had experienced growing hardship in sustaining the war effort. By the time of the signing of the peace agreement in 1992, several localized ceasefires had already begun to be negotiated across the country, reflecting a clear measure of war weariness among local fighting units. A second important factor was the well-calibrated use of material incentives to render demobilization and disarmament attractive. This involved a combination of cash payments and the offer of reintegration packages and other programs. In addition to the specific goods and services (including food and medical attention) received upon arrival and departure from the assembly areas, ex-combatants also received monthly subsidies, calculated according to military rank, for a period of twenty-four months after demobilization. This innovative scheme, financed by international donors and the government of Mozambique, and administered jointly by the UNDP and local branches of the Banco de Moçambique, served several purposes. Income stability for former soldiers helped to militate against the use of force for economic subsistence. It also provided an economic basis for resettlement and for financing longer-term income-generation activities. For soldiers intending to return to agriculture, the two-year subsidy scheme gave them time to acquire land, obtain seeds and implements, and enter local cropping cycles. Psychologically, too, the monthly payments enabled soldiers to end long years of fighting and return to their native communities with a tangible measure of dignity.[26]

A third factor of success was the level of coordination which UNO-

MOZ was able to promote at both policy and operational levels. Aldo Ajello effectively coped with recurring delays and setbacks in the demobilization timetable by making full use of the institutional mechanisms of the GPA (in particular the Cease-Fire Commission and the Supervision and Control Commission) to consult with key donors and political leaders, coordinate policy positions, and address crises as they arose. In the field, logistical challenges were addressed with a reasonably clear division of labour among humanitarian agencies. The World Food Program took on a lead role in coordinating food distributions to assembly areas, while health services were contracted out to selected NGOs. For its part, the IOM ensured transport of demobilized combatants and their families to their chosen resettlement areas and provided reintegration kits containing seeds, tools and basic household items.

Finally, several large-scale reintegration programs were launched to follow-up on demobilization from 1993 onwards. These included a cross-country information referral service (IRS) designed to inform demobilized personnel about work opportunities, a national occupational skills development program (ISD) intended to facilitate employment through vocational and entrepreneurial skills training, and donor-financed provincial funds meant to support local community initiatives facilitating reintegration.

Given the immediacy of their objectives, the longer-term sustainability of these early stabilization programs was legitimately questioned during the period.[27] Nevertheless, despite lingering worries over hidden weapons depots and isolated outbreaks of violence throughout 1994, most agree that the $85 million demobilization program mandated to UNOMOZ largely addressed its stated priorities of rapid demilitarization and pre-electoral pacification.

Elections

The third main component of the UNOMOZ mandate was to provide logistical, organizational, and advisory support for the electoral process. Here again, UNOMOZ retained overall responsibility for managing and supervising the electoral effort, and played a central mediating role in overcoming severe disagreements among the contending parties on electoral financing, monitoring, and post-election power-sharing formulas. The United Nations Development Program (UNDP) was tasked to address the formidable logistical challenge of registering some 6.3 million voters and coordinating the deployment of 2,600 electoral staff,

1,600 civic education officers and 52,000 polling agents to over 7,400 polling station across the country. For its part, the IOM oversaw the deployment of 32,000 electoral monitors recruited from the national political parties. UNOMOZ itself deployed one thousand UN police officers to improve public security and access to registration and voting facilities, as well as three thousand international observers to ensure the international credibility of the electoral outcome. Several initiatives in the area of civic education were contracted out to NGOs, while the National Electoral Commission (NEC), an all-Mozambican body chaired by a respected academic, exercised ultimate authority to apply Mozambique's new electoral rules and verify the legality of the vote.

Two crises dominated the elections from the outset of voter registration in early June 1994. These contributed to mounting tensions in an increasingly politicized setting, and led to uncertainties about the viability of the democratic process until well into the first day of voting on 27 October. The first concerned the option of establishing a government of national unity in the post-election period. The second, more fundamental issue, involved the question of whether the main political parties, and in particular Renamo, would abide by the electoral results.

The option of a government of national unity (GNU) had been debated informally since the beginning of the peace process, and gained public prominence as the elections approached. International support for the idea was boosted in early 1994, following the establishment of a GNU in neighbouring South Africa. Only weeks before the vote, several international donors engaged the local media and political parties in public discussions about the merits of post-election power-sharing, with particular pressure brought by the American mission upon Frelimo to consider the option seriously. In the event, Frelimo strongly rejected the GNU formula on the grounds that it had not been included in the provisions of the general peace agreement, and on the basis of Frelimo's own confidence that it could win a sufficient electoral majority to form a legitimate government. Frelimo's objections also reflected its growing suspicion of the international community's bias towards its Renamo adversaries. For their part, Renamo and the minor opposition parties embraced the formula as an insurance against electoral defeat, and Renamo publicly issued a demand for a pre-electoral power-sharing agreement with Frelimo. However, the strength of Frelimo's reaction was such as to potentially compromise its commitment to the electoral agenda, and international pressures dissipated as a result.

In spite of the parties' repeated public assurances of their commitment to the electoral process, new tensions mounted in the last days of the electoral campaign as Renamo voiced growing suspicions of potential fraud. Fearing that a surplus of over one million unused voter cards might be used to swing the elections in favour of the government, Renamo demanded that they be destroyed ahead of the scheduled vote. Receiving no response from the NEC, Renamo leader Afonso Dhlakama announced his party's unilateral withdrawal from the elections on the eve of the first day of polling. The boycott prompted a flurry of responses from the international community, which by now had an enormous political stake in the successful completion of the elections. Here again, UNOMOZ proved crucial in mediating the crisis. Ajello was the first to re-establish contact with an elusive Dhlakama, and successfully persuaded the diplomatic community in Maputo that Dhlakama might be convinced to cancel the boycott. There followed a succession of international calls to Dhlakama, including from several heads of state, providing assurances that any electoral irregularities would be promptly addressed after the vote. Ajello announced the establishment of a new verification commission, alongside those already in place, to scrutinize the election results. Under intense international pressure, Dhlakama announced his party's return to the electoral process early in the first day of polling. In order to compensate for the electoral disruption, the voting period was extended by a day.

Despite these and other challenges, in early November 1994 UNOMOZ was able to cap its mission by confirming a free and fair vote in Mozambique's first liberal democratic experiment. In the event, Frelimo won a solid victory in the presidential contest, and a majority of parliamentary seats. At the same time, the vote formally confirmed Renamo's dominant political position in five of the country's eleven provinces, solidly establishing it as the main party of democratic opposition. Amid general international and local satisfaction, UNOMOZ began rapidly dismantling its operation in early December 1994, while several UN agencies, donors, and NGOs quickly began to shift their programmatic attention to the next, rehabilitation phase of the postwar transition.

The UN operation produced tangible gains in each of its three main components. In December 1994, as elected MPs from both parties gathered in Maputo for the opening of the first postwar parliamentary session, Mozambique was an altogether different place than it had been just twenty-four months earlier. The ceasefire had held, and post-conflict tensions had been contained. Hundreds of thousands of war refugees had returned home to rebuild their livelihoods, and one of

southern Africa's most destructive fighting organizations had transformed itself into a legitimate political party. Several thousand kilometres of access roads had been rehabilitated, and hundreds of clinics and
primary schools had been repaired. Immediate postwar stabilization,
along with the beginnings of social reintegration, had been achieved.
Yet as UNOMOZ began its rapid withdrawal from the country, the
underlying architecture of the peace, temporarily veiled by pressing
concerns of political stability and humanitarian intervention, became
more readily apparent. It is within this architecture that Mozambicans
have had to address the social and economic challenges of longer-term
postwar recovery and development.

The Political Economy of the Peace

Although the peace plan was formally implemented in the twenty-four
months between late 1992 and 1994, the underlying structure of Mozambique's peacetime political economy had already begun to take shape
under increasing international pressure from the mid-1980s. In a very
concrete sense, the UN peace operation was solidly embedded in broader
movements towards liberal economic and political reform already underway for some time. Yet the bulk of analysis of the Mozambican transition
has tended either to distinguish between the pre- and post-peace periods,
or to examine economic reforms and the political settlement separately
or, at best, as parallel processes.[28] Such distinctions reinforce the idea,
and especially the practice, of peacebuilding as a rather restricted set of
programmatic interventions, and an essentially limited exercise in political reconciliation and stabilization. Yet by linking the pre- and post-war
processes of economic reform, political transition, and aid delivery more
closely, the notion of peacebuilding in the case of Mozambique becomes
richer and more complex, and considerably more problematic. It suggests a comprehensive approach which would require analysts and practitioners to address issues of peacebuilding from a *developmental*
perspective by including structural factors of postwar order, such as the
composition and function of states and economies, the impact of aid and
investment, the coverage and quality of services, and the structure of
socio-economic opportunities, into the peacebuilding equation.

Economic Adjustment

Mozambique's entry into IMF and World Bank membership in late 1984
and its subsequent implementation of the PRE were initiated under cir-

cumstances of multiple duress. Shortfalls in agricultural production had led to an increase in imports to meet national requirements, producing a trade deficit which constrained the government to seek international financing, primarily from the West. At the same time, strong external pressures combined to reduce Mozambican leverage in negotiating conditions for Western credit and aid. One was a steady decline in economic cooperation with Frelimo's traditional Eastern Bloc and Soviet supporters.[29] Another was the intensification of South African destabilization in the latter 1980s. Finally, strong pressure was brought to bear on Mozambique by potential donors and the international financial institutions to accept assistance in exchange for internal reform commitments.[30]

Central to Mozambique's recovery program was a macro-economic stabilization policy based on standard IMF anti-inflation models. Mozambique's currency was devalued substantially in 1987, and in the ensuing period subsidies to state enterprises were reduced while government price controls on agricultural and other commodities were lifted to stimulate marketed output. In total, the provision of public credit to the productive sectors of the economy was reduced by 66 per cent in the five years after 1990, on the assumption the private sector investment would move in to fill the gap. Debt servicing grew consistently as a percentage of GDP between 1994 and 1997, while new public investments fell. Spending on health and education dropped abruptly as a proportion of the state budget in the first years of PRE implementation, and though later recovering, was kept below 1980–1 levels until well into the mid-1990s.[31]

The initial macro-economic impact of these measures was unclear, since they yielded contradictory results: while GDP growth was consistent in the years 1989-94, inflation nonetheless continued to rise and exchange rates to deteriorate. Likewise, although the value of exports grew steadily, imports grew faster, exacerbating the balance of payments problem and increasing the need for external financial support. Crucially, these mixed outcomes are partially attributable to the foreign assistance entering the country. On one hand, a significant proportion of overall economic growth registered during the period was directly linked to the increasing influx of international aid funds, which, as noted, exceeded GDP by 1993. At the same time, the increasing trade imbalance between 1988 and 1994 has been directly associated with growth in domestic demand for imported consumer goods fuelled by a rapidly swelling expatriate aid community after 1987, a pattern compounded between 1992 and 1994 with the deployment of several thousand highly paid UN staff.

The social impact of stabilization measures was much clearer. In a context of ongoing warfare and increasing resource scarcity, the 1987 devaluations abruptly lowered the value of money against marketed commodities, and in particular against basic commercial imports on which Mozambique was becoming increasingly dependent. Likewise, the reduction of subsidized local production and the easing of price controls acted to push up the price of locally produced goods in urban areas. As a result, average annual price increases by 1989 were ranging between 40 per cent and 50 per cent. Overall purchasing power decreased particularly sharply for Mozambicans on fixed, formal sector incomes. According to one report, 'Between 1989 and 1992, real average salaries fell by eighteen percent and the official minimum wage, the principal source of income for 50 percent of Mozambican workers' families, lost 24 percent of its already low buying power.' As a result, the report adds, the overall economic growth (in GDP) which was registered during the period in fact reflected an increasing maldistribution of wealth in urban centres with potentially destabilizing effects:

> Under current policies ... a rise in wealth for a small strata of Mozambique's elite has taken place against a general deterioration in the living standards of much of the country's urban population. [T]he resulting increase in unemployment and the deteriorating buying power of the majority of Mozambicans have occurred within a framework of increasing petty corruption, violent crime and the potential for significant social turmoil.[32]

In rural areas stabilization likewise appeared to complicate the efforts of communities to cope with the already harsh realities of drought and armed conflict, and also to affect adversely remaining commercial links between town and country. In particular, new price uncertainties resulting from the lifting of government price controls added to existing physical and climatic insecurities, and thus further weakened incentives for farmers to generate and market surplus production. Farmers' terms of trade deteriorated, and the removal of subsidies to the state farm sector caused the overall number of rural wage earners to decline.[33] Indeed, even as GDP began to show strong growth in the late 1990s, the number of Mozambicans affected by absolute poverty grew steadily.[34]

In the face of a measurably deteriorating social situation, anti-inflation measures affected the government's capacity to maintain or expand existing social services, to train new staff, or to raise public sector salaries to reflect inflation, in a manner that would provide incentives for raising the quality of services. On the contrary, the declining value of wages for

health workers and primary educators created the conditions for generalized corruption on the front lines of social service delivery. As Susan
Willet observed in 1995, 'The diminishing ability of the state to provide
even the most basic social services and a safety net eroded the well-being
of individuals.' She specified that while per capita income registered at
only US $80 in 1991, diseases spread rapidly as a result of collapsing pre-
ventive healthcare systems, with often fatal effects for vulnerable social
groups such as children, women, and those displaced by war.[35]

Ultimately, this harsh combination of growing social and humanitarian needs and an increasingly limited margin for the state to meet them,
served to compound the effects of war and to generate new aid requirements. Indeed, both net aid flows and the number of foreign aid personnel in Mozambique rose sharply in the years immediately following
PRE implementation, to become a dominant force in the country's
political economy well prior to the peace. Net overseas development aid
to Mozambique nearly doubled from US $355 million in 1985 to US
$700 million in 1987, the year the structural adjustment was initiated,
and rose further to almost US 1.2 billion by 1993.[36] Along with this
influx of money, Willet notes that between 1989 and 1990 'twenty-six
United Nations agencies were operative in Mozambique, in addition to
six non-United Nations multilateral agencies, forty-four bilateral donors
and 143 non-governmental agencies from twenty-three countries.' By
the time the formal peace agreement was signed in 1992, foreign aid
had already become a structural component of Mozambique's liberalizing economy, with in some instances individual aid programs registering as a visible proportion of the national GDP,[37] and with the aid sector
collectively taking over a wide range of social and humanitarian planning, funding and implementation activities. Doubtless international
aid provided a vital lifeline for hundreds of thousands of Mozambicans
at critical a juncture. However, a virtually organic entrenchment of aid
as a core component of the national economy raised serious questions
about sustainability, while the systematic redirection of aid resources
towards parallel service delivery systems led to fundamental concerns
about the capacity of the state to cope with crisis and manage a coherent
national development agenda over the longer term.[38]

Privatization

Plans and mechanisms for large-scale privatization of the economy were
laid out concurrently with the implementation of the PRE, and began to
function in 1989, at which time three hundred firms, amounting to half

of all enterprises in the country, were under state ownership.[39] In the first five years of the program, some 390 state companies and company sub-units had been wholly or partially privatized. By the end of 1997, the number of privatized state assets, which reached 1,248, had generated over US $200 million in additional revenues to the state, and attracted over US $1 billion in private investments.[40] Given these statistics, the privatization process appears to have been successful. However, specific patterns of privatization need to be examined more carefully for their peacebuilding implications.

First, Mozambique's privatization programme has been dominated by foreign investment, despite the existence of explicit legislative measures to ensure a balanced distribution between foreign and domestic investment opportunities.[41] Official records indicate that a numerical majority of privatized state assets have been sold off to Mozambican investors. In reality, the biggest and economically most influential concerns, representing 62 per cent of the value of privatization by 1994 and 78 per cent by 1997, have been conceded to international consortia dominated primarily by South African, Portuguese, British, and American interests. Moreover, several privatized companies classified as Mozambican in fact represent majority foreign interests fronted by minority Mozambican shareholders and, at any rate, proportionately few Mozambicans of African descent (non-European and non-Asian) have found themselves in a position to participate in, or profit from, the privatization process. Revealingly, the implicit bias against Mozambican investors in the distribution of investment opportunities emerged as a direct result of structural adjustment priorities. Mozambican banking institutions, themselves slated for privatisation by the early 1990s, were strongly encouraged to rationalise their lending practices and consequently became increasingly 'reluctant to give credit to small and medium sized firms where nationals are concentrated.'[42] International investors, by contrast, have retained access to international capital markets, and have therefore been able to participate in privatization at a level and pace with which Mozambicans have been unable to compete.

Second, foreign investment has been disproportionately concentrated in the mineral and energy sectors, as well as communications, tourism, and export-oriented agriculture.[43] These sectors are highly valued by foreign markets, and may in effect be beneficial in integrating Mozambique into the global economy and, more directly, into Southern Africa's regional economic grid. Yet they remain essentially extractive and externally oriented. Comparatively little private investment appears to be supporting the expansion of an autonomous, self-generating and integrated *productive* base in the country, which would potentially stimulate domestic economic production and exchange, expand formal employment, produce higher internal valued-added for export, reduce reliance on imports, generate public revenue, and better insulate post-conflict development from eventual external market disruptions. Investors' preferences for export-oriented market development may provide concrete advantages to immediate stakeholders. However, the degree to which it responds to broader requirements for sustainable and equitable national development remains unclear. Crucially, government measures to help protect and expand the internal production base in the context of privatization have met with stiff responses on the part of the international financial institutions.[44]

A third pattern of privatization which, from the perspective of peace-building, should attract closer attention, relates to land security among Mozambique's majority rural population. In the agricultural sector, privatization has involved the granting of concessions of large expanses of territory to large-scale private interests, as the examples of Lonhro in Cabo Delgado, Lomaco in Gaza, and the 1996 Boer land concessions in Niassa provinces illustrate. Likewise, foreign investments in tourism have involved the transfer of large tracts of coastal territory and natural resources to private corporate control.[45] Statistics on the pace and extent of land privatization are particularly obscure, with estimates for 1994 ranging between four and forty million hectares. The impact of privatization on traditional systems of land tenure, and on subsistence and income-generating opportunities, remains a contested issue.[46] Some studies have suggested that private land management by large, reliable companies may be vital in reducing families' dependence on subsistence agriculture by providing supplementary wage incomes, and should thus be considered as part of a strategy for long-term rural poverty alleviation. Others, by contrast, have found that land access will continue, for the foreseeable future, to offer the best guarantee of independent survival, particularly among the poorer segments of the rural population. The land issue, and the politics of land concession, continue to generate some of the most contentious political debates of the post-conflict period, informed at least in part 'by voices of protest emerging from the countryside.' Given the importance of land access for socio-economic stability, particularly among war-affected groups (like resettled refugees and demobilized soldiers) which have been encouraged by aid programs to reintegrate into the rural economy, the complex effects of land privatization stand as a priority peacebuilding issue. With few exceptions, however, land has received comparatively little attention within the mainstream of peacebuilding research initiatives.

Fourth, no less than 82 per cent of the foreign direct investment which privatization attracted to Mozambique between 1989 and 1997 has been concentrated into the single province of Maputo at the extreme south of the country. Historically, superior infrastructure and services, and links to dynamic markets in South Africa, have long been attractive to foreign investment. Pitcher's study of privatization patterns also suggests that the disproportionately high flow of investment to Maputo is related to the location there of sympathetic state ministries, political groupings, and other 'insider' decision-making clusters with material connections to the privatization process. Though understandable from the perspective of both international and domestic capital, such uneven patterns of investment may serve to accentuate existing regional socio-economic differences in the country, thus working contrary to the presumed integrative effects of privatization, and possibly also amplifying divisive sub-national identities in marginalized areas of the centre and north.

Finally, privatization appears to have had a direct effect on the public role and integrity of the state, particularly on leading groups within the state apparatus most exposed to the process and best positioned to profit by it. With the launching of the program in 1989, Frelimo decreed that state and party officials could accumulate capital, and that there would be no limit to the number of workers they could employ privately. Although officials were required to report private earnings to the Departments of Planning and Finance, the latter would not be required to disclose them publicly. The practical effect of these measures was to release well-positioned officials from their exclusive obligations to the state, and to connect them materially to the liberalization process. In the event, senior public officials and ranking military staff have been able to use the influence of office in order to acquire significant shares in privatized companies, board memberships, and lucrative land concessions for themselves and their entourage, and to strengthen clientelistic networks with lower ranking officialdom and former political opponents.[48]

The implications of this process, in terms of state probity and responsibility, are alarming. In two recent studies on the political and institutional aspects of liberalization in Mozambique, Graham Harrison has argued that macro-economic adjustment and privatization have combined to produce a powerful enabling environment for entrenched corruption at all levels of public administration. He suggests that the turbulent socio-economic changes in the late 1980s and 1990s, combined with 'an increasingly assertive discourse which proclaimed the benefits of private enterprise,' have provided high and low ranking officials alike with positive material and normative incentives to engage in corrupt practices. The wider social implications are perhaps equally worrying, as local opportunity structures under an increasingly 'privatized' peace appear to be organically linked to existing power hierarchies within and around the state. Corruption, Harrison warns, 'has become a key component of Mozambique's democratic politics, and it has led to a salient erosion in the legitimacy of the state and the political elite more generally.'[49]

Decentralization

Moves to decentralize public administration have been another important feature of the peacetime political economy. Launched early in the postwar period, they have been justified in terms of better government accountability, higher sensitivity towards local needs, and higher administrative efficiency and flexibility. The direct election of 533 municipal or district councils has been promoted as a means to strengthen community participation in the policy process, and ensure representation by competing local interests. Both processes are ongoing, and together would eventually devolve wide-ranging responsibilities to local authorities.[50]

Mozambique's decentralization measures to date have been strongly supported by donors and the international financial institutions, both in terms of funding and technical advice. At the same time, decentralization remains a highly sensitive domestic issue. The process is viewed with circumspection by many within the ruling Frelimo regime whose power is solidly entrenched in the centralized state apparatus. For Frelimo, decentralization involves a step towards de facto political power-sharing with the former rebel force, a trend which the government has resisted since the outset of the peace negotiations. Not surprisingly, the process has been warmly embraced by the Renamo opposition party as a mechanism to formalize its position in areas, especially rural districts in the centre of the country, where it enjoys strong political support.[51] And indeed, some observers have speculated that international support for decentralization has reflected, among other objectives, 'a wish to tilt the balance of power toward Renamo and "power-sharing" between the two parties, and to circumvent Frelimo power over aid flows.'[52]

The potential benefits of decentralization, in terms of democratic accountability and responsiveness to local needs, are indeed real and could contribute significantly to the quality of the peacetime political economy. However, several observers have pointed out practical risks and warned against the potentially undesired consequences of an accelerated decentralization process in a context of acute state weakness, resource scarcity, and a persistent human capacity deficit. First, critics have highlighted the disparity between the required increase in local administrative responsibilities and the chronically low technical and management resources outside the main urban centres. In resource-poor areas, this may work to widen the gap between public expectations and actual outcomes, thereby accentuating local frustrations, de-legitimizing local authorities, and possibly polarising local politics. Second, observers have wondered about the financial viability of newly empowered local authorities, given a tax base which is extremely restricted or difficult to access, and indeed virtually non-existent in the poorer regions of the country. Decentralization could reinforce, rather than allay, socio-economic differences between those areas able to afford and provide adequate social services, and those which, on the contrary, might see the quality and level of services decline because of a low resource base. Third, political economists have raised the issue of potential 'resource-capture' by local elites benefiting from weakened central authority, and the possible formation of new local power clusters of variable legitimacy and political design. This concern is especially salient where transport and communication links are poor, where weapons circulate with relative freedom, where there are high concentrations of repatriated and demobilized groups, or where there is a historical potential for alternative political projects, possibly hostile to the current peace settlement, to gather momentum. Finally, some have questioned the democratic value of decentralization in the context of a highly internationalized and aid-dependent state, arguing that the process conveys an appearance of power-sharing with lower levels of government, while in actual fact national decision-making authority has been consistently transferred to outside actors.[53]

Because of their importance to long-term stability and development, such considerations should place decentralization squarely within a more comprehensive agenda of peacebuilding research, analysis and strategy formulation. For the moment, despite ongoing uncertainties about the future political and social implications of decentralization, the process will likely continue, under strong international pressures, to be a centrepiece of state restructuring in Mozambique.

Pluralization

The onset of formal political pluralism in Mozambique can be traced to changes in the nation's political climate as far back as 1987. The unexpected death of Samora Machel, a Frelimo founding member and first president of Mozambique, was followed by cabinet changes designed to Africanize the upper reaches of the political leadership – a measure that was seen at the time as moving some way towards democratizing the party structure as a whole. In the same year the party's mass organizations were given autonomy to engage in independent revenue-generating and recruitment activities. Other early signs of liberalization included an opening of the government towards church activities in the country, including those of the Catholic church which had hitherto been marginalized by the socialist project. Previously confiscated church property was returned, and in 1988 church organizations were allowed access to publication and distribution facilities. Also in 1989, Mozambique ratified the African Charter of Human and Peoples' Rights, and began consultations with church groups on the codification of religious freedoms. The late 1980s also saw a gradual withdrawal of overtly socialist vocabulary from key party statutes and policy documents, with a new official language emphasizing free association, civil and minority rights, and decentralization. The 1990 revision of Mozambique's constitution reflected a definitive move towards a fundamentally liberal understanding of the state, and a legal disengagement of its functions from core socialist objectives. The new text paved the way for the legalization of political parties and the rapid expansion of civil sector activities.

Mozambique's first postwar elections provided both the motivating drive and the first practical test of *political* pluralization. And indeed, the years between 1990 and 1994 saw the emergence of a dozen new alternative political groupings claiming to represent a broad range of positions outside of the Frelimo purview. For planners of the peace, the elections also reflected two other strategic objectives: to prompt the conversion of Renamo from a fighting force to a genuine political party, and to secure wide public endorsement for the peace settlement. As noted, the election appeared to succeed on both of these strategic counts, despite heightened tensions and recurring political setbacks. The vote in 1994 was contested by fifteen duly registered political parties, with a turn-out of nearly 90 per cent of eligible voters. Importantly, both leading parties accepted the results of the poll, avoiding Angola's fate, and signalling their commitment to a plural-democratic system.

On the surface at least, subsequent electoral rounds would indicate that this commitment has held over time. In mid-1998 thirty-three municipalities were democratically contested as part of an initial round of political decentralization. In December 1999 a second round of national presidential and legislative elections was completed, despite reported technical difficulties, to the general satisfaction of international observers and local monitoring groups. With some variations in local polling results, Frelimo and Renamo held their respective positions in government and opposition, and both gained a marginal increase in votes at the expense of the minor political parties. However, beneath the apparent success of Mozambique's new liberal democratic process there has emerged a sobering trend of declining voter participation. The 1998 elections in particular were notable for an overall voter abstention rate of over 85 per cent, with balloting dipping below 10 per cent of registered voters in some cities.[54] The higher-profile national elections of 1999, though better organized, better supervised and perhaps more extensively publicised, nonetheless attracted only 68 per cent of eligible voters, 20 per cent less than in 1994.

The reasons for declining voter turnout have received relatively little analytical attention. Media headlines and opinion polls have reported growing levels of voter apathy among urban Mozambicans, resulting in part from a disillusionment 'with politics and politicians'[55] and a perception of leaders' lack of concern for, or inability to address, pressing socio-economic problems. In rural areas, a 1997 survey of ex-combatants in central Mozambique has indicated growing dissatisfaction with the democratic system. Specifically, the survey found a growing gap between initial expectations about the potential for democracy to enhance socio-economic opportunities on one hand, and, on the other hand, the ongoing hardships of rural life in the post-electoral period. Many rural Mozambicans had been led to identify voting with job-creation, higher wages, stable prices, and more aid projects, few of which have actually materialised.[56]

At another level, rising apathy may be explained by the fact that democracy in Mozambique was designed from the outset to reflect overriding, top-down concerns for immediate post-conflict stability. Harrison has highlighted the irony of an electoral system established in a highly undemocratic environment of closed-door negotiations conducted in distant countries and dominated by national and international elite interests. Multiparty elections, he suggests, were very much agreed upon in 1992 as an acceptable political formula for putting an end to a war that neither side was able to continue fighting. It had rather less to do with creating new opportunities for Mozambicans to participate in shaping the country's political and economic future.[57] Others, like Saul, have argued that the parameters for political competition in postwar Mozambique are, too highly restricted to be associated with any meaningful concept of democracy. Party platforms have been, at their core, identical in their commitment to liberalization since before the 1994 elections, by which time 'any immediate prospect of political contestation over alternative socio-economic visions had been effectively sidelined.' Real decision-making power rests in the hands of international financial institutions, aid agencies and 'a particularly aggressive band of...multinationals' while the state, though 'democratized,' remains relatively powerless to address the concerns of voters. In this context, party competition, the theoretical motor of political pluralism, has assumed a primarily cosmetic function. Indeed, as Carrie Manning recently noted, many political parties in Mozambique appear to have interpreted democratic pluralism in primarily opportunistic terms of acquiring 'offices, houses for party representatives ... office equipment, cars ... and sufficient patronage resources.'[58]

It may perhaps still be a matter of debate whether this situation merely represents a transitional stage towards a more meaningful democratic politics in Mozambique at some future point, or whether it reflects the permanent entrenchment of a rather minimalist form of democracy. However, given ongoing social hardship under the pressures of accelerated liberalization, and an increasingly apparent failure of the party system to generate opportunities for Mozambicans to articulate their grievances and see them translated into policy, it comes as no surprise that public apathy towards the democratic formula has increased in recent years. This has led Sogge, among several commentators, to wonder whether 'formal political processes can retain sufficient credibility and legitimacy' in the future.[59]

Alongside the introduction of a new framework for political competition, Mozambique's postwar transition has been marked by a virtual explosion of independent associational life, the so-called *sociedade civil.* The number of known local NGOs multiplied tenfold to some three hundred in the 1991–4 period, and has since perhaps doubled. Civil groups today represent a wide range of social, economic, professional, and cultural interests, and have increasingly expanded their networks outside of the main urban centres into many peri-urban and some rural areas. They provide public services, raise awareness on issues of general public concern (AIDS, family planning, human rights) and promote special interests (vulnerable groups, veterans, women, business groups). During the emergency and immediate post-conflict reconstruction periods, local organizations became an instrumental component of humanitarian aid delivery, serving both as local logistical agents and, to some extent also, as 'societal' intermediaries between international aid agencies and local communities.

In theory, civil society performs several strategic functions to facilitate transitions from war to peace. By further pluralizing social landscapes, new civic groups help to break the grip of wartime affiliations and to provide peaceful alternatives for social organization and mobilization. Likewise, civil society is expected to deepen democracy by strengthening institutional channels between the state and the broader national society. Finally, because it operates within an independent web of transnational organizational and information networks, civil society is regarded as a vehicle for the normative and material dynamics of globalization to be transmitted and become operative inside post-conflict environments.

As such, civil society development has been a central priority of international aid agencies engaging in humanitarian relief and postwar reconstruction programs in Mozambique. During the UN peace operation, an overall average of 35 per cent of humanitarian funds (amounting to over US $365 million) was channelled into the civil sector. Between 1993 and 1996, USAID spent US $76 million on special programs for 'democracy, governance and civil society development,' and another US $80 million between 1990 and 1996 on a Private Voluntary Organization (PVO) support program aimed at 'multiplying and broadening the opportunities for involvement by Mozambicans at all levels of economic, social and political development activities.'[60] The European Union delegation in 1996 included 'strengthening of the role of civil society organizations within the transition' as one of the three pillars of its country assistance strategy, and directing funding to local organizations under the European Commission Rehabilitation Program more than tripled between 1994 and 1997. Of the twelve European Union donor countries in Mozambique, nine operated specific budget lines for local NGOs in 1997.[61] The World Bank has operated a NGO liaison unit since 1995 to provide advisory support to local organizations, and has coordinated a program through government ministries to build public servants' capacity to work more closely with the local NGO community.[62] For their part, many major international NGOs became engaged in local funding initiatives in the 1990s, and began applying various civil society support strategies, including capacity-building schemes, promotional conferences, and 'civil society replication' activities in rural areas.

Yet, in practice, postwar civil society development in Mozambique has been hesitant. First, national organizations have virtually no local resource base to meet operational costs and fund new initiatives on their own. Local charity contributions have been negligible and prospects for state support are slim, given limits on public expenditure imposed by structural adjustment. The civil sector has thus been largely aid-driven, and, like the state itself, has found itself in a situation of acute external dependence. The organizational survival or growth of local civil groups has depended primarily on their ability to tap into the 'aid market' on a competitive basis, mainly by adhering to international aid priorities and project objectives. Many civil society organizations have thus been drawn closer to donors than to the local constituencies they claim to represent, and their 'participatory' value has clearly suffered as a result. In light of this, any claims to the spontaneous emergence of a genuine, independent civil society in postwar Mozambique must be highly qualified.

Second, most Mozambican civil associations have remained highly averse to coordinating their efforts with government authorities. This is explained partly by lingering suspicions about the Frelimo state's historical tendency to impose central control over the civil sector, and by a genuine desire of each group to maintain organizational independence and establish its identity. It is also due, in no small part, to the neo-liberal climate in which international support for civil society was delivered throughout the 1990s. Aversion to government has had the effect of reproducing and reinforcing the links between civil society and external agencies. It has worked against the potential for civil society organizations to channel grass-roots interests and grievances to appropriate ministries, and slowed the creation of potentially valuable operational partnerships between state and society in important areas of post-conflict development.

Third, aid dependence has strongly influenced the style and content of local civil organizations. Following many of their international counterparts, local groups have adopted a predominantly time-limited, project-based approach to their work, with comparatively little interest in long-term national development strategies appropriately informed by local knowledge and practice. As a result, the potential for local organizations to assist communities to address collectively the serious structural challenges and contradictions of the liberal peace has remained weak. Likewise, while an overriding emphasis on bricks-and-mortar reconstruction projects has provided the immediate, high-profile results required for good donor relations, it has worked against the development of important 'soft' capacities within civil society, including the capacity for organizations to identify, analyse, and mobilize effectively around issues of collective concern.[63]

Pluralization of the political and social landscapes in Mozambique has opened up new organizational spaces for Mozambicans to engage more fully in national political and economic development. Yet by the end of the 1990s, the effect of Mozambique's new political pluralism in creating and distributing concrete opportunities for genuine political expression, social mobilization, and eventual material progress remained unclear. As Manning has recently noted, little attention seems to be given to the current performance and transformational potential of political parties, beyond their capacity periodically to (re)surface and compete at election time. As for civil society, it is appropriate to recall the cautionary point, recently made by Chabal and Daloz, that its rapid growth may, more than anything else, simply reflect Mozambique's institutional adjustment to the changing structure of aid flows: 'The explosion in the number of NGOs is not a reflection of the flowering of civil society in the sense in which it is understood in the West. It is in reality (rather than fiction) evidence of the adaptation by African political actors to the changing complexion of the international aid agenda.'[64]

Assessing the Dividend

Clearly, the above discussion cannot lead to any conclusive evaluation of what amounts to well over a decade of efforts to build peace in Mozambique. However, my cursory review of the main processes of political and economic change since the mid-1980s points to several considerations that would require urgent attention by both analysts and practitioners of peacebuilding.

The potent combination of economic adjustment, privatization, decentralization and pluralization has transformed Mozambique's political economy landscape in fundamental ways. It is far from clear, however, that these changes augur well for peaceful, balanced and sustained development in the country. First, although state weakness or collapse is now generally accepted as an important cause or amplifier of civil violence and developmental failure in Sub-Saharan Africa, there is little indication that the processes discussed above have served in any way to re-capacitate the state. On the contrary, Mozambique in 1992–7 remained one of the most indebted countries in the world. Debt financing has consumed on average over half of the annual government budget, which remains heavily dependent on new international lending. Despite recent debt relief measures, the government continues to pay some $1.4 million per day in servicing costs.[65] Strict limits on public spending, imposed jointly by the international debt burden and by aggressive anti-inflation measures, have curbed capital investments in the social sectors and in infrastructure, both of which continue to depend on international grant aid. The state's capacity to plan and manage a national development agenda has been further eroded, as we have seen, by a transfer of concrete decision-making authority to official international agencies, an increasing concession of social and territorial power to private corporate interests, and a fragmentation of the public realm into myriad localized, uncoordinated and often unaccountable NGO projects. The not so tacit acceptance of high-level and petty corruption as a necessary evil of liberalization threatens to combine with recent decentralization initiatives to produce new centres of private power based on local clientelism and profiteering.

Equally crucial, the emerging structure of socio-economic opportunity under the peace does not seem to have favoured the majority of Mozambicans. Living conditions for large segments of population have remained extremely difficult since the end of the war, and have deteriorated in some cases. Despite peace, much aid, and impressive growth, Mozambique continued to rank towards the very bottom of the 1999 UNDP Human Development Index (169th out of 174 countries). Between 1996 and 2000, the number of Mozambicans living in absolute poverty increased by one million, according to the government's own estimates. At the end of the 1990s, 70 per cent of Mozambicans lacked access to healthcare services, while only 39 per cent of the population could expect to live beyond forty years of age. Overall adult illiteracy hovered at some 60 per cent (75 per cent for women), and under-five child mortality stood at over 21 per cent.[66] What immediate social gains were achieved during the UN peace operation do not appear to have been coherently followed up, and seem increasingly susceptible to pressures for accelerated liberalization. Outside of a semi-predatory informal market and some NGO programs, credit for Mozambicans, essential to revitalizing the country's rural economy and manufacturing base, has been largely unavailable. Rapid privatization and restructuring of public sector companies have eliminated several thousands of industrial jobs, while few Mozambicans seemed positioned to take advantage of the opportunities at hand. As a result, privatized assets have become increasingly concentrated in non-Mozambican hands.

A local entrepreneurial middle class, a key component of liberalization, has been slow to emerge due to adverse economic pressures. Real incomes for most people have fallen consistently, while prices on basic consumer commodities have risen, hitting the salaried middle classes especially hard and forcing many to seek additional income through illicit secondary markets or, more seriously, through generalized corruption. The elimination of minimum price thresholds as part of liberalization, and a tendency towards monopoly buying by city traders, have meant that rural terms of trade have steadily declined since the turn of the decade, requiring farmers to produce almost twice the quantity of crops to buy the same basket of goods, thus leading to their de facto impoverishment. The vulnerability of rural populations to external shocks, including global market fluctuations and natural calamities, remains high.

Many have warned, privately and publicly, of the potential for renewed instability and social conflict in the country. Violent crime rose dramatically in the years after the General Peace Accord, mainly as a result of urban and rural impoverishment, high unemployment, a wide circulation of weapons and, ironically, better geographical mobility brought on by the peace. At the same time, public security became increasingly compromised by low police salaries and systematic judiciary corruption. Although a return to war along old lines is unlikely, chronic social distress and a criminalization of substantial parts of Mozambique's post-war political economy appeared, by the latter 1990s, to have become the norm. A mid-1996 monitoring survey conducted by the Organization for International Migration identified twenty-five districts, including principal urban centres, to be 'at high risk of instability' and another thirty-four districts as 'warning situations.'[67] Organized armed movements were widely reported to be active in remote parts of Mozambique in 1996, in some cases with cross-border connections into neighbouring countries, and may begin to acquire a local ethnic territorial base rooted in material discontent.[68] At the end of 1996, the country director of a major international NGO issued a cautionary warning against the emergence of a 'lawless society where the only things that rule are money and guns,'[69] and in 1997 Sogge reflected on the status of the peace with visible unease:

> This is after all, a country where the social fabric has been badly torn; where many have lost assets while few accumulate them; where criminal mafias, apparently in collaboration with corrupt officials, operate with a free hand; where future prospects for a youthful population are not bright; where the advent of conspicuous consumption by new elites clashes daily with frustrated aspirations of poor majorities (and perhaps, more dangerously, with the frustrated aspirations of downwardly-mobile classes); and where small arms circulate in great numbers.[70]

Indeed, as recently as May 2000, former Renamo combatants in Zambezia reportedly began forming 'brigades who are creating disturbances in various parts of the province,' attacking local police stations and administrative posts and leading to violent confrontations in several districts.[71]

Meanwhile, Mozambique's new political parties and civil society organizations seem ill equipped, for the time being at least, to perform independently the stabilizing or progressive functions normally associated with liberal democratic blueprints. With few exceptions, their capacity to identify and analyse urgent problems in terms that are relevant to their constituents, to bring overarching socio-economic issues to the top of national and international decision-making agendas, to stimulate meaningful debate over the merits of current, versus alternative, development agendas, and especially to forge wider, more inclusive socio-economic opportunity structures over the longer term, remains weak.

There is no question that the political settlement between warring parties has been felt throughout the country. The General Peace Agreement and the costly UN operation implemented in support of it were successful in bringing one of the African continent's most destructive and drawn-out civil wars to a conclusive end. Apart from repatriation, demilitarization, and the establishment of democracy, vital transport and energy networks have been restored while internal trade, travel and communications between town and country have revived. Agricultural production cycles are no longer at risk of military or political disruption while a generalized desire for socio-economic normalization has prompted thousands of displaced communities to revive local economic systems and engage in peaceful subsistence activities. Yet for most people, the peace dividend in Mozambique is under sustained pressure from structural constraints on human and social security.

Implications for Peacebuilding

A central purpose of this discussion has been to call attention to structural changes as important, if not critical, factors for consideration by the peacebuilding community. Though it does not purport to provide any definitive conclusions, my review of the Mozambican experience raises a number of questions not normally considered by peacebuilding analysis, but which nonetheless carry profound implications relating to the long-term social outcomes of post-conflict recovery and, as such, to the quality and durability of peace. By raising these concerns in a very preliminary manner, it is hoped that they might inform discussions on the future priorities and orientations of international peacebuilding programmes.

In a general way, the limits of the current peacebuilding agenda must urgently be addressed. It needs to be recognized that the idea of peace-building is largely a by-product of humanitarian experiences of the 1990s. As such, peacebuilding initiatives have been firmly, perhaps unavoidably, lodged in the logic of short-term humanitarian crisis man-agement, reflecting priorities which, though increasingly complex, are rarely geared towards issues of structural change. Although the language of peacebuilding has often referred to such themes as structural stability and long-term institutional recovery, it remains in practice difficult to prioritize such developmental objectives in the midst of rapidly evolving emergency interventions.[72] Yet if peacebuilding is to begin to address larger questions of postwar development that extend beyond immediate concerns for rapid political stabilization, its conceptual parameters must be expanded. Those involved in the design of peace interventions should consider lengthening time horizons and widening the range of issues to be included in the peacebuilding equation. With a more com-prehensive approach in mind, at least three core questions should be addressed.

First, despite growing evidence that liberalization policies can signifi-cantly complicate national postwar recovery and development, they nonetheless continue to be applied, apparently with increasing oppor-tunism and sophistication, in several current post-conflict settings.[73] Peacebuilding analysis must begin to focus, critically and with a view to a pragmatic assessment, on the objective merits and dangers of acceler-ated liberalization as an underlying framework for post-conflict renewal in war-torn economies.

Second, prevailing assumptions about the role of states in post-con-flict settings need to be reconsidered. Although chronic state weakness and state collapse have been associated with civil war, current strategies for post-conflict recovery do not appear to address the problem coher-ently. On the contrary, recovery strategies such as the creation of non-state social service systems, privatization, and decentralization poten-tially aggravate problems of public sector capacity and integrity, and consequently of state legitimacy. To avoid situations of long-term or per-manent collapse, renewed efforts to restore the technical and political authority of governing institutions must stand as a core peacebuilding priority. Related assumptions about the role of the non-state sector, or civil society, should be reviewed accordingly.

Finally, if peacebuilding is to contribute to meaningful social cohesion and the prevention of future tensions, it must balance its concern for formal transitional *processes* with a stronger focus on concrete *outcomes*, particularly as they affect the redistribution of benefits and opportunities among the majority of war-affected populations. To the extent that social progress is recognized as a factor of long-term stability, better monitoring and analysis of social outcomes could sensitize managers of post-conflict transitions to potential points of deterioration and eventual tensions, and to inform policy adjustments accordingly.

NOTES

1 Graham Harrison, 'Clean-ups, Conditionality and Adjustment: Why Institutions Matter in Mozambique,' *Review of African Political Economy* 81 (1999), 324–8.

2 John Saul, 'Inside from the Outside? The Roots and Resolution of Mozambique's Un/Civil War,' in Taisier Ali and Robert O. Matthews, eds., *Civil Wars in Africa: Roots and Resolution* (Montreal and Kingston: McGill-Queen's University Press, 1999), 123–6.

3 Tom Young and Margaret Hall, *Confronting Leviathan: Mozambique since Independence* (London: Hurst and Co., 1997), 3–11.

4 Ibid., 50. Also see Hans Abrahamsson, *Seizing the Opportunity: Power and Powerlessness in a Changing World Order. The Case of Mozambique* (Gothenburg: Pardigu Papers, 1997), 208.

5 Abrahamsson, *Seizing the Opportunity* 209; Malyn Newitt, *A History of Mozambique* (London: Hurst & Co., 1995), 498.

6 Young and Hall, *Confronting Levialtran*, 55.

7 Ibid., 61–8.

8 Ibid., 95.

9 See John Saul, 'Rethinking the Frelimo State,' *Socialist Register* (London: Merlin, 1993), 139–65.

10 *Mozambique Peace Process Bulletin* 14 (February 1995); William Minter, *Apartheid's Contras: An Enquiry into the Roots of War in Angola and Mozambique* (London: Zed Books, 1994), 39–55.

11 See, most notably, Christian Geffray, *La cause des armes au Mozambique: Anthropologies d'une guerre civile* (Paris: Karthala, 1990).

12 Minter, *Apartheid's Contras*, 205–17; see also Otto Roesch, 'Renamo and the Peasantry in Southern Mozambique: A View from Gaza Province,' *Canadian Journal of African Studies* 26, no. 3 (1992).

13 Olaf Juergensen, *The United Nations Come to the Hinterland: Peacebuilding and*

Reconstruction in Mozambique (Ottawa: IDRC Peacebuilding and Reconstruction Programme Initiative Working Paper No. 2 (1998), 11 (published on www.idrc.ca).

14 Minter, *Apartheid's Contras*, 134–40; 155–9, and 185–99.

15 Abrahamsson, *Seizing the Opportunity*, 217.

16 Young and Hall, *Confronting Levialtran*, 196; Joseph Hanlon, *Mozambique: Who Calls the Shots?* (London: James Currey, 1991), 267–8.

17 David Plank, 'Aid Debt and the End of Sovereignty: Mozambique and Its Donors,' *Journal of Modern African Studies* 31, no. 3 (1993), 410.

18 Young and Hall, *Confronting Levialtran*, 196–7.

19 UNDP 1994–95 Report, 'Development Co-operation: Mozambique' (Maputo: June 1996).

20 On the role of the churches, see Alex Vines and Ken Wilson, 'Churches and the Peace Process in Mozambique' (conference paper presented at University of Leeds, September 1993). For more general reviews of the peace talks, see Moises Venancio and Stephen Chan, ' Roman Talks' in Chan and Venancio, eds., *War and Peace in Mozambique* (London: Macmillan, 1998); Chris Alden and Mark Simpson, 'Mozambique: A Delicate Peace,' *Journal of Modern African Studies* 31, no. 1 (1993).

21 See Sam Barnes, *NGOs in Peacekeeping Operations: Their Role in Mozambique* (paper presented at the 9th Annual ACUNS Meeting, Turin, June 1996).

22 See Richard Synge, *Mozambique: UN Peacekeeping in Action 1992–94* (Washington: United States Institute of Peace, 1997); and Chris Alden, 'The UN and the Resolution of Conflict in Mozambique,' *Journal of Modern African Studies* 33, no. 1 (1995).

23 UNHCR, 'Rebuilding a War-Torn Society: A Review of the UNHCR Reintegration Programme for Mozambican Returnees.' (Maputo, 1996), 3–12.

24 Synge, *Mozambique*, 98–102; Chris Alden, 'The United Nations, Elections and the Resolution of Conflict in Mozambique,' in Chan and Venancio, eds., *War and Peace in Mozambique*, 82–7.

25 The number of troops wishing to join the new armed forces was significantly lower than the thirty thousand anticipated. See Synge, *Mozambique*, 104–8.

26 Cash incentives were likewise used to influence the Renamo leadership. Richard Synge reports that Renamo leader Afonso Dhlakama received monthly cash payments of US $300.000 for a period of thirteen months, beginning in September 1993, from a UN trust fund (*Mozambique*, 59–60).

27 Synge (*Mozambique*, 72–3) records the debate that occurred during the planning phases of the demobilization program between UNOHAC chief Bernt Bernander and some bilateral donors. Bernander had initially argued for a developmentalist strategy of 'reintegrating the demobilized into civilian soci-

ety over a number of years' in conformity with 'a macro-economic frame-work.' By contrast, the United States and other donors were concerned with immediate political stabilisation, a position which quickly prevailed over that of UNOHAC.

28 Notable exceptions include Joseph Hanlon, *Peace without Profit: How the IMF Blocks Rebuilding in Mozambique* (London: James Currey, 1996); Abrahamsson, *Seizing the Opportunity*, and Susan Willet, 'Ostriches, Wise Old Elephants and Economic Reconstruction in Mozambique,' *International Peacekeeping* 2, no. 1 (1995).

29 Hanlon reports a steady decrease of socialist bloc development assistance from 1984 onwards.

30 Ibid., 16–17.

31 Ibid., 57–60, 30; UNDP Mozambique Country Report Report (Maputo: June 1996), 4–14.

32 Oxfam UK/I, *A Preliminary Study of the Impact of Structural Adjustment and the Current State of the Health and Education Sectors in Mozambique* (Maputo: Oxfam UK/I, 1995), 13.

33 Merle Bowen, 'Beyond Reform: Adjustment and Political Power in Contemporary Mozambique,' *The Journal of Modern African Studies* 30, no. 2 (1992), 264–5. On rural 'terms of trade' see Hanlon, *Peace without profit*, 154–6; and Hans Abrahamsson and Anders Nilsson, *The Washington Consensus e Moçambique* (Gothenburg: Pardigu, 1996), 59–60.

34 Government of Mozambique, 'Interim Poverty Reduction Strategy Paper' (Maputo, February 2000), 82.

35 Willet, 'Ostriches, Wise Old Elephants,' 40–1.

36 OECD/DAC, 'ODA Receipts and Selected Indicators for Developing Countries and Territories,' 1999.

37 In 1991 aid contributions by the top twenty non-governmental organizations operating in Mozambique amounted to almost 7 per cent of the national GDP.

38 Aid agency reports clearly show the degree of sectoral fragmentation which took place during the peace transition. For example, under one single European Commission rehabilitation budget line, 112 separate projects were implemented by 72 different NGOs between 1994 and 1997. Taken together, the fifteen members of the European Union financed 694 separately managed projects across all sectors in 1996–7. Between 1992 and 1996, UNHCR employed fifty NGOs to implement of 1,571 different relief and rehabilitation projects.

39 Anne Pitcher, 'Recreating Colonialism or Reconstructing the State? Privatisation and Politics in Mozambique,' *Journal of Southern African Studies* 22, no. 4 (1996).

40 Unidade Tecnica para a Restruturaçao das Empresas (UTRE), 'Privatisation in Mozambique, 1998: Consolidating the Gains' (Maputo: Ministry of Planning and Finance, Information Bulletin No. 5, March 1998).

41 The UTRE bulletin states that foreign direct investment to Mozambique amounted to US $1 billion at the end of 1997, compared to 287 million in national direct investment.

42 Pitcher, 1996, pp. 9-11; 'Recreating Colonization,' 9–11, 15; Hanlon, *Peace without Profit*, 78, 58–9.

43 UTRE, 'Privatization in Mozambique,' 4. In 1997 negotiations were underway for two extractive mega-projects (gas and iron ore) involving a US $2.2 billion bid led by a single US corporation. Likewise, US $750 million project for coal extraction, involving South African and Australian investors, was under consideration, as was an US $800 million tourism project submitted by another American group. Together, these three foreign investment bids amount to almost four times the value of total foreign direct investment between 1990 and 1997.

44 See Joseph Hanlon, 'Power without Responsibility: The World Bank and Mozambican Cashew Nuts,' *Review of African Political Economy* 83 (2000); and Hanlon, *Peace without Profit*, 34–37. Also see AIM/Mozambique News Agency Bi-Monthly Report (No.181), 17 April 2000.

45 As Sogge points out in the case of one international tourist operator: 'management of virtually the entire coastline from Inhaca Island to the South African border has been awarded to a U.S. businessman with designs for a tourism empire.' See David Sogge, 'Decentralisation' in David Sogge, ed., *Mozambique: Perspective on Aid and the Civil Sector* (Amsterdam: Gemeenschappelijk Overleg Medefinanciering, 1997), 92.

46 Anne Pitcher, 'What's Missing from "What's Missing"? A Reply to C. Cramer and N. Pontara, "Rural Poverty and Poverty Alleviation in Mozambique: What's Missing from the Debate,"' *Journal of Modern African Studies* 37, no. 4 (1999), 703. What studies do exist appear to rely on localized surveys in diverse areas of the country.

47 See Christopher Cramer and Nicola Pontara's 'A Reply to Pitcher,' *Journal of Modern African Studies* 37, no. 4 (1999), 712–22.

48 Pitcher, 'Recreating Colonisation,' 13; Hanlon, *Peace without Profit*, 79–80.

49 Graham Harrison, 'Corruption as Boundary Politics: the State, Democratisation and Mozambique's Unstable Liberalisation,' *Third World Quarterly* 20, no. 3 (1999), 542, 547. In a separate article, Harrison notes that elite corruption in Mozambique is presently tolerated by donors as a form of 'opportunity cost' for ongoing liberalization ('Cleaning-ups, Conditionality and Adjustment,' 328).

50 These would cover public utilities, policing, commercial licensing, housing, primary education, health care, and other public services, which would be financed on the basis of local taxation.
51 National electoral results in 1994 showed overwhelming support for Renamo in Sofala, Manica, Tete and Zambezia provinces, but were not reflected in subsequent government nominations to administrative positions in those areas. See UNRISD War Torn Societies Project, *Imagem do Pais* (Maputo: Institute for International and Security Studies, 1996).
52 Sogge, *Mozambique*, 99.
53 For an overview of these and contrasting positions, see ibid., 93–103.
54 AIM Bi-Monthly Report No. 139, 20 July 1998.
55 Ibid No. 138, 13 July 1998.
56 Chris Dolan and Jessica Shafer, *The Reintegration of Ex-Combatants in Mozambique: Manica and Zambezia Provinces. Final Report to USAID* (Oxford Refugee Studies Group, 1997), 153–70.
57 Graham Harrison, 'Democracy in Mozambique: The Significance of Multiparty Elections,' *Review of African Political Economy* 67 (March 1996), 20–2.
58 Saul, 'Inside from the Outside?' 154–5. Also see Joseph Hanlon 'Its the IMF that Runs Mozambique' in Sogge, *Mozambique*, 17–37; Carrie Manning, 'Constructing Opposition in Mozambique: Renamo as Political Party,' *Journal of Southern African Studies* 24, no. 1 (1998), 189.
59 Sogge, *Mozambique*, 102.
60 USAID, 'Assistance to Mozambique' (Maputo, 1996); interview with Director, Democratic Initiatives Project, USAID, Maputo, October 1996; Louis Helling, *PVOs and Local Institutions in Mozambican Rural Development: Identifying Strategies for Sustainability and Effectiveness. A Pre-Design Study for PVO Support II Project* (Maputo: USAID, 1994).
61 European Commission, 'Evaluation of Rehabilitation Programmes in Mozambique,' Maputo, 1998, 20. The overall average of direct funding to local direct NGOs stood at 15 per cent for the period 1992–8. See ibid., 'Follow-up Evaluation' (Maputo, 1999), 18; interview with NGO Unit Co-ordinator, European Union Delegation, Maputo, October 1996; European Union Donor Compendium (Maputo, 1997), Table D.
62 Interview with NGO liaison officer, World Bank Country Delegation, Maputo, October 1996.
63 See Alexander Costy, *The Role of NGOs in Mozambique's War-to-Peace Transition* (Bergen: Chr. Michelsen Institute, 1996); and 'Donor Dollars and Mozambique's NGOs' *Southern Africa Report* (July 1995). See also Hans Abrahamsson and Anders Nilsson, *Mozambique: The Troubled Transition* (London: Zed Books, 1995).

64 Patrick Chabal and Jean-Pascal Daloz, *Africa Works: Disorder as Political Instrument* (Oxford: James Currey, 1999), 22–3.
65 AIM Bi-Monthly Report No. 180, 5 April 2000.
66 UNDP Human Development Report, 1999 (index tables).
67 Organization for International Migration, *The Status of Reintegration in Mozambique* (Annual Report) (Maputo, 1996).
68 UNRISD, 1996, 17, 18.
69 Interview with Director, CARE International, Maputo, October 1996.
70 Sogge, *Mozambique* 102.
71 'RENAMO Members Arrested by Mozambican Police,' Panafrican News Agency, 2 May, 2000.
72 OECD/DAC, *Conflict, Peace and Development Assistance on the Threshold of 21st Century* (Paris: OECD, 1998).
73 See David Moore, 'Levelling the Playing Fields and Embedding Illusions: "Post-Conflict" Discourse and Neo-Liberal Development in War-Torn Africa,' *Review of African Political Economy* 83 (2000).

6

Postwar and Post-Apartheid: The Costs and Benefits of Peacebuilding, South African Style

John S. Saul

Peacebuilding in South Africa? A success-story, surely. Not that the actual transition from the violent and authoritarian society that had been apartheid South Africa was entirely peaceful: South Africa in the early 1990s (after Nelson Mandela's 1990 release and during the 1990–1994 negotiations period) remained a killing-field. And yet, through those negotiations and the 1994 election that brought the African National Congress (ANC) to power, South Africa was to realize and to stabilize the shift to a constitutionally grounded and securely institutionalized democratic order – building peace without suffering the potentially crippling backlash from the right-wing, both black and white, that many had predicted, and without suffering the collapse into chaos or dictatorship that some had seen to be threatened by the establishment of majority rule. Moreover, this political stability was sustained through the five years of Mandela's presidency, reconfirmed by the very mundaneness of the 1999 election, and carried over unscathed into the presidency, after that election, of Thabo Mbeki. A clear cause for celebration on a continent where apparently lesser contradictions have proven far more difficult to resolve.

And yet, equally surely, this has been a most ambiguous success-story. For it must be emphasized that this seemingly benign resolution of centuries' old contradictions in South Africa has itself been scarred by contradiction – with the impressive realization of political stability and a democratic restructuring linked, at the very heart of the transition process, to the simultaneous embrace by the ANC of a singularly narrow socio-economic programme. This outcome is far less promising, in the realm of political economy, for the future health and well-being of post-apartheid South Africa than any more narrow political evaluation might suggest. Indeed, it is difficult to escape the conclusion, in the wake of the country's 'successful' 1999 election, that a tragedy has been enacted in South Africa, as much a metaphor for our times as Rwanda and Yugoslavia, and, even if not so immediately searing of the spirit, perhaps a more revealing one. For in the teeth of high expectations arising from the successful struggle against a malignant apartheid state, a very large percentage of the population – amongst them many of the most desperately poor in the world – are being sacrificed on the altar of the neo-liberal logic of global capitalism.

Moreover, it can be argued that it was precisely the willingness of the ANC – presenting itself as acting on behalf of the vast popular movement for change in South Africa that it came to lead – to substantially moderate demands for any real socio-economic transformation that helped secure the brand of peaceful political transition that did occur. This is unfortunate because there is absolutely no reason to assume that the vast majority of people in South Africa will find their lives improved by the policies that are now being adopted in their name by the present ANC government. Indeed, something quite the reverse is the far more likely outcome. Can we not foresee that, despite the peaceful hiatus that the currently stable political situation has produced, a society so scarred by profound inequalities runs the very real risk of rising tides of violence (already exemplified in surging crime rates, for example) and negative long-term political outcomes that threaten any peaceful future for the country?

War and Peace

We will return to such questions. Let us begin, however, with war, peace, and peace-making. Is a society at war an accurate description of the South Africa of the produced 'peace' and a transition to democratic rule in South Africa in the 1990s? The victory of democratic forces in South Africa took place within a violence-plagued domestic polity certainly and within a war-torn region. Still, as Jackie Cock has demonstrated, the question of whether a war was occurring in South Africa in the waning decades of the twentieth century had become something of a political football under apartheid, she notes that the state itself tended to argue both sides of the definition. Thus, in a 1988 treason trial a state spokesperson advanced the position that the ANC could not 'be regarded as being at war with the South African government. Instead, he argued, the government is facing a 'revolutionary onslaught.' This argument was advanced

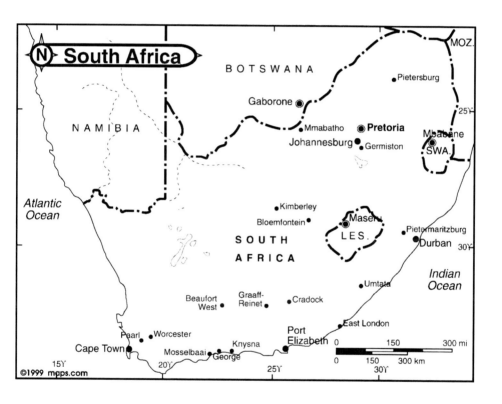

South Africa

in order to deny ANC members prisoner-of-war status which, in terms of the Geneva Protocols of 1977, is granted to people engaged in wars against colonial powers.' Yet, as Cock further documents, 'in contrast, during the same month, in a different court case, the state did describe itself as being at war. It argued that the activities of the South African Defence Force (SADF) fell outside the court's jurisdiction because the Defence Force was on a "war footing."' Meanwhile, much more unequivocally, the ANC spoke openly from exile of waging 'armed struggle' and a 'people's war,' while veteran anti-apartheid campaigner and general secretary of the South African Council of Churches, the Reverend Frank Chikane, could state in 1986 that 'We in South Africa have a war going on. Those who have not realized it are foolish.' As for Cock herself, she is prepared to concede that, as compared with 'nuclear or high-intensity war,' the South African war was indeed 'low intensity.' But she concludes, nonetheless, that this was a situation that produced a substantial militarization of society – and, of course, provided little room for 'peace.'[1]

Note, too, that whatever the language one might wish to employ to codify our understanding of the struggle inside South Africa itself, the southern African region more broadly defined was marked, in an even more straightforward manner, by thirty years of unremitting warfare – warfare that defined, across the sub-continent, a grim record of carnage and destruction. It is well to bear in mind that the chief agent of this regional war was the apartheid state through its strategy of destabilization of neighbouring countries. Thus, in the sections of the Truth and Reconciliation Commission report that deals with the regional war we are told 'that the majority of victims of the South African government's attempts to maintain itself in power were outside of South Africa. Tens of thousands of people in the region died as a direct or indirect result of the South African government's aggressive intent towards its neighbours. The lives and livelihoods of hundreds of thousands of others were disrupted by the systematic targeting of infrastructure in some of the poorest nations in Africa.'[2] Elsewhere, John Daniel, principal author of this volume of the report, bewails the fact that this aspect of the TRC's work was criminally under-reported in the press at the time of the report's publication and also went virtually uncommented upon in the parliamentary debate on the document.[3] All the more reason to remind ourselves that, whatever else it may or may not have achieved inside South Africa, the transition from apartheid served, cumulatively, to neutralize South Africa's capacity to inflict violence on its neighbours, a key contribution to continental peace-making, albeit one beyond the immediate geographical scope of the present essay.[4]

Moreover, to repeat the obvious, the transition to democratic rule inside South Africa was in fact a sharply contested, even violent, one. From the 1970s a struggle, less military than political perhaps but one that, nonetheless, involved a high level of physical confrontation with the state, took place. Launched by such key events as the Durban strikes of the early 1970s and the Soweto uprising of 1976 a considerable mobilization of popular forces occurred. The response from the powers-that-be was a mix of reform and repression, the repression designed to neutralize any political forces that were seen to hinder black embrace of the kinds of reforms the apartheid state had to offer. The catch was that such reforms were extremely limited, stopping far short of granting the vast majority of the population the franchise. And yet no other outcome would really suffice. This became particularly clear with the near-insurrection of 1984–5. Although the regime did buy further time for itself through the implementation of the brutal Emergencies of 1986 and 1987, the handwriting was finally on the wall. With the resurgence of the Mass Democratic Movement, growing out of a United Democratic Movement (which, although banned, refused to die) and buoyed also by a resurgent labour movement centred on the Congress of South African Trade Unions (COSATU), that 'handwriting' was even more visible by the end of the 1980s.

Resistance was a crucial variable in keeping the prospect of a transition from apartheid on the agenda, then. Equally fateful, though not unrelated to the near revolutionary mobilization of popular forces against the established system that marked the 1980s, was the fact that real cracks had begun to appear in the white polity itself. Thus it was precisely when faced with political crisis that Anglo-American business executive Zac de Beer could enunciate in his 1986 classic warning that 'years of apartheid had caused many blacks to reject the economic as well as the political system.' His corollary: 'We dare not allow the baby of free enterprise to be thrown out with the bathwater of apartheid.'[5] Armed with this sensibility, capitalists, both world-wide and local, prepared themselves to sever the marriage between the structures of capitalist exploitation and of racial oppression that had proven so profitable to it in the past and, from the mid-1980s, began to develop a counter-revolutionary strategy designed to shape the socio-economic transition that would now parallel the necessary political transition.

In fact, increased interaction with Nelson Mandela in prison and Thabo Mbeki and others in exile merely helped confirm the growing sense that the ANC might be a potential participant in (and even possibly the best guarantor of) a transition that, while necessarily ensuring a genuine transfer of political power, would safeguard the essentials of the established economic order. The fact that a powerful stratum of Afrikaner capitalists had by now joined the upper echelons of South Africa's business community was also important here. These groups were to become a protagonist within the National Party itself for reformist strategies for a deracialization of capitalism that began to jettison the interests of those Afrikaners – less well-off and most vulnerable to a colour-blind competition for jobs and other privileges – who had once formed its chief political base. True, President F. W. de Klerk held out until quite late in the day for firmer guarantees of continuing racially-defined privilege. And this approach did have its effects, as we will see. Nonetheless, it proved to be much less important to the outcome of negotiations than the underlying pull on the part of capital towards the granting of extensive concessions on the racial-cum-political front.[6]

Enemies of Promise

When it became evident to both dominant business circles and sufficient numbers within the ruling political elite that a situation of relative stalemate had been reached, a strategy of attempting to incorporate the ANC into the circle of legitimate political players took shape. Here were the makings of a class compromise to be reached between the leaders of the ANC on the one hand, and the wielders of capital on the other – a compromise that would blunt the promise of any more sweeping socio-economic transformation. Ultimately this compromise would become institutionalized politically in a liberal constitution and in a democratic electoral system that could pose no real immediate threat to capitalists in South Africa. The fact remains, however, that the political terms of this liberal (ultimately neo-liberal) compromise were not to be so easily won. After all, the South African capitalist system and its attendant class structure had come, over a long period of time, to interweave in very complex ways with South Africa's distinctive format of racially-premised political domination. Many beneficiaries of this latter system could not be expected to yield gracefully to the ANC's political goal of 'one person, one vote in a unified South Africa' just because it now made some sense to leading capitalists both at home and abroad to risk doing so.

Many within the National Party itself, together with the various wielders of bureaucratic state power (especially those in the police and military) whom they ostensibly controlled, constituted one such force. A second was a white 'ultra-right' comprised of political actors to the right of the NP, some organized as parties of formal opposition (the Conservative Party), some as rogue groupings like the Afrikaner Weerstands Beweging (AWB), and also interacting in various unpredictable ways with certain elements in the official state structures (notably within the security branches) to form a variegated group of white extremists. Thirdly, both of these forces (the National Party in power and the white ultra-right) intersected with a black right-wing, spearheaded by some of the leaders of the existing Bantustans, most notably Chief Gatsha Buthelezi and his Inkatha Movement in KwaZulu. The capacity for action, both realized and potential, of these various players would have a significant impact both on the nature of the transition process and on the constitutional/political outcomes it produced. Certainly the ANC, in emerging to centre-stage, had to take such forces seriously. For, as SACP/ANC leader Joe Slovo emphasized at the time:

> We are negotiating because towards the end of the 80s we concluded that, as a result of its escalating crisis, the apartheid power bloc was no longer able to continue ruling in the old way and was genuinely seeking some break with the past. At the same time, we were clearly *not dealing with a defeated enemy* and an early revolutionary seizure of power by the liberation movement could not be realistically posed. This conjuncture of the balance of forces (*which continues to reflect current reality*) provided a classic scenario which placed the possibility of negotiations on the agenda. And we correctly initiated the whole process in which the ANC was accepted as the major negotiating adversary.[7]

In this context we must consider, first, President de Klerk and his associates. As suggested, pressures upon the latter to move towards adoption of the logic of a colour-blind capitalism were real enough. Nonetheless, the National Party was not to drop overnight its preoccupation with the safeguarding of white privilege and the trappings of racial rule. It is clear, for example, that when Nelson Mandela was released in 1990 and the ban on the ANC rescinded, de Klerk and company, still holding the reins of state power, had by no means reconciled themselves to the notion of the ultimate establishment of an ANC government. Indeed, despite their repeal of some of the most offensive of apartheid legislation, they still held hopes well into the transition period of safeguarding various attributes of the existing racial order within any new constitutional/political dispensation that was likely to emerge from negotiations. Moreover, De Klerk was almost certainly knowledgeable of various ongoing attempts by the South African military and police, in ways both direct and indirect (including the strengthening of the hand of Chief Buthelezi and his Inkatha Freedom Party in the harsh jockeying for political positioning that now occurred), to undermine the capacity of the ANC to emerge as a hegemonic force in a new South Africa. Levels of violence rose precipitously, particularly in Natal and the East Rand.

Foot-dragging thus became the NP's main tactic in the pre-negotiation and early negotiations phases over a range of issues regarding the process, substance, and timing of change – with the consequence that the Convention for a Democratic South Africa (CODESA), created as the initial forum for formal negotiations in 1991, broke down on several occasions.[8] Even as such sparring dragged on, however, it was becoming increasingly apparent that the NP could hope only to moderate, not deflect, the drive towards the ANC's goal of 'one person, one vote, in a unified South Africa.' This was true not only because of a crystallizing international consensus on the need for a new political dispensation but also because, internally to the country itself, the ANC continued to consolidate itself at the head of the forces pressing for change. Then, in mid-1992, there occurred a massacre at Boipatong and the shooting of demonstrators at Bisho in the Ciskei, as well as a massive trade union-led general strike in support of meaningful progress. Both parties central to the process (the NP and the ANC) now sensed the need to guide a volatile situation towards compromise, their respective leaderships in effect acknowledging a shared vested interest in a smooth transition under their own joint control: the 'Record of Understanding' they signed in September 1992 produced more serious negotiations at Kempton Park in 1993.[9] Their intentions further focussed by the mass outcry that followed the assassination of popular SACP leader Chris Hani by white extremists, the negotiators now produced guidelines for a transition premised on the holding of national elections in April 1994, the appointment of a Transitional Executive Council to help supervise the interim period, and an agreement on a set of constitutional guidelines designed to structure the final constitution-making process after the elections.

Such acceptance by the NP government of an ever greater proportion of the apparently inevitable was twinned, it should be emphasized, with concessions made by the ANC itself. Certainly NP negotiators, denied the more direct guarantees of minority privilege they might have hoped for, now battled for a federal division of powers as one means of hamstringing any future ANC government. Although such proposals were sometimes presented as being designed to check any future tendency on the part of the ANC (and its SACP ally) towards establishing an abusive one-party state, what these negotiators principally feared was an ANC that would, with victory, use the central government actively for purposes of genuine socio-economic transformation. Another parallel line of defense of established socio-economic inequalities was the effort to bind the ANC to a constitutionally prescribed protection of human rights, a high-sounding enough goal to be sure but one invariably cast by such actors in terms of the most narrowly individualistic definition of such rights and, in particular, in terms of the right to property. With the agreement that the interim constitutional accord reached through the present negotiations would have considerable legal force (through the ministrations of a newly formed Constitutional Court) on the final round of constitution-making (to be undertaken by a new post-elections parliament sitting as constitution-making body) concessions made on such fronts by the ANC were potentially significant ones. In addition, the so-called sunset clauses safeguarded for a period the positions of whites in public employment, the agreement on a Government of National Unity gave promise of positions for both National Party and Inkatha politicians (including de Klerk and Buthelezi) in the cabinet formed by the ANC if it were to win the forthcoming election, and an amnesty offered some protection to those who had committed various gross abuses of power in defence of apartheid (albeit an amnesty that was sufficiently qualified to prepare the ground for the subsequent establishment of the Truth and Reconciliation Commission).

In these ways the ANC and its allies were quite self-consciously seeking to 'minimize the threat to stability and democracy' (as the key strategic document of the movement, entitled 'Negotiations: a strategic perspective,' put it in November 1992[10]), explicitly juxtaposing 'the preferred option of the liberation movement' to more 'immediate objectives.' Moreover, the ANC was well aware that any such threat also sprang from actors further to the right than the NP, actors within both the white and black polities. Indeed, many of the 'concessions' sketched above were directed as much to accommodating/undermining these forces as to facilitating agreement with the government itself. Amongst whites, as we have noted, both the Conservative Party and more overtly fascist organizations such as the AWB remained players to be reckoned with, committed as they were to rolling back the clock to the days of unqualified apartheid. Moreover, their apparent constituency of relatively marginalized whites likely to be the most directly challenged by the emergence of a more colour-blind society – white workers in the lower and middle echelons of state and private sector institutions, platteland farmers, and many rural townspeople – was a potentially volatile one. As Jonathan Hyslop has convincingly argued, however, by far the greatest danger from the White Right was represented by General Constand Viljoen. He, not Ferdy Hartzenberg of the CP or Eugene Terreblanche of the AWB, had lines into a security establishment not otherwise inclined towards putschist activity and also had a much better chance of linking up with potentially divisive forces in the African community (with Buthelezi, for example, and with the Bantustan governments of the Ciskei and Boputhatswana, the so-called Concerned South Africans Group being the chief case in point of such an initiative).

This was because, as a realist, Viljoen had concluded that the Afrikaners' last best hope lay in white separatism rather than the continued pursuit of apartheid overlordship. The foiling of white intervention to shore up Lucas Mangope's regime in Boputhatswana narrowed Viljoen's options, however, and when the ANC skilfully allowed some space in the negotiations for the separatist notion of a Volkstaat to remain a possibility (specifically in the 'Accord on Afrikaner self-determination' struck in April 1994,[11] but also as part of a flurry of concessions, including in the direction of more broadly federalist options, made at the time[12]) the general chose, late in the day but fatefully, to commit himself to the electoral process. Despite a spate of bombings on the eve of the elections, the White Right was thus largely corralled into the fold of peaceful transition. And even though his own last-minute entry into the election did not create quite so peaceful a process in Kwa-Zulu, Buthelezi's decision to participate must surely have been produced, at least in part, by Viljoen's decision to abandon his own resistance.[13]

One might argue that the ANC was equally adept in dealing with Chief Buthelezi and Inkatha. The IFP brought with it a bloody record of harassment of the ANC, often carried out hand-in-glove with the apartheid state, not least during the negotiations years. But it had also developed a significant base amongst many Zulu speakers in the rural areas and squatter settlements of the KwaZulu bantustan and in workers' hostels, especially on the East Rand. Despite the fact that Inkatha largely chose to boycott the negotiations process, the threat it represented was therefore another factor that helped move the ANC towards more concessions than it might otherwise have felt inclined to make, not least in the sphere of federalism. Not that such concessions in and of themselves explain Inkatha's eleventh-hour conversion to participation in the 1994 polls. Here again the broader context of an ineluctable coalescence of forces, local and international, behind a settlement was probably more important. For, in Kwazulu/Natal, familiar patterns of fraud, violence, and considerable chaos were now to mark the electoral process; no-go areas for various of the chief protagonists in the election, especially in Inkatha-dominated rural Natal, imposing a firm limitation on open campaigning, for example. In the end, no accurate count of the vote proved to be remotely possible in Natal: the result was, quite simply, diplomatically brokered and in the IFP's favour. Here, then, was another choice of tactic made by the ANC in order to draw Buthelezi further into the tent of compromise. This result meant that the IFP would form the government in the province of KwaZulu/Natal, one of nine such provincial units established within the new federal system that had been affirmed in the constitutional guidelines.

Democratic Reconciliation or Elite-Pacting?

It bears noting that the federal system of the constitution was not, in and of itself, proved to be much of an impediment to the ANC's undertakings. True, the provinces have provided space for the expression of a degree of diversity in South Africa, even if such diversity has not always been of the most enlightened kind (the KZN government became a formally recognized shelter for the IFP, while the Western Cape government offered a similar outlet for the quasi-racist preoccupations of the white and Coloured constituencies of the victorious National and Democratic Parties there). Most often, however, the provinces have tended to become mere instruments in the hands of those who determine national level budget allocations (and of a depressing brand of intra-ANC infighting) rather than vibrant political sites in their own right. It is surely no accident that the ANC did not seem to push particularly hard in either the 1994 or 1999 elections to win the two-thirds majority that it would have needed in order to change unilaterally the terms of the constitution in this or any other particular (although on both occasions it was actually very close to gaining just such a margin). If long-term constraints on the ANC's freedom of action have existed, or costs have had to be borne for the kind of negotiated transition that the movement did achieve, they have lain elsewhere than in the constitutional realm.

Moreover, some apparent compromises were as appealing to certain elements within the ANC as they may have been to some outside it, albeit for different reasons. Take the tilt within the constitution towards a preoccupation with human rights, for example. Thus many ANC progressives championed a rights-based approach not in any counter-revolutionary spirit, but rather to help safeguard against the danger of abuse of power by an ANC that they knew to be far from immune, given its own hierarchical, even Stalinist, past, from temptations towards high-handedness. There were also those who sought to balance any concession to the privileging of the right to property with the writing into the constitution of a much broader range of economic and social rights, rights designed to give validation to the on-going claims of the impoverished in South Africa. Just how such rights (carefully qualified as they were) might be rendered operational in a post-apartheid South Africa remained to be seen, but that they appeared in the text at all suggests something of the balancing act between defence of privilege and demands for redress of historically embedded wrongs that the constitutional moment embodied. For this was a moment that was also used to pry open space for impressive struggle – often driven by ANC-linked cadres themselves – for the advancing of equality claims made on the basis of gender, sexual orientation, and the like.

A cost-benefit analysis of other kinds of compromise entered into by the popular movement in the name of peace is even less easy to make. Such items as sunset clauses and amnesties no doubt helped buy space for change as the anxiety levels of politicians and civil servants (including the ever-dangerous cadre of 'securocrats') from the old regime were damped down. It could also be argued that a helpful measure of continuity in the ability of state structures to function was thus maintained and that such tricky processes as the blending of cadres carried over from the armed struggle (and the days of ANC's military wing, Umkhonto we Sizwe) into the South African Defence Force without undue backlash on either side were also made that much easier. Needless to say, the record was inevitably mixed in this regard, for retooling apartheid structures to novel purposes was sometimes compromised by this kind of projection into the post-apartheid state of less than progressive attitudes and practices. Further study will be necessary before a detailed balance sheet on the pricetag for peace in these and other spheres can be determined. Nonetheless, it is appropriate even in advance of any such definitive accounting to ask how, more broadly, we can best interpret the compromises made by the ANC in the course of such negotiations.

We have noted the highmindedness that drove much of the rights debate within the ANC itself. A first level of overall explanation would therefore have to take seriously the impact on events of this kind of spirit, including, for example, Mandela's considerable forbearance, after his release from prison, in seeking not revenge but mutual tolerance in his continuing struggle with white South Africa to realize a democratic outcome in his country. Simply put, a degree of statesmanship contributed to producing the peaceful transition that did occur. There was also a second level of explanation, one, echoed above, that has emphasized the importance of more purely tactical considerations. Thus, the ANC was certainly forced to concede considerable ground to established centres of power and to various malign forces that would not yield easily to change. Of course, as we will see, this still leaves plenty of room for debate as to whether the ANC might not have fought harder to achieve more than it did during the transition from apartheid to democracy. Moreover, in such debate, certain analysts have also begun to seek a third kind of explanation, one quite different from an emphasis on either the highminded or the more strictly tactical as possible reasons for the embrace of compromise.

At this third level of explanation, the accent is on the manner in which key actors within the several negotiating parties are pulled towards recognition of their mutual interest in an outcome that services their joint concern to place limits on change. Theorists of democratic transitions like Adam Przeworski have termed this, famously, 'elite-pacting,' a process that finds (using his terms) 'Moderates' within the camp of established power distancing themselves from the 'Hardliners' to their right and 'Reformers' from the camp of change distancing themselves from the 'Radicals' to their left in order to strike a 'realistic' and restrained compromise.[14] Suggesting (with enthusiasm, it should be noted) that this is precisely what has transpired in his own country, well-known South African analyst Steven Friedman then writes that under such circumstances leaders must continue with efforts to 'strike a compromise that is finely balanced and sturdy enough to prevent destabilization *from both left and right* and then to maintain support for it through a series of severe trials.'[15] But what a grim suggestion this is if the goals of those on the left are primarily to prevent the interests of the poorest of the poor from being sacrificed in the name of peace-making. Elite-pacting must then seem a far more sordid business than Friedman implies.

The unfortunate truth is that there are any number of ways in which an explanation cast in terms of the centrality of elite-pacting can help us to understand the nature of the South African transition. Note, for example, that some have cited even the workings of the Truth and Reconciliation Commission as evidence in this regard. As suggested earlier, the TRC was designed to complement the amnesty dictated by the logic of negotiations with the establishment of an investigative process that could, despite the amnesty, allow the truth about historical responsibility to facilitate a deeper level of societal reconciliation. There has been much written about the strengths and weaknesses of the TRC process. As dramatic and morally searing as the proceedings sometimes were, they may well have helped many whites to open their eyes to a record of abuse of power that apartheid epitomized – although it may also have been rather too easy for such observers merely to offload responsibility onto the shoulders of the professional killers-qua-policemen who chiefly appeared in the dock.[16] Polls also suggest that Africans were not overly enthusiastic about the substitution of 'truth' for 'justice' when, from time to time, the most heinous of crimes were actually unveiled.[17] In short, the question will continue to be asked: How much 'reconciliation' actually has occurred in South Africa whether through the TRC or by other means?

But there is another question, even more relevant to our present purposes: what kind of 'reconciliation' would this actually be expected to be even if it were to work on its own terms? Here the criticism (offered by such writers as Colin Bundy, Mahmood Mamdani and Steven Robins) that the TRC's primary focus, case-by-case basis, on abuses of power by malignant state operatives blurred any focus on the far more important and powerful social institutions that had underwritten the unjust structures of the apartheid era. While noting the rather perfunctory hearings that did occur on the role and responsibilities of such institutional actors as the judiciary, the media, and the business community under apartheid, Mamdani, for example, suggests that the central preoccupation with perpetrators of violence helped mask the broader sociological distinction between the beneficiaries and the victims of apartheid: 'In its eagerness to reinforce the new order ... the TRC created a diminished truth that wrote the majority of apartheid's victims out of its version of history' and thus 'failed to open a social debate on possible futures for a post-apartheid South Africa.' In fact, as Bundy extends the argument, is not this a brand of 'truth and reconciliation [that is] not merely the product of a compromise, but historically compromised,' one likely to produce a 'form of nation-building ... which can only yield a lop-sided structure – two nations disguised as one, a hybrid social formation consisting of increasingly deracialized insiders and persistently black outsiders?' Hence, too, Robins's concern that if, as he suspects, the TRC has helped permit 'the systemic socio-economic legacies of apartheid to recede from public discourse' this has had 'important implications in terms of contemporary public debate on social transformation and economic policy.' For whatever the range of truths that were revealed by the TRC process, 'we may be forced to admit that these are not necessarily the sorts of truths that are most useful to setting the present generation of impoverished South Africans free.'[18]

When viewed through the explanatory prism of elite-pacting, then, a whole range of compromises entered into in the name of peacebuilding and of 'reinforcing the new order' suddenly seem much less benign. Consider, as another example, the aforementioned incorporation of Buthelezi into the national fold. Here, some would argue, is a particularly graphic instance of the high price paid for the kind of transition that has occurred. Certainly this will seem an even more plausible reading of developments if one takes seriously Mamdani's argument, in another of his recent writings, that a clear distinction should be made between 'citizen' and 'subject' within the theory and practice of democratic struggle in Africa. In particular, he criticizes much thinking about democracy for focusing far too exclusively on urban pressures (by self-conscious 'citizens') for change and overlooking the importance, if genuine democratic transformation is to be realized, of simultaneously helping rural-dwellers who are often still trapped as 'subjects' within quasi-traditional structures of authority to liberate themselves.[19] Does reflection upon Mamdani's model not raise the fear that the ANC, in the name of peace-making, has merely handed over the rural poor (and the poor who are resident in the many peri-urban shanty-towns around Durban and Pietermaritzburg) in KwaZulu-Natal to the ministrations of the caste of abusive chiefs and warlords who cluster around Buthelezi and his Inkatha structures?

This is, in fact, the argument made by Gerhard Maré, the most articulate academic critic of Chief Buthelezi and his Inkatha project. Maré bemoans the extent to which the unsavoury Buthelezi has apparently forced the ANC to accept him as political player more or less on his own terms. Thus, in spite of the fact that Inkatha won a mere 10 per cent of the vote in 1994, and 'in spite of being named in the TRC report as carrying responsibility for 'gross violations of human rights,' Buthelezi has escaped with scarcely a blemish and with apparent absolution from the ANC itself ... his position as elder statesperson acknowledged through the number of times that he has served as acting state president in the frequent absence of both Mandela and [then Vice-President] Mbeki.' As for his cronies, people 'closely associated with horrendous acts of violence,' they have 'simply defied or ignored the storm and survived – often as members of various provincial parliaments or the central parliament, such as warlords David Ntombela and Mandla Shabalala, and the notorious prince Gideon Zulu.'[20] True (as noted above) some might wish to argue that such an outcome merely epitomizes the success of a judicious strategy of incorporation, a legitimate tactical ceding of ground to a dangerous and decidedly ruthless opponent, a purchasing of peace in one important region of South Africa at some real but nonetheless acceptable cost to principle. And yet one might be more inclined to accept such an argument were this not merely an example of the more general pattern of ANC peace-making efforts: an across the board following of the line of least resistance towards centres of established power, a continued broadening of the scope of elite-pacting to consolidate, on every front, a turning away from the interests of the poorest of the poor.

Nor is this a case merely of being wise with the benefit of hindsight. There were those who warned of precisely this danger during the negotiations period itself, even from within the ANC where some argued that the movement should be pressing much harder than it was in the negotiations with counter-revolutionary forces, both white and black, and in doing so be seeking to realize both a less compromised constitutional outcome and the consolidation of a much more militantly democratic politics. In 1992, for example, senior ANC cadre Pallo Jordan responded to the movement's 'Strategic Perspective' document cited above by suggesting that the ANC has begun to lose track of its own broader goals of democratic transformation and, in making the lowest common denominator of constitutional agreement an end in itself, risked gutting the capacity of a post-apartheid government to sustain any serious attack upon the severe socio-economic inequalities that characterize South African society.[21] There was, of course, a plausible, if predictable, response to this – the claim that Jordan ran the risk of substituting mere rhetoric for political realism. Thus Jeremy Cronin, SACP activist and one of the most prominent theorists in the camp of the democratic movement, wrote in criticism of Jordan that, 'to be sure, there are sometimes epic, all-or-nothing moments in politics. But when one is simply not in such a moment, then all-or-nothing tactics are liable to yield ... nothing.'[22]

And yet it was also Cronin who, during this same period, raised closely related questions regarding the dangers of a negotiations process in which mass action came to be viewed merely as a tap to be turned on and off at the ANC leadership's whim as short-term calculation of advantage at the bargaining table might dictate.[23] As he further argued, 'It is critical that in the present we coordinate our principal weapon – mass support –

so that we bring it to bear effectively upon the constitutional negotiations process ... Democracy is self-empowerment of the people. Unless the broad masses are actively and continually engaged in struggle, we will achieve only the empty shell of a limited democracy.[24] Another ANC activist, Raymond Suttner, had a similar sense of the direction in which things were going:

> JS [Joe Slovo] is absolutely right to underline the massive victory we have scored at the negotiations. He fails, however, to mention that the past three years have also seen the transformation of our organizations, particularly the ANC. This transformation could have a serious, long-term impact. In particular, the negotiations have had a dissolving effect on mass organization, a tendency for our constituency to become spectators. If we conduct the coming election campaign in a narrow electoralist manner, the dissolution could be deepened. Whatever the victory, we should not underrate the strong sense of demoralization in our organizations.[25]

In fact, elections have been, as Suttner feared, fully revelatory of what little has become of popular mobilization in South Africa, as has been the virtual collapse of the ANC as a mass political organization (although not as an electoral machine) since 1994. True, the 1994 election had the distinction of being a "freedom election": one could not have asked for much more than that such an election would ratify, through a massive African vote for the ANC, the coming into the political kingdom of a population that had been denied any such voice for centuries. By 1999, however, it was difficult to miss the significance of the fact that that year's election had become a mere popularity contest, the ANC still floating to a considerable degree on its legitimacy amongst Africans as a successful liberation movement rather than on any record of delivery on popular expectations during its first term in office. Meanwhile, the vote in KwaZulu/Natal continued to fall along quasi-ethnic lines, producing, once again, a narrow victory for the IFP; in Western Cape the vote was along racial ones, once again revealing a distancing of many in the Coloured community from the ANC and that forging of links with white voters that produced an NP government in 1994 and now an NP/DP (soon Democratic Alliance) government in 1999. Nationally, the Democratic Party became the official opposition (albeit with only 11 per cent of the vote compared to the ANC's near two-thirds poll): it did so, significantly, on the basis of a nation-wide campaign pitched to whites, Coloureds, and Indians, in terms of issues of crime, corruption and the dangers of abuse of power inherent in a one-party dominant (read, also, African-dominant) political system, issues that were given, tacitly, a racist spin.

Note, however, that this tendency also reflected the fact that there was not so very much more to campaign about. The DP hewed to a particularly business-friendly line as regards socio-economic policy during the election. But by 1999, as we will document in the next section, this did not much distinguish the party from the ANC itself in policy terms: on many potentially important strategic issues the space for democratic disagreement and contestation had by now been papered over by a crippling consensus amongst the main political contenders regarding the presumed imperatives of neo-liberal economic orthodoxy. Small wonder that some observers have found it difficult to avoid a relatively narrow and unenthusiastic reading of what, substantively, was actually being accomplished in South Africa in democratic terms, especially when one turns one's attention to the policy outcomes with which this kind of democracy was actually twinned.

The Second Negotiations

We now return to a consideration of the circumstances in the realm of political economy that framed the constitutional negotiations and evolution towards electoral politics. For such negotiations were paralleled by what was, in effect, a second set of negotiations; the much more informal process that found the ANC, throughout the transition period, reassuring various international capitalist actors (the bourgeoisies of both South African and international provenance, western governments, and the World Bank and the IMF) of the modesty of its claims to challenge the existing economic status quo. As noted above, the road to a successful political-cum-constitutional transition was eased, both locally and internationally, by this increasing domestication of the ANC to the requirements of global capitalism.

Granted, the negotiations in the sphere of economic/class relationships were far less public than the formal meetings of the Convention for a Democratic South Africa (CODESA) and the Kempton Park negotiations but that does not make them any the less important. As one close observer wrote in 1994, 'Since 1990, when the democratization process began, some foreign governments, notably the US and some of its allies – Britain, Germany, Italy and Japan – successfully induced the ANC to move away from its socialist economic policies, including that of nationalization. Instead, they succeeded in persuading the movement to embrace Western-style free market principles which the ANC increasingly, albeit reluctantly, adopted. It is interesting to note, for example, that Mandela's evolving position on fiscal responsibility was a direct response to pressures from foreign investors and governments.'[26] Moreover, this brand of compromise was merely part of a decade-long process of accommodation, one hailed in retrospect by no less a source than South Africa's corporate think-tank par excellence, the Centre for Development and Enterprise (CDE): 'The evolution of the ANC's policy position was ... influenced by foreign perceptions and pressures (from foreign investors, potential investors, the World Bank, IMF and others). Other important policy influences were the *Growth for All* document of the South African Foundation (representing the country's 50 largest corporations) published in February 1996.' The result: 'Throughout the 1990s the ANC's economic policies have shown a clear shift towards greater acceptance of the market ... (one sealed) finally in the Growth, Employment and Redistribution (GEAR) proposals of June, 1996.'[27] But if 1996 was the crucial year for putting the finishing touches on the ANC's capitulation to neo-liberal orthodoxy, it seems plausible to argue that the die had already been cast during the transition period itself. As Hein Marais observes, 'by 1994 ... the left had lost the macroeconomic battle.'[28]

There were counter-tendencies to this outcome. It is true that many within the ANC were caught flat-footed in the sphere of economic policy in 1990, with only some vague if progressive nostrums from the Freedom Charter ('The mineral wealth beneath the soil, the banks and monopoly industry shall be transferred to the ownership of the people as a whole') to fall back upon. Perhaps it was this that allowed Nelson Mandela, immediately upon his February 1990 release from prison, to state militantly that 'the nationalization of the mines, banks and monopoly industry is the policy of the ANC and a change or modification of our views in this regard is inconceivable' – a position Mandela himself would soon so distance himself from that by 1994 he could tell the US Joint Houses of Congress that the free market was a 'magical elixir' that would produce freedom and equality for all![29] And yet even if Mandela himself was not to be counted upon in this respect, there was also available a more considered expression within the ANC (not least in its Research Department) of a radical sensibility relevant to thinking about the macroeconomic sphere. This sensibility produced chiefly a kind of dirigiste neo-Keynesianism perhaps, but it nonetheless contained the possible seeds of a deepening challenge to capital's prerogatives in favour of a prioritization of popular needs in the sphere of production. Its impact was best exemplified by the then prominence of the proposed guideline 'growth through redistribution' in ANC circles.

Such a perspective also found early voice in the ANC's new Department of Economic Policy (DEP), in its very first major policy pronouncement (the 'Discussion document on economic policy' of 1990) in fact: 'The engine of growth in the economy of a developing, non-racial and non-sexist South Africa should be the growing satisfaction of the basic needs of the impoverished and deprived majority of our people. We thus call for a programme of Growth through Redistribution in which redistribution acts as a spur to growth and in which the fruits of growth are redistributed to satisfy basic needs.' Such emphases were reinforced by the report of the Macro Economic Research Group (MERG) crafted, between 1991 and 1993, by ANC-aligned economists working with progressive counterparts from overseas and in writings by such key players as then-DEP economist (and presently governor of the Reserve Bank) Tito Mboweni who argued that 'the ANC believes that a strategy of "growth through redistribution" will be the appropriate new path for the South African economy ... In our growth path, accumulation depends on the prior redistribution of resources. Major changes will have to take place in existing power relations as a necessary condition for this new growth path.'[30] Moreover, this logic appeared compelling. After all, the vast majority of South Africans were desperate in their poverty for a wide range of the simplest goods and services, on the one hand, and a very large percentage of people were equally desperate for jobs, on the other. Why, the ANC seemed poised to ask, can't those two key pieces at the centre of the South African economic puzzle simply be put together? Why must they be joined so indirectly and inefficiently through the circuits of global capital and the process of generating surplus value (profits) for those few who have the power to dictate terms and guarantee their massive cut of the action? But any such questions were very soon lost from view as Mboweni and other young ANC high-flyers – in a rightward shift which was also congruent with that being made, alongside Mandela himself, by older heavyweights like Joe Slovo and Mac Maharaj – increasingly looked elsewhere for economic cues.

For the voices raised against anything like the 'growth through redistribution' model were ferocious.[31] Moreover, a wave of much more capital-friendly scenarios soon washed over the macroeconomic debate,[32] even as other global players 'arranged for key ANC economic advisers and politicians to receive training at business schools and international banks and investment houses in the west where they were fed a steady diet of neo-liberal economics.'[33] As DEP economist Viv McMenamin put the point frankly at the time, ANC economic thinking now registered 'a shift away from policies that may be morally and politically correct, but which will cause strong adverse reaction from powerful local and international interests.'[34] In the end, ex-United Democratic Front (UDF) activist Trevor Manuel, instrumental in pulling the DEP to the right in the early 1990s, and ex-trade union militant Alec Erwin, patron of the COSATU academics, would become, as ministers of finance and of trade and industry respectively, the principal protagonists of the global conformism that had come to characterize ANC economic policy at the turn of the century.[35]

One last throw of the dice by the left within the Mass Democratic Movement was the document that became, in effect, the electoral manifesto for the ANC in the 1994 election campaign, the *Reconstruction and Development Programme* (RDP). To a considerable degree driven from below by the trade unions and civic organizations and adopted only rather more opportunistically by the core group of ANC senior leaders, it emphasized the centrality to the planning process of both the meeting of the populace's basic needs and the active empowerment of that populace in driving its own development process. Nonetheless, the key chapters on macroeconomic policy were already markedly compromised in the direction of free-market premises (the document as a whole being at best characterized as 'less what it is, than what it might become' in the context of further class struggles[36]). Unfortunately, it was the rightward pull that proved predominant, reinforced in a range of government documents, each more neo-liberal in tone and substance than the last, that ran from the RDP White Paper of September 1994, through the draft National Growth and Development Strategy of February 1996, to the 'Growth, Employment and Redistribution, a Macroeconomic Strategy' document of June 1996.[37] As Marais notes of the latter, 'Rhetorically, attempts were made to align [GEAR] with the socially progressive objectives of the RDP. But the central pillars of the strategy were fashioned in accordance with standard neo-liberal principles – deficit reduction, keeping inflation in single digits, trade liberalization, privatization, tax cuts and holidays, phasing out of exchange controls, etc.'[38] And in March that same year the RDP office, until then strategically located in the president's office as cabinet level overseer of what was left of a popularly-driven development mandate, was closed, its activities folded, ostensibly, into the various line ministries.

For many of the government's most sympathetic critics it was the extreme, precipitate, and unqualified nature of the ANC government's move towards a neo-liberal strategy that is so surprising. As Adelzadeh suggests, what has transpired appears to be in significant part a self-inflicted wound, an 'adoption of the essential tenets and policy recommendations of the neo-liberal framework advocated by the IMF in its structural adjustment programs' which is

> all the more remarkable in view of the limited, even negative impact of such programs, especially in southern Africa, the lack of any leverage that the international financial institutions such as the IMF and World Bank have over South African policymakers, the lack of any dramatic shifts in economic and political environment to warrant such major shifts in policy orientation, and the lack of a transparent and fully argued justification for the adoption of an entirely different policy framework.

What there is, Adelzadeh concludes, is merely 'a lame succumbing to the policy dictates and ideological pressures of the international financial institutions.'[39] Moreover, the pronouncements of these documents have been paralleled by a range of concrete policies that epitomize just such a 'lame succumbing.' Crucial in the constitutional negotiations per se – alongside the property rights clause – was the agreement to guarantee formally the independence of the Reserve Bank, a reassurance to capital that removed from government hands any real leverage (especially in facilitating expansionary policies) over crucial monetary decisions. Moreover, as a member of the caretaker South African government, the Transitional Executive Council, the ANC spent most of 1993 signing on as party to a range of decisions that firmly cast the die for future policies once it was in power: inking an extraordinarily market-friendly letter of intent to the IMF in order to guarantee a balance-of-payments loan, for example, and joining the General Agreement on Tariffs and Trade (GATT). Perhaps the most noteworthy aspect of this latter move was the fact that it set the stage, after 1994, for the ANC government to remove tariffs in key areas much faster than even GATT required, with catastrophic effects on many local firms.[40]

These, and a number of other choices made in the early going, were crucial, cumulatively rendering ever more difficult and more unlikely any opting for the plausible alternative policies that existed at the outset of the transition. Left critics would argue that many of the ANC's more recent claims to be powerless in the face of the marketplace have a disingenuous ring when measured against the fact that the movement itself had, early in the game, thrown away so many of the instruments that might have been useful in crafting a more assertive strategy towards capital.[41] Instead, the central premise of South Africa's economic policy could scarcely be clearer: ask not what capital can do for South Africa but what South Africa can do for capital. This was an option marked by an overwhelming preoccupation with foreign investment, an (at best) trickle-down approach to development more broadly conceived, and an attendant encouragement of a culture of stock markets (with even many trade unions becoming substantial players in the game through their own investment companies) and, for more marginal players, of institutionalized lotteries and other games of chance. And the result? Numbers that indicate not the dramatic increase in employment figures forecast by those who launched GEAR but a spiralling downward trend in that regard (a loss of at least a half a million jobs between 1994 and 1999, it has been estimated). Moreover, these figures are paralleled by evidence in such spheres as GDP growth, investment, savings, exports, and interest rates that 'virtually all GEAR's targets were missed' and missed by a very great deal.[42] It is difficult to escape the conclusion that, in the summary of one analyst, 'GEAR has been associated with massive deindustrialization and job shedding through reduced tariffs on imports, capital flight as controls over investments are relaxed, attempts to downsize the costs and size of the public sector, and real cuts in education, health and social welfare spending.'[43]

Note that all this was occurring in a South African context where a sophisticated case can and has been made against the continued prioritizing of supply-side economics and for an approach ('growth through redistribution'?) that highlighted the far more central brake on economic growth that exists on the demand side of the equation.[44] Such an alternative might be expected to embrace the insights of political economists like Greg Albo who, more generally and in explicit response to the negative impact capitalist globalization has had worldwide, argues the case for a 'realistic socialism' that would focus on 'more inward-oriented economic strategies' and the devaluation of 'scale of production as the central economic objective,' goals that 'can only be realized through re-embedding financial capital and production relations in democratically organized national and local economic spaces sustained through international solidarity and fora of democratic co-operation.'[45] And yet, for its part, the ANC has declined to embrace the (admittedly challenging) tasks that such an approach would imply and has chosen instead to ease the political transition by withdrawing from any form of genuine class struggle in the socio-economic realm, thereby abandoning any approach to the economy that might be expected directly to service the immediate material requirements of the vast mass of desperately impoverished South Africans. No discussion of the 'peaceful transition' in South Africa can afford to ignore this fact. Or the attendant reality that the option the ANC has selected (a 'utopian capitalist' one, in Albo's memorable formulation) is so singularly unpromising both in African terms[46] and more globally.

Race, Class, and Counter-Revolution

The coming of peace to South Africa in the manner that it did can thus be seen to have carried a formidable price tag to set alongside the record of considerable accomplishment. For the substance of the transition has been recast both in political and socio-economic terms: narrowed from a project of mass political empowerment to one of mere electoralism and from a prospect of socio-economic transformation to one that has sanctioned the kind of widening inequality inherent in neo-liberal economic policies. Why this outcome? For some it is merely an inevitable result of the new South Africa coming to its majority in an age where the imperatives of global capitalism carry all before them. TINA, as the phrase goes: 'There Is No Alternative.' This is the smug premise of most business-inspired commentary certainly. As the ANC has come increasingly to spurn discussion of any alternative approach to the neo-liberal one they now offer, Ann Bernstein and her big business backers at the CDE can happily conclude that, given the strength of capital and the (for them, benign) workings of the global economy, there is 'at the turn of the century, not much choice for South Africa ... There is only one road to follow if we want to ... put the country on a sustained high growth path.' Evoking the example of 'Britain's Tony Blair [who] has led the Labour Party away from its socialist and union-dominated past ... [and] is ruthless in ensuring that key members of the cabinet and party "toe the new line,"' the CDE suggests that, similarly in South Africa, 'a certain degree of toughness is ... required to impose the new vision on the party and follow through with the chosen policies.' And despite concerns about too slow a pace to privatization and too little government action to meet the need for greater labour flexibility, the CDE survey is nonetheless pleased to cite the fact that 'business leaders who have met Mbeki are positive' and affirm, with minimal qualification, that 'South Africa is fortunate to have a person of Mbeki's quality to lead it into the next century.'[47] Or, as one banker stated even more frankly in the wake of the 1999 elections: 'The ANC are not fools. They know where the balance of economic power lies.'[48]

Still, as we have argued in the previous section, there is little sign that a mere capitulation to capital's dictate will produce significant economic growth in South Africa, let alone some humane form of development. Surely, critics then suggest, the pre-emptive weight of realism/pragmatism cannot be allowed to stand as adequate explanation and/or excuse for the absence of root-and-branch struggle that has defined the transition in South Africa on too many fronts? Why, in particular, has the ANC's choice of socio-economic strategy been quite so unqualified and its capitulation to the world of market signals and market forces been quite so extreme? Why have its policies been marked by a precipitous rush to go much farther and faster to the right than even the most informed concern as to the pressing nature of global constraints might seem to warrant? What has produced the attendant unwillingness to embrace the fact that the existent market-dominated global order, driven, states Albo, by 'a minority class that draws its wealth and power from a historically specific form of production,' is therefore 'contingent, imbalanced, exploitative and replaceable'?[49] Or to contemplate the possibility that alternative ways of approaching South Africa's economic challenges do indeed exist? Faced with these questions, such critics are, understandably enough, tempted to see the ANC's option for neo-liberalism as being at least as much an ideological choice as a realistic/pragmatic one: an ideological choice by a new elite bent on advancing its own interests.

I would argued that a further extrapolation of the explanatory model of elite-pacting is therefore illuminating. The ANC 'Reformers,' having joined hands with the 'Moderates' to produce a 'peaceful political transition,' also appear to have signed up for a simultaneous project of pan-racial class formation, with the movement's upper echelons now making common cause with the white bourgeoisie, both world-wide and local. Under such circumstances, the best point of reference for analysing the South African transition may well be Frantz Fanon's notion of a false decolonization: the rising African middle-class, both entrepreneurial and political/bureaucratic in provenance, merely sliding comfortably into their political positions as intermediaries of global empire and, from these heights, fending off the claims of the poverty-stricken they have left behind. Hence the glee of *The Economist* in writing of the early years of the South Africa transition that

> For all the fears that resentful ANC socialists would confiscate wealth, the new breed shares the same capitalist aspirations as the old. Though black incomes are barely a sixth of white ones, a black elite is rising on the back

of government jobs and the promotion of black business. It is moving into
the leafy suburbs, such as Kelvin and Sandton, and adopting the outward
symbols of prestige – the BMW, swimming pool, golf handicap and black
maid – that so mesmerize status-conscious whites.[50]

Unfortunately, this is a pattern that has only been strengthened subsequently. Hence, for example, the fact that one can find almost no examples of prominent ANC personnel who, when resigning or being
removed from office, announce their return to the ranks of the popular
movement. Instead, like former trade union and ANC grandee Cyril
Ramaphosa, they quickly turn to the pursuit of private advantage as presumptive captains of industry or, like prominent former ANC provincial
governors Tokyo Sexwale and Mathews Phosa, they wind up in the diamond business or as promoters of casino development in Mozambique.
Small wonder that the authors of one careful analysis of the transition
could conjecture that 'the government seems, in a way very reminiscent
of equivalent groupings such as SWAPO in Namibia or ZANU-PF in
Zimbabwe, to resemble a club of old party militants who are more concerned to reap the rewards of their own earlier sufferings than to effect
major changes in society ... [W]ith the disappearance of the revolutionary vision which undoubtedly spurred such militants on in the past, what
is left is largely a class promotion project, the promotion of a new class
of wealthy and powerful African movers and shakers.'[51]
    Some hard-boiled analysts of the ANC's history profess no surprise at
such an outcome, having interpreted the ANC's entire history as a
nationalist movement as the expression, first and foremost, of a narrowly
petty bourgeois project.[52] Recall, they suggest, Mbeki's own forceful
assertion as early as 1984 that 'the ANC is not a socialist party. It has
never pretended to be one, it has never said it was, and it is not trying to
be. It will not become one by decree for the purpose of pleasing its "left"
critics.' True, Mbeki saw fit to add at the time that the ANC represented
the 'notion of *both* an all-class common front *and* the determined mobilization of the black proletariat and peasantry,' with this working class to
be viewed as 'a conscious vanguard class, capable of advancing and
defending its own democratic interests.'[53] Nonetheless, despite this latter utterance, Mbeki seems to have had little trouble in adapting comfortably to a bourgeois milieu. Thus, a columnist in the *Washington Post*,
writing at the time of Mbeki's election in 1999, reassured his readers by
citing a remark made by a prominent London-based investment banker:
'Mbeki holds things close to his chest and makes decisions in a secretive

way. However, he is not a populist, and has been a "Thatcherite" in his fiscal ideas. His experience in exile introduced him to the financial world – he is unlikely to abandon the close ties to business developed in those years abroad.'[54] Although there is no evidence of personal corruption, the account of Mbeki's preferred social circle, frequented on numerous occasions by shady figures from the soccer world and by business hustlers, in a recent biography also makes for sobering reading in this respect.[55] As does the moment, at the public launch of GEAR, when he took particular delight in guying the left by smugly declaiming: 'Just call me a Thatcherite.'[56]

The latter moment, in its smug and self-conscious crassness, seems especially revelatory, its very bravado capturing eloquently the prevailing undercurrent of the ANC-dominated transition. Not the undercurrent represented by Mandela's contribution to that transition, to be sure. As Andrew Nash has imaginatively argued, Mandela evoked a more traditional ethos ('a tribal model of democracy,' Nash terms it) in playing his own crucial role in the first five post-apartheid years, muffling societal contradictions (for both good and ill) within a mythos of consensus.[57] Beyond structural determinations – of economy, of class formation – here was one way in which variables defined in terms of politics and personality must also be part of the explanation of outcomes in South Africa. But Mandela's was not a politics that the younger generation, epitomized by Mbeki, either could or would choose to play. Their sense of self-importance bore no quasi-traditional markings. It was auto-produced: having pulled off the impossible, the overthrow of apartheid, they are very pleased with themselves. So, seeing themselves as much too smart now to be mere ineffectual lefties, they expected to play equally effectively the only game in town: capitalism. It is this kind of coolly self-satisfied, self-righteous, and profoundly ideological thrust on the part of the new ANC elite (sell-out is much too crude a term for it) that is the single most depressing attribute of South Africa's transition.

To this bald project Mbeki has, of course, come to add the rhetorical gloss of the 'African Renaissance." Sometimes presented with genuinely moving flourishes, this notion is at least as often set out in revealingly narrow terms. Take, for example, the startling evocation of black empowerment to be found in a speech by Mbeki to a recent meeting of black managers.[58] There the emphasis was placed, quite frankly, on the need to 'strive to create and strengthen a black capitalist class,' a 'black bourgeoisie.' Since 'ours is a capitalist society,' Mbeki continued, the 'objective of the deracialization of the ownership of productive property' is key to 'the struggle against racism in our country.' Yet how helpful is such a formulation in a society where, across the decade of the 1990s, a certain narrowing of the income gap between black and white (as a grow-ing number of blacks have edged themselves into elite circles) has been paralleled by an even greater widening of the gap between rich and poor.[59] One fears that as the celebrated 'African Renaissance' comes to be more and more about the 'embourgeoisement' of the favoured few it becomes a very tawdry thing indeed.[60] Meanwhile, analytically, it is tempting to set against Mbeki's formulations the frank and unequivocal statement of the brash emergent African entrepreneur, Tumi Modise, interviewed by David Goodman: 'Race is not the issue anymore,' she told Goodman, 'It's class.'[61]

Needless to say, class division in South Africa still bears a racial colora-tion. But if the knot of class exploitation and racial oppression is ever to be untied, it is much more likely to be done from below than by further elite-pacting between white and black bourgeoisies. It may not seem sur-prising, therefore, that when popular voices have been heard (from the unions, the South African Communist Party, the churches, various town-ship-based organizations, and the like) questioning GEAR and the neo-liberal cast of ANC strategies they have been roundly condemned, often in rather threatening tones, by Mandela, Mbeki. and their colleagues.[62] Such a tendency is not surprising however. Within the frame of the South African elite-pacting process that we have traced, there has occurred – as 'Moderates' have linked up with 'Reformers' – a simulta-neous and increasingly counter-revolutionary distancing of 'Reformers' from the 'Radicals' who were once their comrades.

Transition or Transformation?

How then, finally, are we to interpret this kind of peaceful transition that has taken place in South Africa? Most observers have hailed enthusiasti-cally the movement away from apartheid and towards democracy and for many good reasons. Nonetheless, such observers have been able to do so as uncritically as they have in part by narrowing their terms of reference and thus excluding a range of crucial variables. For by splitting the polit-ical science of peace-making in South Africa from the political economy of such peace-making, many commentators, in their evaluations of the transition, have ignored the enabling context of socio-economic compro-mise that framed the apparently successful constitutional and political negotiations in the first place.[63] In doing this they have underestimate the costs to the material and human prospects of the vast mass of impoverished South Africans of the kind of peace that has been achieved. Much closer to the mark than the celebratory tone that tends thus to dominate the literature is, I would argue, a distinction drawn by David Howarth between the 'democratic transition' South Africa has achieved and the 'democratic transformation' that it has not really attempted – using the term democratic transition to refer 'to the process by which negotiating elites manage to oversee the installation of formal liberal-democratic procedures, whereas [democratic transformation] designates the longer-term process of restructuring the underlying social relations of a given society.'[64] Since, in South Africa, these underlying social relations encompass a measure of socio-economic inequality that is virtually unparalleled elsewhere in the world (only Brazil and Guatemala are ever mentioned as being in the same league on the GINI scale), it is not difficult to see what Howarth is driving at.

Since the present ANC leadership has chosen a strategy with singularly limited promise of recasting, in the interests of those at the bottom of South Africa's socio-economic pyramid, the situation in that country, it is tempting to conjecture what kind of politics might yet place democratic transformation on the agenda in South Africa. Elsewhere, I have sought to analyse just what forces may be emerging that bear some such promise, while also speculating as to the likely costs if a revitalization of the struggle for radical change does not occur.[65] In the absence of material advance and the successful grounding of a progressive political project, the situation is unlikely to stand still: it can quite easily get a very great deal worse, deepening already existing conditions of social distemper.[66] There is, for example, the precipitous rise in the crime rate (much of it crime of an extremely violent nature), this being a direct reflection of socio-economic polarization and communal decay. And there is the cruel decline of health standards, most marked by the escalating HIV/AIDS pandemic.

There is also, Hein Marais suggests, the danger of even more dramatic manifestations of the loss of social cohesion, one of these inherent in the ANC's own propensity to shore up its hegemony by pandering to local chiefs, in KwaZulu and beyond, whose power is rooted 'in a blur of ethnicized tradition, coercion and clientelism.' Under what circumstances might such ethnic notables manage to plug into popular desires to find apparently more meaningful cultural anchors in a national society that has not found its way? Might not 'the tension between the modern and the traditional increase, allowing politicized ethnicity to regain its muscle'?[67] Add to this the fact that the venal Winnie Mandela was able, from time to time, find some ground for her racist populism in the gangrenous inequalities that lie untreated in an untransformed South Africa – even as, at the other extreme, some whites seek in the more privatized racism of their guarded suburbs and schools defence against the leveling so necessary in such a society – and one gets a further sense of just how potentially dangerous are the tensions that seethe beneath the surface in that country.

Such facts further underscore the need to generate an alternative politics if a meaningful peace is to be sustained. But is the ANC itself not more likely to fall back on ever more authoritarian methods as its preferred means of seeking to contain, rather than resolve, the contradictions that now scar the South African social formation? Time alone will tell what the Mbeki years can bring. Still, one senses that for all his cocky self-confidence Mbeki is not always quite certain himself as to just how best to ride the whirlwind he has helped create. Despite his apparently unqualified commitment to his chosen role of architect of South Africa's appeasement of capitalism as presumptive engine of South African economic transformation, one can still find him bobbing and weaving rather uncomfortably – as he did, for example, in the run-up to the 1999 election when he permitted himself some pretty radical-sounding formulations of his own. One such instance saw his revealing attack not only on wealthy whites (afflicted, he said, by 'social amnesia') but also on a black elite that abuses 'freedom in the name of entitlement.' This latter group, he charged, 'seek to hijack the sacrifices which millions of ordinary people made to liberate our country for noble purposes, in order to satisfy a seemingly insatiable and morally unbound greed and personal thirst for wealth and comfort, regardless of the cost to our society.' And he concluded by warning of 'the danger of a mounting rage to which we must respond seriously.'[68]

This may be an intriguing statement with which to conclude this essay, but perhaps as much for what it says about present-day South African society as for what it tells us about Thabo Mbeki himself. Does the slightly desperate tone of such pronouncements suggest, for example, an uneasy sense on the part of the leadership of just how impossible it will be to overcome the grim legacy of racial inequality on a capitalist basis? And perhaps, too, a certain subliminal suspicion that even when local elites do everything possible to conform to global market dictate, the dependent capitalism they seek to facilitate simply cannot be expected, these days, to lift off the ground. We return to the question raised earlier: even if Mbeki and his team can continue to dodge these realities, what of others who have begun to recognize that it is precisely in the failure of the promise of neo-liberal deliverance that there lies the dark underside of peace-building South African style. For them the struggle for a just and lasting peace continues.

NOTES

The paper prepared for the June 2000 preparatory workshop for this volume and entitled 'Ambiguous Success Story: South Africa, Post-War and Post-Apartheid' has given rise to two essays: the present chapter and a longer and more explicitly politically-motivated article published as 'Cry for the Beloved Country: The Post-Apartheid Denouement,' *Monthly Review* 52, no. 8 (2001). Despite their different audiences and auspices, there is an overlap of formulation and phrasing in some sections of the two articles. I would like to thank Professor Jackie Cock, her colleagues, and my students in the Sociology Department at the University of the Witwatersrand for providing me with a stimulating environment during the academic year 2000 in which I could develop the argument of the present paper and to thank as well the numerous comrades in South Africa who commented on an earlier draft.

1 Jacklyn Cock, 'Introduction,' in Jacklyn Cock and Laurie Nathan, eds., *War and Society: The Militarisation of South Africa* (Cape Town and Johannesburg: David Philip, 1989). 1, where she also quotes Frank Chikane.
2 *Truth and Reconciliation Commission of South Africa Report* (Cape Town: TRC, 1998), 2: 43.
3 John Daniel, 'The Truth about the Region,' *Southern Africa Report* (*SAR*), 3–7.
4 See my overview entry, 'Colonialism, overthrow of: 30 Years War for Southern African Liberation (1960–1990),' in Kevin Shillington, ed., *Encyclopedia of African History* (London: Fitzroy and Dearborn, in press).
5 Quoted in the *Financial Times,* June 10 1986.
6 See, on this subject, Dan O'Meara's magisterial study, *Forty Lost Years: The Apartheid State and the Politics of the National Party, 1948–1994* (Randberg: Ravan Press; Athens: Ohio University Press, 1998).
7 Joe Slovo, 'Negotiations: What room for compromise?' in *The African Communist* 130 (1992), 36–7 (emphasis in the original). As Slovo added, 'But what could we expect to achieve in the light of the balance of forces and the historical truism that no ruling class ever gives up all its power voluntarily? There was certainly never any prospect of forcing the regime's unconditional surrender across the table.'
8 Somewhat paradoxically, de Klerk's victory for a 'reform' strategy in the

214   John S. Saul

March 1992 whites-only referendum was taken by the NP as actually ratifying their get-tough negotiating stance of the time.

9 The 'Record of Understanding' is reprinted in Hassan Ebrahim, *The Soul of a Nation: Constitution-Making in South Africa* (Cape Town: Oxford University Press, 1998), 588–94; this book, both in its analytical chapters and in its extended collection of relevant documents, serves as an invaluable resource for tracing the negotiations process. See also Johannes Rantete, *The African National Congress and the Negotiated Settlement in South Africa* (Pretoria: J.L. van Schaik, 1998) and Richard Spitz with Mathew Chaskalson, *The Politics of Transition: A Hidden History of South Africa's Negotiated Settlement* (Johannesburg: Witwatersrand University Press, 2000).

10 'Negotiations: a strategic perspective' was adopted by the National Executive Committee of the African National Congress on 25 November 1992 and is reprinted in Ebrahim, *The Soul of a Nation*, 595–605. This document was in turn based on a draft prepared by Joe Slovo of the South African Communist Party.

11 Reprinted in ibid., 613–5.

12 Ibid., 174.

13 See Jonathan Hyslop, 'Why Was the White Right Unable to Stop South Africa's Democratic Transition?' in Peter Alexander, Ruth Hutchinson and Deryck Schreuder, eds., *Africa Today: A Multi-Disciplinary Snapshot of the Continent in 1995* (Canberra: Humanities Research Centre/ANC, 1996), 145–65.

14 See Adam Przeworski, *Democracy and the Market* (Cambridge: Cambridge University Press, 1991).

15 Steven Friedman, 'South Africa's Reluctant Transition,' *Journal of Democracy* 4, no. 2 (1993), 57 (emphasis in the original).

16 As Colin Bundy asks ('Truth ... or Reconciliation?' *SAR* 14, no. 4 [1999], 11), 'Does the TRC's highlighting of individual memories actually facilitate social amnesia? ... Do we run the risk of defining a new order as one in which police may no longer enjoy impunity to torture opponents and failing to specify that ordinary citizens should not be poor and illiterate and powerless and pushed around by state officials and employers?'

17 The ANC made it own surly contribution towards undermining any positive impact the TRC process might have had by quite unfairly denouncing the final report as being fundamentally flawed in its equation of the movement's own abuses of power to abuses committed by the apartheid state.

18 Mahmood Mamdani, 'A Diminished Truth,' *Siyaya* (1998), 40; Colin Bundy, ibid., 11; Steven Robins, 'The Truth Shall Make You Free? Reflections on the TRC,' *SAR* 14, no. 3 (1998), 13.

19 Mahmood Mamdani, *Citizen and Subject: Contemporary Africa and the Legacy of Late Colonialism* (Princeton: Princeton University Press, 1996).

20 Gerhard Maré, 'Makin' Nice with Buthelezi,' *SAR* 14, no. 3 (1999), 10.

21 Pallo Jordan, 'Strategic Debate in the ANC' (mimeo, October 1992); an abbreviated version of this paper appears as 'Committing Suicide by Concession,' *Weekly Mail* (13–19 November 1992).

22 Jeremy Cronin, 'Nothing to Gain from All-or-Nothing Tactics,' *Weekly Mail*, 9; in Cronin's view. 'Slovo reminds us we are dealing with a chastened, crisis-ridden but still powerful opponent. Both sides find themselves locked in a reciprocal siege. From our side the objective remains the total dismantling of apartheid. But we simply cannot will this objective into being. So how do we move from here to our longer term goals? Slovo suggests principled compromises.'

23 See Jeremy Cronin, 'The Boat, the Tap and the Leipzig Way,' *African Communist* 130 (1992). Note also Joe Slovo's own acknowledgment of this shortcoming of the negotiations process: 'The balance between negotiations and mass struggle was not always perfect. We were not always clear of what we were trying to achieve with mass action. Remember the debate about the "tap," our tendency to turn mass action on and off in a very instrumentalist way?' ('The Negotiations Victory,' 10).

24 Jeremy Cronin, 'In Search of a Relevant Strategy,' *Work in Progress* 84 (September 1992), 20.

25 Rayond Suttner, in 'Central Committee Discussion of Joe Slovo's Presentation,' *African Communist*, 135 (1993), 14.

26 Chris Landsberg, 'Directing from the Stalls? The International Community and the South African Negotiation Forum,' in Steven Friedman and Doreen Atkinson, eds., *The Small Miracle: South Africa's Negotiated Settlement* (Braamfontein: Ravan Press, 1994), 290–91.

27 The Centre for Development and Enterprise (CDE), *Policy-Making in a New Democracy: South Africa's Challenges for the 21st Century* (Johannesburg: CDE, 1999), 83; his report was funded by South African Breweries and written by Ann Bernstein.

28 Hein Marais, *South Africa: Limits to Change. The Political Economy of Transformation* (London and New York: Zed Books; Capetown: University of Cape Town Press, 1998), 156; Marais quotes Anglo-American executive Clem Sunter: 'Negotiations work. Rhetoric is dropped, reality prevails and in the end the companies concerned go on producing the minerals, goods and services,' 147.

29 Cited in Andrew Nash, 'Mandela's Democracy,' *Monthly Review* 50, no. 11 (1999), 26. Mandela's reversal of ground on the nationalization question was actually quite rapid after 1990, such that by May 1994 he could assure *Sunday Times* readers: 'In our economic policies ... there is not single reference to things like nationalization, and this is not accidental. There is not a single

slogan that will connect us with any Marxist ideology' (quoted in Marais, *South Africa: Limits to Change*, 146).

30 Tito Mboweni, 'Growth through Redistribution.' in G. Howe and P. le Roux, eds., *Transforming the Economy: Policy Options for South Africa* (Natal: Indicator Project SA, University of Natal Institute for Social Development, 1992).

31 Thus apologists for business like the economist Terence Moll quickly labelled this model 'macro-economic populism' and 'a dangerous fantasy' (T. Moll, 'Growth through Redistribution: A Dangerous Fantasy?' *South African Journal of Economics* 59, no. 3 (1991).

32 The Mont Fleur proposals, for example, and the recommendations of both the Nedcor/Old Mutual 'Professional Economists' Panel' (entitled Prospects for a Successful Transition) and insurance conglomerate Sanlam's own Platform for Investment. These are well described in Patrick Bond, 'Social Contract Scenarios,' in chapter 2 of his invaluable *Elite Transition: From Apartheid to Neoliberalism in South Africa* (London: Pluto Press, 2000).

33 Bill Freund and Vishnu Padayachee, 'Post-Apartheid South Africa: The Key Patterns Emerge,' *Economic and Political Weekly* (16 May 1998), 1175.

34 Quoted in Marais, *South Africa: Limits to Change*, 154.

35 As columnist Howard Barrell wrote in the *Mail and Guardian* (18 June 2000) at the time of Mbeki's announcement of his new cabinet: 'Both [Erwin and Manuel] have won the confidence of the markets and their presence in their current portfolios is seen as a measure of the government's determination to stick to its current economic course.'

36 See my '... or Half Empty? Review of the RDP,' *SAR* 9, no. 5 (1994), 40.

37 Asgar Adelzadeh, 'From the RDP to GEAR: The Gradual Embracing of Neo-Liberalism in Economic Policy,' *Transformation* 31 (1996); see also the accounts of the rise and fall of the RDP in Marais, *South Africa: Limits to Change*, and Bond, *Elite Transition*.

38 Marais, *South Africa: Limits to Change*, 171.

39 Adelzadeh, 'From the RDP to GEAR,' 67. As Patrick Bond has summarized this pattern, 'Much of South Africa's national sovereignty continued to be offered up on a plate to impetuous and whimsical local and international financial markets' *Elite Transition*, 216.

40 Moreover, Patrick Bond argues that the same kind of 'moral surrender' to the market was evident in an on-going propensity to cut back corporate taxation and in such decisions as those 'to repay in full apartheid's $20 billion-plus foreign commercial bank debt and to phase out exchange controls in the name of attracting new foreign finance' (*Elite Transition*, 200). See also Charles Millward and Vella Pillay, 'The Economic Battle for South Africa's Future,' in E. Maganya and R. Koughton, eds., *Transformation in South Africa? Policy Debates in the 1990s* (Braamfontein: IFAA, 1996).

41 A point underscored for me most forcefully by South African economist Oupa Lehulere in private communications.

42 Bond, *Elite Transition*, 193ff. For a further detailed critique of GEAR's performance, see Asghar Adelzadeh, 'The Costs of Staying the Course,' in *Ngqo!* 1, no. 1 (1999).

43 Lucien van der Walt, unpublished communication (June, 2000); the tendency for narrowly market-based premises to choke off more dramatic initiatives in the potentially explosive area of land reform is also worth noting.

44 The point is convincingly argued, and linked to the extreme inequalities of economic power and income that exist in South Africa, by Ashgar Adelzadeh in his 'Looosening the Brakes on Economic Growth,' *Ngqo!* 1, no. 2 (2000).

45 See Albo's seminal essay 'A World Market of Opportunities? Capitalist Obstacles and Left Economic Policies,' in Leo Panitch, ed., *Socialist Register 1997: Ruthless Criticism of All that Exists* (London: Merlin Press, 1997), 28–30, 41.

46 See Colin Leys and John S. Saul, 'Sub-Saharan Africa in Global Capitalism,' *Monthly Review* 51, no. 3 (1999).

47 CDE, *Policy-Making in a New Democracy*, 145.

48 Gordon Smith, an economist with Deutsche Morgan Grenfell bank, quoted in Norm Dixon, 'ANC Reassures Big Business after Win,' *Green Left Weekly* (e-mail, July 1999).

49 Albo, 'A World Market Opportunities,' 41.

50 'South Africa: How Wrong Is It Going?' *Economist* (12 October 1996), 23.

51 Freund and Padayachee, 'Post-Apartheid South Africa,' 1179. As they continue, 'If there was a phrase that captured the imagination of South Africans black and white within a year of the ANC taking power it was that of "the gravy train."'

52 See, for example, Dale McKinley, *The ANC and the Liberation Struggle: A Critical Political Biography* (London: Pluto Press, 1997).

53 I have cited this statement (from 1984) and explored other questions posed in seeking to divine the historical character of the ANC in my 'South Africa: The Question of Strategy,' *New Left Review* 160 (November–December 1986).

54 *Washington Post* (6 June 1999).

55 Adrian Hasland and Jovial Rantao, *The life and times of Thabo Mbeki* (Rivonia: Zebra Press, 1999), chapter 7.

56 Quoted in Bond, *Elite Transition*, 83.

57 Andrew Nash, 'Mandela's Democracy.'

58 Thabo Mbeki, 'Speech at the Annual National Conference of the Black Management Forum,' Kempton Park, November 1999 (ANC website).

59 Indeed, this gap between rich and poor remains among the widest in the world, marking a society in which, as one survey demonstrated, 'the poorest 60% of households share of total expenditure is a mere 14%, while the rich-

est quintile's share is 69%' (Asghar Adelzadeh, 'Loosening the Brakes on Economic Growth').

60 Moreover, the significance of this trend in broader developmental terms has proven to be quite limited, whatever its implications for class formation within the country's black population. The structure of contemporary South African capitalism actually offers little room for the emergence of a vibrant and transformative 'national [and/or "racial"] bourgeoisie,' however much ANC statements (and certain of its affirmative action policies) may seek to imply otherwise.

61 David Goodman, *Fault Lines: Journeys into the New South Africa* (Berkeley and Los Angeles: University of California Press, 1999), 270.

62 I have further documented this in Saul, 'Cry for the Beloved Country,' 33–6.

63 For a more detailed argument on the necessity of wedding political science to political economy in any study of peace-making see my chapter of Mozambique ('Inside from the Outside? The Roots and Resolution of Mozambique's Un/Civil War') in a parallel volume to the present one, also edited by Taisier Ali and Robert O. Matthews and entitled *Civil Wars in Africa: Roots and Resolution* (Montreal and Kingston: McGill-Queen's University Press, 1999).

64 David Howarth, 'Paradigms Gained? A Critique of Theories and Explanations of Democratic Transitions in South Africa,' in D. Howarth and A. Norval, eds., *South Africa in Transition: New Theoretical Perspectives* (New York: St Martin's Press, 1998), 203.

65 Saul, 'Cry for the Beloved Country,' 37–48; see also John S. Saul, 'Starting from Scratch? A Reply to Jeremy Cronin,' *Monthly Review* 54, no. 7 (2002) and Ashwin Desai, *We Are the Poors: Community Struggles in Post-Apartheid South Africa* (New York: Monthly Review Press, 2002).

66 Manuel Castells, *The Information Age*, vol. 3, *End of Millennium* (Oxford: Blackwell Publishers, 1998) who, in a sub-section entitled 'Africa's hope? The South African connection,' speaks of a possible freefall in South Africa into 'the abyss of social exclusion' (122). See also the parallel remarks by Albie Dithlake, executive director of the South Africa National Non-Governmental Organizations Coalition (SANGOCO), quoted in William Marvin Gumede, 'New Seeds of Opposition,' *Financial Mail* (19 May 2000).

67 Hein Marais, 'Topping Up the Tank: How the ANC Has Reproduced Its Power since 1994,' *Development Update* 3. no. 1 (1999), 27.

68 See the article 'Mbeki Champions Poor against Black and White Elites,' *Southscan* 12, (June 1998).

7
Zimbabwe and Sustainable Peacebuilding

Hevina Dashwood

Through an examination of the Zimbabwean case, this chapter sets out to establish the importance of approaching peacebuilding as a long-term, non-linear process. Peacebuilding is generally understood to refer to efforts to help societies that have been torn apart by civil war to build lasting conditions for peace. The literature, and governments such as Canada, tend to approach peacebuilding in post-conflict situations as a short-term proposition spanning two to three years.[1] Yet peacebuilding generally entails fundamental political, economic, and social transformations that cannot be quickly engineered.[2] The central argument being advanced is that only a long-term approach to peacebuilding that goes beyond the confines of the peace settlement is likely to succeed. A key assumption is that peacebuilding is a complex, interrelated package of security, political, and socio-economic arrangements that provide for the ability to manage social conflict without resorting to violence.

A case study of Zimbabwe can be justified because, even though a negotiated peace was achieved after twenty years of civil war with the signing of the Lancaster House Constitutional Accord in 1979, the country again faces violent upheaval. Aside from violence that occurred in Matabeleland in the mid-1980s, Zimbabwe has managed to avoid descending into another full-scale civil war, although such a prospect now appears more likely. As recent developments reveal, the latent potential for serious violent conflict exists in Zimbabwe, pointing to the importance of addressing peacebuilding from a pre-conflict perspective as well.[3] The Zimbabwean case highlights the problems and dilemmas surrounding whether peacebuilding should be understood as a short-term endeavour on the part of international donors involved in promoting it. Sustainable peacebuilding is defined as peace that is maintained over a long period of time with the underlying causes of the original conflict having been addressed.

The approach of this paper is to establish the extent to which the root causes of the 1970s civil war in Zimbabwe were resolved, and to ponder the implications of this for international peacebuilding efforts. A key question to be addressed is: to what extent can the recent violence and instability in Zimbabwe be traced back to the civil war, the compromises reached at the 1979 Lancaster House Constitutional Accord, and the manner of its implementation? The Lancaster House negotiations that took place in London in 1979 led to a peace settlement whose broad features resemble the initiatives normally associated with peacebuilding. If one were to argue that peacebuilding is best defined as short-term efforts to restore peace, demobilize warring factions and establish legitimate government, then Zimbabwe would have to be seen as an example of successful peacebuilding.[4]

However, from a longer-term vantage point, the verdict of success would need to be qualified. There is much turmoil in Zimbabwe at the moment. Since the defeat in February 2000 of the government's new draft constitution in a national referendum, there has been a state-orchestrated campaign of land invasions on commercial farms owned by whites, which quickly turned violent. The June 2000 general elections were marred by violence, fear, and intimidation, and the violence worsened in the run-up to the 2002 presidential elections. The disturbances can be partially explained by Mugabe's desperate bid to cling to power, but the issues relate to deep-seated problems that have never been resolved. The most significant problem is the failure to correct the extreme inequalities in land distribution in Zimbabwe. Inequitable access to land was a root cause of the civil war, and so the failure to settle this question does raise questions about the success of peacebuilding from a longer-term perspective.[5]

This study argues that a link can be made between Zimbabwe's current difficulties, and the outcome of the civil war, suggesting that the root, structural causes of the war were never adequately resolved. Zimbabwe's experience further points to the tension between structural (or socio-economic) causes of violent conflict, issues of political inclusion/exclusion, and the role of the political leadership (human agency). There is a tendency on the part of Western donors to support the security and political dimensions of conflict, at the expense of socio-economic causes.[6] This points to the need to address the complex interrelationship between these different aspects of peacebuilding, to ensure that the root causes, rather than just the symptoms of conflict, are addressed.[7]

Zimbabwe

Still, the current crisis in Zimbabwe can only be partially explained by socio-economic causes; the lack of political inclusiveness and transparency is a major determining factor. Five years ago, all appeared to be going reasonably well in Zimbabwe, but things have since deteriorated quickly. Why is this so? The answer lies partly in the coming together of competing social forces that have taxed the ability of Mugabe to balance them. Mugabe's extreme unpopularity and the lengths to which he has gone to stay in power are a major factor in the timing of the current difficulties. Until recently, there was no serious opposition to Mugabe and ZANU-PF, so the political system appeared open and reasonably democratic. When faced with more serious obstacles to his staying in power, Mugabe has been willing to repress the opposition ruthlessly.

The following section will identify the root causes of the civil war, and provide a brief overview of the Lancaster House Constitutional Accord. The next section will look at the complex interrelationship between socio-economic developments since 1980, and security/political arrangements. The inter-play between structural causes and the part of leadership can then be elucidated. The final section will consider the role played by the international community, including its involvement in more recent developments, where it has played a counter-productive role.

The Civil War and the Lancaster House Constitutional Accord

To be historically accurate, the civil war, or liberation struggle, would have to be traced to the arrival of Cecil Rhodes, his British South Africa Company, and the beginnings of white settlement in the late 1800s. For black Zimbabweans, the 'first Chimurenga' of 1896/97 marked the beginning of the struggle for black liberation. Over the next fifty years, blacks were forced or pushed off their land in order to make way for growing numbers of European (mostly British) settlers, who were allocated large tracts of land. The 'second Chimurenga' gained momentum after 1965, when Ian Smith's Rhodesian Front party issued a unilateral declaration of independence.

The formation of the Zimbabwe African National Union (ZANU) and the Zimbabwe African Peoples' Union (ZAPU) in the 1960s provided the vehicles through which black opposition to white minority rule could be organized. Significantly, the black leadership at that time was concerned mainly about political rights; the right to vote, the right to form political parties, and the right not to be discriminated against on the basis of race in the workplace, and in the provision of social services in health and education.[8] Inequitable access to the land was an important issue, but not the first concern of a largely urban educated, petty-bourgeois leadership. It was not until the 1970s, after the rural peasant population had been mobilized over the issue of land, that the liberation struggle became a full-scale civil war.

During the colonial period, several acts were promulgated to entrench legally an inequitable pattern of land ownership. For example, the 1931 Land Apportionment Act set aside the best farmland for the whites. In 1980, the government inherited a highly skewed ownership structure, where 800,000 peasant households subsisted on sixteen million hectares in the Communal Areas, and 4,500 white commercial farmers owned some eleven million hectares (33 per cent) of prime farmland.[9]

For Zimbabwe's rural population, therefore, land was the single most important issue. When, in 1979, a negotiated settlement was finally reached through the Lancaster House Constitutional Accord, land proved to be the most important sticking point.[10] There were other difficult issues to resolve, such as how to manage the transition period to majority rule, how to surrender weapons, and how to maintain the cease-fire, but these were all problems related to the handing over of power, and not to the causes of the civil war. Significantly, such potentially divisive issues as the political structure of the country were easier to resolve. The various parties to the negotiations even agreed to a temporary separate voters' role for whites, which could only be altered through a constitutional amendment after seven years had elapsed.

The provisions in the Lancaster House Constitution with respect to land redistribution reflected very significant and difficult compromises on the part of the black leadership. The constitution protected private property, and commercial farms were to exchange hands only through the 'willing seller, willing buyer' provision. The Patriotic Front's original negotiating position was that it wanted to be able to acquire land against the owner's consent, and without paying compensation.[11] An impasse was reached in the Lancaster House negotiations over land, threatening to break up the conference. Only the personal intervention of the Mozambican president, Samora Machel, saved the day, as he urged Mugabe not to allow the issue of compensation to lead to the collapse of the negotiations.[12] Promises of financial assistance from the UK and US governments allowed Mugabe (and Joshua Nkomo) to set aside their reservations.

The compromise reached meant that market forces were to determine the availability and price of land for redistribution. At the last minute, a provision was included requiring that land purchased by the government had to be paid for in foreign currency, an onerous provision that was to make land acquisition by the government very expensive. The provisions of the Lancaster House Constitution allowing the land reform process to be determined solely by market forces established a clear bias in favour of the commercial farmers. The British government sweetened the pill by promising millions of pounds in financial assistance towards land redistribution, an amount that proved insufficient to meet the demand for redistributed land in Zimbabwe.

While many factors account for the lack of progress on land redistribution after 1980, the punishing nature of the Lancaster House Constitution with respect to land acquisition clearly placed a limit on how far, and how quickly, the government could implement its program of land redistribution. As with any peace settlement, difficult compromises had to be made to ensure the key parties to the conflict were prepared to accept the terms of peace. In this respect, the protection of private property rights was a core concern of the whites. However, further concessions, in particular, the foreign currency provisions, were excessive. Had the Patriotic Front opted for an outright military victory, rather than a negotiated peace, it is doubtful whether land redistribution would have been left to market forces.

Still, only so much weight can be placed on the terms of Lancaster House. The sheer practical obstacles of moving tens of thousands of people onto acquired land, and providing them with basic services, also proved to be a major hurdle that slowed down the pace of land reform. As the next section reveals, the government's inability to resolve the land issue, and the lacklustre support of the international community for land redistribution, allowed the dominant cause of the civil war to linger on unresolved, undermining the prospects for sustainable peacebuilding in Zimbabwe.

Socio-Economic Dimensions of Peacebuilding

Land Redistribution

The election in February 1980 of Robert Mugabe and his ZANU-PF party was a surprise to many, but what should not have been a surprise was the emphasis placed by his new government on land redistribution. Having mobilized the peasantry in the 1970s over the land, expectations were very high on the part of those who had directly fought in, or assisted, the liberation struggle. While many war veterans found positions in the newly integrated Zimbabwe National Army (ZNA), the police, and the Central Intelligence Organization (CIO), many others found themselves unemployed. As such, war vets were given priority in the government's first efforts at land redistribution.

In the first two years of independence, with the postwar economy booming, the government's land redistribution program got off to a good start. As many white farmers did actually leave, mostly for South Africa, a good number of farms came on the market which the government was able to purchase. Problems began to appear around 1982, however, when the economy experienced some difficulties, including a balance of payments crisis. By this time, fewer farms were coming on to the market, and prices were driven up,[13] so that many war vets still found themselves unemployed and without land. The significance of this in terms of peacebuilding is that a direct link can be made from the failure to adequately provide for the war vets after the war ended, to the difficulties Zimbabwe is experiencing today. A small number of war vets leading the farm invasions are the same as those who fought for ZANLA (ZANU's military arm during the liberation struggle) and ZIPRA (ZAPU's military arm).[14]

In order to understand the problems associated with the government's land redistribution program, it is important to remember that it has two main components: land acquisition and resettlement. The cost of acquiring land is not as great as a properly implemented resettlement program, which requires the provision of infrastructure, schools, extension services, training, and an effective bureaucracy to administer the program. To this day, the government owns farms that have been acquired, but which have not been resettled, due to lack of resources. After 1983, land redistribution slowed down significantly, and the government's ambitious targets for resettlement were not met.

The government has pointed fingers at the international community for failing to provide enough money towards land redistribution. Although the British government has provided millions of dollars towards that end, there was considerable unease on the part of Britain, and other major donors, over the ZANU-PF government's Marxist-Leninist political orientation. The espoused commitment to socialism influenced the government's land reform program, raising questions about the appropriateness of its design. Although the majority of land was resettled under the Model A plan, where individual farmers were leased land for their own production, much attention was paid to the Model B plan.

Model B consisted of farming cooperatives, consistent with the government's socialist vision. However, very few peasant farmers were willing to participate in the cooperatives, so only a small number of cooperative farms were actually established. Their spectacular failure tainted international and domestic actors' perceptions of the entire resettlement program, including Model A. The major donors have tended to ignore studies that reveal that the Model A resettlement program was not a uniform failure, based on household income data.[15]

Partly because of the requirement that full compensation be paid for acquired land, the government was dependent on foreign donors to help finance land acquisition. Although the British government has loaned over US$400 million towards land redistribution (including acquisition and resettlement), the donor community has generally been reluctant to contribute generously to the program. Donor wariness about the socialist features of the resettlement program and the Marxist-Leninist pronouncements of the government meant that the government had to find domestic sources of funding for the program. On the part of both the government and donors, ideology partly drove thinking on the question of how to proceed with land reform.

During the 1980s the government took positive steps to promote overall rural development, including in the communal areas. The government encouraged peasant production by ensuring attractive prices for peasant crops, establishing marketing depots, offering seeds and fertilizer and, during times of drought, relief. The positive response to these efforts led some within government to question whether land redistribution was necessary. Not surprisingly, the Commercial Farmers' Union (CFU), representing the white commercial farmers, added its voice by proclaiming that land redistribution was unsuccessful. Domestic doubts about the viability of the land redistribution program, combined with international wariness, resulted in a significant slowing down of the program after 1983. By 1990, when the government was in a position to make constitutional amendments facilitating land redistribution, members of the ruling elite were no longer committed to a land redistribution program that would benefit the poor majority.[16]

Under the terms of the Lancaster House Constitution, the willing seller, willing buyer clause could be amended after ten years. In 1992 the government introduced the Land Acquisition Act, allowing it to designate farms for compulsory acquisition that were 'underutilized' or derelict, but providing for reasonable compensation to be paid to commercial farmers. The amendments introduced by the government making it easier to acquire land understandably raised expectations on the part of the peasant population that the government was still serious about land redistribution. However, the international donor community, most notably Britain, became increasingly reluctant to finance a second phase of land redistribution. The reasons for this are related to the pressures for indigenization emanating from Zimbabwean society, including the ruling elite's own interest in large-scale commercial farms, and the impact of the Economic Structural Adjustment Program (ESAP) introduced in 1991.

Indigenization

Since the early 1990s, the ZANU-PF government has been hobbled by contradictory societal pressures competing for scarce government resources. Influential blacks both within and outside government came to push for a more concerted effort on the part of the government for indigenization, or black advancement. This translated into a demand for more resources to assist in the establishment of black businesses, and more pertinently, in a desire to allow blacks to participate in large-scale commercial farming. Thus, popular-based demands for a comprehensive and equitable land redistribution program came into conflict with elite-driven demands for the same economic privileges enjoyed by the whites.

The developments that gave political space to these demands can be traced to the government's effective abandonment of socialism through its embrace of market-based reforms in 1990, and the resulting greater legitimacy attached to the aspirations of blacks who wished to emulate the economic success of the whites in the economy. As market-based reforms were implemented in the first half of the 1990s, under the Economic Structural Adjustment Programme (ESAP), it appeared to many that whites, who continued to control much of the economy, were the main beneficiaries. Indigenous organizations, including the Indigenous Business Development Centre (IBDC) and the Indigenous Business Women's Organization (IBWO) were both formed after 1990, in response to concerns about being left out of the benefits of reforms.

Prior to 1990, there were many significant economic impediments to black entrepreneurship, but the political climate was also not conducive to their advancement. In a context of espoused socialism, there was no political support for black entrepreneurs. In theory, the economic impediments to black advancement were removed after 1990; however, the political impediments remained. One possible reason is that the government did not wish an independent power base to be established through the formation of a sizable black middle class.[17] However, senior politicians and bureaucrats, who had a stake in government-owned companies and state-run monopolies, were unwilling to encounter competition from the private sector.

The market-based reforms highlight the fact that whites continue to control much of the economy, a situation that is unacceptable to those blacks who aspire to replace the whites. While it ought to be possible for blacks to become successful entrepreneurs without displacing the whites, there is more of a zero-sum situation with respect to commercial farming. For blacks to become involved in large-scale commercial farming, it necessarily means displacing white farmers.

Starting in 1990, in response to these pressures, the government introduced the Commercial Farm Resettlement Program, to assist blacks who wished to undertake large-scale commercial farming. Under the program, large-scale commercial farms that had ostensibly been acquired for redistribution ended up being redistributed to well-off, and frequently, well-connected, blacks. Despite the public uproar that ensued when it the extent to which the program had been captured by senior bureaucrats and politicians was revealed, a second phase was nevertheless introduced in 1998. Although the program has been used by the government to dole out political favours, the pressures being exerted on the government for indigenization must be distinguished from straightforward corruption or cronyism. The Zimbabwean elite, both inside and outside government, generally believes that the commercial farming sector (and business enterprises) should be de-racialized, even if this means that land is not available for redistribution to peasant farmers. In its 1996 agricultural policy paper, the government indicated a desire to improve the racial balance in commercial farming as one of the objectives of its large-scale commercial farm resettlement program.[18] There is therefore now a black constituency prepared to argue that land redistribution is not necessary, or even that it will not promote poverty alleviation.

An example of the strength of the pressure to allocate entire farms to blacks can be found in the decision to 'undesignate' two hundred black-owned commercial farms originally designated in November 1997 for compulsory acquisition. These farms had been designated because they were either derelict or underutilized, according to the government's criteria. There was a huge political uproar on the part of blacks who felt that there should be greater racial balance in the ownership of large-scale commercial farms. Roughly eight hundred of the farms newly designated for acquisition in 1997 were earmarked for indigenous commercial farmers (or well-connected blacks), thereby further reducing the pool of farmland that would actually be available for redistribution to peasant farmers.[19]

The government's response to pressures for indigenization, and the corruption that has come to permeate the land redistribution exercise, have made international donors very reluctant to help finance the government's new program, launched in 1998, until guarantees of greater transparency are provided. These concerns were raised at the September 1998 donors conference, where pledges were anticipated by the government to support the second phase of land redistribution, but very little was actually forthcoming. The government's response, a radical approach to land redistribution through illegal squatting and confiscation of farms, is not conducive to a fair and orderly process of land redistribution.

Political Dimensions of Peacebuilding

The above discussion reveals that, in the crucial area of land redistribution, economic justice has not been served, and consequently, a core root cause of the liberation struggle has not been resolved. The failure to achieve this final stage of peacebuilding means that there is a latent potential for violent conflict over this issue. A separate, but interdependent problem, is the failure to achieve an open and inclusive political system. Although the link is not as strong, this failure can be partly traced to the legacy of the liberation struggle, and the political arrangements made at Lancaster House. The manifestation of authoritarian tendencies in the system of governance is partly a legacy of the liberation struggle. The challenge of fighting a civil war required unquestioning loyalty to the leadership, and anyone suspected of selling out was dealt with harshly. The accomplishment of black-majority rule basically meant the grafting on to the existing colonial state structures of a more broadly based Western-style parliamentary system. The new Zimbabwe simply inherited a highly authoritarian colonial state structure, complete with repressive state powers that had been employed during the liberation struggle against blacks.

However, there have been other developments since independence which have reinforced the authoritarian tendencies within the Zimbabwean political system. The Matabeleland uprising in the early 1980s led Mugabe to crack down very heavily on the Ndbele population at large, employing the North Korean-trained Fifth Brigade, which committed severe human rights atrocities. Mugabe also had legitimate regional security concerns, with apartheid South Africa posing a threat to Zimbabwe's physical security and economic viability.

The crushing of the predominantly Ndebele political party, ZAPU, revealed that Mugabe and his ZANU-PF party were unable to tolerate any form of genuine opposition. After the Unity Accord was signed between ZANU and ZAPU in 1987, there was no serious threat to ZANU-PF's dominance until the formation of the Movement for Democratic Change (MDC) in September 1999. The 1990 and 1995 general elections were relatively peaceful, because there was no serious opposition. The timing of more recent violence surrounding the June 2000 general elections can be explained by the arrival on the scene of a new and serious threat to ZANU-PF's, and ultimately, Mugabe's, survival.

Based on the pattern of the past twenty years, the evidence suggests that Mugabe's ZANU-PF is prepared to employ brutal tactics in order to crush serious opposition. The serious human rights abuses committed against innocent civilians in Matabeleland, together with the refusal to distinguish between the activities of dissidents and the political party of ZAPU, is one example. The second is provided by the defeat of the party's constitution in the February 2000 referendum, inducing it to resort to violence, fear, and intimidation to neutralize the MDC threat in the run-up to the June 2000 elections. These more recent events are accounted for in some detail below.

Political Realignment

The formal establishment of the MDC in September 1999 and its impressive performance in the elections held in June 2000 marks a fundamental political realignment in Zimbabwe.[20] Although elections are won or lost in the rural areas, ZANU-PF was clearly concerned that the MDC would be able to make inroads in the rural areas, especially in those regions, such as Masvingo and Manicaland, where there has already been considerable regional disaffection with Mugabe and ZANU-PF. On the surface, it might seem miraculous that a newly formed political party could pose such an immediate and serious threat to Mugabe. However, the formation of the MDC reflected a major political realignment which had been taking place over several years.

The MDC poses a significant threat to ZANU-PF in part because it draws its leadership and organizational machinery from the Zimbabwe

Congress of Trade Unions (ZCTU). The ZCTU has been highly critical of the government, blaming it for mismanaging the economy, and accusing the ruling elite of promoting its own economic interests while the majority of people were suffering under the combined impact of drought and ESAP. In December 1997 the ZCTU flexed its muscle by organizing a massive job stay-away in protest over the government's attempt to impose a war vets levy, to finance pay-outs promised to war vets of the liberation struggle. The ZCTU had the full support of employers during the protests. A second round of protests in March 1998 was also hugely successful, and the ZCTU has sought to use the threat of job stay-aways as leverage to get the government to take measures that would be beneficial to workers, such as tax relief. In the budget presented in October 1999, the reduction of the retail tax rate was a clear concession to the working poor, and the demands of the ZCTU on their behalf.

Many of the leaders of the MDC were also heavily involved in the consultative process over the redrafting of Zimbabwe's constitution. Morgan Tsvangirai was a founding member of the National Constitutional Assembly (NCA), established in 1997 to put pressure on the government to undertake broad-based consultations with Zimbabwean society about substantial constitutional reforms. The government countered this by establishing the Constitutional Commission, thereby placing the NCA in opposition to the government. The draft constitution the government ultimately devised was not entirely reflective of the preferences of the majority, especially with respect to extending the life of Mugabe's presidency. The leadership of the NCA and MDC then focused their energies on defeating the draft constitution, which they succeeded in doing. When the referendum on the draft Constitution was held in February 2000, the government was narrowly defeated. This defeat in the referendum provided the immediate backdrop to the widespread violence and intimidation associated with the June elections.

The defeat of the government's constitution in the referendum was a surprise to both the MDC and the government. It revealed to ZANU-PF that its chances of electoral success in the June elections were not a foregone conclusion. The party realized that in order to maintain its dominance in the rural areas, it needed to be seen to have made progress on a longstanding issue over which it was most vulnerable to attack: land redistribution.

The MDC has the support of many non-governmental organizations, such as human rights groups, the churches, professional organizations, the academic community, and the urban middle class. The role of pro-

fessional, urban-based whites and white commercial farmers is significant, as it is the first time since the removal of the white voters' role after
the 1985 elections, that whites have played a public political role. After
the 1985 elections, Mugabe was very annoyed that, after his gesture of
reconciliation following the civil war, the majority of whites continued
to vote for the Conservative Alliance of Zimbabwe (the re-named Rhodesian Front party). He proceeded to remove the separate voters' role
in 1987, which he was legally able to do under the Lancaster House Constitution. Since then, the whites have played a political role only behind
the scenes, such as when they quietly put pressure on the government to
launch market-based reforms at the end of the 1980s.

Due to the MDC's and NCA's opposition to the government's draft
constitution (which contained clauses allowing for compulsory acquisition of farms without compensation), white commercial farmers and
many of their farm workers openly supported the MDC. Based as they
are in the crucial rural areas, this made them vulnerable to attack by
ZANU-PF thugs. When, by mid-March 2000, it became clear to ZANU
that commercial farmers were encouraging their farm workers to support the MDC, the campaign of land invasions began to turn violent,
and white farmers were singled out for attack, and in some instances,
murder.[21] The MDC attempted to make inroads in the rural areas, but
the intimidation and acts of violence presented a formidable challenge.
As with whites, black farm workers have been targeted for violent
attacks, or have been injured whilst defending their white employers.
Here again, one can find links to the liberation struggle, as many farm
workers did fight in militias formed by whites to defend their farms.[22]

Consistent with past practice, the attacks on supporters of the MDC
are designed to intimidate people and create an atmosphere of fear.
During the 1995 elections there were not many violent incidents,
because the opposition was fragmented and ineffective, and therefore,
there was no serious challenge to ZANU-PF. In the 1990 elections, a
noteworthy incident was the attempted murder of Patrick Kombayi, who
ran as an independent in Masvingo.[23] Since 2000, MOC supporters
including white farmers and blacks, have been murdered. The deployment of ZANU-PF thugs against opposition supporters became a central
feature of the government's strategy in the run-up to the 2000 general
elections.[24]

The other plank in the election strategy was to push ahead with land
redistribution, regardless of the cost, in a desperate effort to hold on to
a majority of the crucial rural vote. The results of the February referen-

dum had revealed that only a slim majority of the rural population voted in favour of the proposed constitutional changes. Having lost the referendum, the government proceeded in April 2000 to ram through an amendment that allows it to confiscate farms without providing compensation.

The most unpopular provision of the draft constitution was the one that would have allowed Mugabe to stay on as president after his term expires in 2002. A survey conducted in September 1999 on the state of democracy in Zimbabwe revealed extreme voter dissatisfaction and the immense unpopularity of the president.[25] The defeat of the referendum has more to do with the provisions with respect to the president, than those over land. As was obvious during the 2002 presidential elections, politics in Zimbabwe continues to be marred by violence.

Although the June 2000 general elections themselves took place without too many serious incidents, the process leading up to them was not conducive to the conduct of free and fair elections. Serious acts of intimidation and violence took place in the rural areas, both on and off commercial farms. Anyone suspected of supporting the MDC was beaten up, and voters were told their votes would not be secret. The voters' roll is seriously flawed, with about two million dead people on the list – and they tend to vote for ZANU-PF! Although the voters roll was revised to address this anomaly (amongst others), the revised roll was not published soon enough for the opposition parties to challenge it in time for the elections, in the likely event of irregularities being detected. The MDC contested results in a number of ridings. The slim majority won by ZANU-PF can be at least partly attributed to the severe levels of intimidation and violence that prevailed prior to the elections. The impressive support enjoyed by the MCD, translating into fifty-seven out of 120 contested seats, reveals that a major political shift has occurred in Zimbabwe.[26]

As the elections confirmed, the MDC won the support of a wide cross-section of Zimbabwean society. The most interesting development is that whites are prepared to actively support and work for a political opposition party that has its roots in the labour movement. This is not altogether surprising, as the position papers produced by the ZCTU in the mid-1990s on ESAP revealed that the ZCTU was not advocating the abandonment of market-based reforms, which it perceived to be necessary.[27] The position of the ZCTU was that the government failed to take adequate steps to soften the blow to workers of such measures as the removal of price controls and the introduction of user fees in health and education.

The ZCTU was also concerned that the working poor were disproportionately affected by a high retail tax rate, high personal income tax rates, and various levies introduced by the government to cover expenses, such as the drought levy, and the development levy. The attempt to introduce a war vets levy in December 1997 was the last straw, and clearly positioned the ZCTU, and now, the MDC, in opposition to the war vets, and hence, the government. The growing corruption of the governing elite, and evidence of serious mismanagement of the economy, were major concerns shared by the ZCTU, the MDC, and the whites who were prepared to support it. The public support of many whites for the MDC has been a source of great annoyance for Mugabe and others who are not happy to see this visible minority play a public political role.

The MDC's charges of government mismanagement of the economy resonated with urban supporters, who were angry over the deterioration in their living standards. While a detailed explanation of Zimbabwe's economic problems is beyond the scope of this chapter, the most serious problems began to emerge after 1996. While many might trace the economic problems to the implementation of ESAP in 1991, the serious deterioration in the economy is most notable after 1996.

When the first phase of ESAP ended in 1995, the IMF was very critical of the government's failure to meet a number of the targets set in the reform program. As a result, the IMF suspended further lending to Zimbabwe, on the grounds that the budget deficit was still too large, forcing the World Bank to reluctantly follow suit. The IMF's decision was ill-advised, as the country had experienced another drought in 1995 (having barely recovered from the major drought of 1992), obliging the government to devote further resources to drought relief. The decision was also unfortunate, as the economy was beginning to respond positively to market-based reforms, and to stronger international commodity prices.

Since 1996, a combination of political crises and missed targets has led the international financial institutions repeatedly to cancel promises to resume lending to Zimbabwe. For example, the government's decision in August 1998 to intervene militarily in the Democratic Republic of Congo led to a significant souring of relations with major financial donors. The IMF's suspension of lending, and the government's flagging commitment to reforms, led to significant delays in the launch of the second phase of reforms, the Zimbabwe Program for Economic and Social Transformation (ZIMPREST).

Zimbabwe's relations with the IMF are especially poor. By failing to respect the government's need for ownership of structural adjustment, and by not displaying sensitivity to political impediments, the IMF has made the situation worse. It has recognized that simply cancelling loans has not helped it to increase its leverage with the government. For its part, the government has little incentive to defend market-based reforms. The government's lagging commitment has, in turn, alienated the economic elites, who had supported the government in its initial formulation of market-based reforms. These same elites now support the MDC.

Interestingly, the ZCTU and the MDC have been more critical of the government's mismanagement of the economy than of the role of the international financial institutions. They see the reforms as necessary, but argue that government decisions, such as the 1997 pay-outs to war vets and the intervention in the Congo, have disrupted their progress, and the poor have borne the burden of this. The lack of economic growth and worsening prospects for urban dwellers were a major factor in the MCD's ability to capture the support of the urban areas. Urban voters have not been impressed, or convinced, by ZANU's attempts to blame all the country's economic problems on the international institutions.

The election results of 2000 confirmed that the MDC enjoys a broadly based coalition of support, which is strongest in the urban areas. This support cannot be reduced to any one minority grouping, whether whites or Ndebele. Although the MDC won twenty of the twenty-three contested seats in Matabeleland, it also won most seats in Masvingo and Manicaland provinces, as well as two each in Mashonaland East and West.[28] Only in Mashonaland Central did the MDC fail to win a seat, in Mugabe's heartland.

Security Dimensions of Peacebuilding

One significant feature of post-1980 Zimbabwe is that the military has taken its instructions from the civilian leadership, rather than the other way around. The ZNA is reasonably well-equipped, and very professional. Regrettably, this accomplishment has been marred by the willingness of Mugabe to use the military in his political battles.

The Military's Influence

There were signs by the late 1990s that the military had become increasingly influential in Zimbabwe. The growth in this influence is a disturbing feature of the authoritarian reflex in Zimbabwean politics today.

The first sign came in August 1997, when the War Veterans' Association confronted Mugabe with an ultimatum intended to improve the conditions for war veterans. The showdown was prompted by the release of a report on the findings of a special commission set up to investigate allegations of abuse of the War Victims' Compensation Fund. The fund was set up ostensibly to provide compensation to war veterans who were suffering from injuries sustained during the liberation struggle. It transpired that millions of dollars in fraudulent claims were paid out to members of the ruling elite, senior politicians and bureaucrats, exhausting the fund and depriving legitimate claimants of compensation.

Chenjerai Hunzvi, the leader of the War Veterans' Association, confronted Mugabe at a time when most of his cabinet was away. Several interviews have confirmed that Mugabe was faced with the prospect of a bloodless coup, unless he went ahead and met various demands of the war vets.[29] Among the demands were a monthly stipend for all war vets, whether employed or not, a pension, and most significantly, insistence that a minimum of 20 per cent of all land acquired for redistribution be set aside for war vets. Without consulting his cabinet, or consideration of the budgetary implications, Mugabe went ahead and agreed to the demands. Although Mugabe attempted to target only unemployed and destitute war vets, Hunzvi insisted that all war vets benefit from the pay-outs, and guarantees of land.

The unbudgeted for pay-outs caused the IMF to cancel lending to Zimbabwe, and the IMF sat down with the government to determine where the money was to be found. The government ultimately decided upon a war vets levy, which was to have been rubber-stamped by Parliament in December of 1997. Attempts to impose the levy led to such a public outrage that it had to be abandoned. The ZCTU organized a massive job stay-away in December, which, unexpectedly, enjoyed the support of employers, even though it meant the loss of business during the Christmas season.

Faced with the prospect of losing the support of the powerful war vets, Mugabe was under intense pressure to push ahead with a second phase of land redistribution. Mugabe's alliance with the war vets strengthened the radical elements within the party,[30] which had been marginalized in the late 1980s and early 1990s in the consensus built-up around the adoption of market-based reforms. These radical elements supported the desire of the war vets to move quickly forward with a comprehensive land redistribution program.

It was in this context that in November 1997 the government announced that 1,471 large-scale commercial farms had been designated for compulsory acquisition. A measure of the pressure being exerted on Mugabe is that this announcement was made before the government had come up with a plan on how it would go about resettling peasant farmers. Lacking the resources to finance the land acquisition and resettlement program, and without a clearly developed plan, the IFIs and international donors refused to provide assistance. In light of this, Mugabe began to raise the spectre of confiscating the land without providing the white farmers any compensation.

The second sign of the growing influence of the military was the hugely unpopular decision in September 1998 to intervene in the Democratic Republic of the Congo (DRC). Ostensibly to support the late Laurent Kabila in his campaign to repel Ugandan and Rwandan-backed rebel forces in the east, the motives behind the intervention were primarily economic. Zimbabwe's top military brass, as well as people close to Mugabe, won lucrative defence contracts.[31] Zimbabwean troops are deployed in the southeast of the DRC, the location of much of the country's mining industry, including diamonds. Since Zimbabwe has no direct strategic interests in the country and shares no borders, the prospect of personal enrichment provides one plausible explanation for Zimbabwe's intervention, even in the face of its domestic unpopularity.

A distinction must be made between the rank and file in the military, and senior officers. While senior officers stood to benefit financially from the intervention, many ordinary troops have paid for the intervention with their lives. Reports that some officers attempted a coup against Mugabe in December 1998, in opposition to the Congo war, suggest that there is not wholesale support within the military for the intervention. The reporters who published news of the coup were detained in January 1999 and subjected to torture.

Zimbabwe's decision to intervene in the Congo, at an estimated cost of one million per day, led the IMF yet again to cancel promised disbursements. The decision preceded the important September 1998 donors' conference on land redistribution, and seriously jeopardized the government's efforts to secure funding.

The military played a direct role in the government-orchestrated campaign of land invasions after the February 2000 referendum. Incidents of squatting had been taking place over the previous two years, often at the encouragement of local area MPs. The 2000 campaign, however, was centrally planned by the government, with the military providing logistical support. Army trucks were used to transport war vets (among others) to the farms, and automatic weapons were seen among the squatters.[32] Murders of white farmers and their farm workers took place in a context where the police refused to intervene. In the case of one farmer murdered in Matabeleland, police reportedly prevented people from coming to the farmer's assistance, in a gun battle that lasted several hours.[33]

It is not clear whether the military would have supported the election results had ZANU-PF lost its majority. Interviews revealed disagreement amongst prominent stakeholders with respect to this issue. Although the MDC expressed confidence that the military would have respected its electoral victory, the head of the CFU was less confident.[34]

Despite international pressure, and questioning on the part of some members of his own cabinet, Mugabe continues to condone the land occupations. He clearly feels he cannot afford to lose the support of the strategically placed war vets, who provide a prominent symbol of the main reason why the civil war was fought. Significantly, the police have stood by while the law has been broken, and have refused to enforce two Supreme Court rulings declaring the occupations illegal.

The military has also become involved in supporting the government in areas not normally within its responsibility. The government has ordered the army to help it implement its fast track land redistribution program, which involves quickly resettling thousands of peasants on thousands of compulsorily acquired commercial farms, without providing any infrastructure. The army is assisting the government in conducting surveys, and pegging the farms to be redistributed, as well as in resettling people onto the land.[35] Prior to the 2002 presidential election, the military took over the directorship of the CIO.

As the economy deteriorates, and fuel shortages, and fuel and food price increases take their toll, the army has been deployed with growing frequency to assist the police in quelling the violent demonstrations in the urban areas. The key question now is, once these forces have been unleashed, how easy will it be to rein them in?

The Role of the International Financial Institutions and Major Donors, 1990–7

There were numerous opportunities during the 1990s when the donor community could have taken on more of a leadership role with respect to land redistribution. Had there been some conception of the importance of land to the liberation struggle, and of the need to redress unequal land access as the final stage in the process of peacebuilding, the logic of attaching priority to this fundamental issue might have been more obvious.

As noted earlier, the introduction of market-based reforms served to highlight the continued dominance of whites in the economy, while also legitimizing the aspirations of those blacks wishing to prosper in business and commercial farming. At the same time, ESAP caused severe hardship for urban workers, as well as the rural population, many of whom depend on remittances from relatives working in the urban centres. The ZCTU, while accepting the need for market-based reforms, was critical of the manner in which ESAP was implemented. For example, in 1993, when Zimbabweans were still reeling from the effects of the 1992 drought, the last remaining subsidies on five food staples, including maize meal and cooking oil, were removed.

While the government has played its part in mismanaging the economy, the unhelpful role of the international financial institutions cannot be ignored. There were serious flaws in the design of the structural adjustment program, the most significant of which was the failure to incorporate rural development, including land redistribution, as a necessary and integral part of the structural adjustment exercise. The error of not supporting land redistribution was acknowledged by the World Bank in its own evaluation of the first phase of structural adjustment.[36] Although the financial institutions claimed that they were committed to land redistribution, no resources were earmarked for that purpose. Since the government was being asked to reduce its budget deficit substantially, it was faced with serious resource constraints, allowing the government to allocate only small amounts to land redistribution. By ignoring the centrality of land redistribution to rural development and poverty alleviation, ESAP failed to address a fundamental structural impediment to equitable growth in Zimbabwe. Instead, it helped to reinforce the politically, socially, economically and morally unsustainable status quo.

The introduction of ESAP has added legitimacy to voices that argue that blacks should be able to engage in commercial farming, rather than being relegated to peasant production in the Communal and Resettlement Areas. Thus, not only has structural adjustment ostensibly benefited white owners of capital, it has also helped a black elite more interested in large-scale commercial farming than redistribution. The conceptualization of the large-scale commercial farming sector as essential for the maintenance of agricultural productivity and for foreign exchange earnings has been perpetuated by both blacks and whites with a vested interest in commercial farming.[37]

However, in a 1991 report prepared by the World Bank, it was established that less than 50 per cent of net prime agricultural arable lands in the commercial farming sector were adequately utilized.[38] Based on its findings, the Bank concluded that the commercial farming sector could supply 3.5 million hectares of its current 11.2 million hectares for redistribution without risking present levels of production. The Bank's report indicated, however, a preference that land be transferred through market forces, rather than government intervention (which, of course, would have the effect of maintaining the status quo). In 1992 the Bank offered to support land redistribution, but favoured market principles, together with rules favouring sub-division over compulsory acquisition.

The government, however, was not interested in the Bank's proposals, and was moving in the direction of compulsory land acquisition. In 1992 the government introduced the Land Acquisition Act, which allowed it to compulsorily acquire land that was underutilized or derelict, and provided for compensation to commercial farmers. Yet the act caused an uproar amongst white farmers, whose legal challenges prevented the government from making much progress on land redistribution. White farmers have been slow to accept the need for land redistribution, only changing their stance after the 1997 land designation exercise, and the commencement of squatting in 1998. An important window of opportunity between 1992 and 1997, when the government was still prepared to respect property rights and pay compensation, was therefore lost by white farmers and the international community.

The key donor with historic responsibility for land reform, the United Kingdom, had serious reservations about the first phase of land reform. Even though most of the money promised in 1981 was used up by 1988, Britain refused to contemplate further funding until the first loan phase came formally to an end in 1996. Britain's concerns about land redistribution are centred around three main issues: that land redistribution be squarely focused on poverty alleviation; strong opposition to the Commercial Farm Resettlement Program, which has siphoned resources away from helping the poor to the black elite; and concern that the process of land redistribution respect market principles.[39]

By 1998, the major donors had lost confidence in the government's ability to effectively implement a second phase of land redistribution. The stage was set for a more radical process of land redistribution.

1998–2000

In preparation for the second phase of land redistribution, the government issued a major planning document, the Land Reform and Resettlement Programme, Phase II.[40] A major donors' conference was held from 9 to 11 September 1998, but was clouded by the government's earlier decision to intervene in the Congo. However, in consultations prior to the conference, the donors had signalled serious reservations about Phase II itself. The government's document reflected a serious effort to respond to the deficiencies identified in earlier resettlement efforts, by providing, for example, for the right of private tenure over resettled land. However, the donors objected to the top-down, centrally administered features of the program, which they felt would make it inefficient and unsustainable. Donors favoured a bottom-up, community-driven approach that was consistent with market principles. While donors were prepared to support the need for land redistribution in principle, the consultations leading up to the conference revealed serious disagreements between the government and the donors over the process by which land redistribution should proceed.

During the conference, it appeared that a compromise had been reached. It was agreed that an 'Inception Phase' covering twenty-four months would be immediately implemented. The objective of the inception phase was to test the market-friendly approach to land reform preferred by the donors. The intention was that current government resettlement models be implemented alongside alternative beneficiary-initiated models.[41] A number of principles were agreed to, including that the program be implemented in a transparent, fair, and sustainable manner.

The communique issued after the conference called for the 'immediate implementation of resettlement, beginning with the 118 farms on offer,' referring to farms voluntarily offered to the government, including those not contested from the 1997 designation exercise.[42] The government understood this to mean that the donors would fund the acquisition of these farms. However, the only pledge made at the conference was that of the World Bank. It pledged US $5 million, which was intended to support the market-friendly, complementary approaches to land reform. The failure of the other donors to pledge money left the government with the impression that they were not serious about funding land redistribution. For their part, the donors believed that the government had undertaken not to confiscate farms. However, in November 1998, after the one-year limitation period was over, the government moved to acquire the eight hundred farms remaining on the original 1997 designation list. This greatly soured relations with donors, and effectively stalled the inception phase process. The process was also hindered by the fact that the Commercial Farmers' Union (CFU) failed to hold up its end of the bargain. Both the government and donors were led to believe that the CFU would voluntarily offer land for redistribution. However, the CFU, sensing the lack of donor support for the Phase II program, took a wait- and-see attitude, and is considered not to have been bargaining in good faith.

After the donors' conference, the government launched an extensive consultation process with stakeholders, donors, NGOs, and land reform experts in preparation for the planning document for the inception phase. The Inception Phase Framework Plan was released in March 1999.[43] However, it was not until November 1999 that a technical support unit, which was meant to be a one-stop coordinating unit for land reform, was set up. The slow pace reflected serious divisions within the government over how to proceed, and in-fighting over who should staff the unit, and where it should be located. The donors were also slow to respond to the publication of the inception phase document. In March 1999, the EU urged the United Kingdom to commit to the government's program, but it failed to do so. Without British support, no other donors were prepared to fund the inception phase, and the CFU failed to offer land in support of the program.

By the time the technical support unit was set up in November 1999, the government had taken a stronger stance on land reform. Around that time, the government released its version of the draft constitution, revealing its intention to confiscate farms without compensation, arguing that it was Britain's responsibility. The number of land invasions continued to increase in 1999, but it was not until after the results of the February 2000 referendum that a systematic, government-organized campaign of land invasions began.

After the land invasions turned violent, the donors adopted a highly coordinated stance towards the government. All donors, including the World Bank, froze all funding to the government, in light of the murders and land invasions. The donors are also not supporting any NGOs, including private policy institutes, that appear to be supporting the government. The donors have formulated two minimum conditions that have to be met before any funding will be restored: the restoration of law and order, and a return to macro-economic stability, including a shadow program with the IMF.

The position of the donors over the 1990s reveals a clear preference for the market-driven process. Yet past experience reveals that the market has thrown up only marginal lands for redistribution, which goes a long way in explaining why the first phase of land reform was not uniformly successful. The donors exaggerated the shortcomings of the first phase, in order to support their claim that the government should not be directly involved in the program. Their claim is not supported by the evidence. Furthermore, it is unclear precisely who the communities are that the donors would place their faith in. As research on poverty alleviation projects that rely on local-level initiatives has revealed, it tends to be the better-off in communities, such as teachers and others with salaried jobs, successful farmers, political leaders, including traditional leaders and local council members, that are best placed to devise plans for projects intended to alleviate poverty.

The fixation of donors on the need to protect the private property rights of the commercial farmers also reveals a privileging of civil and political liberties over the right to subsistence. In the cries for a return to law and order, there has been absolute silence on the right of very poor Zimbabweans to subsistence.[44] Nor does there appear to be any concession to the idea that if the rule of law supports an unjust distribution of land that denies the right to subsistence of a substantial number of Zimbabweans, they may well be justified in challenging those property rights.

Implications for International Peacebuilding Efforts

There are no easy answers as to how the international community can play an effective role in peacebuilding, in what often amounts to nation-building. Fundamental questions about how a society should be organized are as much a part of the peacebuilding process as are more transitional concerns, such as the demobilization of armed forces. The ideological preferences of powerful countries in a position to help, and political expediency, can hinder the efforts of war-torn societies to rebuild in a manner that addresses the root causes of the conflict.

As the Zimbabwean case has illustrated, the problems began at Lancaster House, when onerous terms were imposed on the Patriotic Front negotiators. When Mugabe's avowedly Marxist-Leninist party won the 1980 elections, there were real concerns about his intentions, in an international context where the Cold War had heated up again.

The introduction of ESAP in 1991, and the failure of the international financial institutions to address the land issue in the context of structural adjustment, further entrenched the bias in favour of the status quo. As in other countries, structural adjustment has hindered the realization of social goals that are essential to addressing the root causes of conflict. The problem with this line of argumentation, however, is that it assumes that if only the international community did the right thing, then the problems associated with peacebuilding could be resolved. Zimbabwe does not support such an argument.

A variety of factors explain the slowdown in the pace of land redistribution after 1983, and it was not simply a question of inadequate external funding. The reality is that many members of the ruling elite were acquiring farms for themselves, while at the same time, there was growing pressure for indigenization, rather than redistribution of, the commercial farming sector. As the 1997 land designation process revealed, roughly 40 per cent of commercial farms were earmarked for indigenous commercial farming. The activism of the war vets can be explained by the concerns over this trend, as well as the growing evidence that corruption was preventing deserving communal area farmers from benefiting.

In this respect, the international community's concern over who would benefit from the second phase of land redistribution is a legitimate one. Between 1992 and 1998, however, the major donors were far too preoccupied with a structural adjustment program that has been acknowledged to have serious design flaws. Among these was the failure to address comprehensively the land issue.

At another level, the increasing role and influence of the military in Zimbabwean politics point again to the importance that peacebuilding be carried out in such a way that it will be sustainable. Demobilization and integration of armed forces is essential. Once that task has been accomplished, however, steps must be taken to ensure that the aspirations of demobilized war vets are met, to avoid their growing disillusionment over the outcome of the peace. In Zimbabwe, destitute war vets have joined forces with their employed counterparts in the army, police and security apparatus, thereby creating a powerful destabilizing force in the country.

Some of the developments in Zimbabwe could not reasonably have been foreseen. However, the unrest over what was the central issue in the liberation struggle, and what remains a core social, economic, political and moral imperative, points to the necessity that peacebuilding be treated as an on-going exercise, if it is to be sustained over the long term. Peacebuilding needs to be understood as moving through stages, that moves beyond the achievement of negative peace, to confidence-building, to inclusive political institutions and economic growth and justice.

Zimbabwe's experience points to the importance of addressing in a comprehensive way the socio-economic aspects of peacebuilding. There remains a tendency for international donors to prioritize the political and security aspects of peacebuilding. While important, the danger is that the root socio-economic causes of conflict are not addressed. Socio-economic issues, by their nature, require a long time period to be adequately addressed. Donors, including Canada, tend to be constrained by the desire to see quick results from peacebuilding and development initiatives. This makes support for socio-economic aspects of peacebuilding, such as major land reform (a root cause of conflict in many countries), unattractive to donors. Unless they have a direct stake or responsibility in the process, such as is the case with the United Kingdom in Zimbabwe, countries such as Canada are reluctant to invest in a land reform process that usually takes at least a decade for positive results to emerge.

Canadian policy, for example, has been not to devote funds towards land acquisition in Zimbabwe.[45] Although Canada is prepared to help finance resettlement efforts, a policy that forecloses the allocation of funds for purposes of land acquisition poses contradictions for Canada's peacebuilding initiative, and for the government's human security approach to foreign policy. The government has tended to focus its peacebuilding efforts in countries that recently emerged from civil war, such as Guatemala and El Salvadore, and has been slow to recognize the importance of applying peacebuilding initiatives in countries such as Zimbabwe, where permissive conditions for violent conflict exist. The government's approach to peacebuilding has also tended to focus on the security and political aspects, although evidence is mounting that insufficient efforts to address socio-economic aspects of peacebuilding, including land reform, in the above-mentioned countries has led to serious difficulties.

Even within the political realm, the government's approach has been to emphasize the mechanistic aspect of promoting democracy, such as the regular holding of elections, rather than to examine whether political institutions have any legitimacy. For example, even in light of concerns raised over the level of fear and violence surrounding the recent elections in Zimbabwe, Lloyd Axworthy affirmed that 'basically, Zimbabwe is a democracy.' The mere fact, however, that elections are held every five years in Zimbabwe does not prove that the political process enjoys legitimacy, or that opposition forces are allowed to function on a level playing field.

Nevertheless, concerns about sovereignty limit the extent to which major donors can and should interfere in the domestic political process. The perception that donors have directly interfered in the political process in Zimbabwe, notwithstanding the importance of supporting politically inclusive change, has further soured relations with the government. Donors were effectively frozen out as the government pushed ahead with its fast-track land redistribution exercise.

Most of Zimbabwe's commercial farm land has now been 'redistributed.' Should the MDC ever succeed in assuming power, it will have to contend with a fait accompli insofar as commercial farms are concerned. Any government, including a MDC government, would likely find it politically very difficult to reverse the land invasions that Mugabe's government set in motion. Sooner or later, Mugabe will pass from the scene, but regardless, no government will be able to ignore the need for an equitable resolution of the land issue; a lasting peace in Zimbabwe will require that this be so.

The Zimbabwean case suggests that countries such as Canada must embrace a more expansive view of peacebuilding that moves beyond short-term, political-security aspects in the context of post-conflict situations. If peacebuilding is to be understood as a long-term process, that adequately incorporates socio-economic dimensions, it needs to be conceptualized as an integral part of the larger development process rather than being treated as a separate function. In a context of limited funding for peacebuilding and development assistance efforts, development assistance should be considered in light of its impact on peacebuilding efforts.

NOTES

An excerpt of this chapter originally appeared in *International Journal* 57, no. 2 (2002). Funding for this research was provided by the International Development Research Centre. I would like to thank Sam Moyo, director, Southern African Regional Institute for Policy Studies (SARIPS), for providing me with an institutional home during my research stay in Zimbabwe in August 2000. I greatly appreciate the comments of Robert O. Matthews, Cranford Pratt, Richard Simeon, Blair Rutherford, and Pablo Idahosa on an earlier draft of this paper.

1 The Canadian government's peacebuilding initiative is summarized in Department of Foreign Affairs and International Trade, 'Peace in Progress: Canada's Peacebuilding Initiative' (Ottawa: Government of Canada, 1998). An assessment of Canadian peacebuilding efforts can be found in Gregory Wirick and Robert Miller, eds., *Canada and Missions for Peace* (Ottawa: IDRC, 1998).

2 For a comprehensive assessment of the interdependent dimensions of peacebuilding, see Kenneth Bush, 'Towards a Balanced Approach to Rebuilding War-Torn Societies,' *Canadian Foreign Policy* 3 (Winter 1998), 49–69.

3 This approach was affirmed by Boutros Boutros-Ghali in his *Supplement to An Agenda for Peace: Position Paper by the Secretary-General on the Occasion of the Fiftieth Anniversary of the United Nations* (New York: United Nations, 1995).

4 Although there was a serious rebellion in Matabeleland in the early 1980s, this never reached the scale of a civil war, because the central government's authority and control was never seriously challenged. See Hevina Dashwood and Cranford Pratt, 'Leadership, Participation and Conflict Management: Zimbabwe and Tanzania' in Taisier M. Ali and Robert O. Matthews, eds., *Civil Wars in Africa: Roots and Resolution* (Montreal and Kingston: McGill-Queen's University Press, 1999).

5 While equitable land distribution is a necessary condition for sustainable peacebuilding, it is not being argued here that it is a sufficient condition. Land redistribution in an authoritarian, non-inclusive political context is unlikely to be conducive to lasting peace. Ideas on the relative importance of political or economic factors in peacebuilding are discussed in Stephen Ryan, *Ethnic Conflict and International Relations* (Aldershot, UK: Dartmouth Publishing, 1995), 129–52.

6 For example, James Boyce draws attention to the need for donors and the international financial institutions to pay greater attention to the socio-economic dimensions of peacebuilding: see *Economic Policy for Peace Building: The Lessons of El Salvador* (Boulder, CO: Lynne Rienner Publishers, 1996). A more sceptical view can be found in Dane Rowlands, 'International Financial Institutions and Conflict Management,' *Canadian Foreign Policy* 17, no. 3 (2000), 15–35.

7 Some major donors are now beginning to contemplate the need to approach peacebuilding from a broader perspective. For example, Peace and Conflict Impact Assessment (PCIA), a method for evaluating whether development projects are likely to contribute to peace, or exacerbate conflict, explicitly address the socio-economic root causes of conflict. See Development Assistance Committee, OECD, 'DAC Guidelines on Conflict, Peace and Development Cooperation' (Paris: OECD, 1997); Kenneth Bush, 'A Measure of Peace: Peace and Conflict Impact Assessment (PCIA) of Development Projects in Conflict Zones' (Ottawa: IDRC, 1998); Saferworld, International Alert, and IDRC, 'Peace and Conflict-sensitive Approaches to Development: A Briefing for the OECD DAC Task Force on Conflict, Peace, and Development Cooperation and the Conflict Prevention and Reconstruction Network' (Ottawa: IDRC, 2000).

8 For a brief account of the evolution of the liberation struggle, see Colin Stoneman and Lionel Cliffe, *Zimbabwe: Politics, Economics and Society* (London: Printer Publishers, 1989), 16–28.

9 Land acquisition reached its peak in 1982–3, when almost one million hectares of farm land was purchased for ZWD22million. In 1983–4, the amount spent for land acquisition dropped to ZWD4.5million. The government purchased 2.7 million hectares during the 1980s from the large-scale commercial farm sector, at a cost of ZWD76million, or USD13million in 1993 dollars. Over 70 per cent of this land was purchased between 1980 and 1985. See Sam Moyo, *The Land Question in Zimbabwe* (Harare: Southern African Regional Institute for Policy Studies, 1995), 85, and 122.

10 Stephen John Stedman, *Peacemaking in Civil War* (Boulder, CO: Lynne Rienner, 1991); Donald Rothchild, 'Successful Mediation: Lord Carrington and the Rhodesian Settlement,' in Chester Crocker and Fen Osler Hampson, eds., *Managing Global Chaos: Sources and Responses to International Conflict* (Washington, DC: US Institute of Peace Press, 1996).

11 Stephen Nzombe, 'Negotiations with the British,' in Canaan S. Banana, ed., *Turmoil and Tenacity, 1890–1990* (Harare: College Press, 1989), 185.

12 Rothchild, 'successful mediation.' 481.

13 During the 1980s, real prices shot up by 40 per cent in US dollar terms. See Moyo, *The Land Question in Zimbabwe*, 123.

14 Welshman Ncube, interview, August 2000.

15 Bill Kinsey, 'Land Reform, Growth and Equity: Emerging Evidence from Zimbabwe's Resettlement Programme,' *Journal of Southern African Studies* (June 1999), 183–6; Moyo, *The Land Question* 124.

16 Hevina Dashwood, *Zimbabwe: The Political Economy of Transformation* (Toronto: University of Toronto Press, 2000), ch. 7.

17 Scott Taylor, 'Race, Class and Neopatrimonialism in Zimbabwe,' in Richard Joseph, ed., *State, Conflict and Democracy in Africa* (Boulder, CO: Lynne Rienner Publishers, 1999).

18 Government of Zimbabwe, *Policy Paper on Land Redistribution and Resettlement in Zimbabwe* (Ministry of Local Government, Rural and Urban Development, 1996).

19 Economist Intelligence Unit, *Country Report: Zimbabwe* (4th Quarter, 1998).

20 For an analysis of the election results, see Lloyd Sachikonye, 'Just a Victory,' *Southern African Political and Economic Monthly* (July 2000), 5–6.

21 Sam Moyo, interview, August 2000.

22 This fact has been used to signal the disloyalty of all farm workers by some ZANU-PF nationalists. My thanks to Blair Rutherford, University of Regina, for this insight.

23 Lisa, Laakso, *Voting Without Choosing: State Making and Elections in Zimbabwe* (Helsinki, 2000); Jonathan Moyo, *Voting for Democracy: Electoral Politics in Zimbabwe* (Harare: University of Zimbabwe Publications, 1992), 49–51.

24 At least twenty-nine people were killed in pre-election violence. See 'UN Warns Mugabe on Abuses,' *Financial Gazette* 22 June 2000.

25 Chikwanha-Dzenga, et.al., *Democracy and National Governance in Zimbabwe: A Country Survey Report* (Institute for Democracy in South Africa, 2000).

26 The final results of June 2000 elections were as follows: MDC – 57; ZANU – 62; ZANU-Ndonga – 2.

27 ZCTU, *Beyond ESAP: Framework for a Long-term Development Strategy in Zimbabwe* (Harare: ZCTU, 1996).

28 'MDC's Mat Victory Stuns Mugabe,' *Financial Gazette* (29 June 2000).

29 Interviews, 1998.

30 Moyo, interview, August 2000.

31 Economist Intelligence Unit *Country Report: Zimbabwe* (4th Quarter, 1998), 1.

32 Sydney Masamvu, 'War Vets, Army Throw Weight Behind Mugabe for 2002 Poll,' *Financial Gazette* (May 11 2000); Vincent Kahiya, 'Government Directs Farm Invasions,' *Zimbabwe Independent* (March 3 2000).

33 The actual number of war vets involved in orchestrating the land invasions is estimated at about 1,500. Legitimate war vets are now in their forties and fifties, and the violence on farms can be largely attributed to youth recruited by the war vets to intimidate farmers and farm workers. Although there are no official statistics, there were about 70,000 war vets at independence, and there are now roughly 35,000. (Information provided by Annie Chikwanha-Dzenga, lecturer, Department of Political and Administrative Studies, University of Zimbabwe, based on interviews she conducted on 18 May 2001).

34 Welshman Ncube and David Hasluck, interviews, August 2000.

35 Chris McGreal, 'Mugabe Mobilises Army for Huge Farm Invasion,' *Guardian* (2 August 2000).

36 World Bank, *Performance Audit Report: Zimbabwe – Structural Adjustment Program* (30 June 1995), 33.

37 Moyo, 'The Political Economy of Land Acquisition and Redistribution in Zimbabwe, 1990–1999,' *Journal of Southern African Studies* 26, no. 1 (2000).

38 World Bank, *Zimbabwe Agricultural Sector Memorandum*, Southern Africa Department, Agricultural Operations Division, Report No. 9429, (Washington, DC: World Bank 1991).

39 DfID, *Land Resettlement in Zimbabwe: Background Briefing* (2000).

40 Government of Zimbabwe, *Land Reform and Resettlement Programme: Phase II* (Harare, September 1998).

41 Communique, 1998.

42 Ibid.
43 Government of Zimbabwe, *Inception Phase Framework Plan: 1999-2000* (March 1999).
44 For a classic elaboration of the importance of attaching equal weight to both subsistence rights, and the right to physical security, see Henry Shue, *Basic Rights, Subsistence, Affluence and US Foreign Policy* (Princeton: Princeton University Press, 1981).
45 Anne Charles, interview, former Canadian high commissioner to Zimbabwe, August 1998.

Part Three

Peacebuilding under Threat

8
Somalia: International versus Local Attempts at Peacebuilding

Hussein M. Adam

A series of Somali civil wars has led to state collapse and layers of complicated problems. Like Chad in 1980–2, Somali state collapse in 1991–2 essentially resulted from a factional civil war among the United Somali Congress (USC) guerrilla victors who had overthrown the previous brutal Siyad–Barre regime; a war that caused the demise of all the branches of central government. The capital, Mogadishu, became a city divided by armed barricades, resembling Beirut during the Lebanese civil war. Somali minorities escaped by sea to Kenya and Yemen recalling Vietnam's boat people. Chaos and anarchy engulfed Mogadishu, making it the epicentre of Somalia's problems. The situation in northern Somalia, former British Somaliland, which declared a de facto secession under the Somali National Movement (SNM), reflected similarities to the problem of Eritrea with Ethiopia. A deeper tragedy lay in the formerly peaceful Bay region inhabited by the large, yet poorly armed Rahanweyn Somalis. The war came to them simply as a result of their geography. Siyad Barre left Mogadishu but did not leave the country as Mengistu did. He barricaded himself and his remnant loyalist troops in his home region of Gedo, from where he launched spoiler wars like Renamo in Mozambique. What ensued were continuing civil wars between General Aidid's USC and Siyad's remnant forces, fought mostly on Bay (Baidoa) territories. Journalists termed Bay's plight Somalia's Bosnia. The devastating man-made famine that resulted led to the international community's humanitarian intervention in Somalia in the years 1992–5.

One could speculate about various possibilities for external intervention to rescue Somalia from destruction. According to Ali Mazrui: 'Ideally, Somalia should have been saved by fellow Africans – a kind of Pax Africana, Africans policing themselves or policing each other. It has been attempted in Liberia by a West African force drawn from several nations ... A second preference would have been a rescue of Somalia by members of the Organization of the Islamic Conference (OIC), a kind of Pax Islamica ... A third preference for the Somali rescue would have been under the League of Arab States – a kind of Pax Arabica or Pax Arabiana ... A fourth preference would have been a truly multinational task force to both pacify and feed Somalia, a kind of Pax Humania which would combine troops from carefully and sensitively selected countries.'[1] Perhaps the UNOSOM situation in 1994–5, after the departure of most American and European forces, mirrors somewhat Mazrui's fourth option. The fact remains that when foreign intervention to avert the Somali catastrophe came, it was a US initiative under the umbrella of the United Nations. 'What we have instead is a Pax Americana – a primarily American force. It is essentially a Pax Americana with a UN fig leaf.' In the post-Cold War era, with socio-economic difficulties facing most states, the prospects for a single power (other than the United States) to save a collapsing state have diminished considerably. It gives support to the proposition that the more complete the collapse of a state, the greater will be the role and magnitude of foreign intervention aimed at reconstruction. The magnitude and complexities of Somali problems led the OAU, the OIC, and the Arab League to maintain a cautious posture, concluding that it was not realistic to attempt an intervention. The OAU lacked political will and resources, while the OIC and the Arab League lacked political will.

State Collapse

Around January 1991 and during the ensuing months, Somalia experienced a cataclysmic event, virtually unseen since the Second World War. It was not simply a military coup, a revolutionary replacement of a decayed and ineffective dictatorship, or a new, radical regime coming to power through a partisan uprising. Somalia's collapsed state represented the literal implosion of state structures and of residual forms of authority and legitimacy, and the situation has lasted for over a full decade. In some respects, the country seems to have reverted to a nineteenth-century status: no internationally recognized polity; no recognized national administration exercising real authority; no formal countrywide legal and judiciary system; no national banking and insurance services; no national telephone and postal systems; no national public services; no national educational and health systems; no national police and public security services; and no reliable electricity or piped

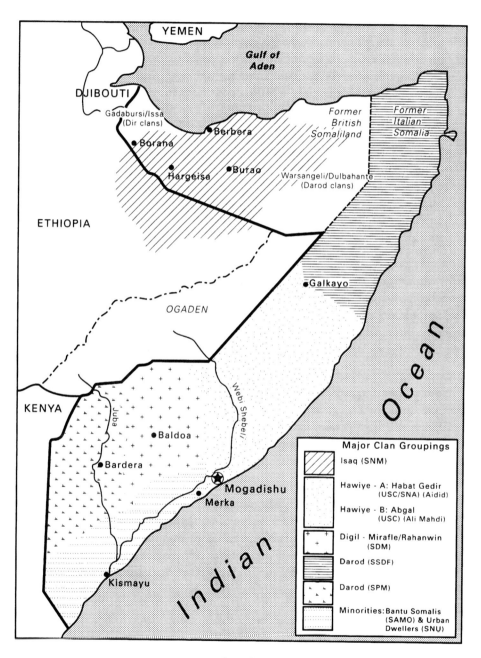

Somalia

water services. Most of the so-called officials serve on a voluntary basis and are often surrounded, in a number of places, by disruptive, violent bands of armed youths.

Like all collapsed states, the Siyad military state disintegrated because it could no longer perform the functions required for it to pass as a state. Siyad Barre's brutal and arbitrary repression and his concentration of power in the hands of his clan elite led to the whole country rising up against him, using their own clans as organizing bases. Such armed clan-based protopolitical organizations were created as the Somali National Movement (SNM, for the northern Isaq clan-family), the Somali Salvation Democratic Front (SSDF, for the Majerteen, Darod clan-family), the United Somali Congress (USC, for the Hawiye clan-family); the Somali Patriotic Movement (SPM, for the Ogaden, Darod clan-family), and so forth. At present there are about twenty-eight such clan-based political factions. As Marina Ottaway put it, 'Competition becomes turf war among political organizations trying to keep each other out. A tragic example is offered by Somalia, where the fragmentation of the elite after the demise of Mohamed Siyad Barre led to the emergence of warlords fighting with each other for exclusive control over territory.'[2] Elite fragmentation has led to political paralysis and continuing conflict or at best negative peace in the central (Mogadishu) and southern (Kismayu) parts of the country. Territorial fragmentation has also led to enclaves of positive peace and progress.

The phenomenon of state collapse represents a major challenge to developmental social sciences. The Siyad case shows a close relationship between state collapse and the role of rogue leadership. A critical cause lay in the mismanagement, pillage of resources, brutal military repression, and abuses by the dictatorial regime that left the majority of the population without a stake in the existing system. Under Siyad Barre, Somalia became one of the most indebted states in Africa; with a debt service ratio of over 180 percent and a meagre revenue base. From a historical perspective, Somali state collapse also represents a mismatch between a seemingly strong state and an amorphous Somali civil society. The problem is not between the state as such, or in the abstract, and concrete Somali civil society; rather, it involves the particular Siyad military state. It is a case illustrating the hypothesis that tyranny, in the end, will destroy its own state. The Cold War sustained Siyad's military regime but in due course, clan-based opposition groups rose up to challenge Siyad's military dictatorship at a time when the end of the Cold War reduced the opportunities for extracting military, technical, and financial resources from external sources. As a result, Somalia became the perfect illustration of the state-civil society contradiction and its implosion, precisely because the Cold War had imposed an exceedingly heavy military state on a decentralized, relatively democratic civil society that was able to survive on meagre resources.

Missed Opportunities

Could the Somali catastrophe have been anticipated and prevented, or at least limited? What pre-emptive measures were appropriate to confront the causes? Ambassador Mohamed Sahnoun the UN's Special Representative in Somalia, raised these issues forcefully in his publication, *Somalia: The Missed Opportunities* in which he concludes: 'if the international community had intervened earlier and more effectively in Somalia, much of the catastrophe that has unfolded could have been avoided.'[3] I hope to dwell on lessons and avoid recriminations. I have tried to base my comments on what was known at that time in order to approach the policy-maker's point of view. I have limited the discussion to selected major instances, which meet the criteria for a missed opportunity. In my judgment, this includes the period of the switch from Soviet dependency to American hegemony (1977–8), the 1988 civil war in northern Somalia; and the scramble on the eve of Siyad's fall in 1990–1.

Following the 1977–8 Ogaden War, Somalia switched sides from being a close ally of the Soviet Union to coming voluntarily under American hegemony. During this period of high tension and flux, the United States missed the opportunity to impose conditions that would have redirected Somalia toward a somewhat different political trajectory. The Americans relied on the IMF and the World Bank to press for market reforms and economic liberalization while remaining silent on political liberalization and issues involving human rights. Interestingly, the United States did impose delay implementation of the agreement on military assistance from 1978 till 1980 because of continued Somali military activities in the Ogaden. In the end, it was Siyad who blinked and restrained such activities in order to receive US military assistance. A clear sign of Siyad's vulnerability to outside pressure is manifested by the offer he finally accepted from the United States. As an opening bid in the negotiations over the former Soviet military facilities, he demanded $2 billion over a ten-year period, but take-it-or-leave-it offer from the United States obliged him to accept a meagre $40 million over a two-year period.[4]

As an observer at the time, I was aware that the regime fully expected to receive not only new economic directives but also pressures for political reforms as the price of its switch to the US camp. Instead, the regime was allowed to get by with insignificant cosmetic reforms, including a meaningless constitution and a bogus election. Perhaps the two most salient reasons for lack of political and diplomatic response then were the overriding concerns of a Cold War mentality and an obsession with economic reforms at the cost of all other reforms. Perceptions of the costs involved in taking action often dim a policy-maker's receptivity to an early warning of an impeding catastrophe. However, in 1977–80 the visible signs did not call for a unilateral military intervention; US and international actions could have limited the problems through military and economic sanctions and diplomatic pressure for tough political reforms.

In May–June 1988 the international community received a crystal clear warning of the impending Somali tragedy in the form of a large and explosive insurrection in northern Somalia. The Ethiopian presidents, Mengistu Haile-Mariam, and Siyad Barre signed a peace agreement in 1988, intended to prevent armed movements directed against their governments from using each other's country as a base. As a result, Mengistu told the Somali National Movement (SNM) that they could seek refuge in Ethiopia but they could no longer use his country as a base for military attacks on Somalia. The SNM returned home to nothern Somilia where they launched a military campaign against Barre. Siyad's response was vicious; he launched full-scaled military and aerial campaigns destroying many cities, towns, and much of the infrastructure in the area. An estimated five thousand people belonging to the northern Isaq clan-family were reported to have been killed in May 1988 alone; about fifty thousand more lost their lives and many more were injured over the following months as revolt and repression spread throughout the region. Over half a million people either crossed the border into the Haud area of Ethiopia or were displaced within northern Somalia. These tragic events were covered by the global media and even in a series of reports by organizations of the US government and by human rights organizations and should have served as a warning signal;[7] There is some evidence to indicate that the US Congress would have supported a drastic cut in all military and economic aid in order to apply pressure for significant political reforms. The Pentagon, however, opposed it and actively lobbied against a change in policy, based on its interests in gaining access to military facilities and the so-called regional security issue.

A third window of opportunity opened up in 1990, on the eve of Siyad's fall from power. The Djibouti conference, analysed below, represents cases of misused opportunity involving Italian and Egyptian responses that were misconceived, harmful, and highly inappropriate given the circumstances. By 1990, armed rebellion had spread like wildfire in most of Somalia's regions and districts, and the international press began to refer to President Siyad Barre as the Mayor of Mogadishu. Nevertheless, Italian and Egyptian officials maintained a single-minded effort to continue and retain a political role for Siyad Barre. The opportunity came with the rise of the manifesto group – a Mogadishu-based civilian opposition movement. The rapid successes of the armed opposition movements encouraged the latent civilian opposition to rear its previously timid head. On 15 May 1990 they launched a protest and issued a Manifesto. This manifesto was signed by 144 well-known members of the post-independence elite: politicians of the parliamentary civilian era, ex-officials of the Siyad regime, well-known religious leaders, business leaders, traders, as well as professional/intellectual elements (lawyers, doctors, teachers and other academics). They established a thirteen-person committee to organize a national reconciliation conference. The committee was headed by Abdullah Osman, the first elected president of Somalia, and Sheikh Mukhtar Mohamed Hussein, a former president of the elected Somali parliament. They called for a peaceful end to the civil wars and for a national conference to launch constitutional changes and guide the nation towards electoral politics and a multiparty system. They advocated the establishment of an interim, power-sharing coalition government to pave the way for multiparty elections. Unfortunately, Siyad's reaction could not have been more predictable. The regime jailed forty-five manifesto signatories, although Italian and Egyptian protests led to their release after a few weeks. Nevertheless, distorted Italian and Egyptian strategies and tactics led them to misuse this window of opportunity that could have led to political reforms that might then have limited the catastrophe. On this issue, Italian political scientist Novati is both succinct and blunt:

> While Somalia was ravaged by civil war, hastening the downfall of Siyad Barre's regime in a dramatic crescendo of bloodshed and despair, Italy sought once more to manage the crisis by offering her good offices. The aim was to effect an orderly transfer of power to a large coalition of forces, parties and persons in which Siyad Barre would continue to play an important transition role in order to avoid, it was argued, a dangerous power vac-

uum. A self-fulfilled prophecy, Siyad's enemies firmly refused to join such a deal, pleading that the President should be personally responsible for crimes, malpractice and political chaos. An eleventh hour reconciliation conference, co-chaired by Italy and Egypt, was called in Cairo but it was doomed from the start and at the last minute was canceled. General Aidid wouldn't forget the activism of Boutros Boutros-Ghali, then foreign minister of Egypt, to 'save' Siyad. The flight of Siyad Barre from Mogadishu deprived Italy of her best card. The setback was definitive. A regime Italy had tried stubbornly to preserve for over twenty years as a token of stability, was in shambles. The University, the jewel of Italian technical assistance, was destroyed and vandalized.[5]

Some observers felt that the Djibouti conference, held in June and July of 1991, constituted another missed historical opportunity. I do not think so; the Djibouti effort was bound to fail even before the conference doors had opened. For one thing, Djibouti was the brainchild of a distorted Italian and Egyptian strategy. During the 1989–90 period, they insisted that foreign powers still had to work with the Siyad regime to create transitional political structures that would facilitate 'stability for a successor regime.' The most positive role the Italians and Egyptians could have played at this point would have been to prevent the Renamo-like spoiler wars and Bosnia-like tragedy in Bay by offering Siyad the incentives to quit Gedo and go abroad into exile. Confusing wishful thinking with rational analysis, their efforts failed and continued to fail after the Djibouti conference had ended. Perhaps the involvement of the United States, considered more impartial than Italy and Egypt by many Somalis, and the United Nations could have produced a relatively better outcome. However, the United States ignored Somalia and concentrated its diplomatic efforts on ensuring a peaceful transition from Mengistu Haile-Mariam to Meles Zenawi in Ethopia. Somali observers felt bitter: after all, they argued, Ethiopia was a Soviet problem while America was significantly responsible for Somalia's mess.

The Decision to Intervene

After showing much reluctance and discouraging others (including the United Nations) from intervening, the lame-duck first Bush administration decided to launch a humanitarian military intervention late in 1992. Why did the Americans refuse to intervene when the circumstances were more appropriate and wait when it was almost too late? Liberal writers and left-wing circles accused the United States of imperialist motives. Some argued that it intervened to protect actual or potential oil resources. However, a number of US oil companies (Conoco, Chevron, for example) were granted exploration rights during Siyad's rule and even earlier. Besides, during this period, most of the Somali elite, either incumbent or in opposition, had generally manifested pro-American attitudes. From a pragmatic perspective they would have welcomed the investment and involvement of US companies as the best guarantee of efficient exploration, production, and access to global markets. It did not make sense for US companies to impose themselves militarily where they would obviously have been welcomed. Had this been a significant motive, the United States would surely have intervened before or just after Siyad fell, not twenty-two months later. Moreover, when military intervention came, none of the US and UN troops were deployed anywhere near the major areas of oil exploration in the northeast and in the de facto Republic of Somaliland.

The United States intervention, some alleged, was motivated by the need to combat the threat of Islamic fundamentalism financed by Sudan and Iran. Since 1991, Somalia and Somaliland had both witnessed pockets of Islamic fundamentalism symbolized by the Islamic Unity group. During that period, their strength lay in northeast Somalia where they tried to gain power but were evicted by the SSDF and a coalition of clan-based forces. Their strength since US and UN forces left, lies in the Gedo region in southwest Somalia near the Kenyan and Ethiopian borders. That this is not a significant issue is demonstrated by the fact that US and UN troops entered Somalia and departed without staging even minor skirmishes with the fundamentalists in Gedo; those in the northeast were too far from their area of operations. More recently, Ethiopian forces have conducted several forays against the Gedo area fundamentalists at the behest of the secular, clan-based Somali National Front (SNF) organization.

Other writers raised the issue of access to Somali military bases. However, as argued above, our knowledge of Somali elites tells us that they would not have denied the US access to military base agreements. The most attractive Somali military installations consist of the Berbera naval and airport facilities in the self-declared Republic of Somaliland. The elites who control Somaliland, according to our information, would only have been too glad to renew Americans access to the Berbera base and facilities, in exchange for recognition or for economic assistance. As of March 1994, US troops and as of March 1995, UN forces had left Somalia without deployment anywhere near the Berbera base. Besides, 'even if one accepts the globalist rationales for ensuring US military access to the region, the Somali bases were unnecessary in the light of other, more extensive, facilities readily available in the region.'[6] An illustration of this is the fact that the massive deployment of U.S. troops and equipment associated with Operation Desert Storm in Kuwait in 1991 did not need the naval facility at Berbera. A more sophisticated version takes the redundancy argument mentioned above and argues that, even though the United States in this highly technological post-Cold War era does not need Somali bases, it simply wished to deny their access to hostile regional powers such as Iran, Sudan, and Iraq. Once again, the evidence is simply not there: intervening forces have come and gone without deploying to protect Somali military bases.

The least satisfactory explanations are those derived mainly from the old Cold War context of US strategic interests. These represent echoes of the general experience of American foreign policy towards the Third World which was shaped by the necessity to control and protect the extraction and supply of raw materials and/or insure access to military bases. Even if one cannot resist the conclusion that American foreign policy has historically been driven by economic and/or strategic determinants rather than by humanitarian considerations, one has to admit that the Somali intervention was a unique phenomenon. Bush administration officials argued that the United States had to intervene because of the 'massive proportions' of the tragedy and because the United States had the means to 'do something' about it. This global vision explanation argued that Somalia could enhance both US and UN credibility in the post–Cold War era, a case study of President Bush's New World Order.[7]

Those who use globalist explanations go on to point to the convergence of vision between Bush's New World Order and the new United Nations Secretary-General Boutros-Ghali's commitment to assertive multilateralism: 'Secretary-General Boutros-Ghali has an ambitious agenda for peace, through which he plans unprecedented UN involvement in peacemaking, peacekeeping, and peace enforcement. He is convinced that the UN now has an opportunity to achieve the great objectives for which it was established ...'[8] There is no doubt that when Bush finally took the decision to intervene, the secretary-general and the UN spared no efforts in its implementation.

However, early in 1992 the United States' mission to the UN did its best to keep the Somali case off the Security Council agenda. The shortcomings of the globalist interpretations have more to do with timing. 'In other words, why did Bush decide to launch Operation Provide Relief during August 1992 as opposed to July 1992 (or earlier), and why did he decide to launch Operation Restore Hope only after (as opposed to prior to) the presidential elections of November 1992?'[9] The dynamics of US electoral politics played a critical role in providing us with a more satisfactory explanation.

Another view advanced to explain the decision to intervene is based on the structural dynamics of American politics. The end of the Cold War has created at least two opposing groups. On one hand are those who want to transcend militarism to promote domestic social progress at home under the slogan of 'the peace dividend.' On the other hand are those who argue that the post-Cold War fragmentation and diffusion of power among multiple actors have made the contemporary situation even more dangerous and volatile. In the unstable, anarchical international system, the United States needs to retain its military establishment in place. In other words, the United States needed the large Somali intervention for its military establishment to retain its size and expenditures.

Obviously globalist and structural militarist explanations were used in retrospect to rationalize the decision but not to trigger it. Domestic politics explanations involve the role of the media, nongovernmental organizations (NGOs) and the US Congress. By 1992 the effects of state collapse manifested themselves in a devastating man-made famine and a brutal multi-sided civil war which collectively claimed the lives of at least three hundred thousand men, women, and children (roughly 25–30 per cent of all children under the age of five). At its peak in 1992, the magnitude of human suffering in Somalia was overwhelming: out of a total estimated population of eight million, approximately 4.5 million Somalis required urgent external assistance. Of those, some 1.5 million people were at immediate risk of starvation, including one million children. American television screens carried the humanitarian disaster in Somalia to saturation point. The sense of urgency about the Somali crisis filtered from the media to the public and Congress, significantly raising pressures on the Bush administration.

The growing media, public, and congressional pressure provided, nevertheless, only a partial explanation for the reversal in US policy. For example, on 3 August 1992, a bipartisan resolution advocating a tangible humanitarian response overwhelmingly passed the Senate; the same bill was adopted by the House of Representatives on 10 August. The most sufficient explanation for President Bush's decision to intervene has to do with presidential politics in an election year. Therefore in his October 1992 address to the United Nations General Assembly, Bush declared that the Pentagon would prepare the US military for a new and more active role in peacekeeping efforts in the New World Order.[13] It is important to observe that his NSC staff began serious preparations for the Somali intervention only *after* Bush lost his re-election bid. 'In an effort to leave office on a high note, President Bush finally decided that something had to be done about the humanitarian disaster in Somalia.'[10] His harsh critics saw the dispatch of American troops to Somalia as a cynical effort on the president's part to deflect domestic and international criticisms for his abject failure to act in Bosnia. In retrospect, the US-led multinational force represented possibly a convergence of interests between Boutros-Ghali and President Bush.

A Critique of Operation Restore Hope (ORH)

Security Council Resolution 794 of 3 December 1992 authorized the United States to lead a Unified Task Force (UNITAF) code-named Operation Restore Hope (ORH) under chapter VII of the UN Charter. Chapter VII sanctions the use of forceful means to enhance UN objectives, in this case the delivery of relief supplies to starving people in Somalia. The resolution gave UNITAF the right 'to use all necessary means to establish as soon as possible a secure environment for humanitarian relief operations.'[11] Resolution 794 authorized the deployment of 24,000 American troops to Somalia; the initial cost of the operation to the United States was estimated at $500 million. More in line with his royal exit aspirations than with his New World Order vision, President Bush wrote Boutros-Ghali to underline that the mission was 'limited and specific: to create security conditions which will permit the feeding of the starving Somali people and allow the transfer of this security function to the UN peacekeeping force.' At another point he seemed somewhat aware that the situation was much more complicated, stating that, 'Our mission is humanitarian, but we will not tolerate armed gangs ripping off their own people, condemning them to death by starvation.'[12] He contradicted himself further by declaring that US troops should depart from Somalia by the time of the inauguration in January 1993 – a forty-day time span that did not allow for the time it takes to settle them on the ground.

Another consequence of the absurd six-week timetable President Bush proposed meant that the US army had to remove the critical civil affairs and military police training components from the ORH program. 'This was unusual; civil affairs officers are specialists in foreign cultures and are used for liaison with local communities. The U.S. military deployed approximately 1,000 civil affairs officers to Panama in December 1989 and about 300 to northern Iraq after the Gulf War. Under UNITAF, the numbers ranged from 7 to 30.' This meant that UNITAF was crippled from the start; it was not able to mount a viable program to demobilize armed youth, train a Somali police force, and revive the legal and court systems. The international intervening force was also doomed to fail because it lacked a credible exit strategy. One key lesson the United States learned from this failure in Somalia led to the positive situation in Haiti, where 'the United States reverted to the immediate and effective use of civil affairs units. In addition to civil affairs troops, more than 800 police advisers were sent to Haiti. Shortly after the initial landing, the United States began a police recruitment and training program.'[13] Under ORH, the Australian force had a civil-military affairs unit and was able to achieve tangible success in rebuilding Baidoa's and Bay's police forces and strengthen its civil society.

At its peak, UNITAF strength reached approximately thirty-seven thousand troops, including eight thousand on ships offshore. The United States provided the largest contingent by far, with a peak strength of about twenty-eight thousand marines and infantry. About nine thousand troops from over twenty countries joined ORH. For example, France provided twenty-five hundred French Legionnaires from neighbouring Djibouti, Australia sent nine hundred elite soldiers, while Pakistan contributed four thousand soldiers, some of whom became embroiled in conflicts with General Aidid's faction.

ORH was implemented in four phases. The first involved the United Nations Task Force, UNITAF. Phase four involved the handoff from UNITAF to UNOSOM II. The troop were deployed in 'the triangle of death,' an area of between a quarter and a third of the whole country and located between Somalia's two main rivers, the Shabele and the Judba. The whole international intervention from 1992 to 1995 was confined to this southern area, between Somalia's two main rivers, the Shabele and the Juba, a zone that is between a quarter to a third of the whole country. Boutros-Ghali's pleadings that troops be deployed in most parts of the country, including the northeast and the northwest (Somaliland) were understandably ignored by the United United and the other members of the Security Council.

There is no doubt that prior to 1992, and even after, ORH and UNO-

SOM represented the most radical and ambitious operations that the United Nations had undertaken in a sovereign state. Since Somalia did not present a military threat to surrounding states, this represented the first time ever that the United Nations organization had intervened in purely domestic affairs involving a humanitarian crisis. The aim was to restore peace, order, reconstitute the state, and promote socio-economic development. The Security Council showed that it was now freed from the paralysis of the Cold War epoch, when the United States and the Soviet Union often blocked Security Council action by their veto. For the first time the Security Council authorized enforcement action under chapter VII of the Charter, bypassing article 2, paragraph 7, which prohibits interference in the domestic affairs of a sovereign state. The world confronted a concrete case of the clash between two international principles: respect for state sovereignty versus the imperative to protect life, to safeguard human rights. The decision goes beyond Somalia since it has potential for much wider application.

It is misleading to conclude that the US/UN humanitarian intervention was a complete failure. The UNITAF/ORH operation permitted the distribution of relief food to previously famished populations. It has been estimated that at least 250,000 lives were saved during the emergency.' However, the operation did not achieve its maximum objectives – that is, reconstituting a viable political system and facilitating democratization and development. Nevertheless, it did achieve as much as could be hoped for under the circumstances; it created an environment that was tangibly better than what would have existed without it, at least in certain respects.

As soon as ORH was on the ground, throughout central and southern Somalia, looting, extortion, and attacks on relief workers dropped sharply. Operations began to shift from emergency relief to development programs, including the revival of agricultural production, restocking livestock herds, restoring some of the country's shattered services and infrastructure. Relief continued to command high priority since 1.5 million Somalis continued to be estimated as still at risk from malnutrition and disease. In March 1993 the United Nations unveiled a comprehensive Relief and Rehabilitation Program for all of 1993, budgeted at $159 million. It included projects ranging from the resettlement of displaced persons and refugees to restoring health, sanitation, water, and administrative services. By 1994 some 130,000 refugees had come back to Somalia from camps in Kenya. The exodus of refugees to neighbouring countries began to dwindle. Seeds and agricultural tools were distributed by United

Nations agencies and NGOs. There was a good rainfall in 1992–3, helping to increase local food production and facilitating the emergence of markets. While relief continued to receive top priority, greater emphasis was being placed on rehabilitation and reconstruction. The mechanism to carry out such activities involved the Civilian-Military Operations Centre located at UNOSOM headquarters: nearly one hundred participants met daily for briefings from the UN agencies, the Red Cross, and NGOs, as well as representatives from UNITAF headquarters and the military commands.

It is on the political front that the international humanitarian intervention met with insurmountable challenges. The United States had no evident reason to favour any one of the several armed factions, and most Somalis continue to believe this in spite of the conflict that ensued. Errors do occur in the conduct of such operations, including those that belong to the inherent structure of the situations in which the intervening (international) forces find themselves. Normally, the intervention freezes the military situation, and thus prevents factions currently victorious or on the offensive from pressing home their military advantage. The intervention therefore favours and aids the faction with the weakest military position that manipulates the intervening force against its rivals. General Aidid had succeeded in defeating President Siyad and his remaining forces and chasing them from Somalia into Kenya in May 1992. Siyad's son-in-law, General Morgan, and loyalist troops, began to cross back into Somalia in November-December 1992, timing his armed faction's movements with the arrival of UNITAF-ORH.

Ambassador Oakley, President Clinton's representative to Somalia during ORH, reports that 'Morgan's forces had been moving toward Kismayu when UNITAF landed in December. They moved back to near the Kenyan border, but after the Addis Ababa cease-fire agreement they began to move south.' Following discussions with UNITAF officers, Morgan 'sounded reasonable and compliant, seemingly reconciled to keeping his forces outside the city,' toward Kismayu in the south.[14] In Kismayu, Morgan's SNF faction confronted Omar Jess's SPM faction allied to General Aidid and his USC-SNA (Somali National Alliance):

In February 1993 ... an anti-Aidid faction managed to seize part of Kismayu by a *coup de main*, catching UNITAF peace keepers by surprise. When Aidid's ally, Omar Jess, tried a similar trick a few days later, peacekeepers were on their guard and managed to foil it. From Aidid's point of view, it was hard to avoid the conclusion that UNITAF had sided with his opponents, but if this particular event had not occurred to create that impression, another incident would have had the same effect.'[15]

General Aidid and his allies believed that there was outright UNITAF-Morgan collusion against Jess. At that point, UNITAF troops in Kismayu were mostly from Belgium. Aidid and his angry supporters mounted demonstrations outside the US embassy compound in Mogadishu. Aidid was also angry at the Nigerian government for having granted asylum to Siyad Barre, and so followed the protest demonstrations with an attack on Nigerian UNITAF forces. 'The arrest of Colonel Jess by UNITAF as he tried to drive from Mogadishu to Kismayu, heavily armed and without permission, only rubbed salt into the wound. More protests and demonstrations followed. Though anti-UNITAF actions by the SNA stopped for a while as cooperation resumed, the Kismayu events marked the beginning of bad blood between General Aidid and UNITAF; it had all the ingredients for 'clanizing' the United States and the United Nations.

The War with General Aidid

The United Nations later mission, UNOSOM II, was mandated explicitly to include enforcement powers, and Boutros-Ghali appointed American Admiral Jonathan Howe as his new special representative. International intervention confronted two broad strategies: one, working with the existing forces, mostly warlords, as a critical source of legitimate authority whose cooperation must be sought; the other, encouraging new institutions and leaders by promoting Somali civil society. Mohamed Sahnoun, as special representative of UNOSOM I, felt that this complicated situation did not call for an either/or policy and he tried his best to pursue a two-track strategy. Ambassador Oakley, representing President Clinton under ORH, leaned heavily on the first strategy and got on very well with all the so-called warlords, especially General Aidid in spite of the suspicions that had begun to emerge. Admiral Howe did not seem to have a strategy; instead he rapidly developed an obsession which he shared with Boutros-Ghali. As John Drysdale and others have argued, Ghali and Howe became convinced that peace and a government could only come to Somalia once Aidid was removed from the political scene.[16] Two cardinal aspects of leadership for such unprecedented operations are the ability to think and act strategically, and the personal aptitude to absorb relevant aspects of indigenous history and culture as well as the diplomatic skills to work effectively with all other actors involved in the peacebuilding effort. Admiral Howe and his team did not appear to have had such qualities.

An attitude of confrontation with Aidid (probably mutual at this point) had set in; the issue became how to find an incident that would provoke him. On the morning of 5 June, Pakistan UNOSOM soldiers were sent to inspect Aidid's armaments near his radio station at very short notice. UNOSOM had already targeted his radio as hostile to UNOSOM's mission. An armed confrontation between this UNOSOM unit and Aidid's militia left twenty-four Pakistani soldiers dead. Did General Aidid give the order to kill UNOSOM soldiers or was this a spontaneous act undertaken by his militia in the heat of tensions and hostile suspicions? There is no clear answer to this question. Under Howe's leadership, UNOSOM took precipitate military action in response to this attack. A far better response would have been to call for an impartial investigation by an esteemed group leading to a judicial decision arrived at in a fair and transparent manner. Before any such assessment had been undertaken, UNOSOM and the United States fixed blame on Aidid and launched an operation to either capture or kill him. Wanted posters with Aidid's picture were displayed all over south Mogadishu, and a price of $25,000 was placed on his head. A clandestine American-led military operation was launched against him. The Italians recommended isolating Aidid while at the same time recognizing and dealing with other leaders of his clan and its protopolitical organization, the Somali National Alliance (SNA). Boutros Ghali and Howe rejected their suggestions, rebuked them for their initiatives and deployed them out of Mogadishu.

Elders and other prominent personalities from Aidid's Habar Gedir clan met on 23 July 1993 to assess their situation and explore various options. US/UNOSOM helicopters bombed the building on the grounds that Aidid could be attending the meeting. As it turned out, Aidid did not attend and at least fifty-four Habar Gedir clan members, mainly civilians, were killed without provocation. Such activities led to the perception that UNOSOM was simply another 'rival clan.' Aidid's hand was in fact strengthened among his clan members, who perceived UNOSOM's activities as an attack against their entire clan. As long as this new external threat persisted, Habar Gedir clan members decided to rally behind Aidid. The clan took heavy casualties while inflicting serious damage and paralysing the whole UNOSOM mission and operations. From June to October 1993, the hunt for Aidid put a hold on most of UNOSOM's work at reconciliation and reconstruction. In October

1993, Aidid's faction shot down at least two US helicopters and in the ensuing combat, eighteen American soldiers were killed, one was captured, and over seventy-five were wounded. This prompted President Clinton to shift both American and UN policy back to politics and diplomacy, as he ordered an end to the manhunt. Even though the hunt for Aidid was aborted, UNOSOM II had been so discredited that it was subsequently unable to play an effective role as interlocutor in the Somali civil wars.

Lessons Learned and Legacy

One can draw preliminary lessons from these experiences. While assisting a country devastated by ethnic conflicts, it is important for international intervention to avoid overt political activities that favour one side over to another. This is not a question of neutrality, but an effort to achieve impartiality to the best extent possible. The Somali case invariably draws our attention to the primary responsibility of leadership in fomenting and sustaining civil wars and also, in initiating and nurturing peace. Leaders have the choice as to whether to manage or exploit ethnic/clan cleavages. A number of the warlords promoted actions and decisions that have perpetuated Somali civil wars. Even though environmental and structural factors played critical roles, what actions leaders decide to take is what ultimately matters. Sahnoun and Oakley's diplomatic instincts allowed them to be flexible and judicious; Howe was rigid, stubborn, and mediocre. A mix of factors led to incorrect UNOSOM decisions: incompetence, personal vanity and ambition, a short-term orientation, and bureaucratic infighting. The leadership of such large operations must be carefully chosen. There is a need for an overall strategy for peacebuilding. With sophisticated, sensitive, pragmatic, and nuanced leadership, the two strategies outlined above could be synchronized and pursued with the long run aim of civilianizing most of the leaders and demobilizing the clan militia. The design and implementation of a peacebuilding strategy should be guided by considered, professional decisions that are responsive to the local cultural and political conditions.

The issue of disarmament also shows that UNOSOM lacked insight into the general situation. To have succeeded, UNITAF/UNOSOM's disarmament strategy would have needed a comprehensive, multidimensional approach: a demobilization program to provide job-training for the youthful militias; a serious program to train and equip local police forces; and a program to equip and restore the courts and legal justice system. The funds the Security Council allocated for UNOSOM troops could not be used to support such developmental efforts. The handful of justice and police systems UNOSOM was able to establish had been reduced in size or disappeared after UNOSOM II's financial support evaporated. On its own initiative, the northern Somaliland Republic has carried out a successful demobilization and disarmament program. Northeast Somalia, or Puntland, has achieved similar success, including the establishment of a police training school. UNOSOM promoted elite level reconciliation conferences in Addis Ababa and Nairobi. The Addis Ababa conference of 15–27 March 1993 resisted UNOSOM pressure to form a centralized state and adopted a regional-autonomy approach. UNOSOM finally backed this plan and speeded up the establishment of regional and district councils as an exit strategy. As of 1994, UNOSOM had assisted in the formation of fifty-three district councils out of eighty-one (excluding Somaliland), and eight out of thirteen regional councils (again, excluding Somaliland). The legacy of these institution-building efforts is mixed. Those that survive are in the process of being incorporated into wide clan-based authorities. Others have been subsumed by alternative indigenous institutions that have emerged without donor support. The UNOSOM method of establishing district and regional councils was based on a top-down approach, rather than being locally generated. UNOSOM was always eager to announce the number of district councils formed, a reflection of its 'product' rather than 'process' orientation. Qualitative rather than quantitative processes that would have eventually led to authentic local governance would have provided a sounder policy to pursue.

Paradoxically, even though UNOSOM moved to support decentralization in Somalia, UNOSOM itself was highly centralized in Mogadishu. It should have been decentralized, with strengthened offices in the various zones and a small mobile headquarters in Mogadishu. Somali civil wars and territorial fragmentation had, de facto, diminished Mogadishu's previous hegemony. In this way, UNOSOM could have avoided becoming hostage to events in a particular part of the country, as it did in Mogadishu. UNOSOM had to learn to overcome serious coordination problems. In military affairs, certain units, the Italians for example, continued to seek directives from their own national capitals rather than from UNOSOM headquarters. UNOSOM tried to create entirely new divisions to carry out its development oriented mandate, rather than seeking to incorporate the efforts and harness the expertise of UN agencies, particularly UNDP, to assist in institution-building and economic reconstruction. There were ups and downs in coordination with humanitarian agencies and the press; this function was later routinized in the form of daily UNOSOM-NGO-press briefings and information exchanges. UNOSOM invested tremendous political capital in the reconciliation process involving factional leaders. Highlighted conferences involving these elements took place in Addis Ababa and in Nairobi. The UN placed a great deal of pressure on the factional leaders to reach agreements quickly, since its own mandate was of limited duration. All such factional elite conferences both before and after the demise of UNOSOM II have failed. Unfortunately, UNOSOM ignored the need to support, simultaneously, grassroots peace and reconciliation conferences like the one that was held in Borama, Somaliland. In such conferences, more indigenous methods of reconciliation were applied, and sufficient time was allowed for agreements to be reached. One of the negative legacies of UNOSOM is that it did not give much attention to and provide support for areas that were more stable and peaceful, such as Somaliland and Puntland.

The lack of a comprehensive and consistent strategy meant that the UNOSOM mission faced serious difficulties in pursuing an appropriate sequence of actions: Should, for instance, reconciliation and institution-building precede or follow disarmament? Should re-establishment of law and order (e.g., police) precede establishment of local or national authority or follow it? There was no reason not to pursue a two-track reconciliation process: bottom-up and top-down. However, for a bottom-up approach to succeed, demobilization and disarmament would have to be pursued consistently and energetically. This would have provided the necessary political space for civil society. Unfortunately, UNOSOM did not have either a clear strategy or resources. Continuity in both policy and personnel, which is essential for the success of a peace operation, was lacking. Investment in indirect peacebuilding, such as the promotion of business, professional, and communal associations, is a critical element in building a web of bridges across conflict lines, and should be a major component of future peace operations, with appropriate budget and expertise. UNOSOM had a negative impact on both Somali political and economic life. UNOSOM's massive presence caused indigenous and sustainable Somali employment to decline while an artificial service sector mushroomed. At the same time, UNOSOM preferred to import many items that were in fact available in local markets.

The international community's preference for local NGOs rather than local business, led to a mushrooming of inauthentic Somali 'NGOs.' All

this led to resource-driven mentalities and opportunists and a revival of
the culture of dependency of the Siyad era. Had UNOSOM been in the
business of promoting sustainability, its approach would have resulted in
a series of initiatives, beginning with institution-building assistance to
Somaliland, which had formed its own civilian government, followed by
efforts in the Puntland areas and other relatively stable clan-controlled
zones. This strategy involves building on the stable and authentic cases
and expanding to surround and eventually include more and more of
the war-torn areas.

UNOSOM and the war with Aidid left a significant and broader legacy
in international affairs: it dimmed, some would say extinguished, ambitious dreams for a New World Order.[17] Proposals advocating the creation of a separate UN standing military rapid response mechanism
were put on hold and, even though Boutros-Ghali failed to win a second
term as UN secretary-general for other reasons as well, it was also evident that he was made the scapegoat for the Somali debacle. The
United States promptly drew the wrong conclusions from the Somali
experience and delayed the Haiti mission to restore elected President
Aristide when Haitian mobs bearing Aidid's pictures demonstrated
before US ships. The United States went so far as to prevent or delay
others from taking humanitarian action. Obviously Rwanda became the
tragic outcome of the wrong reading of the Somali lessons. As Thomas
Weiss observed:

> Somalia cast an ominous shadow on Washington, where the Clinton team
> and the commander in chief in May 1994 issued Presidential Decision
> Directive 25 (PDD25). Supposedly the remaining superpower had 'wisely
> retreated from the overly sanguine expectations held by the administration
> when it began its term.' The first real test of the policy was Rwanda. As one
> senior State Department official close to human rights policy quipped dur-
> ing an off-the-record discussion, 'It was almost as if the Hutus had read it.'
> The new restrictive guidelines made it possible for the United States not
> only to remain on the sidelines but also to prevent others from getting
> involved while genocide proceeded apace.[18]

The Somali experience has also thrown new light on debates about
Africa's 'juridical' versus 'empirical' sovereignty and rhetoric about
recolonization and trusteeship: 'As anachronistic as it may seem, we
need to consider ways to recommit countries (like Somalia) to the good
offices of the UN Trusteeship Council.'[19] The war with Aidid's faction

(actually only one clan out of a potential hundred) shows that recolonization advocates must be willing to pay a heavy price in casualties and must possess unlimited resources. There is, after all, a residual empirical sovereignty in African civil society even after the collapse of the state. Should the society choose to reject foreign intervention, recolonization, or absorption into another state, this residual sovereignty is manifested in the resistance movement and the sacrifices involved.

Let us recall that the most positive and dramatic legacy of the US and UN involvement and that of their NGO partners in Somalia was the success in defeating a man-made (civil war-induced) famine. Reaching a peak in 1992, the magnitude of human suffering in the triangle-of-death zone was overwhelming, as captured and transmitted by the international press. More than 250,000 lives are estimated to have been saved during the famine emergency. There has been no recurrence of a famine of even half such a magnitude.

The Post-Siyad Environment

There are several lessons to be learned from the Somali experience. UNOSOM came to admit that the roots of the Somali crisis were much deeper than originally believed. Further, the international community and the UN lacked adequate knowledge of Somalia and the UN did not have adequate means and institutional mechanisms for learning about the country. The most critical aspect of this knowledge consists of a deeper understanding of the nature and mechanisms of Siyad's dictatorial rule and the emergence of various manifestations of anti-Siyadism. This is the dialectic that shapes the post-Siyad environment. The collapsed state has also produced unique formations as well as survival and coping strategies. Powerful new forces make it virtually impossible for foreigners and Somalis to revive the old collapsed state. So great was Siyad's malevolence and abuse of power that virtually all Somalis now hold a deep-seated fear and distrust of any centralized authority. Any notion of a central army is met with bitter hostility. An Islamic revival draws its inspiration from the need to resist Siyad's anti-Islamic measures. Donor-driven attempts to bring a quick-fix unitary form of government actually have prolonged the civil wars and facilitated fragmentation. UNOSOM could have delved deeper into Somali society to appreciate certain enabling conditions that reflect a new spirit that is reconstructing a new Somalia – one which is prepared to accept a shorter-term modus operandi at district, regional, and even zonal levels as an efficient and necessary step towards building the national coherence that donors, and most Somalis, seek. Future prospects could involve a federal or confederal state or even two states.

The immediate impact of UNOSOM II's departure did not result in the violence that many had predicted. During the post-UNOSOM period, donors have become more pragmatic and flexible. They have come to provide rehabilitation assistance in a more decentralized manner – to units of variable size, as long as they provide security and effective local counterparts. With the collapse of UNOSOM-sponsored institutions, more authentic entities, including authoritative local leaders, have emerged. With the distortionary effect of UNOSOM no longer present, the process of both political and economic transformation has been facilitated. In certain places, including northern Mogadishu, alternative institutions have emerged without any external support. One such significant institution has been the Sharia court movement. A number of these Sharia courts have effectively performed policing and judicial functions. Such indigenous initiatives provide the framework for what one might call enabling conditions or factors. UNOSOM's admitted lack of knowledge of Somali culture and politics prevented it from grasping the dynamics of these enabling factors which, in turn, offer 'leverage points' to initiate constructive action.

It is now possible to list a number of enabling conditions upon which sound governance for Somalia could be built.

- *Autonomism:* A spirit of regional and zonal authority pervades Somali society and ought to be enhanced and formalized. In Somaliland, this spirit of autonomy has been pushed, by specific circumstances, to attain the extreme form of de facto independence.
- *Power-sharing:* People seek broad-based power-sharing both as an echo of the pastoral past and as a key to a more participatory future. This aspiration should be reinforced and information be provided about various power-sharing models.
- *Decentralization:* People favour decentralization and devolution of power. The UN and even the faction leaders were obliged to pay lip service to this preference at the March 1993 Addis Ababa conference.
- *Role of women:* Women are playing an increasingly prominent and constructive role in Somali society, both at home and in the diaspora. They have been building bridges between hostile clan groups. Supporting their efforts enhances reconciliation and lasting peace.
- *Islamic revival:* There are pockets of Islamic fundamentalists on the

margins of Somali society (the Gedo region bordering Ethiopia and Kenya). For most Somalis, however, a spirit of revivalism reflects core values, based on the Somali Sunni tradition of avoiding radical politicized Islam. Somalia's Islamic revival promises to strengthen civic values and institutions of civil society and should be reinforced. Unlike the centrifugal politics of clan division, Islamic beliefs and behaviour manifest a latent centripetal political tendency of integration.

- *Market economy:* With the demise of Siyad's controlled economy along with its numerous parastatals, the post-Siyad period has witnessed a vibrant, free, and unregulated economy. Its growth should be encouraged and facilitated. However, there is also a need to encourage the development of necessary and select regulations to protect the environment and to protect resources for future generations.

- *Local adaptation:* The civil wars and the resulting lack of goods and services that used to be imported have fostered a spirit of innovation and self-reliance. This creativity needs to be encouraged and expanded.

- *Traditional institutions:* The new environment has also obliged Somalis to resort to their rich cultural traditions and institutions to handle grazing and agricultural systems, conflict mediation, legal adjudication, and a number of other related functions. Somaliland has provided an example of innovative governance by establishing a National Assembly with two houses, one of which, the Guurti or House of Elders, comprises traditional clan and religious elders. Traditional law – the *xeer* – is now widely practised in both rural and urban areas. Traditional law and practices are part of the support system needed to make new settlements effective and sustainable.

- *Free Press:* The pre-Siyad Somali Republic was well known for having a tradition of an irreverent free press. That tradition has returned. Mogadishu has fourteen private newspapers while Hargeisa in Somaliland has about four. They present various perspectives on the current situation in the Somali language. A number of them are often critical of the political elements, often using cartoons to drive home their points. All of them would be more effective with training and technical assistance. Free speech and open debate have to be encouraged to promote lasting peace, accountability, and the gradual civilizing of the political elite.

- *Regional links:* Independent Somalia, with its policy of irredentism, engaged in confrontational and hostile relations with Ethiopia and Kenya. All that has changed as relations with neighbouring states have improved greatly. There is, however, a minor danger signal posed by

Ethiopia's forays into parts of Gedo to combat pockets of Islamic fundamentalists.

Somalia is gradually healing, but it remains a fragmented entity. The northern zone, ex-British Somaliland, has proclaimed itself the independent Republic of Somaliland. The northeast zone, now called Puntland, is seeking only internal autonomy in a future Federal Republic of Somalia. After the departure of UNOSOM II the Rahanweyn and related clans of Bay, Bakool, and parts of Gedo and Lower Shabelle regions formed a governing council for the Digil Mirifle. This is another example of the civilianization and autonomy process. Unfortunately, this process in Bay was interrupted by Aidid's invasion of the area in September 1995. The Rahanweyn have continued to organize against Aidid with the formation of a Rahanweyn Resistance Army (RRA) and the struggles persist to this day. While the Somaliland, Puntland and, hopefully, Bay zones have managed to control violence and ensure the establishment of relatively peaceful societies, strongman (warlord) solutions continue to prevail in Mogadishu with Hussein Aidid, Ali Mahdi, Musa Sudi, and Osman Ato; and in the Kismayu and Lower Juba areas with Siyad's son-in-law General Hersi Morgan, General Gabio, and Ahmed Omas Jess. Post-UNOSOM factional leader conferences have been held in Addis Ababa (Sanaa), Nairobi, Sanaa (Yemen) and Cairo, but they have all failed to achieve reconciliation and coordination.

These contrasting outcomes of positive peace in northern Somalia and at best negative peace in central and southern Somalia can, in part, be accounted for by the different approaches adopted towards negotiations. In the north peace has been built upwards from local Somali development on the ground, while efforts in the south have frequently been the result of externally-injected, top-down approaches. The former is best represented by the Borama conference held in February–May 1993, while the latter is captured in the Djibouti-hosted, elite-oriented conference of 1991 and, more recently, 2000.

It was at the Borama conference in that peace was restored in Somaliland. Considerable time was spent adjudicating clan conflicts and disputes between neighbours since peace and reconciliation were considered primary tasks. Discussions were held on the major provisions of an anticipated constitution and it was recommended that the structure of government be based on a president/vice-president model rather than a president/prime minister one. The conference also recommended the strict separation of the judiciary from executive and legislative powers and bodies, and formally endorsed a National Assembly or Parliament consisting of two chambers: a Council of Elders and a lower popular Chamber of Representatives. On an interim basis, both of these were to exist together with a president (Isaq), vice-president (non-Isaq from the Borama area), and a cabinet selected by the president, who was to be sensitive to issues of merit and clan representativeness.

The Guurti, or Council of Elders, was to be chosen according to traditional rules of protocol, historical precedent, and proportionality. The Borama conference elected an electoral body of 150 (elders, politicians, SNM cadres, civil servant and civil society leaders) who went on to conduct competitive elections resulting in the selection of veteran politician Ibrahim Mohamed Egal as the second Somaliland president (Abdurahman Tuur was president from 1991 to 1993) and veteran SNM leader Abdurahman Aw Ali as his vice-president. As a variant of liberal democracy, consociationalism stresses process over product. It is indeed an irony of history that the person delegated in 1960 to consummate union with ex-Italian Somalia is today charged with the task of guiding Somaliland out of that union! Somaliland claims to favour radical decentralization. Indeed, it regained its independence in 1991 with a vigorous civil society that obstructed the formation of a coherent and efficient central state. It took the wily veteran Mohamed Egal to win the credit of bringing the state back in. Finally, popular country-wide elections for local and national bodies, including presidential elections, were being held during January and May 2003. With Egal's death, two of his former ministers, each from different clans, competed to replace him. In the end, Dohir Riyale Kahin, who had served under Egal as vice-president, was elected president.

Somaliland has thus brought an end to generalized fighting and introduced an atmosphere of trust and confidence. It has created a number of political institutions and political arrangements, some of which, like the Guurti, are highly original. It has fostered a relatively open and inclusive political culture. The mini-civil war (within Somaliland) of 1994-5 demonstrated that the evolving arrangements and political culture were capable of fostering reconciliation among previously warring communities and thus helping to build a sense of common identity.

The experience elsewhere was quite different. In 1991 President Hassan Guled, with Italian and Egyptian support, called the first Djibouti conferences as soon as Siyad had fallen from power. In May and again in July 1991, the Italian and Egyptian governments backed the USC faction of Ali Mahdi and the Manifesto Group in organizing two conferences in

Djibouti with the objective of forming a national government. The Aidid USC group and the SNM refused to attend. This top-down approach was intended to confirm Ali Mahdi as interim president and reject Somaliland's independence. The July conference advocated reviving the 1960 constitution and its 123-member Parliament for an interim period of two years, with Parliament electing a president nominated by the USC.

This attempt at parachuting state power from Djibouti to Mogadishu proved unworkable. Ali Mahdi was too impatient to await the parliamentary nomination process; he had himself sworn in soon after his return. The method of filling Parliament seats was never spelled out. Ali Mahdi renominated the northerner (Isaq) politician Omar Arteh as prime minister, but his eighty-three ministerial appointments could not obtain parliamentary and full USC approval. The two leaders hoped to obtain quick injections of foreign aid to be able to function. They ignored the realities of post-Siyad Somalia. Open warfare and banditry had made Mogadishu ungovernable, and they ignored the spirit of decentralization and autonomism at large in post-Siyad Somalia.

Djibouti I (1991) and Djibouti II (2000) share common characteristics and a few superficial differences. Both were top-down projects privileging the modern elites: ministers, politicians, civil servants, military and police officers. Whereas Djibouti I favoured the elites of the parliamentary pre-1969 era, Djibouti II was overwhelmed by the predominance of Siyad-era elites: numerous ministers, diplomats, civil servants, police and military officers (including many of the most notorious). That is why the constitution that was approved included the Siyadist principles of a unitary, centralized state. Djibouti I did not claim to involve civil society representatives, while Djibouti II included a certain number of so-called representatives of civil society.

Djibouti II elected Abdulkassim Salad Hassan as the president of Somalia. In kinship terms, he is a relative of the late General Aidid. Specifically he is of ayr (subclan), Habar Gedir (clan) and Hawiye (clan-family). He was one of the few long-serving ministers under Siyad. His many portfolios included information and interior. Paying lip service to clan power-sharing, he appointed as prime minister Dr Ali Khalif Galied, a Dulbahante, Darod from eastern Somaliland. A veteran of Siyad's service, he was once minister of industries. His deputy is a distinguished veteran of the Siyad regime, a minister serving for many years as minister of fisheries. Osman Jama is from the Habar Yunis, Isaq clan-family. Hasan Abshir, from the Issa Mahamud, Mijertein, Darod clan-family, first served as the new minister of natural resource, and now is currently prime minister, having replaced Dr Ali Khahf Galied. He worked closely with Siyad, once as a mayor of Mogadishu. There are few in this newly proposed cabinet who have not worked closely with former dictator Siyad Barre. Djibouti II has established a Transitional National Government (TNG). Headed by former ministers of General Siyad's discredited regime, the new 'government' includes notorious figures as well as others almost unknown to the Somali public.

Professor I.M. Lewis, a longtime student of Somalia, described this intervention in Somalia's internal affairs by the UN as 'extremely untimely.' Prior to the Djibouti conference 'the situation in Mogadishu and the south was relatively calm, with signs that local peace-making efforts (the only kind that ever work in Somalia) were producing results, and the model for local state-formation provided by Somaliland and Puntland in the north was attracting increasing attention in the turbulent south. Now thanks to the UN intervention, the scales are tipped again toward violence. With the provocation of the new faction, it is difficult to see how serious bloodshed can now be avoided.'

Somalia is indeed made up of two distinct parts. One, involving Somaliland, Puntland, and Bay and constituting the largest part of the country, forms a zone of peace. Here, there exists a dynamic process of peace-building in which civil war antagonists have learned to resolve their differences nonviolently, developed a common set of objectives and a common identity, and moved towards the creation of a just society. Elsewhere, in the capital of Mogadishu and the central regions, in Kismaya and Gedo in the south and southwest, the situation is not nearly as stable. At best, it can be described as a condition of negative peace, where violence, if not effectively controlled, is at least limited. If peace is to be consolidated in the south, it will likely arise from spontaneous developments from civil society, such as it did in the north, rather than from what Professor Lewis described as 'imported Eurocentric quick political fixes.'

NOTES

1 Hussein Adam and Richard Ford, eds., *Mending Rips in the sky: Exploring options for Somalia Communities in the 21st Century* (Lawrence, NJ: Red Sea Press, 1997), 9–10.
2 Marina Ottaway in I. William Zartman, ed., *Ripe for Resolution: Conflict and Intervention in Africa* (New York: Oxford University Press, 1995), 236–7.
3 Mohamed Sahnour, *Somalia: Missed Oportunities* (Washington, DC: United States Institution Press, 1994), xiii.

4 Samuel M. Makinda, *Seeking Peace from Chaos: Humanitarian Intervention in Somalia* (New York: International Peace Academy Occasional Paper Series, September 1993), 55.

5 Giampaolo Calchi Novati, 'Italy and Somalia: Unbearable Lightness of an Influence,' in Adam and Ford, eds., *Mending Rips in the Sky*, 567.

6 Peter Schraeder, 'The Horn of Africa: U.S. Foreign Policy in an Altered Cold War Environment,' *Middle East Journal* 46, no. 4 (1992), 17.

7 Terrence Lyons and Ahmed I. Samatar, *Somalia State Collapse, Multilateral Intervention and Strategies for Political Reconstruction* (Washington, DC: The Brookings Institution, 1995), 33–4.

8 Makinda *Seeking Peace from Chaos*, 59–60.

9 Schraeder, 'The Horn of Africa,' 18.

10 Walter Clarke and Jeffrey Herbst, eds.. *Learning from Somalia: The Lessons of Armed Humanitarian Intervention* (Boulder, CO: Westview Press, 1997), 8–9.

11 *The United Nations and Somalia: 1992–1996* (New York: United Nations Department of Public Information, 1996), 214.

12 Cited in John R. Bolton, 'Wrong Turn in Somalia,' *Foreign Affairs* 73, no. 1 (1994), 60; see also Lyons and Samatar, *Somalia State Collapse*, 34.

13 Clarke and Herbst, *Learning from Somalia*, 9, 35.

14 Robert Oakley and John Hirsch, *Somalia and Operation Restore Hope: Reflections on Peacekeeping and Peacemaking* (Washington, DC: United States Institute of Peace, 1995), 76, 77.

15 Christopher Clapham, 'Problems of Peace Enforcement: Some Lessons from Multinational Peacekeeping Operations in Africa,' in Jakkie Cilliers and Greg Mills, eds., *Peacekeeping in Africa* (South Africa: Institute for Defence Policy, 1995), 2: 146.

16 John Drysdale, *Whatever Happened to Somalia? A Tale of Tragic Blunders* (London: Haan Associates, 1994), 4.

17 Boutros Boutros-Ghali, *An Agenda for Peace: Preventive Diplomacy, Peacemaking and Peacekeeping* (New York: United Nations, 1992).

18 Quoted in Clarke and Herbst, *Learning from Somalia*, 207–8.

19 Robert Rotbert, quoted in ibid., 233.

9
Failures in Peacebuilding: Sudan (1972–1983) and Angola (1991–1998)

Taisier M. Ali, Robert O. Matthews, and Ian S. Spears

In this chapter we describe two cases in which a peace settlement was reached but subsequently broke down. The Addis Ababa Agreement was signed and ratified by the government of Sudan and the rebel Anya-Nya force in 1972, only to be undermined over the next decade and eventually annulled in 1983. In Angola, the MPLA government and the UNITA opposition reached an agreement to end fighting on two separate occasions, in 1991 and again in 1994, but in each instance, the agreement did not hold and the two protagonists returned to the battlefield.

By comparing the failed peace experiment in the Sudan between 1972 and 1983 with the collapse of two negotiated agreements in Angola between 1991 and 1998, we hope to reflect on the fragility of such settlements, the reasons why civil wars so easily recur, and the general lessons to be drawn for present and future exercises in peacebuilding. Our analysis of these two cases suggests that the difficulty in reaching a negotiated settlement and in maintaining the resulting peace is related to the sense of physical, economic, and political insecurity that the parties to a civil war feel, both as individuals and as collectivities. Specifically, this insecurity finds expression in the difficult task the parties face in reaching and sustaining an agreement on the formation of a new national army; in the efforts undertaken to fashion a mutually agreed upon mechanism for the sharing of natural resources in an environment of scarcity; and in the lengthy process of establishing political institutions that are broadly based and open. By identifying these areas of insecurity and the manner in which they feed on each other so as to finally undermine the peace process, we hope to be able to draw insights that will be of value to other experiments in building a lasting peace.

The Sudan, 1972–83

The Addis Ababa Agreement, signed by representatives of the government of Sudan and the Southern Sudan Liberation Movement on 27 February 1972, brought an end to seventeen years of violent conflict. Hailed by Africans and non-Africans alike as a beacon for all nations similarly divided along racial, religious, and ethnic lines, the agreement created a new framework within which the Sudanese people would hopefully work out their differences and resolve their controversies.

The agreement merged the three southerly provinces into one self-governing region, with its own elected Assembly and High Executive Council whose president was to be chosen by the Assembly. The regional government was granted responsibility for the preservation of 'public order, internal security' and local administration 'in cultural, economic and social fields' in the south and was empowered to develop its own budget, the revenue for which was to be drawn from local taxes and fees, direct transfers from Khartoum, and external assistance.[1] While Arabic was recognized as the official language for the Sudan, English was designated as the principal language for the Southern Region and southern schools could also use indigenous languages for purposes of instruction. Any attempt to amend the Addis Ababa Agreement, which was incorporated into the Southern Provinces Regional Self-Government Act of 1972 and then entrenched in the 1973 constitution, required both a three-quarters majority vote in the People's National Assembly and a two-thirds majority in a referendum held in the three Southern provinces of the Sudan. In addition to this double protection against any arbitrary changes by the dominant majority to regional self-government, the constitution also recognized the 'dual Arab and African identity of the Sudan,' expressed the need to respect Christianity and 'noble spiritual beliefs' as well as Islam, and prohibited 'any form of discrimination on the basis of religion, language, or gender.'[2]

The Addis Ababa Agreement did make a difference. Writing four years after the civil war ended, Nelson Kasfir remarked that despite the distrust and antagonism that continued to 'separate Southerners and Northerners ..., the agreement ... amounted to far more than a mere interlude in war.' At the very least, it represented 'the framework of first resort for resolving political controversies between North and South and within the region.'[3] Reflecting on the post-Addis Ababa Agreement period, Bona Malwal commented that 'For most Southerners the ten year period

Sudan

between 1972 and 1982 was almost heaven-like compared with what (had) gone both before and after ... At that time, the South was prepared to forgive and forget.'[4] At least in its first few years of operation the agreement appears to have responded to the Southerners' sense of insecurity, both in their capacity as individuals and as part of a larger community. Since independence all central governments, whether military or civilian, had denied the existence of Sudan's ethnic, linguistic, and religious diversity and sought to eliminate other ethnic national groups by assimilation or by repression. By contrast, the Nimeiri regime, in accepting the Addis Ababa Agreement, seemed prepared to acknowledge the existence of groups other than the dominant Arab majority in the North and to accommodate their needs and demands for physical and material security, a measure of economic prosperity and a degree of political autonomy.[5]

But by 1983 Sudan had returned to full-scale civil war. Indeed, we will argue that the policies and practices of the Nimeiri regime had begun to erode the faith Southerners had in the Addis Ababa Agreement as early as 1977.[6] What were the issues around which the process of peacebuilding came unravelled? We will focus on three areas of concern: the integration of guerrilla forces within the national army of Sudan, the promotion of economic development in the South with a view to narrowing the gap between North and South, and the maintenance of a political balance between the central government and the southern region that protected the South's special character. We will show how the manner in which these issues were resolved tended to feed on each other, gradually eroding any goodwill that the signing of the original agreement might have produced and enhancing the suspicions and sense of insecurity felt by most Southerners.

The task of merging the armed forces of former enemies is, as Nelson Kasfir points out, 'extraordinarily delicate.'[7] Given the legacy of the past, it was understandable that both sides were anxious to negotiate airtight security arrangements before being prepared to reach a final settlement and lay down their arms. From a Southern perspective the North had used its dominant position in all national institutions, including the army, to impose its culture, language, and way of life on the South; if Southerners were to preserve their autonomy in a future Sudan and guarantee the security of the agreement, they would have to establish control over the army in the South. Indeed, the Southern delegation initially proposed that each of the two regions should have its own army. Northerners, on the other hand, were concerned that an independent military force controlled by Southerners would ultimately lead to secession and could threaten the physical security of citizens of the North living in the South. If the two sides had not been able to negotiate a mutually acceptable arrangement on security matters, it is highly unlikely that they would have been able to reach an overall settlement.[8] In the end it took a last-minute intervention by Emperor Haile Selassie of Ethiopia before the two sides could reach an acceptable compromise. The army in the South, the Southern Command, was to be made up of twelve thousand officers and men of which six thousand would be recruited from former Anya-nya fighters. The Southerners were to be absorbed – that is, deployed as separate units within the armed forces – and only fully integrated after a period of five years, provided that 'an atmosphere of peace and confidence (prevailed).' Control of the Southern Command was to be exercised by the president of the republic but on the advice of the president of the High Executive Council of the Southern Region. It was agreed as well that Southern recruitment into the National Army would be proportional to the size of the population of the region and so better reflect the actual social make-up of the country.

To understand how this issue generated tension and ultimately the recurrence of civil war it is essential to appreciate the difference between absorption and integration. Immediately following the ratification of the Addis Agreement a Joint Military Commission began the process of recruiting two thousand former Anya-Nya soldiers from each of the three Southern provinces. These Southern soldiers, made up of 'absorbed units,' were stationed in such a manner as to avoid any contact with troops from the National Army. According to one author, 'There was no resistance to absorption from the Anya-Nya and the Southern public. In fact it went on very smoothly.'[9] If there were any complaints at all about absorption it was that not all Anya-Nya fighters had been selected. Even after 4,500 more had been absorbed into the police and prison services, there were, according to Abel Alier, as many as 7,290 'leftovers.' While some of these undoubtedly refused to accept this arrangement and went back into the bush, some of them 'were resettled on land in traditional farming and others were employed as wage earners in government establishments, mainly in the wildlife department as game scouts (500), local government (900), agriculture, forestry and fisheries (3,700) and roads (2,500).'[10]

By contrast, the policy of integration precipitated considerable opposition, friction and even outright resistance. There was even a dispute over whether this process should be completed after five years, that is by 1977, or simply be initiated at that time. According to Alier, it was generally believed that five years was enough time to complete the process of integration, although he admits in retrospect that more time would have been preferable. What integration meant was the merging of the two separate forces into a single national force in the South, 'mixing men from the two recruitment streams in the same units under a single chain of command at field level.'[11] At the first stage, integration involved the training of the absorbed forces, often within the region of the South but as time went on, with increasing frequency at headquarters in the North. Phase two of the process involved the internal integration among absorbed forces, both within and across provinces. Finally, during the third and most controversial stage, absorbed units and so-called old units from the People's National Army were integrated. Former Anya-Nya officers were suspicious of being asked to integrate with their former enemies and when asked to transfer to the North, either for training or for active duty, often refused to go or even worse, mutinied. A number of the mutineers involved in particularly violent incidents at Akobo in March 1975 and at Wau in February 1976 fled to Ethiopia and joined the ranks of disaffected Anya-Nya guerrillas who had rejected the Addis Ababa Agreement in 1972.

Although most of the absorbed units with the Southern Command were sceptical and even fearful of integration, Johnson and Prunier are probably correct when they argue that by and large they remained 'loyal to the government up through 1982.' But as it became increasingly apparent that Nimeiri was prepared to repudiate both the letter and the spirit of the Addis Ababa Agreement. When he set out to abolish the Southern region, to deny Southerners their share of the oil resources discovered in the South, and when finally he imposed Islamic laws on them, any last vestiges of loyalty were removed. The Bor mutiny, which began in January 1983 when soldiers of the 105th battalion refused to hand over their arms and be transferred to the North, 'was thus the culmination of a long process of disaffection both within and without the armed forces.'[12]

The next challenge facing the new regional government was to develop an economy that had been sadly neglected by colonial authorities and Northern elites alike and had suffered from the destructive impact of a lengthy civil war. With the promise of central government funding and control over and revenue from resources and development, there was some hope that the prior neglect of the South would end and the North-South socio-economic gap might even narrow.

In fact, although the repatriation and resettlement of refugees and displaced persons were successfully concluded and some improvements made to agricultural production and the basic infrastructure, the overall picture is rather gloomy. As one author summed it up, most development that did take place 'was concentrated in and around the traditionally favoured Khartoum-Gezira zone where political power had been concentrated since independence.' Meanwhile in the South, projects initiated and financed by the central government never materialized; access to higher education by Southerners declined; while basic educational facilities remained virtually unchanged.[13] In effect, the economic foundations of an enduring peace were not established. The Southerners' growing sense of economic discrimination and neglect was further strengthened by controversies over the exploitation of natural resources.

Following the end of the civil war the first and immediate task confronting Sudan was the resettlement and rehabilitation of the more than one million people that had fled their villages in the South during the civil war, taking up temporary residence in the bush or in camps in neighbouring African countries. Even before the agreement was signed the Ministry of Foreign Affairs had organized an international conference to enlist financial support for the resettlement of refugees and the rejuvenation of the South. Pledges made at that conference formed the core of a special fund set up in 1973 to finance the repatriation of refugees. By the end of 1973 nearly 180,000 refugees had returned from outside the country in an operation that Prince Sandruddin Khan, High Commissioner for Refugees, described as 'the largest return movement in Africa.'[14] The United Nations High Commission for Refugees played a key role in this exercise, coordinating the activities of a large number of UN agencies and voluntary organizations. At the time of the second anniversary of the Addis Ababa Agreement, on March 3, 1974, Abel Alier, by then President of the Southern Regional Government, announced that the process of resettlement had been completed. He did register his disappointment in the international community's response: instead of the $50 million he had counted on from abroad, the South had only received $4.9 million, with further pledges of $9.7 million.[15]

But the South's focus on relief was soon replaced by the pressing need for development. One of the underlying sources of discontent ever since independence had been what Southerners saw as the neglect, even exploitation, of their economy by the North. If the peace restored at Addis Ababa were to take root, Khartoum would have to transfer resources and encourage investment on a significant scale in the South. In fact, the expected funds never materialized. B. Yongo-Bure has clearly demonstrated that during the first five years actual development expenditure amounted to only 20.1 percent of the funds allocated in the special development budgets. Many factors accounted for the 'poor execution of development projects,' but clearly the single most important 'cause of failure during these five years was lack of financial resources (both in local and foreign currencies).' The new regional government could not be expected to raise much revenue from local taxes and fees; in any case, it faced the enormously costly task of building a new civil service. Without question it was bound to rely heavily on funding from the central government. However, transfers from Khartoum fell far below of what was needed for development and social services, and so the shortfall had to be made up by foreign assistance. Often earmarked for individual projects, most foreign funds were not available for 'the special development budget, which incorporated the bulk of development projects in terms of numbers and geographical distribution.'[16] And to make matters even worse, in many instances individual projects proposed by external donors could not be undertaken as the regional government did not have sufficient local counterpart funds for their implementation.

In 1977 the South launched a six-year plan for economic and social development. The same pattern that emerged in earlier development budgets appeared here as well, with the levels of realized investment over six years falling considerably below what was planned. Once again development financing fell short of what was needed. The South itself could not raise much revenue from its low income base and what was essentially a subsistence economy. The central government identified and even started several development projects, such as the White Nile Brewery in Wau, sugar enterprises in Mongala and Melut, the Jonglei Rice Scheme, and the Juba Hydroelectric Power Project, but in most instances they were never completed. Financial institutions such as banks and insurance companies were all based in the North and transferred the funds they collected to Khartoum. As Yongo-Bure points out, these private financial institutions behaved like Northern traders, the Jellaba, who didn't have any genuine interests in the South and therefore didn't reinvest what profits they made in southern agriculture or industry.[17]

As a consequence, many of the projects developed over this period were undertaken by foreign nongovernmental organizations. These organizations did have funding of their own. In a study of the Norwegian Church Aid (NCA) activities on the east bank of the Nile in Equatoria Province, one author pointed out that this organization alone had spent US $20 million more in that one area from 1977 to 1986 than the regional government had invested in the whole region.[18] However, with this development funding came certain adverse effects. In the first place, the various NGOs tended to do what they considered to be most important, rarely if ever coordinating their operations with the activities of other NGOs or the local government. Secondly, they seem to have made few plans to sustain these projects once they left, 'as there are neither exports nor input production in the South which could then continue to service the foreign projects when they are handed over to the southern administrators.'[19] Finally, their most significant impact seems to be the effect they have had on the local state structures. These NGOs did make a positive contribution to the economic reconstruction of the South and provided emergency assistance to hundreds of thousands of refugees, but they also 'contributed unintentionally to the erosion of the very weak state ... Basically they themselves became local substitutes for state administration.' They tended to establish their own administrative and authority systems and in doing so they undermined existing state institutions. As Tvedy succinctly put it, the 'NCA had become not only a state within the state, but the "state."'[20] To the extent that building the basis for an enduring peace requires the building of state institutions and structures with requisite levels of capacity, authority, and political legitimacy, one must question the real contribution that these NGOs have made to the development of the South.

In contrast to its overall indifference and neglect of general development in the South, the North displayed much greater enthusiasm for two specific projects: the Jonglei Canal and the exploitation of oil at Bentiu. Both investments involved external finance and both resulted in controversies that reawakened and strengthened Southern suspicions and fears that what motivated these projects were Northern and foreign (Egyptian in the case of the canal and American in the case of oil) rather than Southern interests. As Douglas Johnson pointed out, these development schemes, on which 'the central government spent most time, energy and money ..., seemed designed more to extract resources from the south than to develop services and opportunities for local communities.'[21]

Sudan and Egypt reached an accord in 1974 to build the Jonglei Canal through the Sudd swamp and in doing so to reduce the loss of water through evaporation. This project generated considerable unease in the South, where it was believed that most of the benefits would accrue to northern Sudan and Egypt while the South would have to bear all the costs. In response to Southern concerns a number of rural development projects within the proposed canal zone of benefit to the South were incorporated into the plan. Regrettably, however, while by 1985 most of the canal had been dug, even the studies of these projects remained incomplete, not to speak of their implementation. Although Abel Alier had initially been an enthusiastic supporter of the project, he too became suspicious of the two governments, who seemed far more interested in 'getting the water into the Canal in order to execute projects downstream than for providing capital investment for social production schemes in the South.'[22]

The discovery of oil in Southern Sudan in 1978 unearthed a political controversy as well, offering Southerners an avenue to economic recovery,' while enhancing the fear of Northerners that this new economic wealth would fan the flames of Southern separatism. The real roots of this conflict can in fact be found in the financial arrangements provided for in the Addis Ababa Agreement. That settlement 'assigned all central government revenues in the South, realizable from commercial, agricultural and industrial activities and services, to the regional treasury.' Such revenues 'included profits accruing to the central government as a result of exporting products from the Southern Region.'[23] The central government could have negotiated with the Southern regional government a new resource- sharing agreement, but instead it did everything it could to maintain control over the oil and thus deprive the South of this new wealth. First, it introduced a new map that redrew the boundary lines in such a manner that the oil was located in the North. Faced with stiff opposition, Khartoum decided to build a refinery in the North (Kosti) rather than in the South (Bentiu), later reversing that decision and opting for a pipeline to the Red Sea. Uncertain as to whether that would assure its control of the oil, the central government took the final step of breaking up the Southern Region, thus ending 'what was left of southern autonomy once and for all.'[24] While all this was going on, the central government replaced the Southern soldiers that had manned the military garrison at Bentiu until then with Northern soldiers from the West, thus signaling that if all else failed, it was prepared to use brute force to resolve this conflict.

The discovery of oil and the conflict it set off occurred at the very time that the balance of forces along the North-South fault line was shifting. In 1972 Nimeiri had sought an accommodation with the South, not so much out of any belief in the sanctity of national unity but as a countervailing force against his political enemies in the North, the traditional sectarian parties as well as the organized forces on the left. By settling the war in the South Nimeiri hoped 'to placate the army, enhance his prestige at home and abroad, and win for himself the Southern support that all Khartoum regimes had lacked since independence.'[25] But to win over the South he had to pay a political price: the signing of the Addis Ababa Agreement. Whether or not that agreement created a de facto federal system is open to debate, but no one would question that in its early years the agreement worked to protect the South's special character. Working closely with Abel Alier, who became a vice president of the Republic and the first President of the High Executive Council of the Southern Region, Nimeiri allowed the regional government to function fairly smoothly. With the help of Alier and Joseph Lagu, he intervened to resolve incidents arising from the integration of Anya-Nya forces into the national army and to provide funding for the Southern Region's budgetary needs. But even in those early years, he was anxious to control the Southern Region's autonomy. 'He was,' as Bona Malwal reminds us, 'the one and only supreme authority in the Sudan and he was going to find a way to reverse the situation in the South.'[26] By that Malwal meant that Nimeiri wanted to exercise control over the regional government and to ensure that his candidate for president of the High Executive Council was selected. Contrary to the constitution, Nimeiri had notified the Regional Assembly in 1973 that his choice for president was Abel Alier. The Regional Assembly finally chose Alier, and in all likelihood they would have done so anyway, but Southerners resented what they considered to be improper, if not illegal, interference in Southern affairs. Later, in 1980 and 1981, Nimeiri intervened in a similar manner by arbitrarily dissolving the Regional Assembly and imposing General Qasmalla Abdalla Rasa as president.

The turning point came in 1976 when the United National Front, made up of the two sectarian parties, the Democratic Unionist Party and the Umma Party, together with the Muslim Brothers (later known as the National Islamic Front), stormed Khartoum and took over government installations. Realizing how close they had come to overthrowing him, Nimeiri decided to forge an alliance with the National Front, pursuing a policy of national reconciliation with the very forces in the North who had vehemently attacked the Addis Ababa accord and the granting of regional autonomy to the South. As they gradually gained access to Nimeiri's inner councils, these Northern forces were able slowly to erode his adherence to the Addis Ababa Agreement. According to Alier, Nimeiri promised the National Front leaders to undertake 'a substantial review of the Addis Ababa Agreement, especially in the areas of security arrangements, border trade, language, culture and religion.'[27] This shift in the balance of forces was first reflected in Nimeiri's appointment in 1977 of a committee 'to recommend revision of the constitution and legal system to bring these into line with Islamic law.'[28] The chairman of that committee was none other than Hasan Al-Turabi, head of the Muslim Brothers and soon to become attorney general. Although Southerners were alarmed by these developments, by November 1981 there were no Southerners left in the cabinet to protest those moves and Nimeiri was prepared to run roughshod over any objections that may have come from the Southern Region.

In a flagrant violation of the Addis Ababa Agreement, Nimeiri redivided the Southern Region into three new regions. He had tried to secure Southern support for this redivision and, indeed, Joseph Lagu and other Southern politicians approved the idea on the grounds that it would allow Equatoria to escape from Dinka domination. But in the end the Regional Assembly rejected redivision and Nimeiri was forced to impose this change by presidential decree on 5 June 1983, without any vote in the Regional Assembly or in the National Assembly and without a referendum among the people of the South. As Ann Lesch points out, the collapse of the agreement was total: under the new act 'the president appointed the governors, cancelled direct elections for the regional assemblies, and withdrew their control over revenue derived from trade and natural resources.'[29] All this was made easier for Nimeiri by the division within the ranks of Southern politicians. Had they remained united in the face of Nimeiri's erosion of the Addis Ababa Agreement, they would have at least made it more difficult for him to accomplish. But their differences, in part ethnic, in part personal, played into Nimeiri's hands, allowing him to intervene in Southern politics by appealing to their personal interests.

The final nail was driven into the coffin of the Addis Ababa Agreement in September 1983, when Nimeiri imposed his version of the Islamic laws. These laws represented the culmination of Islamic reforms begun in 1977 and were the result of his need to stay ahead of the religious right in appealing to Muslim opinion. That Nimeiri would introduce such reforms should come as no surprise for, as Mansour Khalid, his former foreign minister, wrote: 'Nimeiri had never been genuinely committed to the principles of the Addis Ababa Agreement.' He approached the problem of the South instrumentally: when it served his purpose of staying in power, he signed the agreement, but when it did not, he had no compunction about tearing it into pieces. That Nimeiri could annul the Addis Ababa Agreement should not surprise us either, for, as he said when asked about procedures for amending the agreement, 'The Addis Ababa agreement is myself and Joseph Lagu and we want it that way ... I am 300 percent the constitution. I do not know of any plebiscite because I am mandated by the people as President.'[30] Nimeiri's regime was a military dictatorship, not a democracy. Just as Nimeiri had made the agreement in 1972, he could unmake it in 1983.

The implications of the September laws for the Addis Ababa Agreement were profound and immediate. By reducing all non-Muslims to the status of second-class citizens, Nimeiri had effectively annulled that agreement. Although divided on many issues, Southerners were united in their opposition to any attempt to impose the Islamic religion on all the people of Sudan. At that moment, the three policy areas converged. The fears and suspicions of the absorbed and integrated Anya-Nya that they would be forced out of service or compelled to relocate to the North were made real when it became apparent that Nimeiri was prepared to rob the South of its wealth and to eradicate its cultural, linguistic, and religious identity, by force if necessary. Any loyalty the Anya-Nya soldiers may have felt towards Sudan, Nimeiri, or the Addis Ababa Agreement had evaporated. In a manner strangely reminiscent of the Torit mutiny of 1955, which had resulted in the first civil war, the refusal of the Southern soldiers in Bor and Pibor to transfer to the North triggered in 1983 a series of mutinies that ultimately led to the creation of the Sudan Peoples Liberation Movement and Army and the recurrence of Sudan's civil war.

Angola: The Collapse of the Bicesse and Lusaka Agreements

The experience of peacebuilding in Angola would appear to have had one important advantage over that in the Sudan. Within a relatively short period of time, the principal disputants in Angola, with the assistance of the international community, had *two* opportunities to make peace. If there had ever been any doubt, the urgent need to find a solution to the Angolan conflict had been apparent following the first failed peace process and the post-election return to war in 1992. In his subsequent report to the Security Council on the situation in Angola, the United Nations secretary general stated that 'to all intents and purposes, Angola has returned to civil war, and is probably in an even worse situation than that which prevailed before the Peace Accords were signed in May 1991.' Angola's deputy foreign minister, Jorge Chikoti, agreed, stating: 'Things are worse now than they've ever been ... We have never seen

Angola

so many refugees, so many deaths, so much destruction in a short period of time.'[31] How is it that a peace agreement could lead to a worse situation than that which existed previously, particularly when, like the Addis Ababa agreement in the Sudan, the early days of the peace process had looked so promising? More importantly, why did what appeared to be clearly identifiable errors learned from the failure to consolidate peace under the Bicesse Accords, from 1991–2, *not* help avoid a similar outcome during Angola's second peace process under the Lusaka Protocol, from 1994–8?

Part of the answer may lie in the context and manner in which political decisions on whether to agree to and abide by negotiated settlements were made. An examination of both of these moments of peace and the actors involved suggests that both the ruling MPLA government and the UNITA rebels framed their respective outlooks to these peace processes in terms of their bitter experiences in the past. References were constantly made to previous events and the manner in which decisions made at that time enhanced their security or jeopardized it in ways neither movement could afford to repeat. Consequently, the focus shifted from cautious optimism on the prospects of peace to ensuring survival in the midst of a shaky peace agreement. The manner in which previous peacebuilding experience informed subsequent decisions on what actions to take to protect themselves during the second transition process suggests that any advantage Angola may have had in terms of a second opportunity for peace was at the very least illusory. In this section, we will look at the ways in which the decisions made reflected each movement's preoccupation with the three principal issues considered in our discussion on the Sudan: the physical, political, and economic security of the disputants.

The civil war in Angola had long been driven by the Cold War. Each of the central parties in the conflict, the MPLA and UNITA, had the backing of one of the superpowers and their respective allies, Cuba and South Africa. Consequently, the end of the Cold War was expected to result in a relatively straightforward resolution of the Angolan war. Such an outcome appeared to have been realized in May 1991 when the leaders of the two parties, Jose Eduardo dos Santos for the MPLA and Jonas Savimbi for UNITA, signed the Bicesse Accords and pledged to respect the result of general elections to be held within sixteen to eighteen months of the ceasefire. 'If I lose the election, this is my country and I am an ordinary citizen,' declared Jonas Savimbi. 'No one will push me to go back to the bush anymore.'[32] Particularly in the days following the signing of the accords, few seemed to doubt that the agreement would last. 'Maybe it was the fact that at that point people were just tired of the war,' noted Marcus Samondo, a senior member of UNITA, 'but [the agreement] was something that everybody embraced ... The country was really going through what UNITA had fought for.'[33]

On 17 October 1992 the UN special representative, Margaret Anstee, declared the elections, which gave the incumbent MPLA victories in both the presidential and legislative races, to be 'free and fair.' By this time, however, Jonas Savimbi had already determined that the electoral process had suffered from massive electoral fraud. With the United Nations and other elections observers refusing to acknowledge any sort of systemic vote rigging, and given UNITA's failure to substantiate its own claims, UNITA's accusations were widely viewed as a reflection of its unexpected loss at the polls. Despite the fact that President dos Santos had failed to capture a clear majority – and therefore would need a second run-off vote – as well as frantic efforts to persuade Savimbi to refrain from the military option, Angola returned to war.[34]

Angola's second moment of peace began with the signing of the Lusaka Protocol in October 1994 in the Zambian capital. The agreement sought to avoid many of the weaknesses of the previous agreement by pledging both parties to a power-sharing agreement, by completing the disarmament and demobilization program initiated under the Bicesse Accords, by forming an integrated Angolan Armed Forces (FAA), and by having UNITA hand over territory to central administration in exchange for a side agreement on wealth-sharing. While some of the agreement's provisions were met – most notably the swearing in of sixty-three UNITA deputies and four ministers in a 223-member Government of Unity and National Reconciliation (GURN) in April 1997 – the implementation of other provisions soon bogged down. UNITA refused to fully disarm and to hand over Andulo and other towns under its control in central Angola Fed up with UNITA's intransigence, the government launched a new major offensive in December 1998 to reclaim these territories and, as ultimately occurred, to decapitate UNITA's leadership.

These experiences provided each party with compelling reasons for why they should *not* trust their adversary in any peace agreement. From the government's perspective, that UNITA had rejected the elections of 1992 was indicative of the fact that it could never accept a decision made by Angolans in a free and fair election (of course, by some accounts, UNITA never intended to honour an unfavourable election outcome); secondly, UNITA did not fulfill the requirement that it disarm and, on the contrary, looked to the peace agreements to provide an opportunity to increase its strength; and finally, UNITA had refused to hand over territory as required under the Lusaka Protocol. UNITA had its own reasons for not trusting the government: first, following the 1992 elections, MPLA-sponsored militias killed some of UNITA's senior members who had risked being in Luanda at the time of the elections (an action which some UNITA officials maintained was deliberately intended to decapitate UNITA); secondly, following the initialing but prior to the formal signing of the 1994 Lusaka Accords, the government undertook one 'final push' to capture the UNITA stronghold of Huambo, a violation of the spirit if not the letter of the Protocol; and finally, government actions during the process of handing UNITA-held territory over to central administration were seen as tantamount to that of a conquering army and suggested to UNITA that control over resources (control which UNITA saw as central to its survival) in future would not be conducted in a way which reflected concern for UNITA's security interests.

In her article on the difficulties in resolving civil wars, Barbara Walter argues that peace agreements force parties into a 'paradoxical and unfortunate dilemma.' Because civil war adversaries cannot maintain independent armed forces following the implementation of a peace agreement, any attempt to proceed with a peace process necessarily leaves at least one of the parties vulnerable. In her words, 'as soon as they comply with a peace treaty they become powerless to enforce the terms over which they had bargained so hard.' Alternatively, it is frequently safer and less risky to continue fighting – or at least to keep one's arms – than to negotiate or abide by an agreement which ultimately leaves one at the mercy of an adversary. In short, because the resolution of civil conflicts almost always requires at least one of the parties to relinquish their weapons, they are extremely reluctant to commit to an agreement or follow through on its implementation. With no external guarantor nor any means to protect themselves should their opponent 'defect' from the agreement, parties have little reason for confidence in either the peace process or their adversary.[35]

These problems are exacerbated when, as in Angola, each side believes it has reason not to take its adversary at its word. Indeed, perhaps the biggest obstacle to peace in Angola has been the reluctance of both sides to disarm as was required under both the Bicesse and Lusaka peace agreements. The US special representative to the Angolan peace process, Paul Hare, notes in his record of the events that Savimbi would ask rhetorically, 'What leader had ever given up his army and survived?'[36] While UNITA worried about the formation of a new government paramilitary unit of anti-riot police known as the *ninjas*, rumours circulated that UNITA was maintaining its own 'hidden army' of some twenty thousand men. It was no surprise, then, that by the time of the 1992 elections, only 65 percent of the MPLA and 26 percent of UNITA forces had been processed.

Indeed, for the Angolan government, the obvious and unfortunate lesson of the 1992 elections and subsequent return to war was that it was to no benefit, and at considerable risk, that they followed their pre-election demobilization orders. As a consequence, Luanda remained paranoid about UNITA's future intentions and determined not to let itself be caught again in such a weakened position. 'The Government played largely by the rules, and lost big time,' noted a Western military analyst following the elections and the return to war. 'You can be assured they won't make that mistake again.'[37] Following the signing of the Lusaka Protocol in 1994, the Angolan government sought to create a set of conditions which would assure its legitimate claim to power and reduce the likelihood of UNITA mounting another major challenge against it. It did this by undertaking a massive rearmament program and seeking to isolate UNITA diplomatically. Following the collapse of the Mobutu regime in Zaire in May 1997, Angola defended his Luanda-friendly successor, Laurent Kabila, as a means of precluding UNITA from using it as a rear base from which to arm itself. Luanda also assisted in the overthrow of UNITA-ally Pascal Lissouba in Congo-Brazzaville in October 1997, and made a number of thinly veiled threats against the Zambian government to discourage arms shipments coming from there. Even within the context of the Lusaka Protocol, militant members of the MPLA regime continued to emphasize the need for vigilance against a possible UNITA offensive. 'UNITA only understands one language – force, hard line!' noted the former Angolan foreign minister, Paulo Jorge. 'When we took these hard positions, UNITA became more flexible.'[38]

While the threat and implementation of sanctions did, on occasion, bring UNITA around, it also further confirmed that the government's intentions were not benign. And given its own unpleasant experience at the time of the 1992 elections, many UNITA officials remained wary of a trap in the subsequent effort to form an integrated army. While UNITA did send five of its generals to Luanda to join the FAA, there was considerable scepticism among those who stayed behind that history was about to repeat itself. 'We've been lured to Luanda twice before, in 1975 and 1992, and our men were killed both times,' noted one UNITA official. 'We won't make that mistake again.'[39]

Indeed, both sides could not but believe that their actions were legitimate or logical defensive measures taken in light of the undoubted malfeasance of their adversary. The MPLA's efforts to surround and isolate UNITA were matched only by UNITA's innovativeness in finding new ways to get diamonds out of the country and weapons in. UNITA's former representative to Washington, Jardo Muekalia, noted that, 'While UNITA was [facing] an embargo on arms and petroleum, the government was being given the green light to continue purchasing weapons. And our question was always, if there is a peace agreement – this *is* a peace agreement – why are they so busy purchasing weapons?'[40] For the government, however, and indeed the international community, the MPLA had a right to acquire weapons because, having won the 1992 elections, the government had a legitimate right to defend itself – which included the acquisition of arms.

In short, disputants simply will not disarm if it means that they will then be made vulnerable to attack from their adversary. And a peace agreement which is contingent on disarmament, then, cannot move forward. Regardless of whether one perceives UNITA's actions as acts of belligerence, in a climate of insecurity generated by the fact that the emasculation of UNITA was clearly in the MPLA's interest, it is not hard to understand why UNITA refused to disarm. And it was not hard to appreciate why the elected government in Luanda found this situation unacceptable.

The decision by both parties to enter into the Bicesse Accords and the refusal to consider in advance power-sharing or any other form of accommodation for the post-election period was based on the conviction of each party that they would win the elections. For both the MPLA, who achieved power at the time of Angola's independence thanks largely to Soviet arms and Cuban troops, and for the UNITA rebels, who had failed to gain power at the time of Angola's independence in 1975 and had had to endure the albatross of being supported by apartheid-South Africa, the 1992 elections were embraced because they provided an opportunity to finally have their legitimate authority recognized. On the other hand, both parties were sufficiently familiar with electoral processes in other parts of Africa to be concerned that this might be a one-time event and that there might not be an opportunity to contest elections in future. 'I think that the perception was that this was the *one* election,' noted one election observer. 'I don't think there was a tremendous amount of confidence that the party that wins the elections would not find an excuse to change the constitution to maintain their power.'

In contrast to the elections in South Africa nineteen months later, where there was little doubt that the ANC would be victorious, the situation in Angola became increasingly precarious as election day approached. While his government was held in contempt for its corruption, inefficiency, and incompetence, President Jose Eduardo dos Santos did enjoy personal popularity as the leader who had secured peace for Angola. Once the campaign was under way the Angolan government hired a Brazilian public relations firm to direct its electoral strategy. As the MPLA's perceived electoral support increased and UNITA struggled, the election itself became a tremendous source of tension. Of particular concern were the speeches and statements to the media of the mercurial Jonas Savimbi, which sounded increasingly belligerent. 'If I lose, then the elections were rigged,' Savimbi reportedly told a British television crew. 'I will send my men back to the bush to fight again. We will not accept defeat.'[41]

Peace was sustained during the pre-election period, however, in spite of the animosity and bellicose rhetoric between the two movements. Elections still provided the most direct and least costly means by which one side or the other could legitimately gain complete political power and neither UNITA nor the MPLA was prepared to jeopardize this opportunity by undertaking overt violent actions. The UN special Margaret Anstee, noted that 'the cease-fire held – even if sometimes by a hairline – simply because when push came to shove, neither side wanted to imperil the elections, which each expected to win (at least in the latter stages).' The elections would be, noted Anstee, the 'critical watershed.'[42]

For ordinary Angolans, the election promised to provide a much longed-for bridge to a more peaceful Angola. One election observer, John Marcum, noted that 'Whether citizen or international observer, it was difficult not to get caught up in the desperate, wishful thinking of the moment and believe that just possibly Angola and Angolans were on the brink of the political peace and economic reconstruction for which they had long yearned.' Indeed, 90 percent of the registered voter population lined up for hours often after having walked for miles to their nearest polling station and cast ballots on what turned out to be a peaceful election day. Angolans were undoubtedly concerned about what a possible MPLA victory and UNITA defeat would mean in terms of a possible return to war. But there were other factors impinging on their decisions. Marcum has argued, for example, that voters in regions outside of the traditional UNITA and MPLA strongholds were more fearful of a potential UNITA despotism than a corruption-plagued MPLA in power.[43] Savimbi's anti-white and anti-*mestiço* rhetoric and UNITA's own actions – including setting up roadblocks in some cities – also alienated many Angolans. Finally, Savimbi's pledge to purge state-sector employees who had supported the MPLA in the past led many Angolans who were dependent on government employment to believe that support for UNITA could be costly.[44]

As a result, the anticipated UNITA sweep turned into a situation where the two main contestants for power were described as neck and neck. 'There was a general consensus across the board that UNITA would win those elections up until June 1992,' noted one election observer in Angola at the time. 'It was only in August that the MPLA mounted a brilliant campaign and UNITA mounted an abysmal campaign. Up until election day, I could not have told you who was going to win.' When the election results were finally released there was genuine incredulity among UNITA supporters and officials after they had convinced themselves and repeatedly been assured by their international supporters that their electoral prospects were good. While the government had portrayed UNITA as a band of terrorists who could not be trusted, UNITA saw themselves as a genuine liberation movement who had made tremendous sacrifices for the country. Electoral victory, Savimbi claimed, had been the only expected victory after 'sixteen years of suffering, of humiliation, of torture and above all of theft.'[45] Now, once the election was apparently lost, UNITA's tactics changed. If the political route had been the only acceptable strategy prior to the elections, now the military path remained UNITA's only option.

The subsequent Lusaka Protocol, which was eventually worked out following the 1992 elections and the return to war, called on the government to open a new 'political space' for UNITA. By all accounts the GURN proved to be an institution of open and free debate. One Western diplomat in Luanda noted that the GURN is 'a very open and exciting institution. It gets reported in the national press and UNITA deputies speak openly and criticize the government. It functions like any good parliament should with a good opposition.' Even UNITA's own deputies conceded that the GURN has been 'very important as far as the country is concerned.' Marcus Samondo, the UNITA deputy who served as the minister of geology and mines, noted that 'We work as a team. Once you are here, you are not invited as a minister from UNITA. You are a Minister of Angola.'[46]

Despite these sentiments, however, many senior members of UNITA, most notably Jonas Savimbi, remained outside of the GURN. Several roles were considered to get Savimbi to be a part of the political process, including that of a vice-presidency, leader of the largest opposition party, or some other 'special status.' That Savimbi refused to come to Luanda and assume his unspecified posting reflected the ambivalence within UNITA towards the Protocol.[47] With encouragement from the MPLA, dissident UNITA deputies formed their own breakaway UNITA-Renovada party, while another faction, under the leadership of Abel Chivukuvuku, committed itself to a non-violent political process but refused to be seen as a government stooge.

It was also possible to discern more nefarious motivations behind both the government's concessions on power-sharing and Savimbi's refusal to commit to the peace process. For example, the government's efforts to encourage the emergence of UNITA dissidents and to share power with them were meant to further isolate Savimbi and undermine his strength. Alternatively, for UNITA, the Lusaka Protocol was certainly appealing to Savimbi if the only alternative was military defeat. From his perspective, the protocol could be used as a refuge until a more advantageous military situation emerged.

Finally, regarding issues of economic security, the MPLA and UNITA have looked to, respectively, Angola's vast oil and diamond wealth as their primary source of funding. Since neither party had been able to rely on the generous aid it previously received from their respective superpower patrons, both had become dependent on these resources. 'The diamond issue is the key for UNITA because it determines the survival of the party,' noted Jardo Muekalia. 'Most of the political opposition parties in Africa die of financial asphyxiation before they die of political asphyxiation.'[48] Indeed, in a multiparty system, UNITA's continued access to its revenue base could not be denied if it was to play an effective counter to the dominant position of the MPLA.

In order to reduce the stakes associated with Angola's peace process, a number of initiatives were taken to try and resolve the problem of control over Angola's diamond fields. According to UN spokesman David Wimhurst, 'Luanda recognized that the only way to get UNITA to agree to the return of territorial administration to central authority was to do a deal on the diamonds.' Following talks, which began in mid-1995, an exchange of sorts was worked out whereby UNITA allowed government territorial control to be extended in return for UNITA's right to legally exploit the diamond resources. 'It's a pragmatic solution to a thorny problem,' Wimhurst continued, 'but we recognized that if they can't solve the diamond thing we won't move much further.'[49] UNITA's own legal diamond mining company, SGM, was given two potentially profitable concessions in the southern province of Cuando Cubango and near the town of Andulo.[50] But negotiations over other more exploitable alluvial diamond deposits in Lunda Norte stalled in 1997.

The ability to deny an adversary such access has had obvious military consequences as well. UNITA's military victory in the key oil town of Soyo in the northwest in January 1992, along with its control of the diamond areas in the northeast, assured that the government was at least temporarily unable to generate revenues that had financed its earlier military efforts. Indeed, the capacity of each party to continue arms purchases in times of war and peace only furthered the sense of insecurity of the other. Oil revenues allowed the government to finance the massive rearmament program which began following the 1992 elections. For UNITA, diamonds proved to be a 'guerrilla's best friend' insofar as their indestructibility, high value, and ease of transport made them an ideal currency with which to covertly fund its own war effort. Consequently, any action which limited access to these resources was regarded by each party as the gravest of threats.

Indeed, the implementation of the wealth-sharing agreements – which required the extension of central administration to UNITA-controlled diamond areas – proved to be the most difficult aspect of the Lusaka peace process. UNITA officials likened the MPLA's takeover of certain territory to a 'conquering army.'[51] Such heavy-handedness, from both the UN and UNITA's perspective, did not bode well for the prospects of wealth-sharing. 'The government was not looking for a situation to make room for a political UNITA,' noted one UNITA official. 'It was actually looking for a situation to strangle [UNITA]. We basically had a situation where this agreement was no longer possible to implement – unless UNITA was willing to give up completely.'[52]

From the MPLA's perspective, however, diamonds were being used not only to ensure UNITA's *political* survival but to rebuild its military might so that it could once again challenge the government. While the Lusaka Protocol called on UNITA to demobilize its troops, aircraft continued to ferry military hardware – paid for with UNITA-mined diamonds – from Eastern Europe to UNITA-controlled airstrips. The international community imposed a series of sanctions in 1997 and 1998 which was meant to slow UNITA's capacity to carry out diamonds-for-arms transactions, but these only strengthened UNITA's resolve to deny the government the territory which remained under its control. Meanwhile, UNITA diamond wealth was used to induce other African leaders to continue to help facilitate UNITA's arms acquisitions.

Well before the government's December 1998 offensive against the UNITA-held towns of Andulo and Bailundo, the peace process had reached an impasse. Knowing that it would eventually provoke an attack, UNITA refused to give up the remaining territory under its control. The government could no longer tolerate a movement which refused to abide by its protocol commitments and, worse, posed an increasing threat by using its $400 million in yearly diamond revenues to pay for its rearmament. The government concluded that the most effective guarantee that UNITA would not be able to continue the fight was for it to retake the territory which had allowed UNITA to fund its military activities and to kill or capture its leader, Jonas Savimbi. This it did when Savimbi was killed in a shoot-out with government troops in February 2002. After thirty years of civil war, peace came to Angola not as a result of a negotiated settlement but as a result of the violent death of one of the principal protagonists to the conflict.

Conclusion: Lessons Learned

One of the central lessons arising from these two experiments in peace-building relates to the problems associated with demobilization and demilitarization of the combatants during the peace process. Both the Angolan and Sudanese cases underline the difficulties that result when one or both parties must make themselves vulnerable in order to carry out their side of the peace agreement. Indeed, Barbara Walter presses this point even further in arguing that negotiations rarely end in the peaceful settlement of civil wars because, in the absence of a legitimate central government and legal institutions to enforce the terms of an agreement, adversaries are unprepared to lay down their arms.[73] The natural fears and suspicions associated with the requirement to disarm were present in both of our cases and ultimately contributed to the recurrence of civil war. Clearly innovative ways must be found to ensure that the physical security of both disputants is maintained, particularly throughout a transitional period. In this context the distinction made between absorption and integration in the Addis Ababa Agreement and the delay of considerable time before reaching full integration may have some value as a transitional arrangement for other cases. In other instances, it may be helpful to forego disarmament entirely, at least until greater confidence is established between the disputants. According to Jeremy Ginifer, in Zimbabwe's transition to majority rule, for example, 'none of the parties would contemplate disarmament. The CMF [Commonwealth Monitoring Force] and the British government did not see it as a viable option; indeed, disarmament was never seriously entertained.'[53] What our study suggests is that there may well be other solutions than Barbara Walter's call for an outside enforcer, to the enhanced insecurity facing civil war adversaries both during and after the negotiation of a peaceful settlement.

Concerning the question of economic security, it may be helpful to distinguish between two separate but closely related issues. On one level, we observed in both cases widespread poverty but a poverty distributed unevenly across each country. The economic foundations of an enduring peace must, we are convinced, involve the gradual elimination of that poverty and, at the same time, the narrowing of the gap between the less developed and the more developed regions of each country. The failure of the central government in the Sudan to address the South's economic needs and concerns left Southerners with a strong feeling of being neglected. The economic security of the disputants is affected, on another level, by the discovery and exploitation of key natural resources – in our two cases, diamonds and oil. Who owns those resources? How are they developed? And how are the revenues derived from their exploitation shared? The manner in which these questions are answered in practice may well serve to exacerbate or even to initiate civil wars. Khartoum's strategy of seizing control of the oil at Bentiu and arrogating to itself the right to deploy the revenues as it saw fit contributed significantly to the recurrence of civil war in the Sudan. The wealth-sharing agreement worked out at Lusaka for the Angolans was a promising step in the right direction but, in the context of on-going military struggle between UNITA and the MPLA, it too proved to be unstable. If there is to be an enduring peace, the parties must come to a mutually acceptable agreement on how such resources can be fairly distributed.

Granting mineral concessions to a political party or movement also raises serious questions about accountability and democratization. In both our cases the political arrangements resulting from the peace settlements proved to be highly unstable. In Angola, the winner-take-all elections of 1992 created an unstable situation insofar as it essentially left one of the parties with no guarantee of political or even economic security. Subsequently, progress was made towards creating a more stable power-sharing agreement between UNITA and the MPLA, but this too was undermined by Savimbi's unwillingness to come to Luanda to assume his role in the government of unity. Other events – most notably, the FAA's invasion of Huambo in 1994 – shaped his decision on whether or not the government could be trusted to protect his personal security, even in the context of a power-sharing arrangement. In the Sudan, the granting of self-government and a measure of democracy to the Southern Region alone was also extremely precarious, depending as they did upon the will of one man, for it meant that this experiment could be overturned by Nimeiri when it no longer suited his own political calculations. It would seem that peace can only be achieved through the establishment of political institutions and a political process that are both broadly based and open. The creation of these institutions in principle is far distant from the realization in practice of compromise and cooperation across a war-divided society.

Regional autonomy may, however, offer an arrangement that can help to diffuse tensions within a state marked by deeply entrenched divisions within its society. Regionalization can help alleviate disputants' security needs and, for this reason, is frequently called for. In the case of Sudan the Addis Ababa Agreement accorded a measure of self-government to the South, which proved to be an important ingredient in the realization of the final settlement. That regional autonomy in Southern Sudan ultimately collapsed should not lead us to the conclusion that regional devolution of power does not work, for between 1972 and 1977 it did work reasonably well. As a longtime observer of Southern Sudan remarked, 'For the first time in the post-colonial era the Southern Sudanese actually governed their own affairs or at least many of them.'[54] While regional self-government has not seriously been considered as an issue of discussion in the case of Angola, regionalization should still be a possible ingredient in the peacebuilding process. As Jardo Muekalia, a UNITA spokesman, put it, 'Part of a confidence measure, I believe, would be to say ... we'll allow some kind of regionalization of the country. In other words, it's not just decentralization, it's actually investing real powers in different regions within a unitary state.'[55] The establishment of some form of regional autonomy should, therefore, be actively considered as a way to ensure that the people of a vulnerable region are accorded a measure of control over their own lives and a mechanism by which to protect their cultural, religious and linguistic identity.

Lastly, the international community has an important role to play in the peacebuilding process, both in deploying resources to a country emerging from civil war, especially in support of its underdeveloped regions, and in pressing the combatants to comply with the pledges they made at the time of the settlement. In the case of Sudan the international community was noticeable for its absence. While non governmental organizations did provide some, if not sufficient, resources, the international community failed completely to apply any pressure on Nimeiri as he gradually undermined the terms of the Addis Ababa Agreement. Both Egypt and the United States established close economic, political, and military ties with Khartoum, especially after 1977. Preoccupied with external threats to Sudan's security, Washington and Cairo became too closely identified with Nimeiri and his own personal security to feel free to criticize him. The international community's experience in Angola, though for the most part unsuccessful, was in marked contrast to this general neglect of the unfolding crisis in the Sudan during the 1970s and early 1980s. The UN's early bitter experience in Angola was in part based on having drawn incorrect lessons from earlier peace processes in Namibia and its successful work in monitoring the withdrawal of Cuban troops from Angola during the late 1980s. The subsequent mission, however, was underfunded and undermanned. UNAVEM III sought to correct many of the earlier errors associated with the Bicesse Accords and was generally successful in maintaining peace for a while. But following Angola's return to war in December 1998, the achievements of even this latest effort have once again been called into question. The lessons to be drawn from the international community's response to these two civil wars are quite simple: it cannot remain on the sidelines, as it did in the Sudan, but it must rethink carefully how it can most effectively contribute to ensuring that once the fighting has stopped the combatants find ways to resolve their differences peacefully through the political process rather then by reverting back to armed struggle. Moreover, as should be clear from the Angolan case, being afforded the luxury of a second opportunity to make peace is of little benefit if the parties must overcome mistrust generated and reinforced by the first unsuccessful effort in peacebuilding.

Successful peacebuilding requires a broad-based action program. No single component of that program, military, economic or political, is likely to succeed in restoring security and long-term peace to a country that has been afflicted by civil war. While none of the ingredients found wanting in our two cases would by themselves be sufficient to build an enduring peace, in our view, each is necessary.

NOTES

1 All quotes from the Addis Ababa Agreement are taken directly from the text of the accord, a copy of which can be found in Mohammed Omer Beshir, *The Southern Sudan: From Conflict to Peace* (New York: Barnes and Noble, 1975).

2 Ann Mosely Lesch, *Sudan: Contested National Identities* (Bloomington: Indiana University Press, 1998), 47.

3 Nelson Kasfir, 'Southern Sudanese Politics since the Addis Ababa Agreement,' *African Affairs*, April 1977.

4 In a letter to Sayed Al Saddiq El Mahdi, dated 18 October 1992.

5 Ann Lesch aptly depicts the negotiation of the Addis Ababa Agreement as a shift from what she describes as a 'control model,' in which 'the state tries to undermine and even destroy other ethnic national groups that exist within its boundaries,' towards an ethnic pluralist model, in which group differences are recognized and accommodated. At least in theory, the Addis Ababa Agreement represented this latter model. See Lesch, *Sudan*, 9, 47.

6 In a paper on 'The Political Conceptualization of 'The Sudan' Conflict,' dated 8 May 1994, the SPLM/SPLA argued that the emergence of Anyanya II in 1975 marked 'the start of the second war of national liberation' (13).

7 Kasfir, 'Southern Sudanese Politics," 148.

8 Abel Alier, *Southern Sudan: Too Many Agreements Dishonoured* (Exeter: Ithaca Press, 1990), 106.

9 Deng Awur Wenyin, 'The Integration of the Anya-Nya into the National Army,' in Mom K. Arou and B. Yongo-Bure, eds., *North-South Relations in the Sudan Since the Addis Ababa Agreement* (Khartoum: Institute of African and Asian Studies, 1989), 66.

10 Alier, *Southern Sudan*, 143.

11 Kasfir, 'Southern Sudanese Politics,' 150.

12 Douglas H. Johnson and Gerard Prunier, 'The Foundation and Expansion of the Sudan People's Liberation Army,' in M.W. Daly and Ahmed A. Sikainga, eds., *Civil War in the Sudan* (London: British Academy Press, 1993), 123, 125.

13 See B. Yongo-Bure's Introduction to Arou and Yongo-Bure, *North-South Relations*, 3–4.

14 *African Contemporary Record, 1973-74*, B96.

15 Ibid., *1974–75*, B98. See also Alier's account of the repatriation and resettlement process in *Southern Sudan*, 133–35.

16 B. Yongo-Bure, 'The Underdevelopment of the Southern Sudan Since Independence,' in Daly and Sikainga, eds., *Civil War in the Sudan*, 56, 57.

17 See B. Yongo-Bure, 'The First Decade of Development in the Southern Sudan,' in Arou and Yongo-Bure, eds., *North-South Relations*, 400.

18 Terje Tvedy, 'The Collapse of the State in Southern Sudan After the Addis Ababa Agreement,' in Sharif Harir and T. Tvedt, eds., *Short-Cut to Decay: The Case of Sudan* (Oslo: Scandinavian Institute of Africa, 1994), 93.

19 Yongo-Bure, 'The First Decade of Development,' 401.

20 Tvedy, 'The Collapse of the State, 91, 94.

21 Douglas H. Johnson, 'North-South Issues,' in Peter Woodward, ed., *Sudan after Nimeiri* (London: Routledge, 1991) 124.
22 Alier, *Southern Sudan*, 213.
23 Ibid., 223.
24 Bona Malwal, quoted in Lesch, *Sudan*, 48.
25 M. W. Daly, 'Broken Bridge and Empty Basket,' in Daly and Sikainga, *Civil in the Sudan*, 19.
26 Quoted in Elias Nyamlell Wakoson, 'The Politics of Southern Self-Government, 1972–83,' in ibid., 39.
27 Alier, *Southern Sudan*, 175.
28 Daly, 'Broken Bridge and Empty Basket,' 20.
29 Lesch, *Sudan*, 51.
30 Mansour Khalid, *Nimeiri and the Revolution of Dis-May* (London: Routledge and Paul Regan, 1985), 234, 239.
31 Cited in Kenneth B. Noble, 'A New Crisis Engulfs Angola,' *New York Times*, 29 January 1993, A1.
32 John Battersby, 'Angolans Begin to Disarm under Successful Cease-Fire,' *Christian Science Monitor*, 3 July 1991, 6.
33 Interview with the Marcus Samondo, 5 December 1997.
34 In the presidential vote, incumbent José Eduardo dos Santos won 49.7 percent of the vote – 0.6 percent short of what was required to avoid a run-off; Jonas Savimbi won 40.1 percent. In the legislative vote, the MPLA won 53.7 percent of the vote, to UNITA's 34.1.
35 Barbara F. Walter, 'The Critical Barrier to Civil War Settlement,' *International Organization* 51, no. 3 (1997), 335–64.
36 Paul Hare, *Angola's Last Best Chance for Peace* (Washington: United States Institute of Peace, 1998), 104.
37 Cited in Kenneth B. Noble, 'Angolan Rebels Rebound, Within Reach of a Victory,' *New York Times*, 13 April 1993 1.
38 Interview with Paulo Jorge, 29 November 1997.
39 'Demobilising but Still Divided,' *Economist*, 14 September 1996.
40 Interview with Jardo Muekalia, 17 September 1999.
41 Cited in Andrew Meldrum, 'Hungry to Vote,' *Africa Report*, November-December 1992, 27.
42 Margaret Joan Anstee, *Orphan of the Cold War: The Inside Story of the Collapse of the Angolan Peace Process, 1992–93* (New York: St Martin's, 1996), 78.
43 John Marcum, 'Angola: War Again,' *Current History* (May 1993), 221.
44 Human Rights Watch, *Angola: Arms Trade and Violations of the Laws of War since the 1992 Elections* (New York: Human Rights Watch, 1994), 11.
45 Savimbi's speech on Radio Vorgan, 3 October 1992; cited in *Angola: White Book about Peace Process*, Vol. 1 (Luanda: Republic de Angola, 1995).

46 Interview with Marcus Samondo, 5 December 1997.
47 On the efforts to tie Savimbi into the political process, see Norrie Mac-Queen, 'Peacekeeping by Attrition: the UN in Angola,' *Journal of Modern African Studies* 36, no. 3 (1998), 413–14.
48 Interview with Jardo Muekalia, 7 July 1999.
49 Interview with David Wimhurst, 6 February 1998.
50 See Christian Dietrich, 'Inventory of Formal Diamond Mining in Angola,' in Jakkie Cilliers and Christian Dietrich, *Angola's War Economy: The Role of Oil and Diamonds* (Pretoria: Institute of Security Studies, 2000), 148–9.
51 This term was used in separate interviews by both the UNITA spokesman, Jardo Muekalia, 7 July 1999, and by UN spokesman David Wimhurst, 6 February 1998.
52 Interview with Jardo Muekalia, 7 July 1999.
53 Jeremy Ginifer, *Managing Arms in Peace Processes: Rhodesia/Zimbabwe*, Disarmament and Conflict Resolution Project, UN Institute for Disarmament Research (New York: United Nations, 1995), 9. For a similar view that short-term focus on demilitarization may be harmful to long-term peace, see Fred Tanner, 'Bargains for Peace: Military Adjustments During Post-war Peacebuilding,' in Michael Pugh, ed., *Regeneration of War-Torn Societies* (London: Macmillan, 2000).
54 Robert O. Collins, 'The Blood of Experience,' paper presented to the conference on 'The Conflict in the Southern Sudan: A Search for Common Ground,' Conrad Grebel College, Waterloo, 14 February 1997.
55 Interview with Jardo Muekalia, 17 September 1999.

Part Four

General Themes

10

Development and Peacebuilding: Conceptual and Operational Deficits in International Assistance

James Busumtwi-Sam

Peacebuilding as a distinct concept and strategy applied in the context of intra-state war (as distinct from inter-state war) is relatively new. It was only added to the existing repertoire of United Nations peace operations after 1989.[1] Since then, peacebuilding has evolved to include three inter-related elements: the relief and reconstruction of societies torn by armed conflict; the creation of political and socio-economic institutions and mechanisms to build trust and increase a sense of security; and timely and effective interventions by external actors to create the conditions conducive to peace. Integral to the notion of peacebuilding, therefore, is an apparent linkage between political, social, and economic development on one hand, and achieving sustainable peace on the other. But what exactly is the relationship between development and peacebuilding? What types of economic policies, political and institutional reforms, and changes in incentive structures are needed to build and sustain peace? What assistance can donors provide to promote development for the purposes of building peace?

This paper has two interrelated objectives. The first is to explore problems in the prevailing understanding of the relationship between development and peacebuilding, and to outline an alternative conception of the development challenges in post-conflict reconstruction. The second is to identify operational problems in the kinds of development assistance provided by the international donor community in support of peacebuilding, and to offer recommendations on strengthening aid and other institutional responses.

My main argument is that although the conceptual bases of the two main development cultures in contemporary peacebuilding, humanitarian relief and conventional development, are reasonably clear and differentiated, the conceptual basis for development in the period of post-conflict recovery remains ambiguous. This period, described as rehabilitation, is supposed to provide a bridge between relief and mainstream development. The concept however, does little to address key socio-economic and political causes and legacies of war. Thus, while aid donors appear to acknowledge that no simple continuum links relief and conventional development in peacebuilding, this has yet to translate into a comprehensive understanding of the specific development needs of post-conflict recovery. A successful transition from war to peace may require the elaboration of a third development culture, conceptually distinct from humanitarianism and conventional development assistance, to address explicitly the causes and consequences of war and prevent a recurrence of violence.

This conceptual gap is reflected in the operations of the major multilateral and bilateral donors. Although donors have made some progress in supporting post-conflict recovery by creating new functional units and departments, and allocating resources for this purpose, existing funds for peacebuilding are still primarily geared towards either relief or conventional development assistance. No institutionalized 'third financing window' specifically targeted towards the requirements of peacebuilding exists. Relief and development funds are approved through different procedures, and the activities they support are funded by different agencies and departments that have different priorities and goals. Institutional and procedural mechanisms for joint decision-making and coordination among the major donors are further weakened by the absence of a widely accepted mechanism to trigger donor responses and of a common entrance strategy to enable them to coordinate their responses in a timely manner. These problems of coordination and resource mobilization are compounded by institutional inertia and myopia, and organizational cultures that at times produce bureaucratic indifference to the problem and consequences of state failure.

I develop my argument in three parts. The first section provides an overview of the development cultures that inform current approaches to post-conflict reconstruction. The second section uses evidence from various wars in Africa to examine critically the assumptions that inform these cultures in peacebuilding, and to show that a different approach to development may be necessary to build and sustain peace. The third section examines the actual operations of key international aid agencies involved in contemporary peacebuilding. The conclusion makes recommendations on improving responses to the challenges of peacebuilding by the donor community.

Development Cultures in Peacebuilding

Peacebuilding and development, some argue, should be kept separate.[2] Peacebuilding is a short-to-medium term strategy aimed at consolidating cessation of hostilities and preventing a recurrence of violence, while development is a long-term process of structural change. Others argue that peace can only be successfully built and sustained if it is linked to a broader and longer-term philosophy of political and socio-economic development. Those who take the former approach tend to limit their analysis of peacebuilding to the steps taken by warring factions to negotiate an end to a civil war, usually with the assistance of third parties, thus limiting the scope of peacebuilding to the short-term measures of two to three years involved in negotiating and implementing a peace agreement.[3] However, while limiting the scope of peacebuilding has merits, particularly in terms of delimiting boundaries, building and sustaining peace does not end with a formal peace agreement or cessation of hostilities. There are lengthier processes intertwined with political and socio-economic development.[4] But what exactly is the relationship between peacebuilding and development?

To date, no consensus has emerged on exactly what development means in post-conflict peacebuilding. Instead, at least two distinct development cultures are prominent in international involvement in post-conflict situations: humanitarian assistance and conventional development assistance.[5] The first culture is represented by the myriad non-governmental organizations (NGOs) and other agencies involved in the provision of emergency relief, and the second by the major multilateral and bilateral donors of official development assistance (ODA).[6] Each of these cultures has a different vision of the post-conflict challenge, and starts from a different perspective and point in time when responding to the needs of war-torn societies. Conceptually, the main distinction between them has been defined temporally (short-term/long-term) and in terms of the locus of activity (top-down/bottom up). Humanitarian actors have focused on the short-to-medium-term needs of individuals at the local level (refugee resettlement, provision of housing, shelter, food, medical attention, and so on), while conventional development actors have focused on longer-term reconstruction and recovery at the national level.[7]

In recognition of the degree of overlap, and in an effort to link relief and conventional development, the concept of rehabilitation was developed to provide a bridge between these two cultures.[8] Here, once the short-term tasks of relief and resettlement are under way, then the focus shifts to reconstructing physical infrastructure and providing interim basic needs of affected populations. Once these rehabilitation activities begin, conventional development activities are launched to establish the foundations of a working economy. However, while rehabilitation does represent an acknowledgment that no simple continuum links relief with conventional development in peacebuilding, as a concept it is still interpreted in different ways by the existing development cultures, leading to distinct conceptions of the nature of the post-conflict challenge and different principles on which aid is based.

Among relief actors, rehabilitation is based primarily on humanitarian considerations.[9] Post-conflict situations are thus interpreted as humanitarian crises with additional challenges, and these challenges are viewed as crises in material supplies (such as shortages of food and medical supplies). Among conventional development actors, peacebuilding essentially entails the application of conventional development models, albeit with a few modifications.[10] These development activities are informed by the so-called Washington consensus based on a neo-liberal orthodoxy, within a broader paradigm of liberal internationalism.[11] The focus is on integrating peacebuilding into existing conventional development thinking and practice. Here also, rehabilitation is conceived mainly in terms of responses to supply problems – rebuilding infrastructure (physical, political and socio-economic) along the lines of post–Second World War reconstruction in Europe.

In the existing approach to post-conflict reconstruction, therefore, whether from the perspective of humanitarianism or conventional ODA, development has been seen as a *separate* but complementary process to building peace.[12] More recently a third perspective is emerging that sees peacebuilding as generating special development requirements that fit neither of the existing cultures. From this perspective, peacebuilding is a form of development that needs to be represented by a culture distinct from humanitarianism and conventional ODA, and elaborates a particular vision of development that is integrated with a vision of the goals of peacebuilding, not as a separate but complementary process to building peace.

Although donors appear to be cognizant of the special development needs of post-conflict reconstruction, their responses have focused less on clarifying the conceptual basis of a possible distinct development culture in peacebuilding, and more on the technical and management aspects of their operations. This, for example, has entailed efforts to merge the activities of relief and conventional development actors and thereby achieve greater coherence in post-conflict operations; efforts to design and administer programs that have 'greater sensitivity' to the challenges of post-conflict recovery; and efforts at reconciling the different procedures for raising and disbursing funds among agencies with different priorities and goals, as well as different planning frameworks and timeframes for engagement.[13] From the perspective of these donors, is it really necessary to create a separate development culture for peacebuilding? The concern is that the creation of such a culture would amount to ghettoizing countries in post-conflict situations. The focus instead should be on mainstreaming – that is, to bring countries emerging from the ravages of war into the mainstream of conventional development as soon as possible.[14]

While this concern has merit, it presupposes that the current mainstream of conventional development is beneficial to maintaining and sustaining peace. The evidence from the experiences of African countries emerging from the ravages of war casts doubt on this assumption. Furthermore, operational problems related to resource mobilization, coherence, and coordination among aid donors have arisen in large part because of the failure to clarify the conceptual basis of development in post-conflict situations. In the absence of such conceptual clarification, all that is likely to occur is that the existing cultures will interpret the challenges of peacebuilding to fit their existing programs and priorities rather than the other way around. This is precisely what has happened to the notion of rehabilitation. For reasons elaborated more fully below, rehabilitation as defined by the existing development cultures is inadequate to meet the development challenges of peacebuilding.

To the extent that peacebuilding is as much a preventative strategy as a post-conflict reconstruction strategy, a necessary first step towards identifying the type of development required for successful peacebuilding is to obtain a clearer conception of the nature, sources, and consequences of war in affected countries. For as Green and Ahmed note, 'peacebuilding involves fundamental questions not only about what to reconstruct but also about how to do so in order not to recreate the unsustainable institutions and structures that originally contributed to the conflict.'[15] The goal is not simply to reconstruct a war-torn country but to do so in such a way as to prevent a relapse into conflict. To this end, the discussion below uses illustrative examples from recent cases in Africa to demonstrate why a distinctive third approach or culture of development may be required for successful peacebuilding and to suggest what such an approach would entail.

Table 10.1
African Countries Facing Challenges of Peacebuilding, 1989–99

Algeria	Liberia
Angola	Mali
Burundi	Mozambique
Central African Republic (CAR)	Namibia
Chad	Niger
Congo	Rwanda
Democratic Republic of Congo (DRC)	Sierra Leone
Djibouti	Somalia
Eritrea	South Africa
Ethopia	Suda
Guinea Bissau	Uganda

Source: adapted from Shepard Foreman and Stewart Patrick, 'Introduction' in Foreman and Patrick, eds., *Good Intentions: Pledges of Aid for Post-Conflict* Recovery (Boulder, CO: Lynne Rienner, 2000), table 1.1, p. 3.

The Causes and Consequences of War and Their Implications for Peacebuilding

Since 1970, over thirty wars have been fought in Africa. In the year 1996 alone, fourteen of Africa's fifty-three states were involved in some form of armed conflict. By the end of 1999, some forty-four countries world wide, twenty-two of them in Africa, were facing the challenges of political and socio-economic reconstruction after protracted wars (see table 10.1).

The Nature and Sources of Africa's Wars

Wars in Africa have assumed many forms that defy neat classification and description. They differ from the traditional Clausewitzian notion of warfare in several important ways. Many have assumed hybrid forms that are not purely intra-state or inter-state. The dynamics of regional politics – rivalries among leaders, porous borders, and ideological differences – have induced regional involvement in what ostensibly are civil wars. Furthermore, many of Africa's wars, such as in Somalia, Sierra Leone, and Liberia, have been characterized by the absence of a clear beginning or end, of clear frontlines and clearly identifiable armies, and of a clear distinction between soldiers and civilians. In addition, Africa's wars have been heavily politicized involving competition not only for power and resources, but also for the hearts and minds of populations. Indeed, in many of Africa's wars, civilian populations have borne the brunt of the casualties.[16]

The diversity and complexity in Africa's wars suggest that their sources will also vary. This makes it difficult, if not impossible, to obtain the exact knowledge of causal factors required to predict the outbreak of a crisis. In the context of peacebuilding, however, arguably the main issue is not the ability to predict exactly when a crisis will occur, but to learn as much as possible about the underlying pattern of such crises in the past, and integrate that information into a context-rich approach to a country or region in crisis. Within the literature, a combination of factors have been identified as sources of war in Africa.

EXTERNAL FACTORS

Earlier discussions of African conflicts emphasized external structural factors over domestic factors. These include the history and legacy of colonialism, where factors such as the arbitrary demarcation of colonial boundaries, ethnic polarization, plus the legacy of authoritarian and repressive leadership, are identified as setting the stage for various wars on the continent, including those in Liberia, Rwanda, Sudan, and Uganda. The dynamics of external intervention – either by reference to superpower competition and proxy that occurred during the Cold War, and/or by reference to regional politics – is also identified as contributing to wars in Africa. Superpower involvement played a significant role in the Horn of Africa, and in Angola. Regional involvement has been significant in the central, eastern and southern regions of Africa.[17]

Although external factors have had an impact on the incidence of war, their importance should not be exaggerated. Even in those violent conflicts such as in Rwanda, where the legacy of colonialism had a major influence by setting the stage for the polarization of society, the colonial legacy is not the only or indeed the most important factor. And external interventions, whether by neighbouring states or extra-regional powers, have had their greatest impact in altering the nature, intensity, and duration of wars, and not necessarily in terms of providing the initial impetus for war.

DOMESTIC FACTORS

Some explanations of war in Africa have looked to the ethnic composition of African societies. In the post-Cold War era, the sheer volume of literature and media coverage on the phenomenon of ethnic conflict has entrenched this notion in the popular imagination. While many communal conflicts and other types of violent civil conflict in Africa do have an ethnic dimension to them, ethnic diversity on its own is neither necessary nor sufficient as an explanation of war. Indeed, recent studies indicate that ethnic diversity may actually contribute to stability and peace by making it more difficult to mobilize for rebellion. Furthermore, virtually all attempts to link ethnicity to war point to the contention for state power among contending groups as a key intervening factor.[18] The focus here is on how weak and exclusionary political institutions, discriminatory socio-economic outcomes, and/or instrumental manipulation of social difference by elites, lead to the mobilization, politicization, and hardening of ethnic identity. These factors played key roles in the mobilization of collective identity in Liberia, Rwanda, Somalia, and Sudan, for example.

Other domestic structural approaches have sought the sources of war in factors such as resource scarcity and socio-economic inequality. Where earlier versions of these approaches emphasized relative deprivation as the motivation for violence, more recent versions focus on greed and predation as motivating factors and see civil wars as akin to organized crime. One World Bank study, for example, suggests that while socio-economic inequality is not directly correlated with the incidence of war, the risk of war is strongly linked to three economic conditions: low incomes or the existence of widespread poverty, slow economic growth, and dependence on primary commodity exports.[19] An additional factor is the existence of diasporas willing and able to finance rebellion. In effect, civil wars are more likely to occur where rebels have the means to be financially viable.

However, economic and resource-based explanations of violent conflict provide, at best, partial explanations. Various studies have produced inconclusive results – socio-economic inequality and resource depletion may have positive, negative or no impact on the incidence of violent conflict.[20] Thus, although economic and resource-based perspectives do shed light on some of the structural and situational conditions that lead to violent conflict, their explanations of the outcome are indeterminate in the absence of a key intervening factor – the contention for state power by competing social forces.

A key domestic political factor identified as contributing to war is the character of the regime in power that shapes its reaction to domestic challenges. In many African countries, military and authoritarian regimes such as in Ethiopia, Liberia, Sudan, and Somalia, were more likely to view internal dissent as representing a military challenge and as necessitating a military response that intensified conflict. Even non-military leaders in Africa adopted a form of personal rule – neopatrimonialism – that saw no distinction between public and private realms, focused on personal aggrandizement, and was characterized by arbitrary and repressive leadership. Other studies have pointed to the issue of regime legitimacy as underscoring the security problem in many African states. The focus here is on the disjuncture between attempts to centralize political power in the formal institutions of the state and the actual exercise of political authority by political regimes, in the face of competing foci of authority that compete with the state for loyalty and legitimacy.[21]

A focus on intersubjective factors such as authority, legitimacy, and leadership draws attention to the importance of agency in understanding the sources of war. At best, structural factors, domestic and external, may be seen as underlying or permissive causes, providing the conditions that enable and constrain but do not determine political choices and outcomes, and thereby make war more or less likely. Within the conditions created by structural factors, African political leaders do make choices that set the tone and character of political relations. And it is in these choices – arbitrary and repressive leadership, exclusionary politics, and the cynical manipulation of social difference – that the proximate or efficient causes of political violence and war are to be found.[22]

The Consequences of War in Africa

While this brief description of the nature and causes of war in Africa is by no means exhaustive, it serves to illustrate the challenges confronting those who would build peace by drawing attention to the question of what type of peace to build. The centrality of this question is further illustrated by examining the consequences generated by wars in Africa that provide the context within which peacebuilding operations are undertaken. Three sets of interrelated and mutually reinforcing economic, social, and political consequences may be identified. The precise nature and intensity of these consequences vary from case to case.

ECONOMIC CONSEQUENCES

Economic consequences of war occur through direct costs of waging war and the opportunity costs of lost or destroyed economic production and infrastructure. For example, in 1985 arms imports were 81 and 64 per cent of total imports for Ethiopia and Mozambique respectively.[23] The war in Mozambique left industry operating at only 20–35 per cent capacity and left only 5 per cent of arable land under cultivation; and in Angola, 80 per cent of agricultural land was abandoned due to the war.[24] A recent study has attempted to establish a more direct correlation by comparing over a specified period of time selected indicators (GDP growth, infant mortality, life expectancy, and medical personnel) of 16 African countries involved in wars, with 16 countries not involved in war. It found that non-warring countries performed significantly better on three of the four indicators (GDP, mortality and life expectancy) than warring countries. And as a World Bank study notes, armed conflict is one of the main factors responsible for the estimated 250 million people in Africa (out of an estimated population of 600 million) living in poverty.[25]

Africa's wars have created disincentives for certain types of economic activity, but have also created incentives for others. A new political economy of war has emerged in Africa in which factions turn to trade in high-value commodities (diamonds, gold, oil, timber) to gain access to foreign exchange to finance their war effort. This has been particularly evident in Sierra Leone, Liberia, Sudan, Angola, and the DRC.[26] This new political economy of war has been sustained by a combination of demand and supply in the external environment. On the demand side, a global economic order with unregulated markets creates economic opportunities for those who profit from war. Warlords have access to international networks that purchase commodities and provide safe havens for depositing the gains from such controversial trade. On the supply side, one of the legacies of the end of the Cold War is an unregulated global arms trade in which military hardware is readily available to anyone with the means to purchase. The role of diasporas in providing finance to warring factions and thereby helping to sustain wars is also an important supply factor.

SOCIAL CONSEQUENCES
Wars in Africa have also had a devastating impact on the social fabric of affected societies in terms of societal disintegration, psycho-social trauma, and the legacy of human suffering. Societal disintegration is manifest in the breakdown of social institutions, erosion of community bonds, and disintegration of the bases of social reproduction and exchange. Wars tend to heighten awareness of existing social differentiation, hasten processes of collective identity formation, and have the effect of transforming collective groups into corporate groups. While most wars in Africa may not have their origin in such bases of differentiation, hardened corporate

group identities do come to define the contours of many of these wars, and leave a legacy of polarization and mistrust.[27]

Furthermore, Africa's wars have been accompanied by some of the most gruesome violations of human rights and humanitarian law. In many of the conflicts listed in Table 10.1, accepted rules for the conduct of warfare, including the prohibition on the use of child soldiers and avoiding unnecessary suffering to civilian populations, were regularly and routinely violated. Estimates placed the number of refugees and displaced persons in Africa at about 8.1 million in 1997.[28] War also affects populations living in fragile natural environments; many of the food shortages and famines in drought-stricken areas such as in Sudan, Ethiopia, and Eritrea, have been compounded by armed conflict.

POLITICAL CONSEQUENCES

Two broad sets of related political consequences may be identified; state failure, and the centrality of relative gains considerations in political processes and outcomes. The extent of state failure in Africa varies from case to case. However, at least two elements are common. The first occurs when the state's realm of legitimate domination is contested and weakened by countervailing sources of authority, manifest in the loss of control by those exercising authority in the centre (primarily the capital city) over those on the periphery. Into this vacuum alternative loci of authority emerge that compete with the centre for loyalty and legitimacy. The second element is the breakdown of coherence in governmental policy-making and administration due to a preoccupation with maintaining or regaining power rather than with running the actual tasks of government.[29] State failure can be a consequence as well as cause of war. For in some instances, such as in Sierra Leone, failure of the state preceded the onset of widespread violence. Whether a cause or a consequence of war, state failure is manifest not only in the destruction of physical infrastructure, but more importantly in the de-legitimation of political and administrative institutions of the state.

War also intensifies the pursuit of relative gains among actors. Wars heighten perceptions, especially among divided elites and the polarized groups they lead, that political outcomes are zero-sum. This perception is reinforced by several aspects of a post-conflict situation. The first is a security dilemma that is particularly acute when conflict ends in a negotiated settlement rather than an outright victory, which leads to lingering mistrust and fear among the erstwhile warring factions and polarized groups.[30] The second is infrastructural and institutional where state institutions and agents such as the police and armed forces, are either too weak to enforce rules, or act arbitrarily. The third is the erosion of boundaries on the use of violence as a political tool. Indeed, state failure and the collapse of the formal economy actually serve the interests of warlords in society to the extent that the disorder that ensues creates avenues for maintaining their power and profits. These three factors have been amply evident in Angola, Liberia, and Sierra Leone, for example. In such instances, the war does not really end with a formal peace agreement or cessation of hostilities; instead the violence becomes more decentralized.

Implications for Peacebuilding
In view of these causes and consequences of war, what type of development is needed to build and sustain peace? Do the challenges identified necessitate a separate development culture in peacebuilding? While the evidence presented above is anecdotal and therefore by no means conclusive, it does suggest the following observations, recognizing that the precise requirements of each peacebuilding case does differ.

A first step towards a clearer conception of the development requirements of peacebuilding is to move from a negative conception of peace as simply the absence of war, to a more positive conception. With such a reconceptualization, the focus is on addressing not only the direct behavioural dimensions of violence, but also the infrastructure – political, economic, and social – that enables and constrains violence and war. Development in post-conflict situations is about rebuilding and modifying this infrastructure to support the emergence and institutionalization of more stable and responsive political, economic, and social relations within states, and preventing a relapse into intense and generalized warfare. Building peace requires certain enabling conditions that address explicitly the causes and consequences of war.

Thus, while some of the consequences of war are applicable to almost all countries in Africa, countries in post-conflict situations are differentiated by the severity and immediacy of state failure, economic collapse and societal disintegration. In addition, although virtually all African regimes and their populations face a degree of instability and insecurity in view of the precarious bases of regime legitimacy throughout the continent, the security challenges in the aftermath of a civil war are more immediate and tangible. The erosion of boundaries on the use of violence that occurs during a civil war, and lingering animosity among polarized groups that threatens to reignite violence, implies that post-conflict countries have a greater risk of violence recurring. As a recent World Bank study notes, once a civil war has erupted, the chances of it erupting again are very high.[31]

From this perspective, the distinction between development in peace-building and mainstream development is not simply temporal as suggested by the language of transitions in the existing literature, but functional and substantive.[32] Development activities in peacebuilding are not designed to solve the problems of mainstream underdevelopment generally. That is supposed to be the task of conventional development assistance programs. Development for the purposes of achieving peace is a matter of addressing the immediate consequences of war (e.g., economic collapse, centrality of relative gains, hardened group identities), and those aspects of mainstream underdevelopment implicated as permissive causes (e.g., widespread poverty, resource-scarcity, discriminatory political institutions and socio-economic outcomes) and/or efficient causes (e.g., arbitrary and repressive leadership) of war in the first place.

Table 10.2 below provides an illustrative, not exhaustive, summary of what these development activities would entail. They include two inter-related sets of activities: *post-conflict redevelopment* entailing the reconstitution of the foundations of a working polity, economy and society; and the *abatement/prevention of violence*, in which measures are taken to forestall the re-emergence of hostilities.

What is different about development in peacebuilding, then, is knowledge of and sensitivity to the causes and consequences of war, and the enabling conditions of a functioning peaceful society. This is the type of knowledge and emphasis lacking in the conventional development and humanitarian cultures that currently dominate peacebuilding efforts. Space does not permit a full assessment of the limitations of these cultures in light of the observations above. However, some of the more glaring conceptual gaps evident in these cultures are illustrated in the discussion below.

POLITICAL REDEVELOPMENT

Existing peacebuilding measures approach political reconstruction by attempting to enhance mechanisms of transparency (to ameliorate a security dilemma among polarized factions); reconstructing the institutions and functions of government (administrative and enforcement capacities); and creating formal procedural mechanisms of democracy (multiparty elections) to enhance popular participation. The assump-

Table 10.2
Examples of Development Activities in Peacebuilding

Post-Conflict Redevelopment

Political
Establish foundations for the reconstitution of state (public) authority both spatially and
  functionally.
  – restore political capacities of the state (regime legitimacy) through inclusive political
    arrangements.
  – restore administrative, managerial and enforcement capacities of the state.

Economic
Establish foundations of a working economy.
  – restore a degree of macro-economic stability and conditions for economic growth.
  – generate opportunities for employment and re-training.
  – establish clear targets for reducing poverty and inequality.

Social
Establish foundations of a functioning society.
  – reconciliation of alienated and polarized groups.
  – encourage formation of non-corporate associations.
  – encourage local ownership, autonomy, and participation in redevelopment projects.

Abatement/Prevention of Violence

  – demobilize and reintegrate armed forces.
  – institutionalize mechanisms for peaceful political change and peaceful dispute
    resolution
  – remove incentives for resort to force domestically and internationally.
  – create early-warning mechanisms and procedures for joint decision-making in
    response to threats to the peace.

---

tion is that the two main goals of political development – aggregating
power to achieve stability and distributing that power to achieve responsive and representative government – would operate in complementary
fashion to sustain peace.[33] However, at least two problems weaken this
approach: the tendency to de-emphasize the political in the effort to
reconstruct state institutions and capacity, and a particular approach to
democratization that may be destabilizing.

   Excessive emphasis is placed on replacing physical infrastructure and
restoring administrative and managerial proficiency of state institutions
in the current approach to post-conflict reconstruction. When the
World Bank, for example, identifies the establishment of a framework of
good governance as one of the key elements of its reconstruction strat-

egy, it means 'the management of public resources on behalf of all citizens with fairness and openness.' While the restoration of technical and managerial capacities of the state is necessary, it is clearly insufficient. For the real problems of state failure lie in political variables and not merely in administrative and technical deficiencies. Instead of engaging in a sound political analysis of the political requirements of peace, resort is made to voluntarist notions such as political will, which tends to ignore the structural dimensions of state failure and problems of relative-gains seeking.[34]

In fairness to the Bank, the restriction on explicit involvement in the political affairs of member states specified in its Articles of Agreement may account for its tendency to de-emphasize the political in its approach to post-conflict reconstruction.[35] But what of other multilateral actors involved in peacebuilding, such as the UN? The UN has been a major advocate of democracy as key to building peace in post-conflict situations. However, democratization in certain post-conflict situations may actually be destabilizing. Analysts have shown how democratization in places such as Angola and Rwanda, particularly the insistence on holding multiparty elections soon after the cessation of hostilities, exacerbated existing political cleavages, thereby undercutting the peacebuilding process.[36] At a more general level, Gurr has shown that 'ethnopolitical' conflicts are more numerous and intense in newly democratic states; and that periods of democratic transitions are most prone to various forms of violent civil conflict.[37]

The real problem, however, may not lie in democracy per se, but in a particular understanding of and approach to democratization. While democracy, once established and deepened, may be positively correlated with peace and stability, periods of democratization are not, particularly when they occur in post-conflict situations. Democratization in post-conflict situations encounters serious challenges that may accentuate the potential trade-off between stability and responsive/representative governance. A key to managing these challenges more effectively is a better understanding of processes of political legitimation.

When the UN and other agencies that sponsor peacebuilding talk of democracy as an important requirement of peace, they have in mind a particular notion of democratization based on *procedural* legitimacy.[38] With procedural legitimacy, authority is recognized and accepted because those in positions of power are judged to have acquired that power and to exercise it through accepted means or procedures. The focus here is on the means by which political power is acquired, and not necessarily the ends. Democratization is conceived rather narrowly in terms of holding competitive, free, and fair elections in order to enhance this dimension of legitimacy. However, where relative-gains considerations are high, insisting on a uniform formula of holding competitive elections where the winner-takes-all system will simply reinforce the perception that political outcomes are zero-sum. In such an environment, multiparty elections may become a recipe for disaster. This is precisely what occurred in Angola.

For democratization to proceed and for democracy to flourish as an instrument of peace in a post-conflict environment, the relevant political actors must perceive some absolute gain from the political order and thereby come to see its maintenance as in their interest. Thus, in addition to procedural legitimacy, successful peacebuilding also requires attention to *substantive* and *performance* legitimacy. Substantive legitimacy focuses on achieving agreement and consensus on desired goals and values that inform the political game. With performance legitimacy, political authority is accepted based on the ability of those exercising political power to achieve certain ends/goals, even if they did not acquire power through the formal procedural mechanisms of democracy. Here the legitimacy of government is based on the extent to which it can deliver the goods. Substantive and performance legitimacy, by focusing on values and goals not simply on means and procedures, draw attention to the important demand side of the peacebuilding equation that is often overlooked – the demand by disaffected and marginalized groups for recognition, status, representation, and a means of livelihood. Simply focusing on supply problems – whether in terms of restoring managerial capacities of the state, in terms of creating formal procedural mechanisms of democracy, or in terms of creating market incentives as is the current emphasis in peacebuilding – is insufficient.

The point is that meeting the requirements of peace may necessitate a different approach to democratization in post-conflict situations. Posing it as a choice between a legitimate democratically elected government and an illegitimate authoritarian one based on a single criterion of procedural legitimacy (competitive elections), establishes a false opposition that may produce instability. Avoiding such an outcome may require constitutional guarantees of minority rights and/or representation of specific groups in some form of power-sharing arrangement, as occurred in Zimbabwe's first postwar constitution, for example.[39] It may also require postponing competitive multiparty elections altogether, which may not be such a bad thing as long as a degree of accommodation and reconciliation is achieved with alienated and polarized groups. In this respect, the experience of Uganda, touted as one of the successful cases of peacebuilding in Africa, is instructive. While Museveni's government may not be considered democratic in the formal procedural sense, through a politics of inclusion that sought to include representatives of various political groups in a broad based government, his government has enjoyed a degree of substantive legitimacy.[40] In addition, the remarkable turnaround in the Ugandan economy since the late 1980s has no doubt contributed to enhancing the performance legitimacy of Museveni's regime.

Thus, the evidence suggests that in the aftermath of a civil war processes of democratization that address issues of substantive and performance legitimacy – meeting demands for recognition and status, and delivery of goods and services (especially in regards to poverty reduction) – are just as important, if not even more so, than democratization that focuses exclusively on a single dimension of formal procedural legitimacy. When the economic and social dimensions of post-conflict reconstruction are factored into the equation, the importance of this observation becomes clearer.

ECONOMIC REDEVELOPMENT

Once rehabilitation activities begin, conventional development activities informed by a neo-liberal orthodoxy are launched to establish the foundations of a market economy. The assumption here is that a country loses social capital in addition to other forms of capital in the aftermath of war. Peace dividends will accrue through macroeconomic reforms and the rebuilding of the institutions of civil society. Underlying this process of macroeconomic reform is the transformation of ex-combatants and ex-refugees into market actors. The focus is exclusively on using supply incentives to boost confidence of agents who are to be transformed into market actors (i.e., reduce fear and mistrust of each other and the government). The assumption is also made that economic growth will produce positive distributional consequences. How valid are these assumptions in post-conflict situations?

When viewed in the light of the causes and consequences of war, doubts are raised about the efficacy of applying this approach to economic redevelopment in post-conflict situations. The first lies in the potential trade-off between growth and distribution (equity). Although economic growth is necessary to provide resources to finance economic reconstruction and recovery, and to address aspects of group grievances by providing opportunities for those affected by wars to earn productive livelihoods, the heightened awareness of social differentiation makes the question of how these resources are distributed also paramount. In post-conflict situations, therefore, how the pie is sliced can be just as important, if not even more so than how large the pie is, or how fast it grows. To achieve peace, more than lip service needs to be paid to achieving growth with equity, and to poverty reduction. It cannot be assumed that economic growth will ultimately produce positive distributional consequences.

The second and related set of problems arises from the types of macroeconomic reforms instituted under conventional stabilization and structural adjustment, which can produce important trade-offs that may undermine the consolidation of peace. One important trade-off emerges from the short-run goals of macroeconomic stabilization on one hand, and the need for governments in post-conflict situations to increase current expenditure (for job creation, health, and so on) on the other.[41] This, for example, occurred in Mozambique where tensions were heightened in 1995 when the IMF and World Bank insisted on monetary and fiscal contraction. Other trade-offs arise from the emphasis in structural adjustment on trade and price liberalization, and privatization and deregulation. For example, trade liberalization might result in an influx of cheap imports that could price peasant producers out of their livelihoods. Privatization and divestment of state enterprises could result in increased unemployment, and produce disruptions in the provision of services, thus deepening existing inequities and raising social and political tensions. The issue, then, is not the need for economic stabilization and adjustment in post-conflict situations, both are required. The issue is the type of stabilization and adjustment and how they are achieved. Whatever the wisdom of conventional macroeconomic adjustment, which is a matter of considerable debate even in the context of mainstream development in Africa and elsewhere in the developing world, in post-conflict situations the content and efficacy of conditions must be tailored in light of the requirements of peace.

SOCIETAL REPAIR

The discussion thus far has focused on highlighting some of the conceptual limitations of the culture of conventional development as applied in post-conflict settings. What about the culture of humanitarian assistance? Since the early 1990s, NGOs have emerged as key players in development and peacebuilding. This has occurred in part as a result of deliberate policy among official development donors, which have funded NGOs and integrated them into aspects of aid planning and delivery. For example, by 1996, 10 per cent of Canada's overall development financing was channelled through NGOs; the figure was around 20 per cent for the United States.[42] The increasing role of NGOs is also in part attributable to the broader influence of neo-liberalism on conventional development thinking and practice in the contemporary period, which has devaluated the state as a key agent in the development process.[43] This devaluation is manifest not only in the emphasis on the market, privatization, and deregulation, but also in the emphasis on civil society in development.

In the context of peacebuilding, NGOs are said to possess several comparative advantages that make them important partners, especially in the area of societal repair. These advantages include their relative speed and efficiency in delivery of emergency aid; their ability to mobilize resources at local levels; and their role in the creation of alternative means of economic and social exchange and reproduction at the local level, thereby facilitating local ownership of initiatives for post-conflict recovery beyond relief delivery. In short, NGOs are seen as vital instruments in the emergence of a domestic civil society in post-conflict countries, which in turn is seen as a key ingredient in the consolidation of democracy and a market economy, and hence of peace.[44] Upon closer examination, however, there are very good reasons to question these assumptions.

The culture of humanitarian assistance can only go so far in meeting the requirements of peace for the simple reason that it is based on narratives designed for natural disasters. This conceptual lens provides no mechanism to distinguish between the challenges created by famines, earthquakes, floods and so on, and the kind of man-made political and socio-economic challenges that are the legacies of Africa's wars. Both are seen primarily as material supply crises. While addressing material shortages is required in post-conflict situations – in terms of alleviating human suffering, and in the resettlement and reintegration of refugees – it does little to meet some of the key requirements of peace such as addressing group grievances or structuring political choices towards accommodation and reconciliation.

Indeed, in some instances NGO activities may inadvertently undermine peacebuilding efforts. External aid, even relief aid, is not neutral politically, socially, and economically in its effects. Aid invariably goes to some groups and not others, and thus affects distributional issues. Despite assumptions to the contrary by some of the major international NGOs and their supporters within donor governments and multilateral agencies, what passes for civil society in many post-conflict environments in Africa and elsewhere, and the social relations that underpin it, are not inherently peaceful or democratic. Not all private organizations in so-called civil society are working towards a common objective of peace. Thus, provision of aid directly to support local initiatives may inadvertently support the kinds of corporate social relations that are inimical to democratization and peacebuilding. Hence, NGO activities in peacebuilding can be destabilizing if they deepen existing bases of social differentiation, create economic incentives for those still willing to engage in war, or serve to further undermine the substantive and performance legitimacy of the state.[45]

Furthermore, the view that NGOs foster the emergence of civil society in post-conflict countries is based on a rather simplistic version of liberal pluralism. Civil society is seen as the realm of organized private social life represented by non-governmental actors and associations, which emerges spontaneously as individuals and groups in society organize and form associations to pursue their interests. Insights from recent research suggest that civil society is not simply that realm of autonomous associations, and questions whether a domestic civil society can be created from the outside.[46] The existence of a viable civil society is a product of two factors: recognition of a state's legitimacy by those in society, and a viable political community in which participants recognize certain boundaries of common destiny and interests. Civil society simultaneously engages the state in setting the boundaries of public authority and power, and resists the state in limiting encroachment on various private interests. State and civil society are thus mutually constitutive: a capable state is required to institute public authority both spatially and functionally, and a robust civil society is required to legitimate and limit that public authority.

Thus the artificial separation between state and civil society prevalent in contemporary discourses on development and on peacebuilding is untenable, and efforts to bypass the state in the attempt to reconstitute civil society in the quest for peace are misguided. Whatever the misgivings about the African state, the reality is that in contemporary peacebuilding, problems of development and social change have to be addressed within the framework of a political community that is territorially demarcated and administratively encompassed within the state – however arbitrary, weak, and fictional these may be. And although peace and security are objectives or conditions that ultimately apply to individuals, these objectives can only be attained when those individuals act in a collective political process. To achieve the objectives of human security in peacebuilding, then, there is no alternative to the reconstitution of state authority.

Development Assistance and Peacebuilding: Operational Deficits

Three sets of official actors play a central role in mobilizing resources internationally for post-conflict recovery: agencies within the UN system, the Bretton Woods institutions, and the member states of the

Development Assistance Committee (DAC) of the Organization for Economic Cooperation and Development (OECD).

The Institutional Framework

THE UN SYSTEM

The UN, despite the pronouncements of prominent figures such as its former secretary general Boutros-Ghali, has tended to emphasize the diplomatic-military dimensions of peacebuilding or emergency relief. This has reflected the separation between security issues and development issues in the UN Charter, and the functional scope of activities of the specialized agencies and commissions. The main players within the UN whose activities are relevant to the development dimension of peacebuilding are the office of the secretary general, the High Commission for Refugees (UNHCR), the Children's Emergency Fund (UNICEF), the Food and Population Agency (UNFPA), the World Health Organization (WHO), and the Food and Agriculture Organization (FAO). These agencies, however, are primarily focused on relief.

The lead development agency in the UN system is the United Nations Development Programme (UNDP). The primary role of the UNDP is to assist member states build self-reliance through various forms of assistance, with a focus on basic needs and human development. The UNDP currently has such projects in over 166 countries. In response to the challenges of post-conflict recovery, a series of programmatic and organizational changes to improve the allocation and delivery of aid were undertaken. These included the establishment of an Emergency Response Division (ERD) in 1996 which was upgraded to the Bureau of Crisis Prevention and Recovery (BCPR) in 2002. A fast- disbursing Thematic Trust Fund for responding quickly in countries affected by crises was created in 2000, and by the end of 2002 it had disbursed $180 million to support rehabilitation efforts in various countries.[47] The UNDP also operates a fast-disbursing special fund for responding quickly in countries affected by crises and for supporting rehabilitation efforts. These funds, however, are relatively modest (about $50 million in 1998).

THE BRETTON WOODS INSTITUTIONS

The World Bank – the International Bank for Reconstruction and Development (IBRD) and the International Development Association (IDA) – is by far the single most important international financial institution involved in peacebuilding.[48] The IBRD was established in 1945 as part of a strategy to build and sustain peace in the aftermath of World War Two.

The intention at the Bretton Woods conference in 1944 was to integrate the IBRD and IMF into a global economic system that would help prevent another hegemonic war by promoting economic growth and stability. In the immediate postwar period, western European countries and Japan were the major beneficiaries of IBRD reconstruction assistance, which together with the US-inspired Marshall Plan, channelled billions of dollars' worth of capital investment into these regions and countries.

Despite its history in the reconstruction and development field, World Bank operations were not specifically geared towards post-conflict recovery in intra-state wars. The vision of peace that informed the creation of the Bretton Woods institutions was based on inter-state war, not today's complex political emergencies. Aside from the early postwar period, the World Bank was not involved to any significant degree in post-conflict reconstruction, although it did provide funds for reconstruction in the aftermath of natural disasters. Between 1989 and 1998, however, World Bank lending for post-conflict recovery rose by 800 per cent. By mid-1998, it had committed $6.2 billion dollars to support 157 reconstruction projects in eighteen countries, and had provided grants worth $400 million. By 1997 nearly one-quarter of all World Bank concessional lending to countries other than China and India went to countries either experiencing or emerging from conflict.[49]

In 1995 the Bank began to target its programs specifically for post-conflict recovery. A new Post-Conflict Unit (PCU) was established within the Bank's Social Development Department in 1997, and a $8 million Post-conflict Fund was created. Between 1998 and 2002, the latter disbursed a total of $50.9 million in grants to support peacebuilding activities worldwide, 34.91 percent of which went to Africa. In addition, the Bank became the trustee of a $16 million grant provided by the Japanese government for post-conflict recovery. However, overall responsibility for peacebuilding remains with the Bank's various country departments and teams.

Unlike the World Bank, the IMF is not directly involved in post-conflict recovery. This is due in part to its narrower mandate that focuses on maintaining stability in exchange rates and in the balance of payments of member countries. Its role in the immediate context of peacebuilding is to provide technical assistance in establishing governmental activities in macroeconomic policymaking (establishment of a reliable system of gathering economic statistics, and the organization of the central bank, for example). Prior to 1999, access to IMF resources on concessional terms was limited to 25 percent of quota. In April 1999 its executive board doubled this to 50 percent of quota under Emergency Post-conflict Assistance, and introduced new terms that allowed loans to be made retroactively concessional after one year. Beyond this, IMF assistance for post-conflict recovery has come in the form of lending for macroeconomic adjustment.

BILATERAL DONORS

A large portion of bilateral assistance for peacebuilding is provided by the member states of the DAC, a loose association of major donors established to secure 'expansion of aggregate volume of resources made available to developing countries and to improve their effectiveness.'[50] A DAC meeting in May 1995 focused attention on the need for development cooperation to contribute more proactively to conflict prevention and post-conflict reconstruction. In 1997 the DAC issued a policy statement and *Guidelines on Conflict, Peace and Development Cooperation* that call for greater flexibility and more innovative approaches to peacebuilding.

In addition, several donor countries have individually established functional units within specific government departments. In Canada, for example, a Peacebuilding Initiative was launced in 1996, a joint undertaking between the Canadian International Development Agency (CIDA), and the Department of Foreign Affairs and International Trade (DFAIT), and a special Peacebuilding Fund was created. The US government created the Office of Transition Activities (OTI) within the Bureau for Humanitarian Response in USAID, with a regular budget of about $40 million. These initiatives, however, occurred in a context in which bilateral donors, including Canada and the United States, reduced their overall ODA levels.[51] In terms of total disbursements, aid from the major DAC countries fell by over 15 percent between 1992 and 1998.

Problems in the Institutional Framework for Peacebuilding

international donors have made some progress in recognizing the special needs and circumstances of post-conflict recovery, and have created new functional units and allocated resources for this purpose. However, funding remains relatively modest and is based on a rudimentary understanding of the development needs of post-conflict recovery. In addition, no effective leader to coordinate international peacebuilding efforts has emerged. Thus, currently two sets of problems weaken the institutional framework for peacebuilding. The first set arises from the types of financial resources provided for post-conflict recovery, the

terms on which they are available to countries in need, and the purposes
they serve. The second set of problems arise from how these resources
are raised and disbursed.

THE TYPES, TERMS AND PURPOSES OF POST-CONFLICT ASSISTANCE

Development in peacebuilding is designed explicitly to institutionalize
peace as a condition or outcome by facilitating the emergence of more
stable, non-violent, and responsive forms of political, economic, and
social relations within states. Thus, to the extent that civil war and its consequences represent an interruption or a break in the life of a nation, it
generates distinctive development needs that require special attention
and a special response with a distinct category of funds. The problem is
that the bulk of the existing financing mechanisms among donors are
geared towards either humanitarian assistance (including rehabilitation
assistance, which is considered part of humanitarian relief) or ODA.
While donors appear to recognize the special financial needs of peacebuilding, they have been reluctant to create and institutionalize a 'third
financing window' to provide flexible, fast-disbursing funds to facilitate
performance of the kinds of activities listed in table 2. The kinds of
reconstruction activities called for in this context fall outside the guidelines of traditional humanitarian assistance where rights and duties are
relatively well clarified in international humanitarian law. They also fall
outside the guidelines of enforcement, pacific settlement and traditional
peacekeeping, as well as traditional international trusteeship. Peacebuilding is, after all, explicitly political, which brings it potentially into
conflict with established norms of negative sovereignty – self-determination and non-intervention.[52]

A second reason for the reluctance or unwillingness to institutionalize
a third financing window is that many donors do not see a need for it.
Despite mounting evidence of structural roots, donors have approached
each peacebuilding case as a unique event, and emphasized the mainstreaming of post-conflict countries. However, the mere fact that since
1989, twenty-two of Africa's fifty-three states have faced the challenges of
building peace suggests that these are not isolated and unrelated events.
While the particular circumstances and specific requirements of each
peacebuilding case certainly do differ, certain commonalities exist across
cases. The relevant differences, as far as donors are concerned, have more
to do with the types of aid required, and the content, phasing, and
sequencing of particular recovery measures, than with the fact of state failure and the necessity of an institutionalized approach to peacebuilding.

Insofar as the donor community persists in treating each case as unique, it localizes the issues, provides justification for inaction, and obviates the need for an institutionalized third financing window. The situation is further compounded by the fact that assessments of peacebuilding cases by donors are conducted independently of each other. Among DAC members, for example, no binding rules or set procedures exist regarding how each member state evaluates the needs of aid recipients and the kinds of resources pledged. While the World Bank has played a key role in providing resources for peacebuilding, its knowledge of affected countries is limited and its responses have been cautious. A recent Bank report acknowledges that virtually no learning process has occurred in its response to post-conflict reconstruction.[53]

Another reason for the reluctance among donors to commit resources to and institutionalize a distinct financing window is the risk involved. Take the World Bank for example. Most of its loans for peacebuilding in countries affected by war (which are also the poorest countries) are in the form of IDA credits, where funds are provided by donor governments, in contrast to regular IBRD loans that are financed by borrowing on international bond and capital markets. Nevertheless, concerns have been raised within the World Bank that possible defaults on loans by risky countries could hurt its credit rating on these bond markets, and thereby raise its costs of borrowing. This would cut into profits used for overhead and for the creation of special programs that could be used to assist the poorest countries.

The World Bank claims that funds for post-conflict recovery 'have reached such a magnitude they are reducing funds available for development.' This is an interesting claim coming from an organization that lends in excess of $20 billion annually but has only managed to set aside $8 million specifically for peacebuilding in its post-conflict fund. From the Bank's perspective, since most countries facing the challenges of peacebuilding do not qualify for conventional financing, setting aside new resources for peacebuilding (which would have to come from its limited grant funds) would limit its ability to provide technical and concessional assistance for poverty alleviation in the more numerous developing countries that are at peace. Perhaps the real issue here is not a trade-off between concessional financing for poor countries at peace and concessional financing for poor countries emerging from the ravages of war, but the trade-off between resources devoted to adjustment lending and resources devoted to project and investment lending.

Adjustment lending – designed to shore up the macroeconomic foundations of borrowers – was incorporated into the Bank's lending portfolio in the late 1970s and early 1980s, in response to the developing country debt crisis. The Bank's lending was originally targeted towards technical assistance and financing capital-intensive projects, especially in the mining, energy, and transportation sectors (project lending). Adjustment or policy-based lending heralded a shift from the long-term emphasis of project lending to short-to-medium-term lending under structural adjustment. During the 1980s, in terms of net disbursements, adjustment lending accounted for 33 per cent of IBRD disbursements (18 per cent of total lending) and 12 per cent of IDA lending.[54] Critics have suggested that the World Bank reduce its involvement in adjustment lending an area that was traditionally the realm of the IMF. This would free up resources that could then be used to provide technical assistance, finance conventional development projects, and promote good governance in countries at peace, as well as provide finance for the special development needs of countries facing the challenges of post-conflict reconstruction.

With respect to the terms upon which assistance is made available, in the context of peacebuilding, all forms of external assistance (beyond emergency relief) are subject to some form of conditions, even grants and concessional loans. These conditions may include the signing of a peace accord, holding elections, and so on. The types of conditional lending that generate the greatest problems in peacebuilding are those relating to conventional macroeconomic adjustment as prescribed by the IMF and World Bank, where formal conditionality is embodied in performance criteria that tie disbursements to specific targets. Problems can also be created when donors insist that certain institutional reforms (such as competitive multiparty elections) be implemented as a condition for assistance, which are based more on ideological convictions than actual assessments of the realities of a post-conflict situation.

PROBLEMS OF RESOURCE MOBILIZATION AND COORDINATION

Addressing the development dimension of peacebuilding not only requires a distinct and institutionalized third window of financing, it also requires that donor responses be prompt, flexible, coherent, and coordinated. Donor responses to peacebuilding in Africa, however, have been slow and fragmented, and have occurred with a great deal of selectivity, reflecting the interests and priorities of donors. Currently, significant international assistance beyond emergency relief does not begin to flow until after a multilateral fund-raising or pledging conference is called that brings together UN agencies, the Bretton Woods institutions, bilateral donors, and representatives of a recipient country. The two most important pledging conferences in the context of peacebuilding are World Bank–led Consultative Groups, and UNDP-led Roundtables and Consolidated Inter-Agency Appeals (CAPs).

Pledging conferences do have some advantages for donors and recipients. To a degree, they allow donors to shape recovery plans and priorities to the needs of recipients. They increase burden-sharing among donors, and thus help to overcome the problem of free riding. By raising the profile of a particular crisis, pledging conferences may help increase domestic support within donor countries for the provision of foreign aid. Pledging conferences also provide a forum for recipients to articulate their particular needs and priorities to donors. Donor conferences, however, have some weaknesses that reduce their efficacy as the primary medium of resource mobilization for peacebuilding.

Currently no widely accepted triggering mechanism has been developed that allows donors to recognize when a window of opportunity exists for effective intervention into a post-conflict situation, and allows them to implement a common entrance strategy. Indeed, the independent role of the media in covering (or ignoring) a particular crisis is often what provokes a response. A lag often exists between making a pledge, making a firm commitment, and the actual disbursement of funds. As a result, aid pledged at conferences often arrives after considerable delays. In Rwanda, for example, of the $700 million pledged over one year at the January 1995 Roundtable Conference for Rwandan Reconstruction, only $68.1 million had been disbursed by the middle of the year. In addition, pledge inflation occurs where donors dress up aid pledges by exaggerating their generosity or by double counting aid previously promised. As the World Bank notes, the problem of lack of sustained commitment, where donors tend to disengage once a conflict has receded from public attention, also poses problems.[55]

To an extent, delayed disbursements may reflect the limited absorptive capacity of recipients. The problem of absorptive capacity, however, is a function less of the quantity of funds and more of the types of funds that are pledged. The danger is always present that the type of aid pledged at donor conferences is dictated not by the needs of recipient countries, but by the interests of donor agencies and governments pursuing their national or organizational interests. While this may appear to cast a pall over what undoubtedly are good intentions, the reality is that aid invariably serves the interests of donors. And within aid-granting agencies, organizational interests factor into any calculation. Of the $12 billion spent annually on technical assistance in Africa, for example, about 90 percent is spent on foreign expertise.[56]

Bias or selectivity of funding priorities also poses problems. Preference is often given to the more visible or high-profile aspects of a post-conflict situation, such as the reconstruction of urban infrastructure rather than rural agricultural projects, and the demobilization and reintegration of soldiers rather than the rehabilitation of civilians. The World Bank, for example, has been involved in the demobilization and reintegration of ex-combatants, but is reluctant to be involved in civilian rehabilitation and refugee reintegration for it considers the latter to be emergency relief and hence the purview of relief agencies.

Another major problem is the lack of effective coordination among the various agencies and bilateral donors. The DAC *Guidelines* of 1997, while they articulate high-sounding principles on aid coordination, do little to address, in an operational way, the problems outlined above. Indeed, the views on aid coordination expressed in the guidelines appear contradictory. On one hand, they call for greater coordination and the creation of an independent authority to monitor donor adherence to agreed principles. On the other hand, they emphasize the voluntary nature of aid coordination, and that preventing conflict requires ad hoc approaches. The guidelines look to the UN system rather than the Bretton Woods system to take the lead in coordinating aid for peacebuilding.

Within the UN system, however, no institutionalized lead agency for peacebuilding exists. Instead, lead agencies are selected on an ad hoc basis by the secretary-general, who lacks the authority to ensure effective coordination. Tensions have surfaced between the Department of Political Affairs (DPA) and the Department of Peacekeeping Operations (DPKO) over primary responsibility for peacebuilding operations. And the UN's lead development agency, the UNDP, lacks the authority to coordinate UN responses in post-conflict recovery. Various UN agencies and offices have protected their decentralized independence. Problems are compounded as the various agencies have different charters and mandates. Agencies involved in different aspects of peacebuilding compete for a slice of the action in a given situation and for credit for whatever is achieved. In dealing with national governments they try to protect bureaucratic and budgetary prerogatives. The UN's own Joint Inspection Unit describes the UN system as 'a fragmented configuration of competing organizations' that 'spend an inordinate amount of time jockeying for responsibilities and resources rather than assessing their relative strengths and comparative advantages and exploring a fruitful division of labour on those bases.'[57]

In the effort to improve coordination, in July 1997 Secretary-General Kofi Annan issued a report, *Renewing the United Nations: A Programme for Reform*, that elevated post-conflict peacebuilding to the top of the UN's global agenda. This report sees the DPA becoming the focal point of the UN's peacebuilding activities, reflecting a recognition of the political nature of peacebuilding, with the DPKO dealing with the peacekeeping aspects of missions. The latter is to play a lead role when this becomes a core aspect of the mission. In July 1998, the UN adopted a strategic framework to improve coordination and streamline resource-mobilization among its various agencies and departments, including a proposal for an expanded CAP. In addition, Annan promoted the idea of a Peacebuilding Support Office (PBSO), first established in Liberia, to strengthen and harmonize UN peacebuilding efforts on the ground while also mobilizing international political support.[58] It remains to be seen whether any of these proposals can be effectively implemented.

The Bretton Woods institutions have fared better in coordinating their regular lending activities. The World Bank-IMF Development Committee, a joint ministerial committee with delegates from twenty-four countries representing the full membership of the Bank and the Fund, for example, was instrumental in launching the Highly Indebted Poor Countries Initiative (HIPC) in 1996, designed to alleviate the debt burden carried by poor countries. In 1997 Uganda was one of the early beneficiaries of the HIPC initiative with a debt reduction package of $338 million, a factor that no doubt made a significant contribution to that country's peacebuilding efforts. Indeed, debt relief should become an integral part of any peacebuilding assistance package. This kind of substantive cooperation, however, has not occurred between the Bretton Woods institutions and UN agencies. The World Bank and the UNDP in particular have had disagreements over development activities in peacebuilding. The Administrative Coordinating Committee (ACC) – a body that brings the heads of all the UN agencies, and the IMF and World Bank together twice a year – has been little more than a forum for general dialogue, rather than for substantive coordination.[59]

These problems of coordination among aid agencies should not come as a surprise. The literature has shown that organizations tend to be slow learners, and are more inclined to adapt existing measures to new situations than to devise new strategies.[60] The solutions and strategies developed are sometimes defined, not necessarily in terms of what would best solve a problem, but in terms of the organization's goals, mandate, and its existing tools and routines. In addition, organizational culture can produce 'bureaucratization of indifference' that occurs when an organization establishes a boundary of differentiation determining who is on the inside and outside, who will receive attention, and who its main constituents are. Michael Barnett who was a member of the US Mission to the UN in 1994, has provided a persuasive account of how the organizational culture within the UN produced bureaucratic indifference that led the Secretariat and the Security Council, despite ample warnings of impending genocide in Rwanda, to treat the warnings as a 'routine bureaucratic matter' and to conclude that the needs of the organization overrode those of the targets of genocide.[61]

The reality is that African countries are on the margins of the global political-economy and the problems of civil war and state failure in Africa do not pose any significant threat to the established order. The lack of understanding of the nature, causes, and consequences of war in Africa gives little cause for optimism that the problems of aid mobilization and coordination, and institutional myopia, inertia, and indifference are likely to be solved any time soon – in spite of the good intentions of donors.

Conclusion: Lessons on the Political Economy of Peacebuilding

More research is needed to obtain a fuller understanding of the development requirements of successful peacebuilding. Two areas that cry out for clarification are the question of what peace as a substantive outcome entails, and research into the type of development needed to build and sustain peace with an emphasis on understanding problems of legitimacy that underscore state failure in Africa. In the absence of the knowledge that comes from such research, contemporary practices by donors in peacebuilding will continue to be experiments, which could be costly when based on questionable assumptions, and preconceived notions about the causes and consequences of war. Peacebuilding is not, or should not be, about moulding countries in a particular image (i.e., western market democracies) based on ideological convictions. International assistance for peacebuilding is about helping local actors establish the conditions that will enable them to make choices in an atmosphere that is relatively free of large-scale violence, fear, deprivation, and predation.

Two sets of lessons and recommendations may be offered. The first summarizes the main observations on the relationship between development and peacebuilding. The second summarizes the main recommendations for enhancing the effectiveness of donor responses to peacebuilding in Africa.

Reconceptualizing the Relationship between Development and Peacebuilding

While donors do appear to recognize no simple linearity exists between relief and conventional development, their activities and resources are still overwhelmingly devoted to one or the other. The concept of rehabilitation, intended to bridge the activities of these two cultures in peacebuilding, is inadequate to meet the development challenges of peacebuilding for it fails to address the causes and consequences of war. The evidence suggests that a reconceptualization of the development needs of countries struggling with post-conflict recovery is necessary. To the extent that civil war and its consequences represent a break in what would have been the normal development path of a nation, it generates distinctive development needs that require special attention, special responses, and a distinct category of funds.

Development for the purposes of building and sustaining peace, then, differs from mainstream development in that it is designed explicitly to institutionalize peace as a condition or outcome by facilitating the emergence of more stable, non-violent and responsive forms of political, economic and social relations within states. This reconceptualization could then be represented by a distinct culture differentiated from humanitarianism and conventional development. Indeed, this is the direction in which peacebuilding already appears to be heading, as evidenced by the creation of special functional units and departments specifically geared towards post-conflict reconstruction by bilateral and multilateral donors.[62] However, this trend could be made more explicit and institutionalized, and the units given the support necessary to enable them to emerge into a distinct and coherent culture with the full range of rights and responsibilities central to successful peacebuilding.[63]

Enhancing Donor Responses in Peacebuilding

Meeting development challenges in peacebuilding may also require the creation of a category of funds distinct from humanitarian assistance and conventional ODA – a third window of financing built on a distinct culture of peacebuilding. Funds from such a window would be fast-disbursing and available on concessional terms, to support the kinds of development activities outlined in Table 10.2. These funds could be tied to specific performance criteria based explicitly on a comprehensive knowledge of the needs of the country in question. Disbursements of funds would be based on the achievement of specific targets, a sort of peace conditionality designed to facilitate what Boyce has termed an 'adjustment towards peace.'[64] The question of the duration of these funds (short, medium, long-term) cannot be posited in the abstract. Their duration would vary depending on the specific targets to be met. Such funds could be institutionalized in the form of a 'Global Reconstruction Fund' or 'Strategic-Recovery Facility'. A precedent already exists for the creation of such a specialized facility in the Global Environment Facility created in 1991.[65]

In the absence of such an institutionalized window, or perhaps in addition to it, other reforms are needed to enhance effectiveness of donor responses. In the process of macroeconomic reform, the efficacy of the conditions attached to adjustment measures must be viewed through the lens of the enabling conditions for peace. Donors need to devise a common entrance strategy and agree on a common triggering mechanism for pledging conferences. Greater cooperation and coordination are needed particularly between the two lead agencies in the development field – the World Bank and the UNDP. In addition, more coordinated efforts are required to address aspects of demand and supply in the global political economy, which sustain civil war by creating avenues for trade in commodities obtained in controversial circumstances, and by providing safe havens for profits and a ready supply of arms to warlords.

While the recent efforts undertaken by the IMF to draw attention to military spending and arms imports is a step in the right direction, it does not go far enough. With respect to commodities, in response to increasing international pressure including several Security Council and General Assembly resolutions, the global diamond industry created the World Diamond Council in July 2000, and instituted a system of import and export controls to stem the trade in so-called blood diamonds. It remains to be seen how effective this regulatory system will be. In addition, more private corporations are developing voluntary codes of conduct. These, however, are designed for domestic stockholders and usually only express intent. Since pressures for competitiveness can undermine adherence to voluntary codes, they need to be mandatory and independently monitored with restrictions on certain types of commercial activity with countries at war, not voluntary and self-regulating.

In the final analysis, given the complexities in the causes and consequences of war in Africa, donors cannot realistically be expected to be wholly able to achieve the conditions for peace. Ultimately, the success or otherwise of peacebuilding lies in the hands of domestic actors and groups. However, donors need to build a more comprehensive knowledge of war and its consequences, based on a context-rich understanding of a country or region in crisis, into the vision of development; and integrate that vision with their operational responses in peacebuilding.

NOTES

1 The origin of the concept/strategy is generally associated with the publication of *An Agenda for Peace* (New York: United Nations, 1992) by the UN secretary-general, Boutros-Ghali.

2 Charles-Phillipe David, 'Does Peacebuilding Build Peace? Liberal (Mis)steps in the Peace Process,' *Security Dialogue* 30 (1999), 26–9, provides an overview of this debate.

3 See, for example, Fen Osler Hampson, *Nurturing Peace: Why Peace Settlements Succeed or Fail* (New York US Institute of Peace Press, 1996); Stephen Stedman and D. Rothchild, 'Peace Operations: From Short-term to Long-term Commitment,' *International Peacekeeping* 3 (1996), 17–35; Roy Licklider, ed., *Stop the Killing: How Civil Wars End* (New York: New York University Press, 1993).

4 Carnegie Commission on Preventing Deadly Conflict, Executive Summary of Final Report (New York: Carnegie Corporation of New York, 1997); Timothy M. Shaw, 'Beyond Post-conflict Peacebuilding: What Links to Sustainable Development and Human Security?' *International Peacekeeping* 3 (1996), 36–48.

5 On development cultures in peacebuilding, see World Bank, Post Conflict Unit (PCU), *Conflict Prevention and Post-Conflict Assistance: Perspectives and Prospects* (Washington DC: World Bank, 20–21 April 1998), 4. Development cultures influence the way problems are defined, what is seen, as well as the responses to those problems.

6 I include as part of the conventional development culture all the bilateral and multilateral agencies and departments that provide grants and concessional loans (official development assistance, ODA) as well as non-concessional official development finance (ODF). The major bilateral donors of ODA/ODF include the member states of the DAC-OECD. The major multilateral donors include the World Bank, the various regional development banks, and the development agencies within the UN system such as the UNDP. And although not normally considered a development institution, I

also include as part of the conventional development culture the kind of conditional lending for macroeconomic adjustment provided by the IMF. In the subsequent discussion, I use ODA to include both official development assistance and official development finance. For more on the different types of official financial flows for development purposes, see World Bank, *Assessing Aid: What Works, What Doesn't and Why*, (New York: Oxford University Press, 1998).

7 World Bank–PCU, *Conflict Prevention and Post-Conflict Assistance: Perspectives and Prospects*, 4.
8 See Joanna Macrea, Mark Bradbury, Marc Duffield, et. al, 'Conflict, the Continuum and Chronic Emergencies: A Critical Analysis of the Scope for Linking Relief, Rehabilitation and Development Planning in Sudan,' Disasters 21, no. 3 (1997).
9 See, for example, European Union, *Linking Relief, Rehabilitation and Development* (Brussels: Commission of European Communities, 1996).
10 See Report of the Secretary General, *The Causes of Conflict and the Promotion of Durable Peace and Development in Africa* (New York: United Nations, 1998), 63–4.
11 See John Williamson, 'What Washington Means by Policy Reform,' in John Williamson, ed., *Latin American Adjustment: How Much Has Happened?* (Washington: Institute for International Economics, 1990); and Moises Naim, 'Washington Consensus or Washinton Confusion?' *Foreign Policy* 118 (Spring 2000), 87–103. On liberal internationalism, see J. Busumtwi-Sam, 'The Role of the IMF and World Bank in International Development,' in E. Fawcett and H. Newcombe, eds., *United Nations Reform* (Toronto: Dundurn Press, 1995), 248–66; and Roland Paris, 'Peacebuilding and the Limits of Liberal Internationalism.' *International Security* 22 (1997), 54–89.
12 See, for instance, Report of the Secretary General, *The Causes of Conflict* (United Nations, 1998), 63–4.
13 World Bank-PCU, *Conflict Prevention and Post-Conflict Assistance: Perspectives and Prospects*, 4, 13.
14 I am grateful to Necla Tschirgi and Howard Adelman for raising these points at the conference on 'Peacebuilding in Africa: Cases and Themes' held at the University of Toronto, 23 and 24 June 2000, at which this paper was first presented.
15 Reginald H. Green, and I. Ahmed, 'Rehabilitation, Sustainable Peace and Development: Towards Reconceptualization,' *Third World Quarterly*, 20 (1999), 189–206.
16 Mohammed Ayoob, 'State Making, State Breaking and State Failure: Explaining the Roots of 'Third World' Insecurity,' in Luc van de Goor et. al.,

Between Development and Destruction (London: Macmillan, 1996), 67–90; Jonathan Goodhand and David Hume, 'From Wars to Complex Political Emergencies: Understanding Conflict and Peace-building in the New World Disorder,' *Third World Quarterly* 20 (1999), 13–26.

17 See, for example, Chris Alden, 'The UN and the Resolution of Conflict in Mozambique,' *Journal of Modern African Studies* 33, no. 1 (1995), 103–28; and Assis A. Malaquias, 'UN Peace Operations in Lusophone Africa: Contrasting Strategies and Outcomes,' *Journal of Conflict Studies* (Fall 1998): 66–88.

18 See Rhoda Howard, 'Civil Conflict in Africa: Internally Generated Causes,' *International Journal* (Winter 1995–6) 27–53; Paul Collier, 'Economic Causes of Civil Conflict and their Implications for Policy,' World Bank Development Research Group, 15 June 2000; Ted Robert Gurr, 'Peoples Against States: Ethno-political Conflict and the Changing World System,' *International Studies Quarterly* 38 (1994), 347–77.

19 Paul Collier, 'Economic Causes of Civil Conflict' (2000).

20 Mark Lichbach, 'An Evaluation of 'Does Economic Inequality Breed Political Conflict' Studies,' *World Politics,* 41, no. 4 (1989), 431–70; Homer Dixon, 'Environmental Scarcities and Violent Conflict: Evidence from Cases,' *International Security* 19 (1994).

21 Mohammed Ayoob, *The Third World Security Problematic* (Boulder, CO: Lynne Rienner, 1995).

22 Michael Brown, *The International Dimensions of Ethnic Conflict* (Cambridge: MIT Press, 1996).

23 World Bank, *World Development Indicators,* CD ROM, 1999.

24 John Stremlau and Francisco Sagasti, *Preventing Deadly Conflict: Does the World Bank Have a Role?* (New York: Carnegie Commission on Preventing Deadly Conflict, 1998).

25 Lila Ammons, 'Consequences of War on African Countries' Social and Economic Development,' *African Studies Review* 39, no. 1 (1996), 67–82; Nat Colletta, et al., *Transition from War to Peace in Sub-Saharan Africa* (Washington, DC: World Bank, 1997).

26 World Bank, 'From Reconstruction to Development,' Special Report on the New Wars (Washington DC: World Bank, 1999); David Keen, 'The Political Economy of War,' in F. Stewart, ed., *The Social and Economic Costs of Conflict in Developing Countries* (London: ECOSR, 1997); see also *Africa Confidential,* Special Report, 'Chronology of Sierra Leone: How Diamonds Fuelled the Conflict' 23 March 2000; Ian Smillie, Lusana Gberie and Ralph Hazelton. *The Heart of the Matter: Sierra Leone Diamonds and Human Security* (Ottawa: Partnership for Canada, 2000); Paul Atkinson, 'The War Economy in Liberia: A Political Analysis,' *Relief and Rehabilitation Network Paper,* 22, London, ODI,

1997; David Keen, 'The Political Economy of War' (1997); and Mats Berdal and David Keen, 'Violence and Economic Agendas in Civil Wars: Some Policy Implications' *Millenium* 26, no. 3 (1997), 795–818.

27 Kenneth D. Bush, and E. Fuat Keyman, 'Identity-Based Conflict: Rethinking Security in a Post-Cold War Order,' *Global Governance* 3 (1997), 311–28; Lapid, Josef, and F. Kratochwil, eds., *The Return of Culture and Identity in International Relations Theory* (Boulder, CO: Lynne Rienner 1996); and Francis Deng, 'Anatomy of Conflicts in Africa' in Luc Van der Goor, et al., eds., *Between Development and Destruction.*

28 UN Africa Recovery 'Promoting a Durable Peace' (1998).

29 On state failure, see I. W. Zartman, 'Introduction: Posing the Problem of State Collapse,' in Zartman ed., *Collapsed States: The Disintegration and Restoration of Legitimate Authority* (Boulder, CO: Lynne Rienner, 1995), 1–11; Jeffrey Herbst, 'Responding to State Failure in Africa' *International Security* 21 (Winter 1996/97), 120–44; and Tonya Langford, 'Things Fall Apart: State Failure and the Politics of Intervention,' *International Studies Review* 1 (1999), 59–79.

30 See Caroline. A. Hartzell, 'Explaining the Stability of Negotiated Settlements to Intrastate Wars,' *Journal of Conflict Resolution* 43, no. 1 (1999), 3–22; Marina Ottaway, 'Democratization in Collapsed States,' in Zartman, ed., *Collapsed States*, 235–50; and Barbara Walter, 'The Critical Barrier to Civil War Settlement.' *International Organization* 51 (1997), 335–64.

31 Collier, 'Economic Causes,' 21.

32 Hence peacebuilding involves a security transition from war to peace; a democratic transition from authoritarian to democratic government, and a socio-economic transition involving the rebuilding of capacities and creation of a market economy.

33 On the goals of political development, see Samuel P. Huntington, 'The Goals of Political Development,' in Myron Weiner and Samuel Huntington, eds., *Understanding Political Development* (Boston: Little, Brown 1987) 437–90.

34 World Bank-PCU, *A Framework for World Bank Involvement in Post-Conflict Reconstruction* (25 April 1997). See also 'Conflict Prevention and Post-Conflict Reconstruction: Perspectives and Prospects' (Washington, DC: World Bank, 20–21 April 1998), 8–9.

35 World Bank, *Articles of Agreement*, section 10, article 4.

36 See John Saul, 'Inside from Outside? The Roots and Resolution of Mozambique's Un/Civil War,' in T. Ali and R.O. Mathews, eds., *Civil Wars in Africa: Roots and Resolution* (Kingston and Montreal: McGill-Queen's University Press, 1999), 123–66; Chris Alden 'The UN and the Resolution of Conflict in Mozambique,' *Journal of Modern African Studies* 33, no. 1 (1995), 103–28; and Paris, 'Peace building,' 54–89.

37 Ted Robert Gurr, 'Peoples Against States: Ethno-Political Conflict and the Changing World System' *International Studies Quarterly* 38 (1994), 359–63.
38 See, for example, B. Boutros Ghali, '*An Agenda for Peace*' (New York: United Nations, 1992). For different views on legitimacy, see Rodney S. Barker, *Political Legitimacy and the State* (New York: Oxford University Press, 1990); and William Connolly, ed., *Legitimacy and the State* (Oxford: Blackwell, 1984).
39 See Hevina Dashwood and Cranford Pratt, 'Leadership, Participation and Conflict Management: Zimbabwe and Tanzania,' in Ali and Matthews, eds., Civil Wars, 233–54.
40 See John Kiyaga-Nsubuga, 'Managing Political Change: Uganda under Museveni,' in ibid., 13–34; and Kiyaga-Nsubuga, 'Politics of Reconstruction in Uganda,' this volume.
41 A recent World Bank report acknowledges that if undertaken improperly and without special attention to social needs, the adjustment process may exacerbate conflict or create new disparities from which conflict may arise. See World Bank, *The World Bank's Experience With Post-Conflict Reconstruction*, vol. 1, Synthesis Report. (Washington, DC: 4 May 1998).
42 See Ian Smillie, 'NGOs: Crisis and Opportunity in the New World Order,' in Jim Freedman, ed., *Transforming Development: Foreign Aid for a Changing World* (Toronto: University of Toronto Press, 2000), 119–20.
43 For an overview of debates on the role of civil society in development, see Donald Harbeson et al., eds., *Civil Society and the State in Africa* (Boulder: CO: Lynne Rienner, 1994).
44 Ken Hackett, 'The Role of International NGOs in Preventing Conflict,' in K.M. Cahill, ed., *Stopping Wars before They Start: Preventive Diplomacy* (New York: Harper Collins, 1996).
45 See J. Okola-Onyango and J.J. Barya, 'Civil Society and the Political Economy of Foreign Aid in Uganda,' *Democratization* 7 (1997), pp. 113–38; Cathy McIlwaine, 'Contesting Civil Society: Reflections from El Salvador,' *Third World Quarterly* 19, no. 4 (1998); and Chabal and Daloz, *Africa Works: Disorder as Political Instrument* (Oxford: James Currey, 1999), 17–30.
46 For overviews of the evolution of conceptions of civil society, see John Keane, ed., *Civil Society and the State* (London: Verso Press, 1988); Goran Hyden, 'Civil Society, Social Capital, and Development: Dissection of a Complex Discourse,' *Studies in Comparative International Development* 32, (1997), 3–30; and Peter M. Lewis, 'Political Transition and the Dilemma of Civil Society in Africa,' *Journal of International Affairs* 46 (Summer 1992), 31–54.
47 UNDP, *Introducing the Organization* (New York: United Nations, 1998), 9.
48 The IBRD was established in 1945, and the IDA was set up in 1960 as an affiliate of the IBRD to provide concessional assistance to low-income countries.

Together they are known as the World Bank. Other affiliates of the Bank
include the International Finance Corporation (1956) and the Multilateral
Investment Guarantee Agency (1986). In the subsequent analysis, the name
World Bank will be used to refer to both the IBRD and IDA.

49 World Bank–PCU, *A Framework for World Bank Involvement in Post-Conflict
Reconstruction* (25 April 1997), 1; Stewart Patrick, 'The Donor Community
and the Challenge of Post-conflict Recovery,' in Forman and Patrick, eds.,
Good Intentions, 44–5.

50 DAC/OECD, *Geographic Distribution of Financial Flows to Aid Recipients, 1992–
96* (Paris: OECD, 1997). Members of the DAC are: Australia, Austria, Belgium, Canada, Denmark, Finland, France, Germany, Ireland, Italy, Japan,
Luxembourg, Netherlands, New Zealand, Norway, Portugal, Spain, Sweden,
Switzerland, the UK, USA, and the Commission of the European Communities.

51 For a critical look at Canada's development assistance policies, see R.C.
Pratt, 'Alleviating Poverty or Enhancing Security: Competing Rationales for
Canadian Development Assistance,' in Jim Freedman, ed., *Transforming
Development: Foreign Aid for a Changing World* (Toronto: University of Toronto
Press, 2000), 37–59.

52 See Duane Bratt, 'Peace Over Justice: Developing a Framework for UN
Peace Operations in Internal Conflicts,' *Global Governance* 5 (1999), 63–81.
On negative sovereignty, see Robert O. Jackson, *Quasi States: Sovereignty, Inter-
national Relations and the Third World* (Cambridge: Cambridge University
Press, 1990).

53 World Bank-PCU, *A Framework for World Bank Involvement in Post-Conflict
Reconstruction* (1998).

54 World Bank, *Adjustment Lending: Policies for Sustainable Growth* (Washington
DC: World Bank); Stremlau and Sagasti, *Preventing Deadly Conflict* 22–3.

55 Foreman and Patrick, eds., *Good Intentions*, 7–8, 21.

56 UN Africa Recovery, *Promoting a Durable Peace.*

57 United Nations, Joint Inspection Unit, *Coordination at Headquarters and Field
Level Between the United Nations Agencies Involved in Peacebuilding: An Assessment
of Possibilities* (September 1997).

58 United Nations, *The Causes of Conflict and the Promotion of Durable Peace and
Sustainable Development in* Africa, Report of the Secretary-General (1998).

59 Stremlau and Sagasti, *Preventing Deadly Conflict*, 35.

60 See, for example, William Ascher, 'New Development Approaches and the
Adaptability of International Agencies: The Case of the World Bank,' *Interna-
tional Organization* 37, no. 3 (1983); and Ernst B. Haas, *When Knowledge Is
Power* (Berkeley: University of California Press, 1991).

61 See Michael Barnett, 'Peacekeeping, Indifference and Genocide in Rwanda,' in Jutta Weldes et al., *Cultures of Insecurity* (University of Minnesota Press, 1999), 173–202. See also Philip Gourevitch, 'Letter from Rwanda: The Return,' *New Yorker* (20 January 20, 1997).

62 See World Bank–PCU, *Conflict Prevention and Post-Conflict Reconstruction* (1998), 17.

63 The World Bank's PCU, for example, is a very small unit buried under several layers of bureaucracy within the Social Development Department.

64 James Boyce, 'Adjustment Towards Peace: An Introduction,' *World Development* 23 (1995), 2067–116.

65 The GEF is a special facility created to assist developing countries in their efforts to implement sustainable development programs. It is reliant on existing institutions – the UNDP, the United Nations Environment program (UNEP) and World Bank – as its implementing agencies. For more on the GEF, see Busumtwi-Sam, 'International Cooperation in Sustainable Development,' *Encyclopaedia of Life Support Systems* (Paris: UNESCO, 2001).

11

Structural Deficits and Institutional Adaptations to Conflict and Peacebuilding in Africa

James Busumtwi-Sam, Alexander Costy, and Bruce D. Jones

This chapter discusses the nature and evolution of institutions, both official and unofficial, involved in managing post-conflict interventions, and identifies the important historical and contemporary challenges they face in orchestrating effective interventions in Africa and elsewhere. It places the specific challenges of African peacebuilding within the wider setting of international institutional change.

The first section opens with a critical overview of the historical evolution of peacebuilding since World War two, with particular emphasis on the implications of institutional continuity and change for contemporary post-conflict interventions. The section argues that the institutions through which post-conflict efforts are currently organized were originally developed in response to the very different challenges of the post–Second World War era, and have become increasingly discordant with the new challenges of peacebuilding in the post–old War period. The result is a 'structural deficit' manifest in a confusion of roles, vagueness of purpose, and weak coordination among leading states and international organizations.

The two following sections consider different aspects of institutional adaptation to the new challenges of post–Cold War peacebuilding. They critically assesses the increased role and perceived comparative advantages of civil society organizations in post-conflict settings and explore several recent organizational and policy reforms in the United Nations system. The concluding section explores briefly a number of recent innovations and options for further strengthening the institutional framework of post-conflict interventions.

Three core themes recur. First, the paper is unambiguous in its conclusion that reconstitution of state institutions is a sine qua non of effective postwar recovery. Secondly, it recognizes the essentially political nature of post-conflict reconstruction. Finally, it expresses a degree of concern for the long-term politicization of aid, and suggests the need for a renewed balance between political objectives and the concrete developmental requirements of post-conflict recovery.

Institutional Continuity in a Changing World: A Structural Deficit in Peacebuilding

The problem of international engagement in peacebuilding is often posed in terms of a lack of political will and interest among the major western donors and the multilateral agencies they control. This analysis takes a different approach: it focuses on the institutional and normative basis of collective action that shapes how problems are defined and understood, and on the roles that are prescribed to address those problems.[1] In so doing, contemporary efforts at peacebuilding are placed within a broader historical context to show how the institutional structure of contemporary world politics, constructed in the aftermath of the Second World War, enables and constrains efforts at building and sustaining peace.

States do not act on interest alone any more than they act on principle alone. Even when engaged in a rational calculation of interest, their notions of interest depend on the ways they define the problem to be addressed and their perceptions of their own identities (in relation to others). Rational calculations are likewise mediated by behavioural traditions and other sources of conduct. While interests provide a primary motivation for action, they can be advanced in different ways and the choice among them is strongly conditioned by the institutional context of interaction. Roles assumed in pursuit of interests are often defined and circumscribed by prevailing international norms.

Thus, if the way policy-makers define the problem greatly affects what they see and how they respond, then the problem for peacebuilding is not simply a lack of political will. The problem lies in an underlying structural deficit evident in a lack of available and feasible roles for external actors that do choose to respond to a local crisis. The end of the Cold War failed to produce a new vision of peace that matches the realities of intra-state war and state failure. While various attempts have been made since 1989 within the UN, the multilateral aid agencies, and among major bilateral donors to articulate new principles and roles and to adapt existing institutional practices, to date these efforts remain under-institutionalized.[2] Peacebuilding in the contemporary period thus occurs within an institutional framework that has failed to delineate appropriate roles to provide coherent and coordinated responses to state failure. When the challenges of peacebuilding are viewed in this historical and institutional context, the evidence reveals contemporary world politics is, to large extent, under-governed.

Building Peace in Historical Context

Viewed historically, contemporary efforts to build peace are not necessarily new. In the history of the modern state system, various attempts have been made to build particular forms of peace. The approach that emerged after 1945 was only the latest in a series of peace experiments to have occurred with varying degrees of success, notably Vienna in 1815, and Versailles in 1919. Each of these followed the conclusion of hegemonic wars between major powers in which the victorious imposed a vision of peace defined in large part in opposition to the practices of the losing side. These peace settlements were state-centric. They were based on the presumed autonomy of the political-military security sphere from other spheres of social and economic life. Building peace was essentially about dealing with the organization of legitimate force among states in order to preserve state sovereignty.

The post-1945 settlements were distinctive in the development of an elaborate institutional framework that attempted to link a vision of peace with a vision of economic development. By the end of the Second World War, it became obvious that the presumed autonomy of the political-military sphere that had informed earlier postwar settlements was no longer valid, and that the regulation of the use of force between states was only one out of a host of externalities created by the domestic organization of states. Thus, in the settlements of the Second World War, in addition to the elaboration of principles and norms that delegitimated the aggressive use of force and created a framework for joint decision-making in response to threats to peace, for the first time, recognition was given explicitly to the potential impact of economic forces on political-military security. This informed the creation of the Bretton Woods institutions. The intention, based on lessons from the inter-war period, was to prevent another world war by creating financial mechanisms to introduce stability in current international transactions and thereby prevent a recurrence of economic depressions (the role of the IMF). As well, the economies of the major powers (including the defeated powers, Germany and Japan) were to be redeveloped through a program of economic reconstruction (the role of the IBRD).[3]

Debates will continue as to whether this elaborate framework was indeed successful in building and sustaining peace among the major powers.[4] What is undeniable is that the type of war this institutional framework was primarily designed to prevent declined dramatically in the postwar period. While major wars between great powers declined, other types of wars that are the primary focus of contemporary peacebuilding increased in number and intensity. As the analysis below shows, the challenges of peacebuilding in response to these newer types of wars are not readily reconciled with the range of third party roles institutionalized in the post–Second World War settlements.

Peacebuilding in the Context of Intra-State War and State Failure

Several important differences exist between building and sustaining peace in the context of traditional inter-state war and contemporary intra-state war. These differences and the challenges they pose are analysed in their political-military, socio-economic, and societal dimensions. Although in practice the three dimensions are interrelated, greater insights into the challenges of contemporary peacebuilding are obtained by analysing them separately.

THE POLITICAL-MILITARY DIMENSION OF BUILDING PEACE

In the context of preventing inter-state war, the postwar institutional framework embodied a reasonably clear understanding of what peace entailed. Peace existed when territorial boundaries of states were recognized and stable and there was no attempt to revise borders through the use of force. This type of peace would be built and maintained by removing incentives for forceful territorial revisionism, institutionalizing procedures for joint decision-making in response to challenges (UN Charter chapters 6, 7, 8), and making illegitimate all unilateral uses of force except in self-defence.

This territorial covenant was buttressed by a cluster of norms centred on a particular interpretation of self-determination. Self-determination meant a peoples' (defined territorially, not ethnically) right to independence from external domination/interference, or anti-colonialism (i.e., *external* self-determination).[5] This particular meaning of self-determination was strengthened by other rules stabilizing states' territorial property rights, including the principles of sovereign equality, non-aggression,

and non-intervention of the UN Charter.[6] Henceforth, external predation was prohibited, and people under foreign domination had a right to
independent statehood. Nothing, however, was said about the nature of
the community within states, or of their internal political arrangements.

To realize this vision of peace, a set of roles was institutionalized that
revolved around third parties becoming external guarantors of external
self-determination. These included two primary roles and two subsidiary
ones. These roles may be described with a certain degree of imagery as
sheriff and *umpire* as primary roles, and *trustee* and *samaritan* as subsidiary
ones. Activities under the role of sheriff involved collectively applying
force in an escalating ladder until aggression was reversed. Umpire
activities included traditional peacekeeping to overcome coordination
problems between belligerents, and other forms of third party diplomatic intercession to facilitate negotiated solutions to conflicts between
states. Since a challenge to peace occurred through a forceful deviation
from a status quo, these two primary roles were designed to preserve
existing territorial and political arrangements. The role of trustee, a
remnant of the League Mandate system, involved placing a population
formerly under colonial domination, under the benevolent management of an external authority until they were ready for full political
independence.[7] The role of samaritan involved the provision of humanitarian relief to victims of natural and man-made disasters. Each of these
roles was governed by institutionalized norms.[8]

Contemporary peacebuilding has attempted to apply elements of
these four roles in the aftermath of intra-state war without a great deal of
success. This has generally entailed international efforts to provide relief
to victims of civil war (samaritan), monitor and if necessary enforce
adherence to peace agreements (umpire/sheriff?), supervise national
elections, and assist in the political and socio-economic rehabilitation
and reconstruction of societies torn by armed conflict (trustee?). Yet
state failure and civil war produce certain consequences that are not
readily reconciled with roles originally designed to support external self-
determination in the maintenance of a territorial covenant. For example, in the aftermath of inter-state war, ex-combatants were separated by
a border, and victims of aggression did not have to live in the same place
as their aggressors. In intra-state war and other forms of organized group
violence in the contemporary period, perpetuators of violence are difficult to distinguish from their victims and often they have to live together.
In Rwanda, for example, survivors of genocide have to live virtually next
door to people who participated in genocide. As a result, in many con-

temporary conflicts the outcome is often ambiguous, and lingering animosity among communities threatens to re-ignite hostilities.

Furthermore, in many contemporary conflicts in Africa and elsewhere, the status quo itself – the existing political and territorial arrangements – is at issue. These kinds of war concern the question of statehood itself and the nature of the political community within those states. Achieving peace in this context requires roles that facilitate and support a transition to more stable and responsive forms of political relations within states rather than roles designed to oppose external aggression and preserve the political and territorial status quo. Building peace within states is thus a very different proposition from building peace between states.

To the extent that the way the problem is defined by third parties influences what they see and how they respond, an important difficulty in developing effective peacebuilding roles in Africa lies in how state failure and civil war are interpreted. The latter did not suddenly emerge after the Cold War ended in 1989, despite their sudden discovery by the UN and the mainstream academia and media in the west. As Holsti argues, the tendency to employ spatial and socio-political dichotomies in the characterization of African conflicts (such as the zone of conflict and the coming anarchy) results in an unfortunate bifurcation of the world and an ethnocentric conception of peace that equates it with the development of western-style market democracies.[9] Consciously or otherwise, such characterizations establish a new basis of differentiation among states (us and them) that serves to further marginalize and isolate African countries, localize issues, and downplay the influence of the broader global political-economy in either supporting or undermining peacebuilding efforts.[10]

During the Cold War, most of the conflicts in Africa were viewed through the lens of superpower competition and proxy. In the post–Cold War era, ethnicity, pejoratively called tribalism in the African context, has become the new master variable. However, in many of Africa's so-called ethnic/tribal wars, such as in Somalia and Rwanda, the designation by outsiders of tribes ignores the history of those societies and obscures important social relations and modes of social differentiation that define how affected groups stand in relation to each other.[11] Thus, despite evidence of structural roots – at the end of the 1990s some forty-four states worldwide faced the challenges of peacebuilding after experiencing some type of intra-state war, and almost an equivalent number were hovering on the brink of state failure – the international community persists in seeing each instance of state failure as a unique and unrelated event.

While the exact causes of civil war and other forms of political violence within states vary from case to case, many of them arise from disputes over internal, not external self-determination.[12] In some of the most protracted conflicts, such as in Sudan, the problem arises not from external violations by an invading army across an internationally-recognized frontier, but from increasingly assertive demands by disaffected groups provoked by repressive governments and socio-economic deprivation. According to Gurr, over nine hundred million people belonging to 233 increasingly assertive minority groups exist around the world.[13] Unresponsive governance could turn such demands into organized violence. Roles designed to guarantee external self-determination cannot readily be grafted onto such situations.

Currently, no international political framework has been elaborated that specifies appropriate roles for third parties and local actors in internal political conflicts. For example, while existing international norms prohibit the unilateral use of force among states, no rule of international law forbids insurrection and the use of force within states. In cases of violent rebellion by a people against an unpopular government, international law has traditionally held that no faction is competent to speak on behalf of the state as long as the outcome remains uncertain. The expediency of this view rests on two foundations. The first is to prevent third parties from unduly influencing the outcome of the contest over internal self-determination through intervention on behalf of one warring side or the other. The second is to prevent the civil war from becoming an international war, the premise being that civil wars become international wars through competing external recognitions and interventions.[14]

Contemporary peacebuilding thus occurs in an international environment that has largely been oblivious to questions of domestic governance, permissive of the use of force within states, and constraining of the kinds of roles third parties may play in attempting to build peace. The only recognized exceptions are when the conflict is 'internationalized' through, for example, a transborder spill-over, and when certain peremptory norms (*jus cogens*) such as the norms against genocide, are violated.[15] In all other cases, the international community has had to walk a tightrope. However, to the extent that successful peacebuilding is as much a preventative strategy as a post-conflict reconstruction strategy, in the absence of a coherent attempt to define the scope and domain of third party roles in intra-state conflicts, timely and effective intervention may not occur even where there is evidence of genocide. The genocide in Rwanda unfolded, in spite of ample warnings, in part because major states insisted on defining the problem as a civil war – a resumption of fighting following the breakdown of a ceasefire – not genocide, thereby justifying inaction.

To conclude, it is safe to say that in cases of internal political conflict the traditional focus of international law and organization, as manifest in the practices of the UN, has been preserve the political and territorial status quo, avoid influencing the outcome of internal self-determination where the outcome is uncertain, and prevent escalation into an international war. The continuing influence of this approach is well illustrated by the UN's actions or lack thereof in the conflict in Democratic Republic of the Congo that began in 1996. At the same time, however, UN actions in the conflict in Sierra Leone point to efforts at redefining this traditional paradigm. While attempts are being made by agencies within the UN system and by regional organizations to define a more coherent approach to contemporary peacebuilding, institutional adaptation to the challenges posed has been slow and hesitant. Section three examines in more detail some of the challenges of recent organizational and policy reform in the UN system.

THE SOCIO-ECONOMIC DIMENSION OF BUILDING PEACE

In addition to addressing the political-military dimension, the postwar settlements attempted to build peace by promoting a particular type of socio-economic development, reinforced by an open multilateral trading system. Today, no specific strategy to meet the particular socio-economic needs of countries emerging from intra-state conflict has been articulated. Rather, what passes for strategy is the application, regardless of circumstances, of a conventional development model informed by a neo-liberal orthodoxy. The importance of a clearly-specified set of policies to address explicitly the socio-economic dimension of peacebuilding is illustrated by examining the differences between the postwar era and the contemporary period.

In the aftermath of WWII, the initial beneficiaries of IBRD loans were the war-torn economies of Europe and Japan. The first IBRD loans in 1947, for example, went to finance reconstruction in France, the Netherlands, and Denmark. And as late as 1964, Japan was the Bank's second-largest borrower. Beyond this, a single hegemonic state, the United States, exercised structural and entrepreneurial leadership to provide collective goods that addressed the needs of sixteen recipient countries (primarily western Europe and Japan). In June 1947 the US secretary of state, George C. Marshall, called for a major bilateral assistance program for Europe. The European Recovery Program (ERP), or Marshall Plan was instituted in 1948, and by 1952 it had dispensed over $13 billion in US aid – over 90 per cent in the form of grants – to Western Europe.[16] The United States not only dominated the entire postwar economic reconstruction effort, it also 'had a strategic vision and explanation for its undertakings that satisfied its own citizens and its old and new partners in Europe and Asia.'[17] Most aid recipients already had well-advanced capitalist economies, with impressive human and physical capital. Recipients engaged in free riding, but this did not impede collective action for the reconstruction of their economies was viewed as vital to the continued economic growth of the United States and to its strategy of containing communist expansionism.

In addition, the role of the state in post 1945 economic development was clearly defined: the IMF and IBRD were to accommodate and promote Keynesian stabilization policies and social welfare goals. There was explicit commitment to full employment. A small set of unifying principles emerged: trade liberalization would be pursued; transactions on the current account would be freed of controls but capital movements would be restricted, exchange rates would be pegged and their adjustment would be subject to supervision. The original Bretton Woods compromise broke down in the early 1970s.

In contemporary peacebuilding, no single state or international organization exercises leadership comparable to the United States after 1945. What exists for peacebuilding today is a complex mix of bilateral donors, multilateral aid agencies, and civil society organizations. Collective action problems among these donors abound: delayed aid disbursements after pledging conferences are held, lack of sustained commitment beyond the provision of emergency relief, and lack of effective coordination among multilateral and bilateral donors and aid agencies. Most post-conflict countries do not qualify for conventional IBRD lending, and most have weak and underdeveloped economies and are peripheral to the economic interests of the major donors.

Furthermore, contemporary peacebuilding occurs in an environment where the role of the state in economic development has been devalued. Since the early 1980s emphasis has been placed on the role of the market and the private sector in development. In the 1990s the major bilateral donors and multilateral financial institutions embraced financial liberalization, including capital account convertibility as the key to attracting private capital flows and hence to fostering economic growth. Private international financial flows are the primary vehicles for development finance and investment in the contemporary globalized economy. At the same time, bilateral ODA declined. In 1996 ODA as a share of donor GNP declined to 0.27 per cent, down from 0.34 per cent in 1992, the lowest level in forty-five years (the target set by the UN in 1974 for ODA is 0.7 per cent of GNP). Total net disbursements of ODA to sub-Sahara Africa actually declined from $17.3 billion in 1993 to $16.3 billion in 1996.[18] The attempt by donors to transform war-torn societies into market economies via IMF and IBRD- inspired macroeconomic adjustment is informed by this faith in private capital and markets.

The reality is that many sub-Saharan African countries, whether relatively peaceful or emerging from war, are economically isolated, and are not in a position to attract substantial private capital flows. In 1996, 80 percent of the estimated $235 billion in private capital flows to developing countries, went to only twelve countries, primarily in southeast Asia and Latin America. The growth of international trade and capital flows has brought little benefit to African countries. According to World Bank figures, as of the beginning of 1998, approximately 1.2 billion people worldwide were living in poverty (less than $1 a day) with the greatest regional concentration of poverty being in sub-Saharan Africa, where average incomes in 1997 were 1.4 per cent lower than they were in 1992.[19] It is certainly more than a little coincidental that as of the end of 1998, twenty of the world's thirty-five poorest countries were in Africa, and of this number, fourteen had experienced a major war.

LONG-TERM SOCIETAL RECOVERY

The difference between post-1945 and contemporary peacebuilding can also be seen in the importance of a third dimension of recovery, namely long-term societal recovery. Alongside state failure, an extensive erosion of local social fabric has been identified as a core dynamic of protracted conflicts.[20] Here, a breakdown of societal institutions relating to family, community, labour, and exchange relations has been understood to lead to a generalized failure to meet basic material, psychological, and cultural needs, and thus to enable or perpetuate violence. Normalizing and repairing the economic, political, and cultural conduits of local social interaction, otherwise referred to as building social capital or promoting civil society now stands as a cornerstone of contemporary peacebuilding.

Such issues were not prominent features of postwar stabilization in Europe, nor are they challenges for which the UN or the Bretton Woods institutions have any particular competence. This fact highlights the very different kinds of problems posed by the internal conflicts characteristic of the post–Cold War period. As such, it also points towards one form of institutional adaptation to the new peacebuilding challenges, namely the increased roles played by civil society organizations (CSOs) in contemporary post-conflict settings, an issue to which we now turn.

Institutional Adaptation to Conflict in the 1990s: The Civil Society Option

The abrupt rise to prominence of civil society organizations in conflict interventions from the mid-1980s onwards may be seen as one form of programmatic response to the insufficiencies of traditional institutional arrangements in addressing the domestic political and economic challenges of post-conflict recovery.[21] Once relegated to the radical margins of the North-South dialogue, CSOs have become an integral part of the post-Cold War global conflict response framework, serving partially to fill the structural deficit left by the multilateral agencies. An early illustration was provided by events in Somalia in late 1991, in what was to be the first major experiment in post-Cold War intervention: when factional warfare hit the streets of Mogadishu, the UN and other official agencies withdrew, and the CSOs stayed behind. By the mid-1990s, CSOs had emerged as institutions of choice for executing official humanitarian and post-conflict development programs. Many have been regularly consulted by bilateral donors, the EU, and the UN system on a wide range of aid management and strategy issues. According to OECD data, CSOs transferred over $ 44 billion in official and private aid to recipient countries between 1990 and 1997, while the share of total ODA earmarked for local civil society development nearly doubled, from 6.4 per cent to 12.2 per cent, between 1996 and 1998.[22]

International Responses in Conflict Recovery: Why Civil Society?

At a very general level, the increasing prominence of the civil sector in international aid may be understood as a by-product of recent trends in global political and economic reordering. In a concrete sense, privatization, decentralization, and a pattern of withdrawal by states from the public domain have combined with the advance of communications technologies to open up new spaces for private groups to engage in social, cultural and economic interaction across national boundaries.

Global social relations have intensified as CSOs have capitalized on opportunities to construct knowledge and action networks and, in some instances, to become effectively trans-nationalized. The massive presence and influence of CSO delegations at global conferences on the environment (Rio, 1992), population and development (Cairo, 1994), women (Beijing, 1995) and trade and investment (Seattle, 1999), have illustrated the growing scale, intensity, and organizational potential of civil society relations within the globalizing context. By the mid-1990s the appearance of some fifteen thousand recognized CSOs operating in three or more countries was taken as emblematic of a de facto pluralization of global governance.

At the same time the adverse social effects of globalization are concretely felt. The erosion of national autonomy has challenged the ideological, administrative, and territorial coherence of many states, leading to internal fragmentation and new conflicts. The disruption of traditional systems of production and exchange, and increasingly pronounced global inequities, have produced reversals of previous socioeconomic gains, and in many cases unprecedented levels of hardship and marginalization. The rise of CSOs is thus regarded as a spontaneous organizational reaction, from the bottom-up, to the growing social needs arising from the globalization process. 'More and more people who are bypassed by the new world order are crafting their own strategies for survival and development, and in the process spinning their own transnational webs.'[23] In brief, then, the growth of civil society is partly explained as a broad, yet decentralized, institutional adaptation to both the opportunities and objective needs generated by rapid political and economic change in the global sphere.

At another level, the rapid proliferation of CSOs in conflict interventions reflects purposeful policy choices within the aid community itself. As noted, official agencies have used aid funds deliberately to integrate CSOs into the core of aid planning and delivery systems. Their rationale for doing so in the 1990s reflected a broad consensus around several programmatic and strategic considerations.

Operational Advantages of Civil Society Organizations

From the operational standpoint, CSOs have been widely regarded as possessing key comparative advantages that facilitate aid delivery in volatile and politicized environments.[24] These are contrasted to the perceived stasis and inflexibility of the traditional, state-centred international institutions noted earlier. In particular, CSOs are considered less bureaucratized and more flexible than official aid agencies, and therefore capable of mobilizing human and material resources more quickly and efficiently. Their freedom from official mandates or security protocols has meant that they are less constrained by potential legal or political obstacles to intervention. Their direct engagement with recipient populations is seen as increasing both the sensitivity and the efficiency of aid delivery, while comparatively lower operational overheads helps to reduce program costs.

Unlike official organizations which must balance contrasting strategic priorities, CSOs involved in aid delivery are widely perceived to operate on the basis of straightforward humanitarian and developmental commitments. As such, CSOs generally are attributed a higher degree of probity than governments in managing aid efforts in post-conflict situations. Likewise, CSOs have claimed a higher degree of political neutrality in conflict environments. Channelling aid through local CSOs has emerged as an option to promote longer-term recovery while avoiding direct support for national political factions. This is a critical issue in contexts where the authorities who emerge at the end of conflict are seen as only partially legitimate and risky partners. In contrast to traditional institutional arrangements of the postwar period, interventions through CSOs enable external powers to engage with local actors without conferring upon the latter any appearance of international legality or legitimacy.

In practice, the operational comparative advantages of CSOs have proven to be problematic on many counts. In the late 1990s donor agencies and analysts became increasingly concerned about the efficiency, cost effectiveness, accountability, and coordination weaknesses of CSO aid delivery. And although there are few doubts about CSOs' fundamental humanitarian commitments, aid analysts have expressed a growing unease with the effects of 'contracting out,' a pattern associated with the privatization of aid services and the consequent intensification of competitive market behaviour among CSOs. Others have suggested that CSOs' superior sensitivity to local needs may be compromised by standardized needs-assessment routines, short-term project cycles, and other organizational imperatives.[25] Finally, perhaps the most passionate policy debate since the mid-1990s has surrounded the issue of CSOs' political neutrality. Complex political emergencies in Africa throughout the 1990s have revealed the real vulnerability of CSOs to local political intsrumentalization. More recently, many CSOs and aid analysts have become concerned about the politicization of aid 'from above' and have begun seriously to question their growing dependence on donor funding, which looks increasingly tied to foreign policy interests.[26]

The Strategic Value of Civil Society–Based Aid in Post-Conflict Settings

Beyond stated operational advantages, a number of core strategic functions are attributed to the civil sector, corresponding to presumed economic and political requirements of post-conflict recovery. These strategic attributes became embedded in the aid policy mindset of the 1990s, and appeared as an integral part of most post-conflict aid programming. They are broadly divided into protective and reproductive functions. The former relate to immediate priorities for postwar political and economic stabilization, while the latter are concerned with the longer-term structural transformation of transitional political economies.

ECONOMIC PROTECTION

This function relates to the role of the civil sector in protecting and consolidating the immediate socio-economic gains generated by post-conflict settlements, and can be broken down into two main activities. The first is welfare provision, whereby CSOs move quickly into affected areas to distribute commodities, provide essential services, and eventually assist in the rehabilitation of destroyed or neglected service systems. A key objective here is to provide immediate and tangible social benefits to affected populations, and thereby strengthen local incentives against a reversion to conflict. The second type of activity involves the accelerated reintegration of vulnerable or potentially destabilizing groups, such as former soldiers, displaced persons, or war victims belonging to identifiable political or ethnic groupings, into normal socio-economic activities. The focus here is on creating new opportunities for income-generation (agricultural extension, vocational training, credit, rural market support). Here again, the strategic objective is to strengthen incentives for a rapid societal buy-in to post-conflict settlements, although, unlike welfare provision, reintegration places additional emphasis on local participation and individual initiative. It is particularly in this area of activity that CSOs are assumed to perform their most characteristic functions as enablers of a social economy and promoters of coping strategies that are sensitive and appropriate to local needs and practices.

ECONOMIC REPRODUCTION

While safeguarding the immediate economic gains that accompany the resolution of conflicts, civil society is understood to play an equally important function in generating long-term conditions for market-based economic development in post-conflict transitions. As already noted, one way that civil society does this is by standing in for the state in large areas of public responsibility, thus helping to ensure against regulatory encroachments by the public sector over the private. A more positive function is that the requirements for self-regulation and individual initiative, the social internalization of which are considered necessary to the development and consolidation of civil society, are identical to the requirements of a market economy. Civil society, in this sense, socializes people to the market, by promoting the acquisition of behavioural patterns and decision-making preferences, and by supporting the functional social networks which are needed in order for markets to work more smoothly. For countries undergoing political transitions from war to peace, civil society functions positively to promote a simultaneous process of economic liberalization.

POLITICAL PROTECTION
Civil society is also assumed to serve important political functions in post-conflict environments. As in the economic realm, these functions can be divided into protective and generative categories. Its primary protective function rests, in the first instance, on the effect of civil society forces in de-politicizing social relations, by recasting personal interests in private, individual and functional terms, and by pluralizing existing political landscapes, loyalties to the state and other nationalistic, ethnic or class identities, which are seen as potentially conflictual or destabilizing. Wartime political affiliations are broken down in civil society to reflect multiple cross-cutting loyalties. Through this process, old lines of divisive political competition fade into a one-world scenario, in which politics is no longer exclusively mediated by governments and political organizations, but through the civil society itself, on the basis of more issue-based, trans-nationalized identity networks and perceived harmonies of interest. To the extent that potentially conflictual collective identities like class, ethnicity or nationalism do survive, they are diluted by competing interests within a 'level' civil society playing field, and thus effectively lose their original political momentum. Activating a dynamic local civil sector, then, serves to contain the risks of return to violent conflict.[27]

POLITICAL REPRODUCTION
The key generative function most commonly attributed to civil society relates to democratization. Dynamic civil sector activism is seen as one way of addressing the lack of accountability, transparency, and sensitivity of governments. In countries recovering from violent political conflict, it

is generally recognized that party political representation and periodic electoral competition are by themselves insufficient to ensure meaningful democratic practice, and rather pose the risk of monopolization of government policy by competing elite interests. In this context, civil society is seen as a key ingredient for deeper forms of democratic practice. In his work on international electoral monitoring, Vikram Chand has emphasized the point that civil society institutions, including 'civic associations, religious institutions and the free press' are necessary to peacefully represent social interests in the political realm, and thus to build or restore confidence in democratic structures.[28] Indeed, local civil society organizations have received considerably more international attention as agents of post-conflict democratization than have national political parties.

Issues and Challenges Raised by the Civil Society Option

Together, the presumed operational advantages and strategic functions attributed to civil society organizations by the aid policy community help us to understand, in part, why post-conflict aid was increasingly channelled through the civil sector in the 1990s. Yet as a form of global institutional adaptation to the challenges of civil conflict and peacebuilding, the civil society option has raised several critical concerns for analysts, practitioners, and stakeholders of post-conflict recovery.

CSOS AND STATE RECOVERY

State failure and collapse has been widely identified as a root cause, as well as a consequence, of protracted internal conflict in many African countries. In view of this, analysis suggests that the resolution and sustainable settlement of internal conflicts must rest in large measure on the success of strategies to restore state capacity, legitimacy and authority.[29]

In many post-conflict settings, the inability of states to implement decisions and ensure the equitable allocation and management of resources has constituted a powerful rationale for the international community to channel aid directly into the civil sector as a functional substitute to the state. Yet the effects of this strategy on the longer-term potential for failed states to recover requisite levels of capacity, authority, and political legitimacy are problematic. The diversion of aid to parallel CSO delivery systems potentially further reduces state capacity, by causing a dramatic decline in direct transfers of knowledge and funds to public sector institutions, and by attracting valuable human resources away from public sector employment. Furthermore, CSO-channelled aid is well known for its potential to fragment national public services into large numbers of projects. This significantly increases the management and coordination burdens of recipient government institutions, and further reduces their monitoring, assessment and planning capacities.[30] Recently, the aid community has developed new strategic policy frameworks to help rectify the problem of parallel and fragmented service delivery by CSOs and other external agencies. Interestingly, however, these new strategic frameworks appear to emphasize better coordination among external actors rather than a concrete restoration of state capacity.

The colonization by CSOs of vast areas of public responsibility also potentially erodes states' ability to recover political legitimacy after the fighting ends. Several cases in Africa show how political credit for aid projects is sought by competing local factions in order to influence local public opinion in their favour. The sheer financial magnitude of CSO projects may simply highlight the shortcomings of the state as a provider of public goods, and accordingly weaken its credibility among local communities.[31] Moreover, aid has been provided within a powerful normative framework which emphasizes the risks to recovery posed by states, while highlighting the positive contributions of civil society. This normative bias, transmitted into post-conflict environments by CSOs themselves, further reduces the scope of government authority and credibility in the public sphere, and has fostered chronic tensions, rather than constructive developmental relationships, between state and civil sectors.

It is thus far from clear whether increased external assistance through CSOs adequately addresses the issue of state restoration as a basic requirement of postwar recovery. On the contrary, there are indications that such assistance, though justified in terms of state collapse, may perpetuate low state capacity, authority and legitimacy over time.

CSOS AND SOCIETAL REPAIR

John Prendergast has identified several areas of societal repair and renewal in which CSO efforts have been particularly salient. These include initiatives to address psycho-social trauma, support for community-level problem-solving processes, peace conferences, conflict management training, reactivating indigenous conflict resolution practices, encouraging collaborative community activities, and the promotion of democracy and human rights. From the material standpoint, too, there is a strong emphasis on the role of CSOs in rehabilitating local services, and strengthening local economies of as a means of promoting post-conflict reintegration. Together, these efforts are meant to provide 'space and motivation for local people to disengage from the conflict' while building on 'existing local capacities for peace.'[32] Societal failure, then, has combined with state collapse to generate a powerful rationale for bilateral and multilateral donors to support local civil society development in war-torn countries.

Here again, however, the overall impact of CSO strategies to repair societal structures ruined by conflict is unclear, as are their implications for long-term social development. In particular, the issues of compatibility between imported models of organization and psycho-social analysis on one hand, and local practices and cultural frameworks on the other, remains problematic. The degree of normative absorption of, or accommodation to, desirable systems of social interaction is, at best, difficult to assess, given both the complexities of local social reality and the short time frames in which most CSOs implement their projects. The long-term effects on local social processes, over five- or ten-year periods, have not been systematically assessed.

Recent evidence has suggested that uncritical international funding of local civil society initiatives may in fact contribute to accentuate power imbalances within the existing social structures, or to reinforce local societal hierarchies not historically inclined towards progressive development. This may be particularly the case in volatile post-conflict situations where resource competition is intense, and where local elites are well positioned to manipulate associational efforts to maximize material or political gain. Indeed, rather than responding to objective needs, the intense proliferation of CSOs in Africa must be understood as a local form of institutional adjustment to changing international aid priorities. Civil society has partially replaced the state as a key mechanism for gaining access to resources and opportunities, and for determining their redistribution within the broader society. In this context, CSOs may represent new structures within which 'Africans can seek to establish an instrumentally profitable position.' The use of CSO resources 'can today serve the strategic interests of the classical entrepreneurial Big Man, just as well as access to state coffers did in the past.'[33]

Chabal and Daloz strongly warn that the growth of CSO activities in a context of state collapse 'is eminently more favourable to the instrumentalization of disorder than to the emergence of a Western-style civil society' and that rather than strengthening the latter, CSOs could well facilitate a 'high-jacking of genuinely needed development aid.' Confirming or qualifying such findings would require significant in-depth analysis of the impact of international CSO-support programs. Until this occurs, unresolved questions about the function of CSOs in repairing war-torn societies should, at minimum, encourage a more sober international approach.

CSOS AND THE TRANSITION FROM RELIEF TO DEVELOPMENT

A central priority of the aid community in post-conflict recovery has been to ensure quicker and more coherent transitions between short-term relief and sustainable development processes. The logic of this priority stems from the recognition that the short-term objectives of relief assistance do not necessarily facilitate successful long-term development, but may rather delay development by becoming an institutionalized mode of response to protracted crises. This has led to efforts to bridge programmatic gaps between the two forms of international assistance, reflected in a stronger emphasis on rehabilitation, and in moves to enhance the developmental value of relief operations.[34]

Successful transitions from relief to development are not, however, merely a matter of better program coherence along the relief-to-development continuum. By necessity, they must also allow for a passage from externally-driven programming to domestic planning and long-term agenda-setting. Whereas emergency relief derives, almost by definition, from external sources, long-term national development must come from internal political and economic processes if it is to be both genuine and sustainable. Where this passage fails to occur, authority over national political economies in recipient countries remains at least partially externalized, and risks being tied to the foreign policy preferences of donors, with negative implications not only for self-determination, but also for sustainability, accountability, and the political legitimacy of recipient governments.

In the 1990s CSOs were highly regarded for their ability to facilitate the transition from externally-sourced relief to internally-managed development, mainly by promoting local ownership of post-conflict recovery initiatives. In theory, support for local CSOs opens new opportunities for participatory decision-making among local stakeholders of development, maximizes the use of local knowledge, and helps to build local human and organizational capacities. This reasoning has provided additional momentum for direct international support to civil societies in war-affected countries, particularly where states are considered inappropriate or incapable development partners.

Here again, however, the potential for local CSOs to enable sustained national participation and ownership must be qualified in several ways. First, emergent civil societies in post-conflict situations are themselves largely generated from external sources, and cannot therefore be taken as mechanisms for nationalizing long-term development initiatives. A tendency among CSOs to replicate and implement projects pre-modelled from the outside may not favour the incorporation of local knowledge structures into longer-term recovery strategies. The top-down structure of emergent civil societies, and a high rate of material dependency on external funds, weakens their genuine representation of local interests and favours stronger links with outside agencies. At the same time, dependency on external funding cycles may seriously compromise the sustainability of local development initiatives, while existing tensions between CSOs and state bodies potentially weaken prospects for the implementation of a coherent national development program. Here again, the role of CSOs in enabling the transition from external assistance to internal development has not been consistently assessed. In the meantime, several observers have suggested that CSOs may instead serve to internationalize local developmental processes over time.

With few exceptions, a major impediment to knowing more about the actual impacts of internationally-sponsored civil society promotion has been the absence of rigorous evaluation on the part of donor agencies.[35] What information is available tends to be exceedingly scattered or localized, rendering sectoral, thematic or geographical comparisons difficult to draw. This shortcoming may reflect a lack of analytical tools to properly address the complexity of the issues in question. Possibly, it also reflects an implicit disinterest in questioning convenient conceptual frameworks for international intervention. Nonetheless, towards the end of the 1990s a growing recognition, of the limits of the civil society option has led to a tangible loss of innocence of CSOs in post-conflict settings. The result, in part, has been an increased willingness to return to official, multilateral forums, and a serious push for reform within the multilateral institutions, especially the UN.

Institutional Adaptation at the UN: Towards a More Political Economy

The first phase of UN engagement in post-Cold War peacebuilding brought some modest successes (Guatemala, El Salvador, Mozambique) and some catastrophic failures (Somalia, Rwanda, Angola). One of the starkest realities faced by the UN in the mid-1990s was that several of the worst humanitarian crises of the decade came in the wake of the collapse of UN-sponsored or facilitated peace agreements. The worst fighting in Angola followed the failure of the Lusaka Protocols; and, most dramatically, the Rwandan genocide occurred in the wake of the UN-guaranteed Arusha Accords.

These episodes highlight a wider challenge for the UN – namely the difficulty of consolidating peace and maintaining stability in the wake of conflict and crisis. Learning from such failures has led to a number of changes within the UN, in particular, to a growing recognition of the political factors, as well as the humanitarian features, of recurrent crisis. This has prompted an important policy shift that emphasizes political stabilization in post-conflict settings. Partially as a result, UN political actors have assumed a more robust political profile in post-conflict recovery, alongside existing humanitarian and developmental functions. This widening UN political involvement in post-conflict peacebuilding until recently has reflected a hesitant but discernible revival of support for UN engagement, even leadership, in post-conflict settings. Recent UN engagements in post-conflict situations have fallen primarily into three categories: managing transitional aid, political stabilization, and coordination.

Transitional Aid: Relief-to-Development Linkages

Within the UN, aid agencies have had primary responsibility for managing post-conflict responses. As active conflict receded, so, typically, did those charged with managing conflict resolution processes, including UN mediators and peacekeeping forces. Aid agencies were then tasked with supporting the reconstruction of so-called war-torn societies.

Historically, post-conflict assistance has been managed jointly by UN humanitarian and development actors, and framed in policy terms as the challenge of managing the transition between relief and development. The UN's humanitarian presence in post-crisis settings is led by the big three agencies: the UN High Commissioner for Refugees (UNHCR), the World Food Program (WFP) and the UN Children's Fund (UNICEF). A number of smaller humanitarian agencies, or humanitarian programs of development agencies, also play important roles. These include the World Health Organization (WHO) and the UN Food and Agriculture Organization (FAO). Additionally, the UN Office for the Coordination of Humanitarian Affairs (OCHA) which typically has a presence in early post-crisis situations, is a less significant player than during acute crises.

On the development side, the UN's presence is led by the UN Development Program (UNDP) as well as the WFP, UNICEF, and the UN

Food and Population Agency (UNFPA). Various specialized agencies, including the FAO, the International Labour Organization (ILO) and UNESCO, play small but not insignificant roles in providing advice and support to emergent governments. Additionally, development policy departments of the UN have recently tried to expand their activities in the post-conflict field. For example, the Department for Economic and Social Affairs (DESA) has sought to provide technical advise on fiscal and economic elements of post-conflict assistance. These efforts have been highly constrained by the centralized, headquarters-based nature of such departments.

The UNDP has played a particularly significant role in the development arena, both as the usual in-country coordinator of UN activities and as the UN's lead development actor. However, its specific role in crisis settings remains subject to debate. To date, the UNDP has not defined its own approach to development in a crisis or immediate post-crisis context.[36] Even the question of who is responsible within the UNDP for post-crisis cases has been hotly disputed. On the one hand, a Bureau for Conflict Prevention and Recovery (formerly the Emergency Response Division) has been created for precisely this challenge. On the other hand, the UNDP's geographical departments claim and are often able to exercise lead roles in shaping the UNDP response.

Such competition within the UNDP reflects and contributes to a wider uncertainty among the aid community about how to handle post-crisis development programs. It also represents uncertainties in the legislative framework within which UN development actors must work. This framework is composed primarily of the Economic and Social Council, the General Assembly, and the executive boards of the various agencies. Typically, policy-making in these bodies reflects a careful consensus between OECD states (most of them aid donors) and G77 states (many of them aid recipients). At times, the need to cultivate a consensus with aid recipients has frustrated donor efforts to generate a clearer role for the UNDP within the post-crisis arena. Unlike in the international financial institutions, the G77 states carry a lot of weight in UN decision-making, and some of these states have strongly resisted greater UNDP involvement in crisis and post-crisis settings, regarding it as interventionism.

Many programs that begin in the humanitarian sphere, such as provision of medical care and basic education services, are ones that rightly belong as part of a government or community-led package of social services. In collaboration with CSOs, nascent governments, and bilateral actors, the UN plays a significant role in post-crisis social reconstruction.

The humanitarian dimension of social recovery is the first part of the UN's work to fade out or diminish to a minor scale. Core social recovery programs, including reconciliation efforts, continue either through development channels or through a residual humanitarian presence. However, the speed with which such a shift in UN presence occurs depends on the degree of political and military stability. In fluid, uncertain situations, a major humanitarian presence is prolonged, sometimes for a number of years.

In more stable situations, a fairly rapid shift in the UN's work towards economic reconstruction occurs. Economic challenges in post-conflict typically involve establishing macro-economic stability and a framework for fiscal policy, restoring markets, supporting community development, and reconstructing war-damaged infrastructure. UN efforts in this sphere are usually directed at supporting the nascent government or local authorities. Less emphasis is given to supporting the private sector or to setting the conditions for international investment. This reflects a deep commitment within the UN to the concept of social as well as economic development. It also reflects a preference for a stronger role for the state in development expressed by the G77 and some European states. This contrasts with the more market-oriented philosophy of the international financial institutions.

Of course, the UN's role in economic reconstruction is sharply limited in relation to the roles played by other multilateral and bilateral actors. A major factor in this regard has been the increasing presence of the World Bank as a development actor in post-conflict settings. The World Bank has sought and frequently obtained a lead role in donor coordination in post-conflict settings, formerly one of the UN's most important functions. Bilateral donors also play a significant post-conflict role through their aid programs. Additionally, the European Community is an increasingly important player in this field. The sums of money that are channelled through such actors dwarf those of the UN in most settings, though in some African contexts the sums available to the UNDP represent a significant portion of international assistance.

The challenge of managing humanitarian programs in tandem with both social and economic development is at the core of the relief-development problematique. The manifold challenges range from the highly technical (different systems for raising and disbursing funds, different recruitment and staffing arrangements) to the managerial (different planning frameworks, varying timeframes for engagement) to the political (variable degrees of support for emergent regimes) and the conceptual (distinct conceptions of the nature of post-conflict challenges, different principles on which aid is based). Within the UN, efforts to improve policy coordination in post-conflict aid have focused on strengthening coordination mechanisms, lobbying donors for greater funding flexibility, and ensuring early linkages between planning frameworks for humanitarian and development assistance. In the institutional politics which consumes much ostensible policy-making, the prevalent focus has been on the gap between relief programming and development action. The charge, specifically, has been that UN development actors are too slow to start their programs, leaving relief agencies to take on roles (such as housing reconstruction) that they are ill suited, and under-financed, to play.

Less explicit attention has been paid to the different conceptual bases for the two types of assistance. Yet these are significant. Whereas humanitarian assistance focuses on individual needs and short- to medium-term problems, development aid is more focused on longer-term issues of a national or at least communal nature. Development actors place far greater emphasis on the state and on government than do humanitarians – a repeated bone of contention between the two communities. In the context of joint learning and policy-making efforts across the humanitarian/development chasm, the critical work on forging a conceptual framework which provides guidelines as to what aid is supposed to do has largely been sidelined by an excessive focus on technical and management issues.

Political Stabilization: Towards Peacebuilding

Recent debates over the management of relief-to-development transitions have been increasingly overshadowed by the growth of more explicitly political approaches to post-conflict assistance. Witnessing recipient states revert to conflict has been a significant learning experience for the UN, resulting in far greater emphasis on the fundamentally political character of post-conflict challenges. This in turn has led to an extension of UN political activity in post-crisis settings. Though not yet fully institutionalized within the UN, this is an evolution with significant implications.

Traditionally, the UN's only direct political involvement in post-conflict settings had been in a peacekeeping capacity (under the responsibility of the Department of Peacekeeping Operations). In the 1990s, UN peacekeeping operations covered a range of roles related to the implementation of political settlements, including verification of ceasefires, demobilization and disarmament, mine removal, and provision of physical protection to government and international authorities. Less commonly, tasks have included limited military action against hostile forces or provision of military assistance to the government (Sierra Leone), and the physical protection of all civilians coming under direct threat from combatants (Sierra Leone, Democratic Republic of the Congo).

After the debacles of Rwanda and Somalia, the UN's peacekeeping role declined considerably. In the past few years, the UN has had a minimal peacekeeping role. Even where peacekeeping operations did occur, they were often of limited duration and ended soon after the implementation of a political settlement. Only at the end of the decade was there something of a resurgence in UN peacekeeping, both in Africa and elsewhere. By the end of 2002 the largest UN peacekeeping presence was in Sierra Leone, and a smaller force was deployed to oversee a quasi-settlement in the Democratic Republic of the Congo.[37]

Increasingly, however, even where the UN does not have a peacekeeping role, it has extended its political interventions in other forms, either through UN political missions (i.e. the deployment of special representatives of the secretary-general), or through UN Peacebuilding Support Offices (PBSO), under the Department of Political Affairs (DPA). The roles of these offices include confidence-building and political stabilization efforts, electoral support, efforts to strengthen and legitimate a new government established through political settlement, and the hosting of donor conferences. UN political offices also support the development of national human rights institutions, and promote judicial and constitutional reforms in post-conflict settings.

PBSOs were a hopeful innovation. First used in Liberia in the latter 1990s, they have since been created in Guinea-Bissau (where the UN had no peacekeeping role) and in the Central African Republic, following a brief peacekeeping mission which oversaw elections. PBSOs are the institutional expression of the lead peacebuilding role given to the DPA under the 1997 UN reforms. Of course, similar activities have been undertaken in other contexts by the UNDP, the UN high commissioner for human rights, and other UN actors. However, internal reviews of the performance of PBSOs have pointed to disappointing results. No consistent internal or external evaluation of the impact of SRSGs has yet been conducted, but there is at least anecdotal evidence to suggest that the deployment of senior political officials, operating under the authority of the secretary-general, and therefore bringing his authority to bear in these post-crisis efforts, has been a significant evolution.[38]

The involvement of the secretary-general in peacebuilding potentially lends considerable weight to the UN's efforts in this regard. Though many of the SRSGs and PBSOs deployed to post-conflict settings operate under the secretary-general's good offices, the secretary-general routinely conducts close consultations with key members of the Security Council and involved parties before deploying a political presence. Thus, from the perspective of the host country, the statements or decisions of a special representative (and to a lesser extent the head of a PBSO) can carry with them the weight of the governments who comprise the Council. This political weight can be used to place considerable pressure on local authorities, as well as on regional actors whose actions may have a significant bearing on political stabilization in a post-crisis setting.

The involvement of UN political actors in peacebuilding activities has several other implications. It brings into the management of development-oriented activities the Security Council rather than the General Assembly-based forums which traditionally set policy in the economic sphere, and therefore raises questions about the relationship between the primary organs of the UN. Significantly, the G77's role is much less significant in the Security Council than in the General Assembly, although the presence of China in the Council is an omnipresent check on Western members. Furthermore, the temporary nature of political offices raises concerns about continuity at the end of the mandate. In past instances, the abrupt withdrawal of peacekeeping missions with significant development portfolios – such as UNTAC in Cambodia – meant a sudden end to many ongoing peacebuilding and development-oriented programs, with obvious negative effects. Increased political management of aid could exacerbate this problem.

On balance, however, the longer-term consequences of political management of aid are probably more than offset by more effective efforts to stabilize political settlements in post-crisis contexts. While it may be that social and economic development reinforce peace in the long run, unstable politics and reversions to violence undermine any form of development. In the short term, prioritizing political stabilization over socio-economic development in insecure contexts will arguably be the most effective approach to peacebuilding. In the medium-to-long-term, reducing the politicization of aid and increasing the degree of national ownership over development processes is likely to be an important means of ensuring the sustainability of post-conflict recovery. Indeed, balancing political and socio-economic aspects of post-conflict interventions has been a central challenge for the UN and other actors in the later part of the 1990s. In the UN, this has been tackled primarily as a question of coordination.

Coordination: Balancing Political, Economic, and Social Dimensions of Peacebuilding

The increasing frequency of UN political missions has led to some confusion about the overall coordination of UN efforts in post-conflict contexts. Whereas the UNDP once had an undisputed coordination mandate for aid, and the department of Peacekeeping Operations had the undisputed lead in UN peacekeeping missions, both of these roles are now in dispute. Indeed, the question of who coordinates overall post-conflict activity is among the most contentious of current UN policy debates. Given that the UN in theory coordinates not only its own activity but also that of many non-governmental and other multilateral actors, the question has significant implications for post-conflict assistance as a whole.

Given the stakes involved, several of the different UN entities involved in post-crisis activity have put forward their own framework for overall coordination. Within the development sphere the UN Development Group Office has experimented with the so-called Development Assistance Framework (UNDAF), a tool for enhancing the coherence of the programs of the various UN development and specialized agencies. It is based on a common assessment template, specified program cycles, and joint policy formulation (based on UN standards). The past few years have seen an increase in efforts to use the UNDAF as a policy coordination tool even in countries in crisis. For example, it has been used in Burundi to orchestrate the UN's development plans, notwithstanding the continuing conflict. However, the UNDAF is very limited as an overall coordination tool for crisis since the Development Group Office, which manages it, represents UN development actors but excludes UN humanitarian and political entities.

More significantly on the development side, UNDP and the Development Group Office have consistently supported the role of the UN Resident Coordinator as the overall coordinator of post-crisis operations. However, in 1997 the principle was established that a special representative of the secretary-general, when deployed to a country, would assume overall coordinating authority over the UN. The UNDP's adjustment to this new policy has been slow and partial. In some cases, resident coordinators have been assigned as deputies, bringing the two coordination mechanisms together. By the end of the 1990s, however, increasing policy support was given by the UN leadership to the concept of integrated coordination mechanisms, under the lead of a special representative.

Two distinct versions of this concept have been put forward by the political departments. One, sponsored primarily by Peacekeeping Operations, entails integrated missions. Used first in Kosovo and East Timor, but also planned for use in the D.R. Congo, the integrated mission model involves coordinating all elements of UN peace operation programming, be it in development, humanitarian assistance, human rights, or political spheres, under the direct authority of the special representative. This model emphasizes a chain-of-command approach, no doubt reflecting a certain military culture in the in the Peacekeeping Operations Department. Early experiences with this model in Kosovo and East Timor appeared to be successful in terms of mitigating coordination problems within the UN.

Another coordination model, the Strategic Framework, has been championed by the Department of Political Affairs and the office for the Coordination of Human Affairs. In the late 1990s, this tool was used for overall coordination usually under the lead of the special representatives, who are instructed to ensure that political, aid, and human rights elements of UN programming 'inform and are informed by' one another. Additionally, the special representative, along with the resident coordinator, is instructed to develop coordination mechanisms bringing together the UN agencies, local and international NGOs, bilateral donors, and national authorities. This model has been tested in Afghanistan and, more recently, in Sierra Leone. Early experiences of the Strategic Framework suggests that it suffers from excessive inclusiveness. With so many actors involved, it has proved difficult to make the leap from generic consensus to concrete decisions. Moreover, the mechanisms envisaged by the Strategic Framework take a long time to establish: in both Afghanistan and Sierra Leone, over a year elapsed between the launch of the framework and the appearance of concrete results. On the positive side, the Strategic Framework contains a formal commitment to working primarily through, and in support of, national capacities.

Through these and other institutional innovations, the UN has sought to provide a comprehensive policy framework for post-conflict recovery. To date, these coordination efforts have often been characterized by an emphasis on process over content, and an excessive focus on internal UN institutional competition. The result has been a proliferation of coordination mechanisms, which in some instances has complicated overall coordination efforts. Consider, for example, Sierra Leone. In this context, where there was reasonable donor support for the UN to play a lead role, including significant direct backing from the British government, the UN deployed a multitude of coordinating mechanisms. There was an integrated mission a Strategic Framework, and a resident coordinator plus at times a humanitarian coordinator. While these could all be pieces of an elaborate coordination puzzle, the reality on the ground was overlapping, unclear and excessively complicated coordinating structures, none of which clearly related to one another.

The two coordination models may have comparative advantages in different stages of post-crisis. It may yet prove that the integrated mission model is a more effective political coordination approach for the early phases of post-crisis, and that the Strategic Framework model – where there is greater balance between political and socio-economic aspects of post-conflict assistance – is more effective for medium- to long-term peacebuilding processes.[39]

A third mechanism that has been deployed for post-conflict peacebuilding is that of transitional authority. Although the increase in the 1990s in the number and scale of authority of transitional authority missions is an important issue, it operates so differently than the regular UN post-conflict mechanisms that it warrants separate treatment.

Institutional Innovation and Options for the Future

After three years of intensive reform efforts under Secretary-General Kofi Annan, the UN has strengthened its capacity to engage in peacebuilding activities. However, the UN still faces considerable challenges in implementing mandates in the context of internal war. Some of these challenges, and related reform options, are briefly considered here.

UN Challenges

A major challenge for the UN in its new, more political approach to post-conflict peacebuilding concerns the nature of political authority. Even in contexts of relative political stability, it is often the case that no government can officially be recognized as a fully legitimate political partner of the UN. Even where peace agreements formally enable the UN to support transitional governments, such agreements are usually hampered by fracture, distrust, and paralysis of power-sharing arrangements. Thus, counterparts at the political level are rarely both legitimate and effective, and are often neither. For UN political and development actors seeking to support a national government, this is a major challenge.

There is good reason for outside actors to be cautious about relations with local authorities; premature recognition of quasi-legitimate authorities can lead to excessive centralization of power and diminish prospects for good governance. However, too much caution may entail failure to provide a basis for building adequate national authority over development and social recovery. This kind of dilemma has been a recurrent feature of post-crisis situations. In the absence of a clear international norm, ad hoc solutions have tended to prevail. As yet, no official UN policy has been developed, or guidelines drawn up, on the issue of political authority. Equally significant is the question of the relationship between the World Bank and the UNDP, which have competed for the lead role in coordinating the development dimensions of post-conflict assistance. This, for example, occurred in Rwanda and Sierra Leone. New leadership at the UNDP and new policy in the World Bank have led to a muting of this competition. A growing recognition within the Bank of a need to engage political questions, coupled with restrictions on its capacity to do so in the absence of firmly recognized governing authorities, have led the Bank to seek greater collaboration with the political departments and programs of the UN.

This notwithstanding, no clear division of labour exists between the two entities. No doubt the UN's relationship with the Bank will be crucial in determining its ability to perform an overall coordinating role in post-crisis, its ability to make effective linkages between humanitarian assistance and state capacity-building, and its capacity to ensure coherence between the economic reconstruction efforts of the Bank and its own efforts at political stabilization. An effective relationship between the two is the essential building block for a new, more effective political economy of peacebuilding.

Other Options for Reform

With respect to the broader institutional framework for peacebuilding discussed in the first section of this article, several proposals have been advanced to better integrate the international community's efforts to build peace in divided societies.

A NEW MARSHALL PLAN

Several scholars and policy-makers have suggested creating a special financing arrangement, similar to the Marshall Plan, to direct concessional funds and grants for post-conflict recovery.[40] However, the differences between the post-World War Two period and the current context of peace and development, including the change in the global distribution of power, arguably make this proposal unrealistic.

CREATE ETHNICALLY HOMOGENOUS STATES

Based on realpolitik notions of the balance of power, some scholars have advocated the creation of mutually balancing ethnically-homogeneous enclaves or states, as a solution to civil war.[41] However, even where ethnicity is believed to be a cause of war, it cannot be assumed that secession will result in governments that are more responsive to their populations, or that conflict will end.

A NEW INTERNATIONAL TRUSTEESHIP

Others have proposed elevating the role of trustee to a central place as a possible solution to the problem of state failure. This would involve placing failed states under some form of new international trusteeship or 'conservatorship.'[42] Critics have been quick to denounce this proposal as a new form of colonialism and a denial of self-determination, and thus a violation of international law.[43] A variation of trusteeship that is less intrusive and somewhat less suggestive of colonialism has been labelled 'peace-maintenance' by its principal advocate.[44]

REVISITING SOVEREIGNTY

Others have proposed that the international community revisit the issue of sovereignty and recognize alternative forms of political organization to the sovereign territorial state. These analysts question the wisdom of attempting to rebuild states that have never been viable. Gidon Gottlieb, for example, argues that the dominant interpretation of the principle of self-determination should be supplemented by a new one that is less territorially based. Jeffrey Herbst argues that the fiction of territorial sovereignty in Africa should be recognized and alternatives sought in African history and geography. It is not clear how this goal can be achieved.[45]

A variation on this theme that is more feasible involves the international community differentiating between claims to self-determination that are warranted, and those that are not. Here, the international community would establish a system of incentives and constraints to influence the behaviour of claimants in particular directions, and institutionalize procedures for joint decision-making in response to challenges. For example, states that govern in a responsive, efficient, and accountable manner would be rewarded. Others that violate international standards would face some type of sanctions (e.g., ostracism) or suspension.[46] Standards would also be developed to discourage certain types of claims by disaffected groups. Demands for secession and the resort to force, for example, would not be justified when made against a responsive government. In effect, this proposal calls for the introduction of new criteria for recognition of states, and for the international community to assume the role of external guarantors of internal self-determination. This would provide the institutional and normative foundations for a coherent approach to peacebuilding.

REFORM OF CIVIL SOCIETY ORGANIZATIONS
The strengths and weaknesses of CSOs are not static. But in order for the objective benefits of CSO-based strategies to be maximized, the aid community must begin to consider several steps aiming, first, to qualify basic policy assumptions and reduce the contradictory effects of uncritical support to emergent civil societies. These would include: a more consistent analysis of the domestic political and material forces at play; more attention to the long-term impacts of CSO-based interventions; a more critical selection of international and national partners; and an adjustment of funding strategies to encourage balanced and constructive relationships between CSOs and relevant government departments. This would help to rebuild state and society capacities in a complementary manner, and ensure more durable and coherent domestic frameworks within which to initiate longer-term development programmes.

Recent Innovations: A New Model?

Most recently, the questions of UN reform, CSO reform, and the need for new models have found expression in a growing number of newly-created, or rejuvenated, hybrid organizations. These possess some of the advantages of CSOs – flexibility, adaptability, informality – while retaining something of the authority, legitimacy, and political mandate of the UN.

An early initiative was the War-Torn Societies Project which focused on the use of participatory methodologies for generating local political dialogue around priorities for post-conflict reconstruction. Its particular success has been in identifying and mobilizing moderate and constructive voices in local political circles and civil society, and creating forums for neutral discussion among such voices. Initially a joint project of UN political and development departments and academic institutions, the Project has evolved into a CSO/UN hybrid. Formally a non-governmental entity, it nevertheless has significant UN representation on its board, and the ability to operate as a UN entity in some contexts. Thus, it can engage with non-official political actors within an internal war context without the kinds of limitations that the UN faces, but it can also use its UN identity to shield its staff, create legitimacy for its projects, and bring donor governments and others into the dialogue.

Similarly, the Henry Dunant Centre (now called the Centre for Humanitarian Dialogue), initially founded as a think tank by the ICRC, was recently remoulded with strong unofficial links to the UN system. Focusing on humanitarian law and principles, the Centre has engaged in dialogue with several official and unofficial actors, free of UN constraints, but in ways which ultimately support UN or UN-backed conflict-resolution efforts. In 1999 and 2000, the Henry Dunant Centre engaged with a wide range of political and military actors in Burundi (where UN contact with some rebel factions had been heavily constrained). While the Centre's dialogue with these groups was strictly limited to humanitarian issues, its efforts nevertheless appear to have had a positive impact on the search for peace in Burundi. In July 2000 all the military and political factions involved in the civil war met for the first time face-to-face in UN-supported peace talks in Arusha, Tanzania, facilitated by Nelson Mandela. While other factors combined to facilitate this process, it is likely that these efforts helped to provide momentum for the official peace dialogue.

Finally, the creation of a Strategic Recovery Facility, proposed by the Centre on International Cooperation has recently been discussed at donor consultations concerning the management of transitions from relief to development. The essential notion behind the Facility is to create a forum for coordination between the UN and its agencies, the World Bank, and CSOs. Based on coordinated planning, the Strategic Recovery Facility would provide dedicated funds to support vital post-conflict recovery activities that are sometimes lost in the relief/development gap. Importantly, the it would be constituted outside the UN structure, but would be co-chaired by both the UN and the World Bank. As such it would combine programmatic flexibility with formal international authority and legitimacy.

These innovations and proposals provide strong evidence of trends towards hybrid organizations that seek to marry some of the advantages of CSOs with the authority and legitimacy of official multilateral actors. Alongside further reform within the UN and the civil sector, such institutions are likely to play a significant role in the management of post-conflict interventions in the coming years.

Conclusion

Ultimately, the international community cannot solve the problems of internal war and state failure. Solutions will have to come from within African countries themselves. However, through a more constructive engagement the international community can provide organizations that facilitate the transition from war to durable peace. Important steps in this direction include shedding preconceived notions about the nature and causes of war in Africa that further isolate the continent and its people, recognizing that traditional institutional roles developed to manage inter-state war are not appropriate to modern state failure. More relevant roles must be developed to address the challenges of contemporary peacebuilding.

Vitally, international actors cannot neglect the critical task of supporting the reconstruction of state institutions, or of finding a new balance for the political and socio-economic dimensions of post-conflict recovery. These tasks may be supported by new hybrid organizations or reformed CSOs. Ultimately, however, they will also require deeper reform within the UN, the Bretton Woods institutions, and in the civil sector, as well as more coherent institutional relations among them. And, finally, they must be guided not by ad hoc solutions, but by the articulation of clear international norms and roles governing the management and resolution of internal wars.

NOTES

1 Roles are identity-specific conceptions of appropriate behaviour in specified contexts. They are behavioural traditions, often expressed as norms, that link values to action by specifying appropriate measures actors may take in pursuit of desired goals. All roles are inherently normative since they offer prescriptions about what actors ought to do. See Peter L. Berger et al., *The Social Construction of Reality: A Treatise in the Sociology of Knowledge* (New York: Doubleday, 1966); Richard W. Scott, *Institutions and Organizations* (London: Sage, 1995), pp. 37–40; Michael Barnett, 'Institutions, Roles and Disorder: The Case of the Arab States System,' *International Organization* 49 (1995), 479–510; and Martha Finnemore, 'Norms, Culture and World Politics: Insights from Sociology's Institutionalism,' *International Organization* 50 (1996), 325–47.

2 See B. Boutros-Ghali, *An Agenda for Peace* (New York: United Nations, 1992)

and *Supplement to an Agenda for Peace* (1995); Kofi Annan, *Renewing the United Nations: A Programme for Reform* (New York: United Nations, 1997), and *The Causes of Conflict and the Promotion of Durable Peace and Development in Africa* (New York: United Nations, 1998); OECD/DAC, *Conflict, Peace and Development Co-operation on the Threshold of the 21st Century*, 5–6 May 1997; and OECD/DAC, *DAC Guidelines on Conflict, Peace and Development Co-operation* (Paris: OECD, 1997).

3 Barry Eichengreen et al., 'Managing the World Economy under the Bretton Woods System: An Overview,' in Peter B. Kenen, ed., *Managing the World Economy: Fifty Years after Bretton Woods* (Washington, DC: Institute for International Economics, 1994); John Stremlau et al., *Preventing Deadly Conflict: Does the World Bank Have a Role?* (New York: Carnegie Commission on Preventing Deadly Conflict, 1998).

4 Some have attributed the absence of war between the major powers to the presence of nuclear weapons. Others argue it was due to the normative and institutional effects of democracy. See Bruce Russett et al., 'Normative and Institutional Causes of Democratic Peace,' *American Political Science Review*, 87 (September 1993), 624–38.

5 See Robert O. Jackson et al., 'The Territorial Covenant: International Society and the Stabilization of Boundaries.' Working Paper No. 15, Institute of International Studies, University of British Columbia, July 1997; Patrick Thornberry, 'Self-determination, Minorities, Human Rights: A Review of International Instruments,' *International and Comparative Law Quarterly* 38 (1989), 867–89; Robert H. Jackson, *Quasi-States: Sovereignty, International Relations and the Third World* (Cambridge: Cambridge University Press, 1990).

6 UN Charter articles 2(1), 2(4) and 2(7) respectively. This interpretation is reinforced by the principle *uti possidetis juris* that affirms the sanctity of territorial frontiers within which political independence is achieved, thereby protecting the borders of existing and post-colonial states.

7 The last remaining trust territory (Palau) achieved independence in 1994.

8 The role of sheriff is governed by the enforcement provisions of UN Charter chapters 7 and 8. Umpire activities generally fall under chapter 6, although peacekeeping occupies a somewhat grey area between chapters 6 and 7. Trusteeship is governed by chapters 11–13, and samaritan activities are governed by humanitarian law under the 1949 Geneva Conventions and the 1977 Protocol I.

9 See Kal J. Holsti, 'The Coming Chaos? Armed Conflict in the World's Periphery,' in T.V. Paul and John Hall, eds., *International Order and the Future of World Politics* (Cambridge: Cambridge University Press, 1999), 283–310.

10 See Aristide R. Zolberg 'The Spectre of Anarchy: African States Verging on

Dissolution,' *Dissent* 39 (1996); Neta Crawford, 'Imag(in)ing Africa,' *Harvard International Journal of Press/Politics* 1 (1996). The cover of the influential *Economist* newsmagazine – 'The Hopeless Continent' – in reference to the war in Sierra Leone, illustrated this tendency. See *Economist*, 13–17 May 2000.

11 See Catherine Newbury, 'Ethnicity and the Politics of History in Rwanda,' *Africa Today* 45, no. 1 (1998), 7–24; and Rhoda Howard, 'Civil Conflict in Africa: Internally Generated Causes,' *International Journal* (Winter 1995–6), 27–53.

12 Internal self-determination deals with political, socio-economic, and cultural rights of groups and individuals within states, the nature of the political community, internal political arrangements, and so on.

13 Ted Robert Gurr, *Minorities at Risk* (Washington DC: United States Institute of Peace, 1993).

14 Heather Wilson, *International Law and the Use of Force by National Liberation Movements* (Oxford: Clarendon Press, 1988); John Morton Moore, 'Legal Standards for Intervention in Internal Conflicts,' and Bart de Schutter et al., 'Coping with Non-international Armed Conflicts: The Borderline Between National and International Law,' *Georgia Journal of International and Comparative Law* 13 (1983), 191–9, and 279–90.

15 No widely accepted list of peremptory norms exist, but most analysts agree they include prohibitions against genocide, slavery, and systematic and institutionalized racial discrimination (apartheid). See L. Hannikainen, *Peremptory Norms (Jus Cogens) in International Law* (Helsinki: Finnish Lawyers Publishers, 1988).

16 As a result of the Marshall Plan, the IBRD largely stopped providing loans for reconstruction and shifted its focus to development, beginning with loans to Chile in March 1948, and to Mexico and Brazil in early 1949. See Edward S. Mason et al., *The World Bank Since Bretton Woods* (Washington, DC: Brookings Institution, 1973); and Robert E. Wood, *From Marshall Plan to Debt Crisis: Foreign Aid and Development Choices in the World Economy* (Berkeley: University of California Press, 1986).

17 Stremlau et al, *Preventing Deadly Conflict*, 19.

18 World Bank, *Advancing Sustainable Development: The World Bank and Agenda 21* (Washington, DC, World Bank). Figures from UN Africa Recovery, *Promoting a Durable Peace*, (Department of Public Information, United Nations, 1998). It remains to be seen whether recent anti-poverty initiatives such as the UN's *Millennium Declaration* and the March 2002 Monterrey Declararion in which the major donors pledged to increase aid by 15 per cent, will indeed produce results.

19 World Bank, *Advancing Sustainable Development*, and World Bank, World

Development Report 2000/2001: *Attacking Poverty* (New York: Oxford University Press, 2000), 21–4, table 1.

20 See Edward Azar, 'Protracted International Conflicts: Ten propositions' in Azar and Burton, eds *International Conflict Resolution: Theory and Practice.* (Boulder, CO: Lynn Reinner, 1986); Francis Deng, 'Anatomy of Conflicts in Africa,' in Rupesignhe et al., eds., *Between Development and Destruction: An Enquiry into the Causes of Conflict in Post-Colonial States* (London: Macmillan, 1996); John Burton, *Violence Explained* (Manchester: Manchester University Press, 1997).

21 The term CSO here encompasses the broad array of international and local NGOs, independent associations, unions, church groups and private research networks involved in the aid process as donors, recipients or intermediaries. For clarity, private sector entities and formal political parties are excluded from the designation.

22 OECD/DAC, Annual Co-operation Reports (Brussels, OECD,1999 and 2000), Annex tables 1 and 19.

23 As quoted in Laura Macdonald, 'Globalizing Civil Society: Interpreting International NGOs in Central America,' *Millennium* 23, no. 2 (1994). See also Robert Cox, 'Civil Society at the Turn of the Millennium: Prospects for an Alternative World Order,' *Review of International Studies* 25 (1999); and Jay Mazur, 'Labour's New Internationalism' *Foreign Affairs* (January-February 2000).

24 For a positive assessment of CSO aid delivery, see Leon Gordenker et al., 'Devolving Responsibilities: A Framework for Analyzing NGOs and Services,' in Weiss and Gordenker, eds., *Beyond UN Subcontracting: Task Sharing with Regional Security Arrangements and Service-Providing NGOs* (London: Macmillan, 1998), 30–45.

25 See Jon Bennett, ed., *Meeting Needs: NGO Co-ordination in Practice* (London: Earthscan, 1995); John Whitman and David Pocock, eds., *After Rwanda: The Coordination of United Nations Humanitarian Assistance* (London: Macmillan, 1996); and Michael Edwards and David Hulme, eds., *Non-Governmental Organizations: Performance and Accountability* (London: Earthscan, 1996). See also Sheelagh Stewart, 'Happy Ever After in the Market Place: Non Government Organizations and Uncivil Society,' *Review of African Political Economy* 71 (1997); and Mark Duffield, *Evaluating Conflict Resolution: Context, Models and Methodology*, discussion paper prepared for the Chr. Michelsen Institute, Bergen, May 1997.

26 See Robert Chambers, 'The Primacy of the Personal' in Edwards and Hulme, *Non-Governmental Organizations*, 207–17.

27 Ronnie Lipschutz, 'Reconstructing World Politics: The Emergence of Global

Civil Society,' *Millennium* 21, no. 3 (1992); see also Ken Hackett,, 'The Role of International NGOs in Preventing Conflict,' in K.M. Cahill, ed., *Stopping Wars Before They Start: Preventive Diplomacy* (New York: Harper Collins, 1996); and Harry Blair, 'Donors, Democratization and Civil Society: Relating Theory to Practice,' in Michael Edwards and David Hulme, eds., *NGOs, States and Donors: Too Close for Comfort?* (London: Macmillan/Save the Children Fund, 1997); 228.

28 Vikram Chand, 'Democratization from the Outside In: NGOs and International Efforts to promote open Elections' in Thomas Weiss et al., eds., *Beyond UN Subcontracting: Task Sharing with Regional Security Arrangements and Service-Providing NGOs* (London: Macmillan, 1998), 169–71.

29 See William Zartman, ed., *Collapsed States: The Disintegration and Restoration of Legitimate Authority* (Boulder, CO: Lynne Reinner, 1995).

30 See Joanna Macrae et al., 'Aid Policy in Transition: A Preliminary Analysis of Post-Conflict Rehabilitation or the Health Sector,' *Journal of International Development* (1995); and 'Dilemmas of Legitimacy, Sustainability and Coherence: Rehabilitating the Health Sector' in Kumar, ed., *Rebuilding Societies after Civil War: Critical Roles for International Assistance* (Boulder, CO: Lynne Reinner, 1997).

31 In early phases of post-conflict transition, rebel groups in Angola (1994–7) and Mozambique (1992–5) routinely took political credit for CSO projects, while consistently delaying the extension of the state's administrative authority into areas under their control. On NGOs and political legitimacy in the Sudan, see Terje Tvedt, *NGOs as a Channel in Development Aid: The Norwegian System* (Bergen: University of Bergen Centre for Development Studies/Norwegian Ministry of Foreign Affairs, 1995), 60–1.

32 Cited in *The Experience of NGOs in Conflict Intervention: Problems and Prospects*, Collaborative for Development Action, April 1995), 4.

33 Patrick Chabal and Jean-Pascal Daloz, *Africa Works: Disorder as Political Instrument* (Oxford: James Currey, 1999), 22–4.

34 See Joanna Macraa et al., 'Conflict, the Continuum and Chronic Emergencies: A Critical Analysis of the Scope for Linking Relief, Rehabilitation and Development planning in Sudan,' *Disasters* 21, no. 3 (1997), 225.

35 Notable exceptions include Allison Van Rooy, ed., *Civil Society* Tvedt, *NGOs* David Sogge, *Mozambique: Perspectives on Aid to the Civil Sector* (Oegstgeest: GOM, 1997).

36 Interviews with senior officials of the UNDP's Bureau for Conflict Prevention and Recovery, formerly UNDP Emergency Response Division, New York, April 2000 and March 2003.

37 The United Nations Mission in Sierra Leone (UNAMSIL) was expanded

from six thousand personnel in 1999 to thirteen thousand in May 2000. In the DRC, the UN Organization Mission (MONUC) deployed up to 8,700 personnel in 2002.

38 Interviews with senior officials of UNDP and the Department of Political Affairs, New York, March 2003; Bruce D. Jones, 'The Challenges of Strategic Coordination' in Stephen John Stedman et. al., eds., *Ending Civil Wars: The Implementation of Peace Agreements* (Boulder, CO: Lynne Reinner, 2002).

39 A 2002 study by King's College, and a 2003 study by the Cambridge, Centre for Humanitarian Dialogue reached more nuanced conclusions. However, there are grounds for concern about the methodology of both studies, as they explored coordination issues in a small number of cases where various forms of integrated mission or coordination structures had been deployed, without comparing these cases to others where more traditional mechanisms were in place or where there was no UN political actor interest.

40 See Michael E. Brown, 'Internal Conflict and International Action,' in Michael Brown, ed., *The International Dimensions of Internal Conflict* (Cambridge: MIT Press, 1996); and Shepard Forman and Stewart Patrick, 'Introduction,' in Foreman and Patrick, eds., *Good Intentions: Pledges of Aid for Post-Conflict Recovery* (Boulder, CO: Lynne Rienner, 2000).

41 See Steven R. David, 'Internal War: Causes and Cures,' *World Politics* 49 (1997), 552–76; Michael Lind, 'In Defence of Liberal Nationalism' *Foreign Affairs* 73 (May–June, 1994); and Chaim Kaufmann, 'Possible and Impossible Solutions to Ethnic Conflicts,' *International Security* 20 (Spring 1996).

42 See Charles Krauthammer, 'Trusteeship for Security: An Old – Colonial – Idea Whose Time Has Come Again,' *Washington Post* (October 1992), A27; Ali A. Mazrui, 'Decaying Parts of Africa Need Benign Colonialism,' *International Herald Tribune* (4 August 1994); and William Pfaff, 'A New Colonialism? Europe Must Go Back into Africa,' *Foreign Affairs* 74 (1995); Richard B. Helman and Steven R. Ratner, 'Saving Failed States,' *Foreign Policy* 4 (1992–3).

43 See Ruth Gordon, 'Saving Failed States: Sometimes a Neo-colonialist Notion,' *American University Journal of International Law* 12 (1997).

44 Jarat Chopra, 'The Space of Peace-Maintenance,' *Political Geography* 15, nos. 3/4 (1996), 338–9; and Chopra, 'Introducing Peace-Maintenance' *Global Governance* 4 (1998).

45 See Gidon Gottlieb, 'Nations without States,' *Foreign Policy* 89 (1992–3), 21–35; and Jeffrey Herbst, 'Responding to State Failure.'

46 See Tim Shaw and Clement Adibe, 'Africa and the Global Developments in the Twenty-first Century: An African Perspective,' *International Journal* 51 (1995–6).

Conclusion: The Long and Difficult Road to Peace

Taisier M. Ali and Robert O. Matthews

Building a lasting peace in Africa has proven to be very difficult. Of the ten endeavours in peacebuilding examined in this study, only five were described as successful: Uganda, Ethiopia, Mozambique, South Africa, and Zimbabwe. Even in these instances, their positive depiction was qualified, in some cases quite seriously. In Uganda, for instance, not only has Museveni opposed resumption of party politics, but his government continues to face armed opposition from groups in the north and west, resulting in considerable destruction and human suffering and forcing Uganda to send troops into the Democratic Republic of the Congo. Having abandoned a broad consensus approach, Museveni runs the risk of succumbing to the temptation of holding indefinitely onto power. In Ethiopia, the Ethiopian Peoples Revolutionary Democratic Front has resisted the process of democratization, taking steps that could well lead, as John Young suggests in his chapter, 'to subsequent difficulties and the possibility of future failure and a return to instability and civil conflict.' As well, it has been drawn into a bloody war with its erstwhile ally, Eritrea. In both Mozambique and South Africa the peaceful political transition that they experienced has been marred by a failure to address socio-economic inequalities in their countries, thus exposing them to widespread social unrest and instability. Finally, after almost two decades of relative peace in Zimbabwe, renewed fighting seems increasingly likely, the combined result of Mugabe's abuse of power and the international community's mishandling of the land redistribution question.

The other five cases illustrate even more forcefully how difficult it is to rebuild a peaceful society that has been torn apart by civil war. In Angola and Sudan, the peace that was brokered eventually collapsed and fighting resumed with even more brutality and destructiveness. While life in

Somaliland has returned in large measure to what one might call normalcy, the situation in central and southern Somalia, especially in the
former capital of Mogadishu, is far different, marked by repeated violence and lawlessness. Peace in Rwanda since 1994 has remained elusive,
as Hutu militia, operating from neighbouring Congo, have targeted government officials and Tutsi survivors, prompting in turn the government
to invade the Congo on two separate occasions, to use force to relocate
Rwandan civilians into monitored villages, and generally to subdue the
Hutu population. The election of Charles Taylor as president of Liberia
in 1997 was initially greated with considerable relief by most Liberians,
but it wasn't long before the true nature of his regime had become
apparent. Surrounded by security forces loyal to him and employed to
promote his own personal security and welfare and to pursue and eliminate his rivals, Charles Taylor managed this peace process in such a manner as to reduce personal security, significantly cut access to schooling
and health care, increase unemployment, and undermine regional security. Not surprisingly, war broke out again, Taylor was eventually forced
to flee, and order was finally restored by a UN peacekeeping force.

This record of peacebuilding does suggest that it is no easy task to
learn to live and work together after having fought against each other for
so long.[1] Post–civil war governments need to address not only the root
causes of the civil war but also the full legacy of the war itself. As the cases
in our volume point out, frequently they have failed or been ineffective
in addressing each of these fundamental needs. In the pages that follow
we hope to shed some light on the nature of the peacebuilding process
itself, the obstacles that frequently lie in its path, whether or not the
manner in which civil wars end matters, and the role played by the international community in helping or hindering that process. Finally, we
offer the broad outlines of a peacebuilding strategy. Any peacebuilding
edifice will have to include four building blocks: a secure environment,
new political institutions that are broadly representative, a reconstituted
and healthy economy, and a mechanism for dealing with the past and its
injustices. How these blocks are put together will vary from case to case,
though if they are well designed and carefully arranged to fit the specific
local circumstances, the outcome will likely be self-sustaining peace.

The Peacebuilding Process

Much of the literature dealing with peacebuilding tends to restrict its
focus to a transitional period during which short-term measures, for the

most part dealing with security and political matters and often incorporated in a peace settlement, are implemented.[2] Part of the reason for this is that peacebuilding is perceived by many as essentially an international activity; what external actors are looking for is a political quick fix and an early exit. Elizabeth Cousens, for instance, argues in her co-edited book with Chetar Kumar that 'successful peacebuilding must ... recognize that international actors need "exit strategies" or at least what might be termed "reduced commitment strategies."'[3] What our case histories illustrate, however, is that if peace is to last, the process of building that peace must first of all be extended in time, then widened in scope, and finally anchored in its domestic setting.

In short, building peace is a long-term, complex, multidimensional process during which the previously warring parties lay down their arms, learn to manage their differences without resorting to violence, develop a common set of goals and common identity, move towards the creation of a just and more equitable society, and rebuild relationships that have broken. The ultimate objective of this process is the achievement of peace, not just 'negative peace' or the mere absence of violent conflict, but movement towards 'positive peace,' a condition in which the human security of a country's population is assured.[4]

Despite the primary focus of all our cases on the relatively short period that has elapsed since the end of fighting, the so-called post-conflict phase, all our authors clearly recognize and take into account the impact the past has had on current conditions and point out that the peacebuilding process unavoidably extends well into the future. What may appear like a success today could well be reversed or even collapse tomorrow. Indeed, as Duffield reminds us, the distinction between conditions of war and peace, particularly when countries are just recovering from war, 'can all appear remarkably similar.'[5]

The case studies acknowledge that current events are necessarily shaped by forces unleashed and institutions created prior to and during the civil war. The whole thrust of Will Reno's argument is that Charles Taylor and his National Patriotic Front of Liberia (NPLF) were products of the collapsing state of Liberia, a process that began in the 1980s. Instead of performing the traditional tasks of governance once the elections were held in 1997, Charles Taylor and his cronies behaved more like private entrepreneurs than legitimate rulers, interested only in their own personal security and welfare. Alex Costy points out how 'the underlying structure of Mozambique's peacetime political economy had already begun to take shape under increasing international pressure from the mid-1980s.' It is unhelpful, indeed misleading, to separate the political settlement in Mozambique, implemented between 1992 and 1994, from the economic reforms launched almost a decade before. Hevina Dashwood demonstrates how the unequal distribution of land in Rhodesia played a major role in mobilizing rural African support for the struggle against white rule in the 1970s and how failure to deal with that issue in a satisfactory way during the Lancaster House negotiations of 1979 and since then has provoked a crisis that could well return Zimbabwe to a state of civil war. John Young argues that the very characteristics of the Tigrayan Peoples Liberation Front that made for its success in winning the war may well prove to be a major obstacle to building lasting peace in Ethiopia.

Our case studies suggest as well that peacebuilding is a process that not only extends back to events and forces of the past but also forward, beyond what is often perceived as a transitional period of two to three years. Peace is rarely built in a linear fashion but is subject to reversals, outbreaks of violence, and total collapse. Even the claim that if peace has endured for at least a decade, it can justifiably be described as a success is clearly open to challenge.[6] The reappearance of fighting in Sudan in 1983, eleven years after the first phase of the civil war ended, and the outbreak of violence in Zimbabwe further illustrate how fragile the edifice of peace may be and how easily it can break down if no serious efforts are made to correct the underlying causes of political violence. These two cases underline a broad theme emerging from this volume: peacebuilding is of necessity a lengthy process, our conception of which must be expanded beyond what is essentially a limited and short-term exercise in political stabilization to encompass the transformation of socio-economic structures and the reconciliation of peoples. As John Paul Lederach put it so succinctly, 'we must move beyond a short-term crisis orientation and toward the development of a capacity to think about social change in terms of decades and generations.'[7]

Obstacles to Peacebuilding

THE PEACEBUILDING PROCESS ITSELF

Clearly one of the principal obstacles to enduring peace is the very complexity of the peacebuilding process. Shepard Forman and Stewart Patrick describe postconflict recovery as 'a "triple transition": a security transition from war to peace; a democratic transition from authoritarianism ... to a participatory form of government; and a socioeconomic transition, including both the rebuilding of economic capacities and (frequently) the movement from a controlled to a market economy.'[8] When viewed chronologically, we suggest that peacebuilding is best perceived as a sequence, beginning with negative peace or the mere absence of armed violence, and then moving into differing layers of positive peace, including the cultivation of political processes and institutions that can manage conflict without resorting to violence; the reconstruction and development of a national economy which addresses the underlying issue of regional inequalities; and the rebuilding of society on the basis of justice and reconciliation. Both of these conceptions of peacebuilding describe a process that is extremely complex, subject to reversals and periods of considerable violence.

Several of our cases illustrate how this very complexity can act as an obstacle to the building of peace, with progress on one level serving as an impediment to advancement on another. John Young maintains that the EPRDF's tight control of the political process during the transitional period in Ethiopia may very well conflict with its subsequent need to open up that process in an effort to ensure its future stability. Costy contends that 'accelerated liberalization as an underlying framework for post-conflict renewal' in Mozambique has resulted in increasing violent crime, urban and rural impoverishment and high unemployment, thus serving to undermine the positive gains made in the transitional phase of peacebuilding. John Saul's analysis of peacebuilding in South Africa points out how the compromises necessary to reach agreement on a constitutional settlement shaped and even constrained what the new majority government could and can hope to accomplish at higher levels of peacebuilding. In order to achieve a political accord the ANC was forced to moderate its demands for socio-economic transformation, leaving in place 'a society so scarred by profound inequalities that it runs the very real risk of rising tides of violence and negative long-term political outcomes.' In a similar vein, he argues that any good that was accomplished by creating the Truth and Reconciliation Commission, itself a compromise of justice in the name of security, would be seriously weakened if meaningful change were not made in the lives of the majority of South Africa's population. Finally, the implementation of a structural adjustment program in Zimbabwe has undermined the government's capacity to cope with rural development and poverty alleviation, elements central to building an enduring peace.

The question of timing and sequencing of peacebuilding measures is related to this complexity. Holding elections before the country is prepared for them can jeopardize short- and even long-term peace. The elections following the 1991 Bicesse Accords in Angola took place before demobilization and demilitarization had been completed, thus allowing Jonas Savimbi and UNITA to resort to armed violence once again. Many observers and participants are concerned that multi-party elections encourage competition and conflict in deeply divided societies, particularly ones that have just ended violent civil wars. It is therefore often argued that competitive party elections should not be held, at least not until agreement has been reached on the rules of the game. This argument is still made by the Ugandan government, whose leaders argue in favour of the continuation of what they call a 'movement system' on 'the grounds that political parties had previously shown themselves to be "sectarian" and divisive.' Their view was upheld by a majority of Ugandans in a referendum held in June 2000. Recently, Museveni has had a change of heart and agreed to the resumption of multiparty politics as long as it is accepted by the people in another referendum.

The way in which peacebuilding is conceptualized can also serve as an impediment to its realization. Elizabeth Cousens has argued strongly in favour of setting priorities among peacebuilding goals and of focusing on conflict resolution and opening up political space. Failure to take such an approach, she suggests, 'risks holding peacebuilding efforts to an impossibly high standard, overestimating what international engagement can plausibly and constructively deliver while diminishing the importance of more modest achievements.'[9] We too would link the way in which peacebuilding is conceptualized to a likely outcome, but with quite a different twist. The narrow, short-term focus on the politics of stabilization underestimates what needs to be done and what can in fact be accomplished. More importantly, it ignores important economic structural changes that can have, as Alex Costy points out, profound implications for the long-term outcome of post-war recovery and development, and, as such, for the quality and durability of peace. Failure to recognize and to take steps to counteract the adverse impact of economic liberal reforms on positive peace in Mozambique, South Africa, and Zimbabwe has already resulted in increasing levels of violence in these three countries.

FLAWED AGREEMENTS

In several of the cases examined in our volume the accord signalling the end of fighting contributed to the erosion or collapse of the peacebuilding process. No agreement can anticipate all eventualities, but sometimes specific provisions or arrangements can cast a dark shadow on the future. For example, the Addis Ababa agreement, which ended the first phase of Sudan's civil war, was flawed from the very beginning, for it created a small island of democracy in the South within the overall framework of a dictatorship. The future of the region of Southern Sudan relied entirely on the whim of one man, who could, as he had fashioned the agreement, just as easily break it. And that is precisely what President Nimeiri began to do as early as 1977, five years after the accord was signed.

There were profound flaws in the Lancaster House Constitutional Accord, which brought an end to the Rhodesian civil war. Given the inequitable pattern of land ownership that emerged during the colonial period it is not surprising that for Zimbabwe's rural population land was the single most important issue. Land was also one of the most difficult issues to resolve during the negotiations. The African nationalists originally took the position that the new majority government should have the right to acquire land against the wishes of any owner and to do so without having to pay compensation. In the end they were persuaded to accept a constitution that protected private property, allowed for the exchange of commercial farms only on a 'willing seller, willing buyer' basis, and required compensation, which was to be paid in foreign currency. Clearly the agreement favoured the commercial farmers, even though the British government promised to provide financial assistance towards the redistribution of land. Although other factors helped to shape recent events concerning this matter, Hevina Dashwood is correct in asserting that 'the punishing nature of the Lancaster House Constitution with respect to land acquisition clearly placed a limit on how far, and how quickly, the government could implement its program of land redistribution.'

Lastly, the Arusha agreement of August 1993 brought a brief end to fighting in Rwanda. However, as Bruce Jones has recounted in our earlier volume and in a recently published book, the agreement had within it the seeds of its own destruction.[10] Extremists within the Hutu community were excluded from participating in the coalition government fashioned at Arusha, and yet no provision was made to protect the new government and the Tutsi population from any violent actions taken against them by those same extremists. The absence of an international force with the authority to control extremist Hutu militia left open the door for the genocide that followed and the continuing instability and violence that exist even today.

SPOILERS

Negotiated settlements necessarily constitute compromises. There will always be someone – sometimes a party, more often extremist members of one or both of the parties – that is disappointed with the outcome. Even in cases where civil wars have ended through military victory, the defeated aren't totally without the means to carry on their struggle, particularly if they can find support from governments of neighbouring states. Those who perceive themselves as on the losing side and their vital interests in jeopardy may continue to fight for their goals and thus affect adversely the peacebuilding process. Whether they constitute a serious impediment to peace or merely a mild irritation will depend upon the size, coherence, and strength of the spoilers, the post-conflict government's approach towards rebuilding its war-torn country, and the attitude of neighbouring states.

South Africa stands out as an interesting counter-example. Extremist white groups, such the Conservative Party and the Afrikaner Weerstands Beweging (AWB), and individuals like General Constand Viljoen, were all committed to a return to unqualified apartheid. And yet these potential spoilers were effectively marginalized and rendered impotent by the concessions granted to the white community as a whole by the ANC. Elsewhere in Africa the outcome has not been quite so fortunate. In northern Uganda two armed groups, Joseph Kony's Lord's Resistance Army operating in districts on the Sudanese border and the Allied Democratic Forces situated along the border with the Democratic Republic of the Congo, benefit from deep-seated grievances in the north towards any regime, such as the National Resistance Movement (NRM), that draws its support largely from central and southern Uganda. That those northern groups are able to find a haven and even encouragement in neighbouring Sudan and the Congo only gives greater force to their disruptive impact on peace in Uganda.

In several other countries the disruption of peace by spoilers has been much more extensive, even total. Jonas Savimbi was unwilling to accept a negotiated settlement unless it offered him total victory in Angola. When he unexpectedly lost the elections in 1992, he didn't hesitate to return to the battlefield to secure his ultimate aim of the presidency. Only with his recent demise can that country and its people look forward to a much-awaited peace. In Rwanda, the inner circle of the so-called akazu (members of President Habyarimana's clan family) were unwilling 'to consider a negotiated settlement with the RPF (Rwandese Patriotic Front).' Even after being forced to flee the country by the advancing RPF forces in the summer of 1994, operating from neighbouring countries they continued to wage war against the new government and Tutsi survivors. They were the ultimate spoilers. They cannot alone be blamed for the final collapse into genocide in 1994 but certainly their presence 'complicated the search for peace.'[11]

The last instance of a spoiler, Charles Taylor in Liberia, involved not unreconciled opponents of the new regime but the internationally recognized government headed by the spoiler himself. His regime established a measure of order, but not genuine peace. Most government resources were employed to protect Liberians, but only 'to the degree that their activities contribute to the personal enrichment of Taylor and his associates.' Security was therefore provided selectively; anyone who dared to challenge Taylor's authority was vigorously pursued and, if necessary, eliminated. Beyond bringing a measure of order to Liberians, and even that was supplied arbitrarily, the government of Charles Taylor brought little else. In 1999 the national budget amounted to only '15 percent of reported expenditures in 1988, the last year before the start of the war,' and most of that went to the armed forces and various security agencies. What few social services Liberians benefited from were in fact provided by foreign donors and local NGOs. Taylor's involvement in Sierra Leone and more recently in Guinea and Côte d'Ivoire was an extension of his overall strategy of self-enrichment; by supporting opposition groups in these three countries, he succeeded in destabilizing the region while achieving enormous personal gain. Charles Taylor's regime was not a government whose interest lay in providing security and positive peace for the citizens of Liberia, but a spoiler whose sole goal was personal advancement. His was the rare case of a spoiler who was also the leader of a country. The very nature of his rule led inevitably to his down fall in 2001.

LEADERSHIP

Just as individual leaders who hold the reins of power can play a significant role in causing or averting civil war, they can have an impact on the peacebuilding process. Nelson Mandela and Yoweri Museveni provide excellent examples of leaders who have contributed to the peaceful transition that did occur in their countries, encouraging their citizens to engage in the forward-looking process of rebuilding their societies rather than returning to the past, a process often characterized by recrimination, mistrust, and inter-communal violence. In the case of South Africa it took the combined leadership of Mandela and F.W. de Klerk to make the smooth transition from apartheid to majority rule.

The impact of other leaders has been decidedly more negative. Although Robert Mugabe played a positive role in restoring peace to Zimbabwe in the early years following the Lancaster House settlement, his commitment to hold on to power at whatever costs has led him on a collision course with not only the small and wealthy white community but also a growing number of urban and rural Black Africans. The outcome still remains uncertain, but it has inevitably resulted in a weakening of the rule of law and growing violence. Finally, Nimeiri was never truly committed to the principles of the Addis Ababa agreement that acknowledged Sudan's ethnic and cultural diversity and expressed a willingness to accommodate the needs and demands of Southern Sudanese. Instead, he was driven by the oldest of all motives, the retention of power. When the tides of Sudanese politics swung in the direction of the North, he never hesitated to turn his back on his erstwhile allies in the South and annul the peace settlement.

Leaders do, therefore, matter. Their visions of the future (or lack thereof) can have an impact on the building of peace. Those who are dedicated to ending a costly war, opening up political space to the broadest participation, eliminating economic poverty and regional inequalities, and administering justice to those who have committed crimes in the past will in all probability build a solid basis for lasting peace. By contrast, those who fail to address the root causes and legacies of the war and who continue to exploit the ethnic card will likely face a collapse of the peace process and an early return to fighting.

How Civil Wars End: Does It Matter?

Simply put, it does seem to matter how civil wars end, but only over the short term. The evidence from our volume clearly supports the widely held view that building peace is more difficult to achieve if civil wars have ended through negotiations than if they have been brought to an end by military victory.[12] Of the cases examined in this volume in which peace was restored through negotiations, in at least three instances – Sudan, Liberia, and Angola – warfare was resumed. When you add to that record Rwanda's genocide following the Arusha accord; Zimbabwe and Somalia, where peace has come under enormous pressure. Only in Mozambique and South Africa have such settlements resulted in successful peacebuilding. By contrast, widespread fighting in Uganda and Ethiopia has ended and stability, for the most part, been established. In Rwanda, it is true, there does exist a real threat of renewed fighting.

The explanation for this disheartening outcome would seem to lie in the logic of negotiations and negotiated settlements. Peace is more difficult to achieve through compromise and negotiations because the various parties to the conflict 'retain some semblance of their original identities after the war, even if they are disarmed.'[13] Negotiated settlements too often result in a balance of power, an unstable outcome where former adversaries are anxious about their future and quite prepared to revert back to armed resistance if they think they can get a better deal by doing so or if their interests are placed in jeopardy. This condition of uncertainty and instability is further exacerbated by the adoption or even imposition of a more open political system in which popular participation is enhanced and civil and political rights more fully respected. Democracy does encourage competition and conflict which, in well-established democracies, are channelled 'through peaceful political institutions before they turn violent.' However, in societies that are divided into 'hostile communities,' such competition, especially that which takes place during an election, tends to 'reinforce societal differences,' hinder 'the consolidation of peace,' and even spark 'renewed fighting.'[14]

By contrast, in cases where peace has been restored by military force, the most likely outcome is 'the supremacy of state,' a condition in which all but one faction in the civil war is disarmed and 'the organizational identity of the losers' destroyed.[15] A single authority is thus established with the power to assert and implement its policy preferences in the face of what amounts to an insignificant opposition. In effect, order is often quickly restored and the transition to peace is easily initiated. What this analysis ignores, however, is the underlying long-term threat to the stability and peace of these countries that arises from the concentration of power in the hands of those who have won a military victory and from their apparent readiness to use repression and to inflict reprisals against their adversaries.

The Rwandan case highlights the difficulty of peacebuilding after a military victory. Instead of building support among the many Hutu who had opposed the Habyarimana regime, the Rwandan Patriotic Front chose instead to presere power through political domination. Prevented from expressing their frustration and anger through normal political channels, much of the Rwandan population, including many Tutsi, remains susceptible to violent movements. While it is true that those who won the civil war in Ethiopia and Uganda have shown more tolerance for political diversity and developed broader political bases than the Patri-

404 Taisier M. Ali and Robert O. Matthews

otic Front in Rwanda, they too have displayed many of the same authoritarian tendencies. It is not therefore surprising that the presidents of
these three countries have taken up arms against their neighbours and,
as Longman points out, 'appear increasingly like the old dictatorial presidents with which Africa is all too familiar.'

Those who have led their movements to victory on the battlefields of
civil conflict may be able to offer stability in the short transitional period
from war to peace, but unless they are prepared to adopt more just and
reconciling policies over the long run, they are apt to face increasing
challenges to their authority and to their ability to consolidate peace.
Civil wars that have ended in military victory may be less likely to resume
than those that are settled through negotiations, at least in the short run,
but as the Rwandan case demonstrates so well, if the military authorities
want to avoid the recurrence of war, they must learn to strike a more
equitable balance between the desire to control and the demands for a
more open political process.[16] And as the Ethiopian and Ugandan cases
point out, if the new governments hope to consolidate peace over the
long run, they too must be prepared eventually to remove all remaining
barriers to an open political system. In effect, whether the end to fighting has come through negotiations or military victory the achievement
of lasting peace is more likely in the long run to depend on the will of
the leaders of both warring parties to make the new political arrangements work.

The Role of the International Community

The extent of the external world's involvement in the peacebuilding
processes examined in this volume has ranged from marginal to significant, while the quality of that engagement has varied from helpful to
harmful. Contrary to what one might expect, involvement by the international community is not always essential for peacebuilding to succeed, as
the largely domestic-driven, bottom-up process of building peace in
Somaliland, Puntland and the Bay area clearly demonstrates.[17] However,
neglect by the outside world has often had a harmful impact. The Addis
Ababa agreement, which brought an end to Sudan's civil war in 1972, was
widely applauded by Africans and the world at large. However, once the
refugees had been resettled, the world turned its back on developments
in that country, largely ignoring Nimeiri's subversion of the peace process while the West extended military and economic support to Khartoum in the wider context of the Cold War. The world's failure to

intervene in Rwanda while the Hutu extremists carried out their planned genocidal attack on the Tutsi population is now well documented and openly acknowledged. Less well known is the international community's relative silence concerning the RPF and the present government's policies and practices. While making a considerable contribution to the immediate relief of the people of Rwanda and to the country's longer-term reconstruction, the international community has blamed the former government for all the violence and excused 'any abuses on the part of RPF as somehow necessitated by the post-conflict genocidal situation.'[18] Failure on the part of the international community 'to hold accountable the RPF and the current government for their human rights record and their resistance to democratic reform is,' in the view of Longman, 'a major obstacle to peacebuilding in Rwanda today.'

Just as the world's non-involvement is likely to have a harmful impact on a peacebuilding process, so too might one predict that a significant engagement would have a constructive influence. And yet, in at least two of our cases, Somalia and Liberia, a substantial commitment by the international community actually undermined the peace process. The UN/US intervention in Somalia did succeed in dealing effectively with the immediate problem of relief, distributing food to that country's starving population, but their efforts at building long-term peace in southern Somalia and in the country as a whole bore little or no fruit. Various conferences designed to reconcile rival factional leaders all ended in failure, largely because the model they followed involved a top-down project privileging the national elites, what I.M. Lewis referred to as 'imported Eurocentric quick political fixes.' UNISOM and UNITAF lacked adequate knowledge about Somalia, ignoring or failing to appreciate Somali distrust and fear of any centralized government. In Liberia, anxious to restore stability and order to a country torn apart by civil strife, the international community was quick to extend recognition and foreign assistance to Charles Taylor as the strongest factional leader. Unwittingly, outsiders helped to 'subsidize Taylor's construction of a sort of centralized personal economy.' Only when the true nature of his rule became apparent was the international community prepared to take steps to replace him.

Even in Mozambique, South Africa, and Zimbabwe, where the international community can fairly claim some responsibility for a successful transition from war to peace, measured by such criteria as effective economic recovery, free and fair elections, the repatriation of refugees, the decommissioning of former combatants and their integration into society, external intervention has also had a negative impact. Economic liberalization policies introduced into Mozambique at the behest of the IMF and major donor countries have complicated that country's national postwar recovery and development, reducing the quality of life for most Mozambicans. In South Africa, the ANC was persuaded by major foreign governments 'to embrace Western-style free market principles' within its development policy Growth, Employment and Redistribution (GEAR). The result has been, as one analyst commented, 'massive deindustrialization and job shedding through reduced tariffs on imports, capital flight as controls over investment are relaxed, attempts to downsize the costs and size of the public sector, and real cuts in education, health and social welfare spending.' South Africa has experienced peace, but a peace that sanctions 'the widening inequality inherent in neo-liberal economic policies.'[19] In Zimbabwe, according to Hevina Dashwood, was the failure of the IMF to include land redistribution 'as a necessary and integral part of the structural adjustment exercise,' that undermined the prospects for sustainable peace in that country. In the same way that most countries were being advised to pursue neo-liberal policies, the key donors were ideologically opposed to the idea of land redistribution, involving as it did state intervention, preferring instead to rely on the market to perform that function.

Only in Ethiopia and Uganda has the international community for the most part played a positive role. Uganda launched an Economic and Recovery Program in 1987 with the active support of the IMF, the International Development Association, and bilateral donors. It is noteworthy, however, that in the second phase of that program, beginning in 1996, the government sought to translate the benefits of economic recovery into improving the livelihood of Ugandans, the result of which was a remarkable turnaround in Uganda's economy. The annual growth of its GDP averaged 6 per cent between 1990 and 2000, the number of Ugandans living under the poverty line fell from 56 per cent in 1992 to 35 per cent in 2000, and school enrolment doubled. As one of the largest recipients of international assistance in Africa in the 1990s, Ethiopia too benefited from the strong financial support of the international community, at least until its war with Eritrea in 1999. While it is true that these two countries have profited from positive international contributions to their peacebuilding exercises, they both have been drawn into armed conflicts with their neighbours. This hostile regional environment has weakened their capacity to restore peace.

Why has the international community's involvement in peacebuilding not been more effective? Why has it so often done more harm than good? The answer lies, we believe, in the disjuncture or disconnect that frequently exists between the requirements of peace and the priorities of the donors, between the needs of the countries recovering from civil war and the quality and impact of the international community's intervention.[20]

This mismatch is reflected in what James Busumtwi-Sam, Alex Costy, and Bruce Jones have called a 'structural deficit.' The current institutions through which peacebuilding efforts are organized were developed after World War Two in response to different challenges from those that confront the world today. 'Building peace within states is...a very different proposition from building peace between states.' Efforts to reform those institutions in the 1990s have not yet succeeded in adapting them to the special circumstances of post-conflict transition and recovery. The result is 'a confusion of roles, vagueness of purpose, and weakness of coordination.'

Related to this institutional gap and inertia is the particular conceptualization of peacebuilding that continues to dominate the perspective of most policy-makers and many academics. Focusing on the short-term task of political stabilization, this paradigm emphasizes such projects as a ceasefire, the demobilization, demilitarization and reintegration of former combatants, the resettlement of refugees and displaced persons, the drafting of a new constitution, and the holding of a nation-wide election. At the same time, it ignores the longer-range goals of socio-economic transformation and socio-psychological reconciliation. Stability and order tend to be given preference over the consolidation of peace. While the pressing problems of relief and security must be addressed, so too must the long-run requirements of peacebuilding. Neither short-run priorities nor long-run requirements should be allowed to dominate the peacebuilding process.

The disjuncture between the requirements of peacebuilding and the goals of donors is manifested most sharply in the issues surrounding aid and the conditions attached to it by donor countries. All too often the macroeconomic discipline required of aid recipients has the unfortunate effect of forcing post-conflict governments to cut back on current expenditures just at the very moment that they need to expand them. The risk is that the very objects of peacebuilding – economic recovery and political stabilization – will be placed in jeopardy by the financial and monetary contraction imposed by international financial institutions. This was clearly the case in Mozambique in 1995, when fearing that 'this orthodox prescription' threatened that country's peacebuilding process, several donor countries 'took the "unprecedented step" of writing the IMF to voice this concern.'[21]

What is an appropriate role in the peacebuilding process for the international community? In the years immediately following the publication of *An Agenda for Peace*, it was generally assumed that peacebuilding was an international activity. Together with preventive diplomacy, peacemaking, and peacekeeping, post-conflict peacebuilding was portrayed as the UN and world's approach to the fourth stage in the conflict cycle. Much was then written on the needs of war-torn societies and on the capabilities available to international actors to address them. Peacebuilding was, therefore, seen as belonging to the international community, whose task it was to promote in conflict-ridden countries developments, both political and economic, that were modelled after neo-liberal democratic societies in the West.

More recently, however, an alternative approach has emerged, focusing on local ownership. From this perspective peacebuilding must be firmly anchored in the domestic setting of the countries being assisted. External actors may only be marginally relevant, as in Somaliland, or their intervention may even prove to be harmful, undermining rather than facilitating the peacebuilding process. As one of the editors of *Good Intentions* concluded, 'the critical determinants of successful peacebuilding and sustainable recovery are likely to be internal. The good intentions of the donor community cannot substitute for the willingness of local actors to renounce violence and to devote domestic resources to reconstruction.'[22] At best, the international community cannot reasonably be expected to be able to do more than facilitate a war-torn country's transition from war to durable peace.

We too have come to the same conclusion. Peacebuilding is essentially a domestic activity. Civil wars begin and are fought in countries that then strive for peace and it is there that conflict must be ended and peace rebuilt. The international community's role should be a facilitative one, supporting and encouraging local actors to achieve their goals, not imposing its preferred vision of a peaceful society. As James Busumtwi-Sam expressed it, 'peacebuilding is not, and should not be, about moulding countries in a particular image (i.e., western market democracies) based on ideological convictions. International assistance for peacebuilding is about helping local actors establish the conditions that will enable them to make choices in an atmosphere that is relatively free of large-scale violence, fear, deprivation, and predation.' International proposals and programs should be filtered through 'the special lens of the peace process' to determine whether or not they are appropriate. If they are found to be incompatible or to 'clash with peacebuilding objectives, there is a compelling case for modifying them.'[23]

Even the increasing prominence of civil society organizations in international aid to countries recovering from civil war – a response to the inability of multilateral agencies to address the challenges of post-conflict recovery – has now come under closer scrutiny. As Busumtwi-Sam, Costy, and Jones point out, external assistance through civil society organizations may, instead of helping to restore the local state, have the effect of perpetuating low state capacity, authority and legitimacy. Their impact on societal repair and restoration has also been unclear, as has their role in making the transition from short-term relief to longer-term sustainable development.

There have been occasions in the past, however, and will be in the future, when post-conflict governments engage in activities that undermine the peace. Under such circumstances, the international community should not encourage, facilitate, or support local authorities but instead use whatever leverage it has to pressure local leaders into reversing their policies. All too often, however, the international community has remained detached from such governments or, even worse, continued openly to support them. Had the West paid more attention to events in Sudan in the late 1970s, Nimeiri might have been encouraged to uphold the Addis Ababa agreement. We hardly need to mention the international community's failure to act in the face of Rwanda's genocide. Notwithstanding the horrors unleashed in the spring of 1994, many observers argue that if permanent peace is ever to be established in Rwanda, pressure will have to be brought to bear on the RPF government to give up its monopoly of power and to share it with the Hutu majority. Perhaps learning from this past record of inaction, in 2000 the United Nations Security Council imposed sanctions on Charles Taylor's government in Liberia to bring an end to his involvement in Sierra Leone, in March 2003 the Special War Crimes Court for Sierra Leone indicted Taylor himself for his responsibility in the crimes against humanity committed in that country since 1996, and later in the same year, under pressure from the United States, he was forced to leave Liberia.

A Peacebuilding Strategy

Countries emerging from a lengthy civil war are all confronted by a set of challenges that must be addressed successfully if they are to avoid a return to war. While the particular shape of the policies and programs developed to respond to these problems may differ from one country to another, we are convinced that at some point all war-torn societies will have to deal with the following tasks: creating a secure environment; building political institutions to enable the previously warring parties to resolve their differences peacefully; promoting economic development in such a way as to eliminate abject poverty and overcome the underlying inequalities that often gave rise to conflict in the first place; and coping with injustices, both of the past and those that could potentially arise in the future. These four elements of a peacebuilding strategy are interconnected, for a successful outcome will depend ultimately on advancement in each of these domains. The first two of these tasks are most likely to be addressed in the early, transitional phase, while the latter two may require considerably more time, even generations, to complete.

Creating a Secure Environment

No one would contest that ending the fighting and establishing a secure environment are early prerequisites of peacebuilding. Many of the ex-combatants must first be demobilized and disarmed and then reintegrated into civilian life. This is essential not only because it allows, at least in theory, for a reduction in military expenditures and a release of scarce resources for social and economic development projects (the realization of the so-called peace dividend), but also because in the long run, peace will be impossible to achieve without the disarming of large numbers of ex-combatants and their deployment in peaceful and productive activities. The restoration of order in Mozambique, Ethiopia, and most of Uganda can in part be attributed to the success with which DDR (demobilization, disarmament, and reintegration) programs were implemented in those countries. By contrast, the failure to demobilize and disarm, let alone reintegrate ex-combatants in Angola, southern Somalia, Liberia, Rwanda, and northern Uganda has resulted in widespread disorder, in effect, the absence of negative peace.

The success of DDR programs is clearly related to the availability of resources (both local and international) to cover the costs of demobilization and subsequent reintegration; careful planning involving all those most seriously affected; the development of special projects for women, child soldiers, and the disabled; the willingness and ability of local communities to absorb ex-combatants; and, as most ex-combatants are resettled in rural areas, the availability of land cleared of mines and unexploded ordinances. But, above all else, such programs are most likely to be effective if they take place within what Kees Kingma calls 'an enabling environment.'[24] In other words, demobilization, disarmament and reintegration are not implemented in a vacuum but are part of a larger process of peacebuilding. That process involves a prior political agreement among the previously warring parties; a functioning economy that can absorb ex-combatants as they return to society in search of employment; and a measure of trust that can overcome the parties' insecurities. The Angolan case clearly demonstrates that in the absence of a commitment to political agreement and mutual trust, demobilization and demilitarization are bound to fail, with or without an international presence.

A compelling case can therefore be made to address the entire question of security at the same time, if not after a political settlement has been negotiated. Disarmament and demobilization are only likely to be effective once the parties have re-established a measure of trust. As Ian Spears has argued, rather than focusing solely on security concerns arising from the predicament in which the parties find themselves, they should seek to negotiate a political settlement. By 'eliminating the conditions which led groups to take up arms in the first place,' they could become 'secure enough to end [their] belief in the need to remain an armed movement.'[25] Steps can be taken, short of total and complete disarmament, that can serve as confidence-building measures. The Sudan experience in the 1970s of distinguishing between absorbing and integrating southern soldiers into the national army offers a creative example of what can be done. In the case of Zimbabwe the question of disarming the Patriotic Front and the Rhodesian Security Forces in 1979–80 before the election was consciously avoided; instead, the parties were simply placed at a distance from each other.

Creating a secure environment often requires that steps be taken at a regional as well as a national level, for rarely are civil wars contained within their own borders. Whether through spillover into the region (as in Liberia) or regional intervention in a local dispute (Rwanda and Uganda), civil wars frequently take on a regional dimension. In West Africa, the Great Lakes Region of Central Africa, the Horn of Africa, or Southern Africa, security has become interdependent, thus requiring a regional approach to the building of peace. As long as Charles Taylor was left free to support and profit from civil strife in neighbouring Sierra Leone, Guinea, and Côte d'Ivoire peace in those countries was seriously flawed. In a similar fashion, spoiler forces operating from the

Democratic Republic of the Congo and Sudan continue to undermine stability in Rwanda and Uganda. The creation of a regional system in West Africa to manage conflict and promote enduring peace is the first step in the direction of correcting that flaw.

Constructing New Political Arrangements

Most observers agree that the reconstitution of the state is a necessary prerequisite for successful peacebuilding. Whether a cause or a consequence of civil war, state weakness or state failure is a reality that confronts peacemakers when the fighting has stopped. Thus, one of the most important and earliest of tasks is the development of state institutions and processes that command authority and the loyalty of the majority of its citizens and the restoration of its administrative, managerial, and enforcement capacities.

Some, however, place too much emphasis on the restoration of the managerial and technical capacities of the state. The World Bank, for instance, stresses the importance of good governance in its reconstruction strategy, by which it means 'the management of public resources on behalf of all citizens with fairness and openness.' While this is important, as John Kiyaga-Nsubuga's case study on Uganda demonstrates, it should not be pursued at the expense of building institutions 'that can manage conflict without violence but with authority and, eventually, legitimacy.'

New institutions and processes that can indeed command broad-based authority and loyalty need to be built. One proposal often advanced is power-sharing, a formula that on the surface appears 'to satisfy the desire of civil war disputants for political and economic power' and appeals as well 'to the international community insofar as it reduces the need for a substantive international commitment.' And yet, as Ian Spears demonstrates, power-sharing agreements are at best transitional remedies, certainly not long term solutions.[26]

Spears does cite two instances where power-sharing has succeeded: in facilitating a smooth transition from apartheid to majority rule in South Africa and promoting the evolution of Somaliland into a remarkably peaceful and stable country. In both cases, he argues, there were other factors that accounted for their success; a prior readiness on the part of South Africa's leaders, Mandela and de Klerk, to forego violence in order to attain a mutually accepted outcome; and the threat that southern Somalia posed to Somalilanders. Spears might have added to his short list of successes the case of Uganda, President Museveni actively pursued a strategy of sharing power, anchoring his regime 'by including various contending groups in its political and military structures. In 1996 the Democratic Party left the coalition and together with the Uganda Peoples' Congress put forward a candidate of their own in the country's first presidential election. Museveni's victory marked the end of power-sharing as he began then to rely more on political capital from the processes and institutions that it had fostered. Clearly, power-sharing did work, if only as a measure for easing the transition in Uganda from war to peace.

Notwithstanding the many failed instances of power-sharing agreements, the most egregious of which include Rwanda (from August 1993 to April 1994), Angola (from 1994 to 1998), Sierra Leone (in the early 1990s), and Sudan (1972 to 1983), we should not lose sight of their basic insight, their kernel of truth. If peace is to be restored, political arrangements must be developed that open up the political arena to broadly-based popular participation and thereby create the ability effectively and peacefully to manage conflict and address underlying grievances. This has led many to argue that the solution is the development of democratic institutions and norms. The claim is that by offering all groups in society an effective voice in government, democracy can encourage ethnic accommodation, facilitate political stability and enhance a country's prosperity.

All too often, however, those who sponsor peacebuilding have in mind a particular kind of democracy, one based on procedural legitimacy. The focus is, as James Busumtwi-Sam notes, 'on the means by which political power is acquired ... Democratization is conceived rather narrowly in terms of holding "competitive, free, and fair elections" in order to enhance this dimension of legitimacy.' But in societies that are deeply divided, where civil wars have further heightened insecurities, the competition that takes place during elections may very well aggravate societal differences and increase the likelihood of a relapse into civil war. Opening up the political process to greater popular participation may 'unleash divisive ethnic, regional, and class divisions' and so 'shatter the still-fragile unity of the states.'[27]

Insisting on competitive multiparty elections or procedural democracy may aggravate existing communal divisions within a country. As well, it can also produce apathy, even despair with the inability of politicians to address pressing socio-economic problems. Costy describes how the enthusiasm associated with the first post-war Mozambican elections in 1994, reflected in the 90 percent turn-out of eligible voters, was by the time of the municipal elections in 1998 and the presidential elections in 1999, replaced by disillusionment. As social hardships have grown, both in the urban and rural areas of the country, and as the party system appeared to fail 'to generate opportunities for Mozambicans to articulate their grievances and see them translated into policy,' public apathy has increased and with it the risk that the credibility and legitimacy of the formal political processes will be undermined.

Busumtwi-Sam suggests that our choice need not be 'between a legitimate democratically-elected government and an illegitimate authoritarian one based on a single criterion of procedural legitimacy.' Posing the question in that way forces peacebuilders to choose a policy that is likely to produce instability and to ignore a whole range of choices open to them. Indeed, there are alternatives from which we can draw. In his study of Tanzania and the steps that country took to avert intensified ethnic-centred politics, Cranford Pratt describes how Julius Nyerere developed the idea of a democratic, one-party state, which provided sufficient participation 'as to limit the risk of the regime's becoming severely authoritarian and corrupt,' while averting a serious threat to Tanzania's fragile unity.[28] Similarly, Museveni restricted the resumption of overt political activities during elections, a measure that has led some observers to cast doubt on his regime's genuine commitment to democratization.[29] Whether a democracy in a formal sense or not, Museveni's government has clearly reached out to ensure participation of a wide range of groups in both its political and military structures. In Ethiopia also the EPRDF applied *gim gima*, a system of accountability developed during the liberation struggle, to all levels of government. Although not a feature of Western democracy, *gim gima* gives people a voice in their administration, makes leaders accountable to their citizens, and encourages transparency. These examples illustrate that it is possible to obtain some form of broader political participation and legitimacy while avoiding the immediate adoption of competitive party democracy.

All the political arrangements considered to this point focus on national elites and politics at the centre. Even in our references to democracy the focus was on competitive elections from which emerged a representative national government. Reversing this earlier concentration on power at the centre, African countries have, in some instances, chosen to devolve power to federal units (South Africa and Ethiopia), to autonomous regional bodies (southern Sudan in 1972), or to new or revived local institutions (Mozambique and Uganda). Federalism, regional autonomy, and decentralization all offer, to differing degrees, ways to ensure that the peoples living under a single sovereign authority who are nevertheless strongly differentiated from their neighbours by culture, language, history and in some cases religion as well, are accorded a measure of control over their own lives and a mechanism by which to protect their separate identities. They also hold the potential for creating 'a genuine sense of participation, responsibility, and ownership in the process by a broad spectrum of the population,' a necessary condition for the construction of a durable peace.[30] Only with such a broad underpinning of support is peace likely to be consolidated.

Restoring the Economy

Just as peace is dependent upon a secure environment and a reconstituted state, so too is it reliant on the rebuilding of the economies shattered during violent conflict. Societies that provide for the well-being of their citizens are more likely to reduce the potential for deadly conflict. Indeed, the economic foundations of an enduring peace must, in our view, involve the gradual elimination of widespread poverty and the narrowing of the gap between the less developed and the more developed regions of each country. One particular economic policy of central importance to successful peacebuilding is the promotion of gainful employment for demobilized ex-combatants, returning refugees, and those who were either unemployed or underemployed even before the war began. 'High unemployment is,' as Susan Woodward recently pointed out, 'a threat to peace,' for those without jobs are easily recruited by spoilers or drawn into the criminal networks and activities spawned by the war itself.[31]

Despite the obvious importance of finding jobs for the unemployed and eradicating poverty, there is a tendency on the part of practitioners to downplay or even overlook the central contribution that development can make to peace. In the early stages of peacebuilding, development is overshadowed by issues of military security and short-term emergency relief, by what Busumtwi-Sam calls the culture of humanitarian assistance. In the longer term, the focus has tended to be on integrating peacebuilding into conventional development strategies informed by a neoliberal orthodoxy; the requirements of the peace process are not allowed to interfere with the presciptions of economic policy, and when they do, they are likely to be sacrificed on the altar of the marketplace. Alex Costy's analysis of the political economy of peace in Mozambique reveals how the implementation of such policies as economic adjustment, privatization, decentralization and pluralization has had an adverse impact on Mozambicans and their living conditions, weakening the state and increasing the likelihood of renewed instability and social unrest in the country. Finally, Hevina Dashwood points out that it was the very failure of international financial institutions to address the land redistribution issue within the context of structural adjustment that contributed to Zimbabwe's current crisis. In these cases, then, liberal orthodoxy triumphed over the requirements for an enduring peace.

If economic policies are to have a positive impact on peacebuilding, then, they must be designed or reshaped to address the special circumstances surrounding a country emerging from a lengthy and costly civil war. Civil wars constitute a total break in the life of a country and thus generate special needs – needs that are quite different from those confronting underdevelopment. If development is to address the underlying causes of civil war and repair the damage inflicted on an economy by years of violence, the needs of the peace process must be effectively accommodated as economic policies of the new regime are reshaped.

What does this imply for economic development policy in countries that have experienced a violent civil war? James Boyce's study focuses on El Salvador's problems, but 'many aspects of the Salvadoran experience are of general relevance to the formulation of economic policies in post-conflict transitions.' It is helpful at this point to summarize his findings. In the first place, there is the task of financing the costs of peace. These are likely to include the building of new democratic institutions, the reintegration of soldiers from all sides in the conflict into civilian life, the repatriation of refugees and displaced persons, the holding of elections, the removal of land mines, and the repair of physical infrastructure. Funding must be found to cover the costs of implementing all the measures agreed upon in the peace settlement or that need to be undertaken by the side that has assumed power through military victory. In some cases, domestic resources can be mobilized by shifting government expenditures from the military – for instance, to support social programs – but often it may 'be necessary to ease macroeconomic stabilization targets so as to permit funding of peace programs through deficit finance.' As Boyce emphasizes, 'the soundness of [economic] policies can be ascertained only in light of the political economy of the peace process.'[32] In other cases, these costs of peace cannot be met without support from the international community, and should that not be forthcoming, the peace process may flounder. We have seen how the failure of the international community, in particular the United Kingdom, to provide adequate funding for the transfer of land to the rural black population in Zimbabwe has contributed to that country's current crisis. Even more recently, the Sierra Leone Truth and Reconciliation Commission may be put at risk if the donor community fails to fulfill its funding pledges.[33]

The second set of policies addresses what Boyce refers to as the consolidation of peace. If peace is to be restored, a country emerging from civil war must make every effort to promote economic growth. In at least one World Bank study, the risk of war was found to be strongly correlated with widespread poverty and slow economic growth. The recent deterioration in Liberians' human security and the accompanying growth in social unrest and instability illustrate this point forcefully, while Uganda's record of strong economic growth and its success at peace-building offer a counter example. But economic growth by itself may not be enough to build an enduring peace; the benefits derived from that growth must be shared equitably and widely. As the Carnegie Commission on Preventing Deadly Conflict commented, 'The resentment and unrest likely to be induced by drastically unbalanced or inequitable economic opportunity may outweigh whatever prosperity is generated by that opportunity.'[34] Uganda's success in building peace may have had something to do with the attention its government has given, especially since 1996, to dealing with equitable access to economic growth. By contrast, the collapse of the Addis Ababa agreement in 1983 was in part due to Khartoum's continuing neglect, even exploitation, of southern Sudan's economy over the eleven years of peace. The Southerners' growing sense of economic discrimination was further strengthened by the controversy over the discovery and development of oil.

The consolidation of peace requires that the new government seek to achieve a balance among investments in human, physical and natural capital. Replacing destroyed plant and equipment or building it anew, long acknowledged as crucial to economic growth, is obviously essential to economic recovery or restoration. Investment in education and health is of equal, if not greater significance. It is also important to consider the modernization of the state, not only in the sense in which economic policy-makers usually employ the term, as efforts to streamline and make state structures more efficient, but also in terms of democratization, establishing an equitable distribution of power and protecting democratic institutions. With such reforms it is more likely that the state will intervene in the development process in ways that will help ensure the strengthening and consolidation of the peace process. In effect, the

restoration of a shattered economy is itself dependent upon the reconstitution of the state, just as the authority and legitimacy of the new state
will be strengthened by strong economic performance.

Promoting Justice and Reconciliation

Peace without justice is unsustainable. As South African Justice Richard
Goldstone expressed it, 'when nations ignore the call for justice, they
are condemning their people to the terrible consequences of ongoing
hatred and revenge.' The record of past injustices and human rights violations cannot be forgotten and buried. If 'people regard a political settlement as unjust, they will not support it; and if enough people regard
it as unjust, it will cease to be viable.'[35] A policy of forgetting is likely to
fail simply because not everyone will forget, especially the victims; if the
underlying grievances are not properly addressed in one manner or
another, they are likely to fester, generating anger and mistrust, eventually erupting into violence. In our earlier study of Sudan's civil war we
recounted how memories of the Torit mutiny in 1955, the accompanying massacre of northerners in Equatoria Province and the government's brutal reprisals continued to haunt the country in 1990 and
undermine attempts at resolving that conflict.

Others contend, however, that any serious attempt to accomplish justice is likely to rekindle old animosities, ignite controversies over what is
the 'truth,' and stir up old resentments rather than lay them to rest.
Consequently, they argue it is best to forget the past and its unresolved
grievances, to bury them without a suitable ceremony, to sweep them
under the rug. Indeed, with the exception of South Africa, Rwanda, and
to a much lesser extent in Uganda and Ethiopia, the issue of transitional
justice did not figure prominently in the other cases. 'Let bygones be
bygones' appears to have been the approach taken in Mozambique
where the former combatants have insisted that reconciliation means
forgetting the past. 'Today, if we did a truth commission,' asserted the
former head of the Mozambique electoral commission, 'it would be to
restart the hate,' and presumably a civil war.[36]

Notwithstanding this evidence, we are persuaded of the former view,
one eloquently expressed by Roberto Canas of El Salvador: 'Unless a
society exposes itself to the truth, it can harbor no possibility of reconciliation, reunification and trust. For a peace settlement to be solid and
durable it must be based on truth.'[37] Political accommodation and economic transformation are essential but insufficient ingredients of the

peacebuilding process, for they need to be supplemented by a process of reconciliation, a rebuilding of relationships. Paraphrasing Lederach, Knox and Quirk maintain that '[t]rue reconciliation ... requires a willingness to acknowledge truth and the past injustices – "to remember and change".'[38]

Once a society has chosen to remember rather than to ignore the past, there still remains the difficult task of determining how to deal with its injustices: how in fact to aid and heal the victims of abuse, how to treat the perpetrators of past injustices, and how to reconcile the events surrounding the civil war with the country's past. The policy options available to post-conflict governments range from the granting of absolute amnesty, to the formation of truth commissions, the disqualification of specific individuals from serving in state institutions, criminal prosecution, and finally the offer of compensation to victims. While the policy measures will vary from country to country; the choices made are likely to depend on a range of factors, including 'earlier experiences with post-transitional justice; the international context at the time of the regime change; the presence or absence of organizational resources; and the state of the judiciary.' What seems to be most important in determining how a country deals with the past, however, is 'the balance of power between the forces of the old and the new order during and shortly after the transition.'[39] Where civil wars end with military victory for one side, the risk is great that retribution and revenge may be sought and reconciliation never considered. Similarly, when peace comes from negotiations, retribution and revenge may be ruled out but so also may a quest for truth.

Not surprisingly, then, it is in Rwanda and to a much lesser extent in Ethiopia and Uganda where we find the most aggressive pursuit of justice and retribution. The EPRDF did prosecute and jail a number of the Derg's political leadership and dismissed wholesale the pilots from the Ethiopian airforce as they had been involved in attacks on the civilian population, especially in Tigray. The pilots were not reinstated until their services were required when Ethiopia went to war with Eritrea in 1998. In the initial years following the end of civil war in Uganda, Museveni did exclude from representation in his cabinet the leaders of the Uganda People's Congress, Milton Obote's party, and the former Uganda National Army, who had been closely associated with Idi Amin's regime. In Rwanda, however, the new government adopted a much more aggressive stance: it sought to rehabilitate the domestic justice system so that it could prosecute perpetrators of the genocide. By 1999 the number of

detainees in Rwanda's prisons exceeded 120,000, a number far beyond
the capacity of its judicial system. The genocide trials didn't begin until
December 1996 and by mid-1999 only eighteen hundred detainees had
been brought to trial. It was in part because of the incapacity of its formal
judicial system to accommodate all these detainees that the government
has since developed an alternative system of local courts to deal with
lower-level accused. In addition, of course, the UN Security Council created the International Tribunal for Rwanda in November 1994 to render
justice for the crimes committed during the genocide and to 'contribute
to the process of national reconciliation and to the restoration and maintenance of peace.' Several high-ranking political leaders, senior administrators and businessmen have been convicted and sentenced. These
criminal investigations at both the national and the international levels
have, however, been criticized for being too slow, for failing to include
victims in the process, and for constituting a victor's justice. What might
fairly be concluded is that such a judicial approach of relying on individual trials alone will not suffice in promoting justice, reconciliation and
peace.[40]

The path chosen by South Africa was quite different. Its decision to
establish a Truth and Reconciliation Commission amounted to a compromise made necessary by two different calculations. In the first place,
if the new government had proceeded with an active policy of prosecution, there is a strong likelihood that the courts might have frustrated
popular expectations by deciding in case after case that the prosecution
just had not proved its case, simply because it couldn't. The second concern was, as Justice Richard Goldstone put it, 'If the ANC had insisted
on Nuremberg-style trials for the leaders of the former apartheid government, there would have been no peaceful transition to democracy,
and if the former government had insisted on a blanket amnesty then,
similarly, the negotiations would have broken down. A bloody revolution sooner rather than later would have been inevitable.' The resulting
compromise offered amnesty for any person who was prepared to make
a full public confession and who was politically motivated. They did not
even have to repent for their violent actions or pay any reparation for
the injuries they may have perpetrated. The TRC therefore rejected the
idea of retribution or punishment, and spoke instead of restorative justice, a justice that 'seeks to reincorporate the perpetrators into society,
while restoring the dignity and well-being of the victim.'[41] The TRC may
be praised for many things: for the telling publicly of the truth of so
many individual offences and thus allowing some closure for those

whose suffering had been so long ignored; for promoting coexistence among former combatants and allowing them to sit down and negotiate the creation of a better society; and for opening the eyes of many whites to the record of apartheid. It too has been criticized for failing to address the gross historic un-righted collective offences against the black majority.

If the pursuit of truth and justice is to result in genuine reconciliation and durable peace, post-conflict governments must be prepared to adopt a strategy for promoting such a philosophy, to adjust such a strategy in the face of criticism, and to recognize that this search for reconciliation alone is insufficient. For Rwanda, this might mean finding ways to speed up the genocide trials, incorporating Hutu lawyers and judges in the judicial system, ensuring that Tutsis who commit human rights abuses are prosecuted as well, and in general making certain that justice is seen to be evenhanded rather than belonging only to the victors. But beyond improving the administration of justice, the Rwandan government must open up the political process and allow moderate Hutu to share in the governing of the country. Only in that way are the majority Hutu likely to view the state and the justice rendered as theirs. For South Africa, this might involve recognition that testimony at the TRC hasn't completed the process of healing victims, willingness on the part of the new government to accept responsibility for reparations, and commitment by the ANC to address socio-economic disparities. This latter issue is of particular concern, for, as Brandon Hamber has commented, 'the Truth and Reconciliation Commission is going to be remembered in history as a bad exercise if the government continues in the way it is going – in terms of its economic line and if the gaps between the rich and the poor do not narrow. If people's lives do not change then reconciliation is simply a waste of time.'[42] For other countries emerging from civil war in Africa, there is a basic need to recognize the importance of reconciling with the past.

Promoting justice is an essential part of any peacebuilding strategy but alone it is not enough. It will often require, for instance, that post-conflict governments address socio-economic grievances, ensure that their political systems are open and sensitive to the needs of all citizens, and provide a secure environment. In short, each of the four building blocks of our peacebuilding strategy is essential but none taken by itself is sufficient.

But what does this mean in concrete terms? We need to tie this strategy back into our earlier conceptualization of peacebuilding as a process of moving war-torn societies from a condition of negative to positive peace, a process that necessarily takes place over a long period of time. During the initial period of transition peacebuilders are bound to focus their efforts on building an environment in which the previously warring parties are able and willing to resolve their differences through nonviolent means. Attention must necessarily be directed towards reaching agreement on the rules of the game, establishing political institutions that allow for broad-based participation, at both national and local levels, arranging for the gradual demobilization and disarming of former armed combatants together with their reintegration into civil society, and jump-starting the economy to create opportunities for employment. Simultaneously, refugees and displaced people will also have to be resettled in their former communities. With the conditions of negative peace firmly established the new government will then be able to address the longer-term needs of a consolidated peace, in particular, the promotion of economic development that is equitably and widely shared and the establishment of mechanisms to deal with past injustices as well as to promote respect for human rights in the future. Underpinning these activities should be the engagement of a robust civil society whose presence is bound to play an important role in ensuring a durable peace.

NOTES

1 This focus on the difficulty of building lasting peace can be contrasted to the approach adopted by Pierre Atlas and Roy Licklider, who in their article 'Conflict among Former Allies after Civil War Settlement: Sudan, Zimbabwe, Chad, and Lebanon,' *Journal of Peace Research* 36, no. 1 (1999), seek to explain why civil wars do not recur when they so easily might.

2 See, for instance, Fen Osler Hampson, *Nurturing Peace: Why Peace Settlements Succeed or Fail* (Washington DC: US Institute of Peace, 1996); and Stephen John Stedman, Donald Rothchild, and Elizabeth M. Cousens, eds., *Ending Civil Wars: The Implementation of Peace Agreements* (Boulder, CO: Lynne Rienner, 2002) 12.

3 Elizabeth Cousins and Chetau Kumar, eds., *Peacebuilding as Politics: Cultivating Peace in Fragile Societies* (Boulder, CO: Lynne Rienner, 2001), 12.

4 For a similar understanding of peacebuilding, see John Paul Lederach, *Building Peace: Sustainable Reconciliation in Divided Societies* (Washington, DC: US Institute of Peace, 1997); John G. Cockell, 'Conceptualising Peacebuilding: Human Security and Sustainable Peace,' in Michael Pugh, ed., *Regenera-*

tion of War-Torn Societies (London: Macmillan, 2000); and Report of the International Commission on Intervention and State Sovereignty, *The Responsibility to Protect* (Ottawa: IDRC, 2001).

5 Mark Duffield, *Global Governance and the New Wars* (London: Zed Books, 2001), 188.

6 For such a claim, see Donald Rothchild and Caroline Hartzell, 'The Peace Process in the Sudan, 1971–72,' in Roy Licklider, ed., *Stopping the Killing: How Civil Wars End* (New York: New York University Press, 1993), 63–4. In fact, according to Barbara Walter, most scholars of civil wars are prepared to declare a negotiated settlement successful after only five years. See Barbara Walter, 'The Critical Barrier to Civil War Settlement,' *International Organization* 51, no. 3 (1997), especially 345. Roland Paris in his article 'Peacebuilding and the Limits of Liberal Internationalism,' *International Security* 22, no. 2 (1997), 88, argues in favour of extending peacebuilding operations to between seven and nine years. In a review of literature dealing with policy implementation, Paul Sabatier pointed out that most of the earlier scholars in that field attempted to reach judgements about 'a program's outcomes ... within 2-4 years of the basic policy decision.' However, as it became apparent that changes in the program were subject to a range of different influences, he and others came to the conclusion that 'in order to understand the ability of the public sector to guide target group behavior,' it would be desirable to take a much longer perspective of ten to fifteen years; shorter time spans 'are likely to produce erroneous conclusions about program efforts and to mask the critical process of policy evolution and learning.' See Paul A. Sabatier, 'Two Decades of Implementation Research: From Control to Guidance and Learning,' in Franz-Xaver Kaufmann, ed., *The Public Sector: Challenges for Coordination and Learning* (Berlin: Walter de Gruyter & Co., 1991), 259, 261.

7 John Paul Lederach, *Remember and Change: Peace and Reconciliation Conference* (Enniskillen, Fermanagh District Partnership), quoted in Colin Knox and Padraic Quirk, *Peace Building in Northern Ireland, Israel and South Africa: Transition, Transformation and Reconciliation* (London: Macmillan, 2000), 27.

8 Shepard Forman and Stewart Patrick, eds., *Good Intentions: Pledges of Aid for Post-Conflict Recovery* (Boulder, CO: Lynne Rienner, 2000), 5.

9 Cousens and Kumar, *Peacebuilding as Politics*, 11.

10 See Bruce D. Jones, *Peacemaking in Rwanda: The Dynamics of Failure* (Boulder, CO: Lynne Rienner, 2001) and his chapter in T. A. Ali and Robert O. Matthews, eds., *Civil Wars in Africa: Routs and Resolution* (Kingston and Montreal: McGill. Queen's University Press, 1999).

11 Bruce D. Jones, *Peacemaking in Rwanda*, 46, 158.

12 See Roy Licklider, 'The Consequences of Negotiated Settlements in Civil Wars, 1945–1973,' *American Political Science Review* 89, no. 3 (1995), 684–5. Of the fifty-seven civil wars that occurred in that period, three-quarters ended by military victory and one-quarter by negotiations. Civil war resumed in only 15 per cent of the former cases but in 75 per cent of the latter.

13 R.H. Wagner, 'The Cause of Peace,' in Roy Licklider, ed., *Stopping the Killing: How Civil Wars End* (Boston: South End Press, 1994), 261.

14 Roland Paris, 'Peacebuilding and the Limits of Liberal Internationalism,' *International Security* 22, no. 2 (Fall 1997), 74–5. See also Hevina Dashwood and Cranford Pratt, 'Leadership, Participation, and Conflict Management: Zimbabwe and Tanzania,' in Ali and Matthews, eds., *Civil Wars in Africa*, 246.

15 Wagner, 'The Case of Peace,' 261.

16 In a recent study of Rwanda, Mahmood Mamdani makes a similar point, arguing that if the Tutsi hope to have a common future with the Hutu, they will have 'to give up the monopoly of power.' See his *When Victims Become Killers: Colonialism, Nativism, and the Genocide in Rwanda* (Princeton: Princeton University Press, 2001), 279.

17 Eritrea, though not covered in this volume, provides another example of a peacebuilding process that has largely been autonomous. See Eric Garcetti and Janet Gruber, 'The Post-war Nation: Rethinking the Triple Transition in Eritrea,' in Pugh, ed., *Regeneration of War-Torn Societies*.

18 The ICTR recently announced that as of September 2002 it would start investigating atrocities committed in 1994 by the RPF against the Hutu.

19 Quoted in John Saul's chapter.

20 This mismatch sometimes is made more complicated by disagreement among donors as to their assessment of the post-conflict situation and the steps needed to consolidate the peace. In this regard, see Peter Uvin, 'Difficult Choices in the New Post-Conflict Agenda: The International Community in Rwanda After the Genocide,' *Third World Quarterly*, Vol. 22, no. 2 (April 2001).

21 James Boyce, 'Beyond Good Intentions: External Assistance and Peace Building,' in Forman and Patrick, eds., *Good Intentions*, 376. See also Alvara de Soto and Graciana del Castillo, 'Obstacles to Peacebuilding,' *Foreign Policy*, no. 94 (Spring 1994).

22 See Forman and Patrick, eds., *Good Intentions* 31.

23 James K.Boyce, 'Beyond Good Intentions: External Assistance and Peace Building,' in ibid, 375.

24 Kees Kingma, ed., *Demobilization in Sub-Saharan Africa* (London: Macmillan 2000), 242.

25 Ian S. Spears, 'Evolution in African Conflict: The Impact and Aftermath of the Cold War, 1985-1995' (PhD dissertation, McGill University, 1998), 504.

26 Ian Spears, 'Africa: The Limits of Power-Sharing,' Journal of Democracy 13, no. 3 (July 2002) 123–4.

27 See Hevina Dashwood and Cranford Pratt, 'Leadership, Participation, and Conflict Management: Zimbabwe and Tanzania,' in Ali and Matthews, eds., *Civil Wars in Africa*, 146.

28 Ibid., 241.

29 See Nelson Kasfir, '"No-Party Democracy" in Uganda,' *Journal of Democracy* 9, no. 2 (April 1998).

30 John Paul Lederach, *Remember and Change* (Peace and Reconciliation Conference, Enniskillen: Permanent District Partnership, 1996), 186.

31 Susan L. Woodward, 'Economic Priorities for Successful Peace Implementation,' in Stedman, Rothchild, and Cousens, eds., *Ending Civil Wars*, 201.

32 Boyce, *Economic Policy for Building Peace*, 14, 15.

33 See International Crisis Group, 'Sierra Leone After Elections: Politics as Usual?' 12 July 2002.

34 Carnegie Commission on Preventing Deadly Conflict, *Executive Summary of Final Report* (Carnegie Corporation of New York, December 1997), 25.

35 Richard J. Goldstone, *For Humanity: Reflections of a War Crimes Investigator* (New Haven: Yale University Press, 2000), 60. Nigel Biggar, ed., *Burying the Past: Making Peace and Doing Justice after Civil Conflict* (Washington, DC: Georgetown University Press, 2001), 7.

36 Quoted in Priscilla B. Hayner, *Unspeakable Truths: Making Peace and Doing Justice after Civil Conflict* (Washington, DC: Georgetown University Press, 2001), 2.

37 Quoted in John Stremlau, *A House Divided, A Report to the Carnegie Commission on Preventing Deadly Conflict* (Carnegie Corporation of New York, July 1997), 23.

38 Knox and Quirk, *Peace Building*, 196.

39 Peter Harris and Ben Reilly, eds., *Democracy and Deep-Rooted Conflict: Options for Negotiators* (Stockholm: International IDEA, 1998), 279. In a similar argument, Elin Skaar maintains that 'the government's choice of human rights policy depends on the relative strength of the public's demands for truth and justice and the outgoing regime's demand for amnesty and impunity.' See E. Skaar, 'Truth Commission, Trials – or Nothing? Policy Options in Democratic Transitions,' *Third World Quarterly* 20, no. 6 (1999), 1109.

40 Cited by Stef Vandginste, 'Rwanda: Dealing with Genocide and Crimes Against Humanity in the Context of Armed Conflict and Failed Political Transition,' in Biggar, ed., *Burying the Past*, 230–45.

41 Quoted by Charles Villa-Vicencio in 'Restorative Justice in Social Context: The South African Truth and Reconciliation Commission,' in ibid., 209, 212.

42 Quoted in Knox and Quirk, 219.

Contributors

Hussein M. Adam is professor of political science at the College of the Holy Cross, Worcester, MA. He received his BA from Princeton University in 1996, his MA from Makerere University, Uganda, in 1967 and his Ph D from Harvard University in 1974. Prior to his recent position at the College of Holy Cross, he taught at the Somali National University from 1981 to 1987 and the Brandeis University from 1969 to 1970. He is the author of Adam and Richard Ford, *Mending Rips in the Sky* (1997) and Adam and Ford, *Removing Barricades in Mogadishui*, (1998). His most recent articles are 'Islam and Politics in Somalia,' *Journal of Islamic Studies*, 6, no. 2 (July 1995), 'C.L.R. James and Richard Wright: On Ghana and Nkrumahism,' *UFABAMU, Journal of the UCLA Africanist Association*, 23, no. 1 (1995(, and 'Islam in Somalia,' in the *Encyclopeadia of the Modern Islamic World*, ed. John Esposito (1995). He has also written numerous chapters in books.

Taisier M. Ali received his Ph D from the University of Toronto in 1982 and for the next decade taught political economy at the University of Khartoum in the Sudan. From 1986 to 1989 he was coordinator of the Sudanese peace dialogue with SPLM/SPLA on behalf of the National Alliance for National Salvation. At present, he is a member of the executive and secretary-general of the Sudan Alliance Forces. His publications include *The Cultivation of Hunger: State and Agriculture in Sudan* and *Civil Wars in Africa*.

James Busumtwi-Sam is an associate professor in the Department of Political Science, Simon Fraser University. He specializes in international relations, comparative international development. He has published articles in journals and books on the politics of development finance and the role of international financial institutions, the politics of macroeconomic policy reform and financial

liberalization in developing countries, international organizations and regional
security, the political economy of conflicts and peacebuilding in Africa, and on
homeland security. He is co-editor of *Turbulence and New Directions in Global Political Economy* (2002) and *Global Instability: Uncertainty and New Visions in Political
Economy* (2002).

Alexander Costy is currently serving as head of programmes with the Policy,
Planning and Assessment Unit of the United Nations Assistance Mission in
Afghanistan. He has previously worked with the UN and the European Commis-
sion in Iraq, Angola and Mozambique, and has authored several evaluations and
policy studies on post-conflict recovery, peacebuilding and conflict prevention.
He holds a Ph D from the University of Toronto.

Hevina Dashwood is an assistant professor of political science at Brock University, specializing in international relations and development, Canadian foreign
policy, and African politics. Her publications include *Zimbabwe: The Political
Economy of Transformation.* Her current research focuses on corporate social
responsibility and the role of norms in the dissemination of new values around
acceptable corporate behaviour.

Bruce D. Jones is the deputy director of the Center on International Coopera-
tion, New York University, where he directs research on security and political
institutions. From 2000 to 2002, he served as chief of staff to the UN Special
Coordinator for the Middle East Peace Process. He previously worked at the UN
Office for the Coordination of Humanitarian Affairs, leading policy efforts on
strategic coordination and post-conflict peacebuilding. He was a member of the
UN's Advance Mission in Kosovo and of the UN Department of Peacekeeping
Operations' planning team for East Timor. Before joining the United Nations,
Dr Jones worked with non-governmental organizations involved in conflict
response in Central Africa, and participated in a number of evaluations of NGO
and UN responses. He is the author of *Peacemaking in Rwanda: The Dynamics of
Failure.* Dr Jones was a Hamburg Fellow on Conflict Prevention at Stanford University's Center for International Cooperation and Security, and holds a Ph D
from the London School of Economics.

John Kiyaga-Nsubuga holds a BA (Hons) in political science from Makerere
University, Kampala, Uganda; an M Phil in International Relations from Cambridge University, England; and a Ph D in political science from the University
of Toronto, where he focussed on the politics of developing countries, particularly the reconstruction of societies that have undergone extensive social and

economic dislocation. He is presently deputy director of Uganda Management Institute, a position he assumed in January 2000. Previous to that, from February 1998 to December 1999, he was chief of Division, Training and Staff Development at the Decentralisation Secretariat of the Ministry of Local Government in Uganda. From 1995 to 1998 he was adjunct professor of political science, University of Toronto, visiting professor in third world politics at Ryerson University of Toronto, and also briefly taught at Makerere University, Uganda, before joining the Ministry of Local Government.

Timothy Longman is on leave from his position as assistant professor of political science and Africana studies at Vassar College. He is currently serving as director of Rwanda Research for the Human Rights Center at the University of California, Berkeley. His research and writing have focused on state-society relations and ethnic conflict in Rwanda, Burundi, and Congo.

Robert O. Matthews is professor of political science at the University of Toronto. Former editor of the *International Journal* (1983–92) he is co-editor and co-author of *Civil Wars in Africa: Roots and Resolution* (1999) and author of many articles on African conflicts, both inter- and intra-state. Since 1994 he has engaged, together with Taisier Ali, in a study of the civil war in the Sudan.

William Reno is associate professor of political science at Northwestern University. He is the author of *Warlord Politics and African States* (1998) and *Corruption and State Politics in Sierra Leone* (1995). His current work includes a comparative study of the political economy of warfare in Central Asia and Africa.

John S. Saul is a member of the editorial working group of the Toronto-based periodical *Southern Africa Report* and also teaches social and political science at York University in Toronto. A veteran of the Canadian Southern African liberation support movement, Professor Saul has also taught in Africa, off and on since the 1960s, for almost a decade, most recently as visiting professor of sociology at the University of Witwatersrand in South Africa, January to June 2000. Author or editor of a dozen earlier books on Africa, he has two books forthcoming: *Millennial Africa: Capitalism, Socialism and Democracy* and *South Africa: Apartheid and After* (co-authored with Patrick Bond).

Ian S. Spears teaches political science at the University of Windsor. His work focuses on power-sharing and other form of conflict-resolution in African states. Other research considers the phenomenon of 'states-within-states' in Africa and in the developing world.

John Young was awarded an Honours BA in political science at Simon Fraser University in 1972, an MA in political science at McMaster University in 1974, an MPA at the University of Victoria in 1982, and a Ph D in political science at Simon Fraser University in 1995. With respect to Africa, he has worked as a high school teacher in Swaziland, a journalist in the Sudan, an assistant professor at Addis Ababa University, and researcher with CIDA. His publications include *Peasant Revolution in Ethiopia: Trigray People's Liberation Front 1975–1991* (1997) and articles in the *Journal of Modern African Studies*, *Review of Political Economy*, and *Third World Quarterly*. John Young is currently employed as a political analyst on Sudan based out of the Canadian embassy in Addis Ababa and also holds the position of research associate at the Institute of Governance Studies, Simon Fraser University.

Index

elements of success of peacebuilding in, 151–3; emergence of civil
society in, 169–72; and IMF and
World Bank, 149, 158–9; legacy of
war in, 150; pluralism in, 166–72;
policy towards Rhodesia of, 147;
political disillusionment in, 413–14;
and PRE, 158–9; reconciliation in,
418; roots of civil war in, 143–9;
roots of peace in, 149–51; social
consequences of structural adjustment in, 158–61; and United
Nations, 151; and WFO, 155. *See
also* Frelimo
MPA, 303
MPLA, 282–306 passim
Mubarak, Hosni, 49
Muekalia, Jardo, 300, 307
Mugabe, Robert, 12, 220, 222, 223,
230, 233, 393, 402; election of in
1980, 224
Museveni, Yoweri, 4, 9, 10–11, 65, 86,
87, 105, 330–1, 393, 398, 401, 413,
414

Namibia, 208
National Commission on Human
Rights (in Rwanda). *See* NCUR
National Democratic Alliance. *See*
NDA
National Islamic Front. *See* NIF
National Party (South African), 188,
191
National Patriotic Front of Liberia.
See NPFL
National Resistance Army. *See* NRA
National Resistance Movement
(Ugandan). *See* NRM
natural resources: exploitation of in
Angola, 303–5; exploitation of in

Liberia, 129–32; exploitation of in
Sudan, 290–2

NCA, 289–90
NCUR, 71
NDA, 49
NGOs: in Ethiopia, 31; in Rwanda, 62,
72
NGOs (local), in Mozambique, 169–
70
NIF, 48–9, 52, 292
Nigeria, 268; and peacekeeping in
Liberia, 136; President Abacha of,
124
Nimeiri, President, 285, 287, 291–2,
293, 307, 308, 399, 402
Nkomati Accord, 149
Norwegian Church Aid. *See* NCA
NP/ND government, 199
NPFL, 115, 119, 120, 123, 124, 125; as
product of collapsed state, 120–2
NP (South African), 190
NRA, 65, 89
NRM, 11, 86, 91
Nyerere, Julius, 414

Oakley, Ambassador, 267, 270
OAU, and Somalia, 254
Obote, Milton, 90
ODA, 338
OECD, 375
Ogwal, Cecilia, 87, 92
oil: discovery of in Sudan, 291; signifi-
cance of in Angola, 303–5
OLF, 19, 25, 55; attitude of EPRDF
toward, 32; Eritrean support for,
27; insurrection by, 29
Operation Provide Relief, 263
Operation Restore Hope (ORH),
263, 264, 265–6, 268

tional community and land redistribution in, 238–43; intervention in Congo by, 237, 241; land invasions in, 232; land redistribution in, 224–7, 228, 231–5, 236–8, 244, 399, 416; referendum on draft constitution in, 231; structural adjustment in, 234–5, 238, 397; veterans in, 244; and World Bank, 239–40, 241

Zimbabwe African National Union. *See* ZANU

Zimbabwe Congress of Trade Unions. *See* ZCTU

CPSIA information can be obtained at www.ICGtesting.com
Printed in the USA
LVOW08s0133281115

464076LV00002B/133/P